Read this book online today:

With SAP PRESS BooksOnline we offer you online access to knowledge from the leading SAP experts. Whether you use it as a beneficial supplement or as an alternative to the printed book, with SAP PRESS BooksOnline you can:

• Access your book anywhere, at any time. All you need is an Internet connection.
• Perform full text searches on your book and on the entire SAP PRESS library.
• Build your own personalized SAP library.

The SAP PRESS customer advantage:

Register this book today at *www.sap-press.com* and obtain exclusive free trial access to its online version. If you like it (and we think you will), you can choose to purchase permanent, unrestricted access to the online edition at a very special price!

Here's how to get started:

1. Visit *www.sap-press.com*.
2. Click on the link for SAP PRESS BooksOnline and login (or create an account).
3. Enter your free trial license key, shown below in the corner of the page.
4. Try out your online book with full, unrestricted access for a limited time!

Your personal free trial **license key**
for this online book is:

8q5d-b7uj-6i3r-9mnf

Enterprise Information Management with SAP®

PRESS

SAP PRESS is a joint initiative of SAP and Galileo Press. The know-how offered by SAP specialists combined with the expertise of the Galileo Press publishing house offers the reader expert books in the field. SAP PRESS features first-hand information and expert advice, and provides useful skills for professional decision-making.

SAP PRESS offers a variety of books on technical and business related topics for the SAP user. For further information, please visit our website: *www.sap-press.com*.

Andy Walker, Jagadeeshwaran Ganapathy
Effective Master Data Management with SAP NetWeaver MDM
2009, 403 pp., hardcover
ISBN 978-1-59229-223-3

Helmut Stefani
Archiving Your SAP Data (Second Edition)
2007, 405 pp., hardcover
ISBN 978-1-59229-116-8

Loren Heilig et al.
SAP NetWeaver Master Data Management
2007, 331 pp., hardcover
ISBN 978-1-59229-131-1

Michael Willinger, Johann Gradl
Migrating Your SAP Data (Second Edition)
2008, 373 pp., hardcover
ISBN 978-1-59229-170-0

Gatling, Brague, Champlin, Stefani, Weigel, Bryce, Dharwad, Engel, Gardella, Grewal, Felsheim, Haelterman, Hamer, Jackson, Keilen, Kuppe, McFadden, Seguin, Sinha, Stridinger, Waite

Enterprise Information Management with SAP®

Galileo Press

Bonn • Boston

Galileo Press is named after the Italian physicist, mathematician and philosopher Galileo Galilei (1564–1642). He is known as one of the founders of modern science and an advocate of our contemporary, heliocentric worldview. His words *Eppur si muove* (And yet it moves) have become legendary. The Galileo Press logo depicts Jupiter orbited by the four Galilean moons, which were discovered by Galileo in 1610.

Editor Kelly Grace Harris
Copyeditor Ruth Saavedra
Cover Design Graham Geary
Photo Credit iStockphoto.com/Mr_Khan
Layout Design Vera Brauner
Production Graham Geary
Typesetting Publishers' Design and Production Services, Inc.
Printed and bound in the United States of America

ISBN 978-1-59229-414-5

© 2012 by Galileo Press Inc., Boston (MA)

1st edition 2012

Library of Congress Cataloging-in-Publication Data
Gatling, Ginger.
Enterprise information management with SAP / Ginger Gatling. — 1st ed.
p. cm.
Includes bibliographical references and index.
ISBN 978-1-59229-414-5 (alk. paper) — ISBN 1-59229-414-6 (alk. paper)
1. Information resources management—Data processing. 2. Management
information systems. 3. SAP ERP. I. Title.
T58.64G38 2012
658.4'038028553—dc23
2012008959

FSC
www.fsc.org
MIX
Paper from
responsible sources
FSC® C014174

Contents at a Glance

Dear Reader,

Good decisions are based on good information—with this book, you have the foundation for both. While some books are written by a single expert, some books require a team: And since this particular book is meant to introduce SAP's wide swath of EIM tools, it has an ensemble cast. Your benefit from the varied backgrounds and contributions of true experts will be obvious—but less obvious will be the guidance that was provided by the team lead, Ginger Gatling. There are few people who could turn the work of many experts into a cohesive tome with a clear focus, but Ginger is one of them. Enjoy this product of her work, and all of the expert guidance provided by all the talented authors.

Of course, we at SAP PRESS are always eager to hear your opinion. What do you think about *Enterprise Information Management with SAP*? How could it be improved? As your comments and suggestions are the most useful tools to help us make our books the best they can be, we encourage you to visit our website at *www.sap-press. com* and share your feedback about this work.

Thank you for purchasing a book from SAP PRESS!

Kelly Grace Harris
Editor, SAP PRESS

Galileo Press
Boston, MA

kelly.harris@galileo-press.com
www.sap-press.com

Contents

PART II Working with SAP's Enterprise Information Management Solutions

6 Getting to Know Your Data with SAP Information Steward ... 223

9 Monitoring Data Quality with Scorecards in SAP Information Steward 339

13 Introducing SAP NetWeaver Information Lifecycle Management ... 423

14 Introducing SAP Extended Enterprise Content Management by OpenText 467

Foreword

There's one phrase that has crept into the vocabularies of IT and business professionals alike over the last year, more so than any other: *big data*.

Not only has the variety and volume of structured data in our enterprise systems increased at an unprecedented pace, but we're now challenged to reconcile data from blogs, Twitter, email, and more that can help our businesses ensure we have everything we need to make critical decisions. Consider as well that the pace of business is now real-time. Business leaders want information they can trust now—not in a report run in a week, but in a dashboard they can access on their tablet in minutes or even seconds while on the road.

The data quality imperative has perhaps never been clearer: Data can be the competitive differentiator. As a result, data management professionals are suddenly finding themselves in situations where information management projects, which for years have been put on the back burner in many companies, have executive buy-in.

This book will help anyone who plays a role in managing the inexhaustible and seemingly endless flow of information better understand strategies for getting started and executing successful enterprise information management initiatives at their companies. For those who already have master data management programs in place, the book offers strategies for ensuring they stay successful. The authors detail everything from how to start a data quality initiative, to establishing data governance and stewardship, to deploying and evangelizing master data management programs and policies. They also discuss SAP's EIM portfolio, as well as the role of products like SAP HANA.

In the spirit of the Americas' SAP Users' Group ASUG, this book is a collaboration between SAP and its customer community and is full of real examples from SAP customers with leading EIM strategies. These customers recognize that implementing an effective enterprise information management strategy gives them a clear competitive edge. Many of the customers in this book are also ASUG members, who present an unbiased and balanced view of the challenges and benefits of EIM projects with SAP. Their experiences demonstrate the clear value that customers get from participating in ASUG. These ASUG members have helped influence the development of these products and facilitate feedback with SAP development so that they continue to bring more value to their peers.

In that spirit of giving back, the authors of this book have generously decided to donate all of the proceeds from sales to Doctors Without Borders/Médecins Sans Frontieres, an organization that provides medical care to people living in the most dangerous and desolate places on earth.

I trust that you will find this book helpful in forming the increasingly important enterprise information management strategies that will guide your companies through the big data imperative.

Bridgette Chambers
CEO, The Americas' SAP Users' Group (ASUG)

Preface

Welcome to the first edition of *Enterprise Information Management with SAP*! The goal of this book is to introduce readers to the concepts of enterprise information management, provide examples of how SAP's EIM solutions are used today, and offer technical instructions on performing some of the most common EIM tasks in SAP. Although a significant portion of the book is devoted to SAP Data Services, we also discuss SAP HANA, SAP Information Steward, SAP Master Data Governance, SAP NetWeaver Information Lifecycle Management, and SAP Extended Enterprise Content Management by OpenText.

Target Groups of the Book

This book is intended for both experienced practitioners and those who are new to managing, governing, and maximizing the use of information that impacts enterprises. Specifically, it will be of use to business process experts, architects, data stewards, data owners, business process owners, analysts, and developers who are new to the topic of EIM in SAP. While there are several specific "how to build" and "how this works" sections, the book content requires no previous knowledge of EIM or SAP's solutions for EIM.

This book is also intended for existing information management experts who need to expand their skills from a specific EIM domain to broader information management strategies. This target group will not need to reference all chapters, but will be interested in new capability information provided in many (for example, the latest release information and new products available).

Structure of the Book

This book is divided into two parts:

▶ **Part I: SAP's Enterprise Information Management Strategy and Portfolio**
This part of the book starts by introducing enterprise information management and its main concepts, including information governance and big data. Once you understand the ideas behind EIM, we move on to an overview of the

solutions for EIM within SAP's portfolio, offering brief explanations of the main EIM solutions. Finally, the section concludes with real-life examples of how SAP's EIM solutions are used by several different customers.

▶ **Part II: Working with SAP's Enterprise Information Management Solutions**
This part of the book focuses on how to get started using SAP's solutions for EIM. Part II includes product details on topics ranging from understanding the current state of your data, to managing unstructured content and getting started with master data governance. This section focuses on select parts of SAP's EIM offerings with the goal of providing practical examples and step-by-step instructions for key SAP capabilities. You will learn how to get started assessing your data (SAP Information Steward), build data quality dashboards (SAP Information Steward), use data quality transforms (SAP Data Services), turn text data into data points (SAP Data Services), migrate your data (SAP Data Services), govern your master data (SAP Master Data Governance), manage structured and unstructured content that impacts business processes (SAP Extended Content Management by OpenText), set retention rules (SAP NetWeaver Information Lifecycle Management), and retire information (SAP NetWeaver Information Lifecycle Management).

With the division of the book into two major parts, you can read the different parts as you need them. Part I is critical to understanding EIM and the role it plays in SAP's strategy and portfolio. In Part II, you can access information and insight about the EIM capabilities that are most applicable to your projects, planning, and information management strategy.

More specifically, the book consists of the following chapters:

▶ **Chapter 1: Introducing Enterprise Information Management**
This chapter provides an introduction to the concept of enterprise information management. It defines EIM, discusses common use cases and business drivers for EIM, discusses the impact of big data on EIM, explains SAP's strategy for EIM, and discusses common user roles of people and organizations normally involved in EIM. You will also get an introduction to NeedsEIM, Inc., which is the fictional company used as a basis for examples throughout the book.

▶ **Chapter 2: Introducing Information Governance**
Information governance is the practice of overseeing the management of your enterprise's information. It touches all aspects of EIM and must be considered in any EIM strategy. This chapter provides tips for developing your governance

standards and processes, and maps governance activities to technology enablers for these standards and processes.

► **Chapter 3: Big Data with SAP HANA and Hadoop**
This chapter introduces big data in the context of SAP's solutions for EIM. Specifically, it focuses on the role of SAP HANA and Hadoop.

► **Chapter 4: SAP's Solutions for EIM**
This chapter describes SAP's solutions for EIM, introducing and providing overviews of specific products. After reading this chapter, you will be able to quickly identify which chapters in Part II are of the most interest to you.

► **Chapter 5: Practical Examples of EIM**
This chapter discusses specific examples of EIM application by various customers. Content discussed includes recommendations for your EIM architecture (written by Procter and Gamble), the evolution of SAP Data Services (written by National Vision), and tips for successful enterprise content management projects (written by Belgian Railways). In addition, there are other customer-written sections on data migration, managing master data, data archiving strategy recommendations, and recommendations for positioning different SAP tools for data and process integration.

► **Chapter 6: Getting to Know Your Data with SAP Information Steward**
This chapter introduces SAP Information Steward, which can be used for profiling and getting to know the current state of your data. It will discuss cataloging your data assets, performing data profiling, and monitoring your data quality over time.

► **Chapter 7: Introducing SAP Data Services**
Chapter 7 introduces SAP Data Services as a data foundation for EIM. It describes the components and architecture of SAP Data Services and walks you through specific examples of how to start doing data integration with SAP Data Services.

► **Chapter 8: Managing Data Quality with SAP Data Services**
Chapter 8 describes how you can use SAP Data Services for data quality, including data cleansing, data enrichment, data matching, data quality blueprints, and data quality functions embedded within SAP applications. If you want more information after reading this chapter, advanced data quality capabilities are discussed in Appendix A (available for download from the book's website at *www.sap-press.com*).

- **Chapter 9: Monitoring Data Quality with Scorecards in SAP Information Steward**
  This chapter adds to your data quality knowledge by explaining how to use SAP Information Steward to create scorecards that monitor data quality over time. You will explore a specific example based on NeedsEIM, Inc., and step-by-step instructions for creating data quality scorecards.

- **Chapter 10: Processing Text Data with SAP Data Services**
  This chapter describes the use of the text data processing capabilities in SAP Data Services. It provides an overview of the capabilities, and then walks through an example of using text data processing to analyze and semantically disambiguate unstructured text.

- **Chapter 11: Migrating Data with SAP Data Services**
  Chapter 11 adds to your knowledge of SAP Data Services by describing the use of SAP Data Services for data migration. The chapter focuses on accelerators and enablers, including rapid data migration packages. It also discusses step-by-step instructions for migrating data using SAP Data Services.

- **Chapter 12: Introducing SAP Master Data Governance**
  Chapter 12 describes how to get started using SAP Master Data Governance for your master data governance initiatives. It includes a description of SAP-provided master data governance processes and explains how to create custom governance processes. It also describes the use of SAP Business Workflow and BRFplus for governing master data. Finally, the chapter gives an example of using SAP Information Steward in conjunction with SAP Master Data Governance for monitoring and remediating master data.

- **Chapter 13: Introducing SAP NetWeaver Information Lifecycle Management**
  Chapter 13 provides background information on the concept of information lifecycle management. It then specifically introduces SAP NetWeaver Information Lifecycle Management, offering discussions of retention management, system decommissioning, and how SAP NetWeaver Information Lifecycle Management works to support the lifecycle of information.

- **Chapter 14: Introducing SAP Extended Enterprise Content Management by OpenText**
  Chapter 14 discusses the major features of SAP Extended Enterprise Content Management by OpenText, how it uses SAP ArchiveLink, and how it works with the SAP Business Suite.

▶ **Online Appendices**
There are several appendices to assist you: Appendix A covers advanced data quality capabilities, Appendix B provides details on SAP's migration content, and Appendix C provides tips for your first data archiving projects. The appendices and an example spreadsheet for monitoring your data migration projects can be downloaded from the book's website at *http://www.sap-press.com*.

Acknowledgments

This book would not have been possible without the incredible efforts of a diverse set of authors. I would like to say a special thanks to every author who participated in this project, each of whom made a unique contribution that only he or she could provide. Some of the authors I've known for many years, while others I met during the course of this project—and it was a privilege to work with all of them. I hope you will take the time to learn about them in the About the Authors section of the book.

In addition to the authors, many others played a critical role in this book. From discussing ideas, to reviewing chapters, to providing content, many people have been part of the group collaboration effort to create this book. People to thank include Victor Szczerba, Bob Hagenau, Vish Agashe, Aaron Mahimainathan, Georg Fischer, Markus Ganser, Tammy Powlas, Richard LeBlanc, Paul Medaille, Florian Koeller, Ben Hofmans, Werner Daehn, Marc Diefenbruch, Kristin McMahon, Michael Briles, Abhiram Gujjewar, Trish Harman, Iwona Luther, Jodi Maciejewski, Bob Berntsen, Angel Sasso, Joan Ward, Andrea Thomsen, Mike Eacrett, Prasad Illapani, Justin Martinson, Michael Wiesner, Debbie Labe, Sarah Anderson, Ken Campbell, Jan Zielinski, David Quirk, Olivier Claude, Anil Kumar Rachaputi, and Kiran Kumar Reddy.

I would also like to say a special thank you to Mike Keilen, one of our authors and also my manager. Mike provided his complete support, and his input and guidance enabled this project.

We as an author team also need to say a big thank you to all of the folks who supported us with content and reviews but who wish to remain anonymous.

When we started this book project, we all knew it would take time and considerable effort, but the time taken from family was certainly underestimated. We are all very fortunate in life if we can find people who love us, and when those people encourage us and support us during times when work takes priority, as it did while working on this book, we realize how fortunate we are! So thank you to our families and friends who provided support, encouragement, and patience throughout this project.

As a final note, I hope you have noticed that all royalties from this book will be donated to Doctors Without Borders (Médecins San Frontières). Each author individually decided to donate their royalties. Your purchase of this book helps us support an international medical humanitarian organization that delivers emergency aid in many countries. Thank you for enabling us to provide financial support to this important organization and its critical mission.

I hope to see you blogging about EIM on the SAP Community Network after reading this book!

Ginger Gatling
Enterprise Information Management Solutions Team
SAP Labs, LLC

PART I
SAP's Enterprise Information Management Strategy and Portfolio

This chapter introduces enterprise information management, including common use cases and big data. It also provides an overview of SAP's strategy for enterprise information management.

1 Introducing Enterprise Information Management

All businesses and organizations run on information; businesses that run on timely, accurate, and reliable information run better. The best-run businesses treat information like all other corporate assets: It is carefully managed, thoughtfully governed, strategically used, and sensibly controlled. The opposite is also true; businesses that have haphazard, ad hoc, or sloppy information management practices find that important information gets locked in silos, reports are untrustworthy or practically useless, and vital processes that depend on data all too frequently go awry.

Skillful management of information not only can keep your organization running efficiently, but can greatly improve results by providing key competitive advantages: understanding your customers, getting the most from your suppliers, ensuring compliance without increasing your risk, and providing internal transparency to drive operational and strategic decisions.

SAP is best known for business processing applications such as the SAP Business Suite. Over the past several years, however, SAP has made significant investments in extending the portfolio beyond the Business Suite. One important extension includes the business of managing data and information, referred to as *enterprise information management* (EIM). This chapter will introduce EIM, including what it is, why it is important to organizations, how it fits into SAP's strategy, and some typical user roles. Finally, the chapter concludes by introducing NeedsEIM, Inc., a fictional company that will be used throughout the book to illustrate EIM principles.

1.1 Defining Enterprise Information Management

On Gartner's IT glossary page, enterprise information management is defined as "an integrative discipline for structuring, describing and governing information assets, regardless of organizational and technological boundaries, enabling business insight."[1]

Enterprise information management covers all types of information, including traditional structured data, semi-structured and unstructured data, and content such as documents, emails, audio, video, and so forth.

The management of information with the understanding of its lifecycle yields the best results for use and cost. And more is not always better. The active management and governance of information helps in avoiding the costs associated with blind information hoarding. The risk of having too much information is just as real as not having enough when you need it.

Figure 1.1 shows a typical spend of information over time. Notice that this is a technology *and* resources spend curve. Perhaps the curve surprises you. You know you spend money acquiring data, but is the cost that much more in the off-boarding phase? Yes. Many companies spend a lot of money maintaining information that is out of control. Is the information still used? In what systems? Can you decommission those systems? Are you managing pieces of information that are no longer used?

As illustrated in Figure 1.1, there is an associated cost in bringing information into an organization, using the information, and hopefully retiring the information once it is no longer producing value. The idea that organizations really just do three things with information — on-board, actively use, and then off-board — is powerful when thinking about EIM solutions.

Once information is brought into your organization, it is required for many uses beyond its original purpose. Hence, it is advantageous to prepare it for these manifold uses. That way, the effort to repurpose information during the active-use phase is greatly reduced. Once information is no longer required, it should be off-boarded or retired in a manner that meets your organization's legal and business requirements. The truth is that most organizations do not proactively consider the reuse and eventual off-boarding of information, which ends up costing millions in IT resources due to maintaining systems that are no longer used.

---

1   Source: *http://www.gartner.com/technology/it-glossary/enterprise-information-management.jsp*

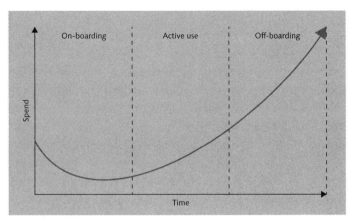

Figure 1.1 Typical Spend on Information Over Time

If you adopt an information strategy, the spend changes to closer to what is shown in Figure 1.2.

Figure 1.2 Spend on Information with an Information Management Strategy

Figure 1.2 also provides detailed examples of the types of activities involved with EIM across the typical lifecycle of information. In the on-boarding phase, activities include the creation of information, either through on-line user creation, integration of processes that involves the creation of new information, import of information, and migration of information. Additionally the on-boarding phase should included lifecycle planning; for example, how long the information should be retained. Implementing governance and retention policies as the information is on-boarded dramatically lowers the cost of information over its effective lifetime. Notice there is still some spend increase as information is actively used. This is from incrementally improving, enriching, and preparing information for alternative uses. The key to bending the cost curve down is understanding that information has tremendous value beyond its original purpose and proactively planning for that in your enterprise information management strategy. The result is that the spend curve goes down over time in the active use phase as information is simply repurposed. Again, this can be achieved because the incremental cost is just the provisioning of existing known and trusted information—as opposed to starting over for each new information initiative.

Next we will look at an example of information flow through a company and then discuss how this relates to information management.

1.1.1 Example of Information Flow Through a Company

NeedsEIM, Inc. is a fictional company based on real customer examples. NeedsEIM, Inc., will be explained in detail in Section 1.7 and again throughout Part II of the book when we demonstrate how to use various EIM capabilities. For now, we want to introduce NeedsEIM, Inc. and the types of information it must deal with, including how information flows through the company. This leads to a discussion about the types of information included in EIM.

Figure 1.3 depicts the business processes of NeedsEIM, Inc. It manufactures retail durable goods, and the majority of its manufacturing is outsourced. This business model results in a complex and diverse supplier network that impacts most departments. The major departments include finance, who must deal with supplier payments, and the engineering and contracts department, who must coordinate contracts and technical spec drawings with the manufacturers.

The IT department must deal with diverse systems, including SAP and non-SAP systems. The procurement department is responsible for the supplier relationship and ensuring the company gets the most from its suppliers. The sales departments is always looking for new and creative sales channels, including opportunities in the supplier population.

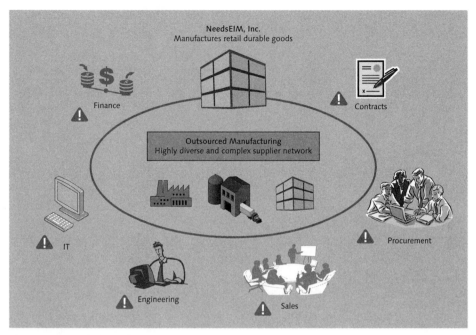

Figure 1.3 NeedsEIM, Inc.

As an example of information flow through NeedsEIM, Inc., let's look at the process of contract negotiations with a supplier:

1. The proposed supplier must be researched for due diligence, including type of products or services provided, similar customers serviced, reference calls with current customers, quality history, financial and credit ratings, reliability and trustworthiness, as well as general reputation.

   ▶ This involves emails, online research, and getting information from external sources such as Dun and Bradstreet.

   ▶ This information is shared between the finance, engineering, procurement, contracts departments.

2. Assuming the due diligence indicates the supplier is approved, the supplier master data needs to be created and distributed to related systems. The scope, projects, pricing, contracts, and legal documents must be created.

   ▶ This involves most departments and includes sales if the durable goods price point might be impacted.

> ▸ The supplier sends and receives legal, technical, financial, and other information.

3. Once the contracts are negotiated, the supplier requires ongoing communication including technical drawings, bills of materials, and other information they require to do their work. In addition, financial documents such as invoices, purchase orders, and so on are exchanged.

> ▸ This includes a lot of collaboration between engineering, contracts, procurement, and the supplier.

Figure 1.4 shows the information as it needs to flow through each department. Departments use the information with their perspective in mind: They store it, update it, download it, and ensure it meets the requirements for their department's role with the supplier.

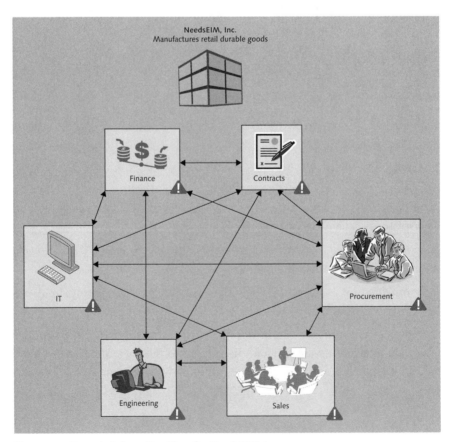

Figure 1.4 Example Information Flow for NeedsEIM, Inc.

As you can see in Figure 1.4, the reality is that information is often required by many departments. Sometimes when the information does not move from one department to another due to application, political, and/or departmental silos, departments create their own "tribal" versions of the information, and each department has a different sense of their ownership of the information. (We'll discuss more about tribal information in Section 1.3.2.)

Earlier we mentioned several examples of information that is needed for negotiations with a supplier. This includes detailed information on the supplier, external references for the supplier, pricing and detailed contract information, engineering documents of what the supplier will provide or build for NeedsEIM, Inc., as well as billing, invoicing, and all the typical supplier interactions. The next section will break this down further into types of information that are required and how this information is included in EIM.

1.1.2 Types of Information Included in Enterprise Information Management

Figure 1.5 shows the types of information that are included in SAP's solutions for EIM that will be covered in this book.

Figure 1.5 Types of Information Included in Enterprise Information Management

These information types are relevant for most companies, including NeedsEIM, Inc. We provide some more information about these types below:

❶ **Structured data**

This includes the familiar data used within an application system (e.g., customers, products, and sales orders); for example, supplier information such as name, address, cre+dit information, contact information, and so on. This also includes all purchase orders, sales orders, and other data related to this supplier.

The following list describes typical activities related to structured data:

▶ Migration of structured data into an application system.

▶ Enforcement of data rules upon data entry when creating new master data, such as a business partner or product. This can include a duplicate check (i.e., checking whether customer, lead, business, partner, or material already exists based on the criteria you supplied) or enrichment of data (i.e., validating the address with the local postal authority).

▶ Central management of data that is used in multiple application systems.

▶ Governance of all major data structures, including the governance and control of master data.

▶ Aligning, transforming, and integrating structured data between both operational and analytical applications.

▶ A legal requirement exists that inactive customer data cannot be stored past a certain number of years; this data must be deleted from all data stores in which it is held.

▶ Legacy systems hold data that are no longer relevant to the business; the data needs to be archived, and the systems decommissioned to keep IT costs manageable.

❷ **Desktop documents**

These include Microsoft Word, Microsoft Excel, Adobe Acrobat, and other desktop application documents. This data is stored across the enterprise, on shared drives and laptops, which means that much of it is not controlled at an enterprise level. This content may be critical to the application data, so you need to manage it with the same importance as the structured data in the database. Examples include:

▶ Purchasing documents (e.g., invoices), which may need to be scanned and associated with the invoice in the application system.

- Contracts with suppliers, which need to be stored centrally and linked to the associated structures in the ERP system.

- Legal documents, grants, and other unstructured to semi-structured data, which must support business processes.

- Resumes, stock options, and employee performance reviews, which are used as part of normal HR processes.

❸ **Pictures, scanned documents, videos, and other images**
These could be scanned invoices, videos, pictures of products that are sold in a catalog, and drawings of products that are being designed and built. These become part of the content that needs to be managed and related to the structured data when required. Managing content associated with a core business process is becoming increasingly important to process efficiency and regulatory compliance. Examples of such content include:

- Engineering documents to be shared with suppliers.

- Pictures of raw materials or finished goods.

- Routine maintenance records in asset management. Also failure case analysis, photographs and video of assets, and all relevant correspondence between employees, customers, and contractors.

- Invoices, expense reports, and other scanned documents in finance.

- Pictures and videos of a new ad campaign in marketing.

- Employee pictures.

❹ **Semi-structured data**
Information such as RSS feeds, blogs, and other semi-structured information that is important to the enterprise. Examples include:

- RSS news feeds about a supplier that are relevant for the purchasing agent responsible for the supplier relationship.

- Blogs and posts. For example, a company might have a large trade show and is interested in the blogs and posts regarding the show. Those comments should be associated with the show and also related to customer structured data.

- Emails associated with purchasing documents, design plans, and contracts, which should be linked with the structured objects in the SAP application.

❺ Text data

In Figure 1.5, ❺ reads "The car should self-drive on the highway." This piece of information may come from a survey or be a comment on a social media or other website, and by itself it might not be important. However, if you are looking at car design over the next five years, and 60% of the comments you receive have something about self-driving, this comment warrants further investigation. Information management includes looking into text you receive and analysis to determine sentiment, feedback, input, or actions that should be taken based on comments. Examples of text data include:

- ▸ Comments from the supplier's manufacturing process that need to be analyzed for either product design or engineering.

- ▸ Feedback from internal departments and even consumers that can be used to build a supplier scorecard.

- ▸ Comments on surveys and service tickets; for example, surveys sent to new car owners or service tickets created for a new product line. These comments should be synthesized and analyzed to provide feedback and sentiment.

As you can see, EIM includes a combination of traditional structured data and nonstructured information, from the moment of creation through retirement. The retirement of data and information has the same value as creation. Once information is no longer needed, it becomes a liability—a legal liability, a cost liability, or some other kind of liability. The entire lifespan of the data and information, and the governance of that information, is covered in enterprise information management.

1.2   Common Use Cases for EIM

There are many use cases for EIM solutions. Three of the primary scenarios include:

- ▸ **Operational EIM**
  Operational EIM focuses on common business processes and increased efficiency of established systems. Business applications, such as SAP ERP, automate crucial processes including order to cash, payroll processing, and accounts payable. Business process applications require EIM for information on-boarding, conversion, facilitating the flow of information across business functions inside and outside the organization, improving the quality of data, management of master

data, and implementing a strategy for structured and unstructured information in a cohesive manner that supports and drives the business process.

▶ **Analytical EIM**
Analytical EIM focuses on preparing and delivering trusted information for analytics and analytical applications. Analytic applications (also referred to as business intelligence [BI] solutions) are geared to support better business decision making to optimize performance. These applications can include drill-down reports, "slice-and-dice" data reports, predictive analysis, and supply chain optimization. All analytical applications require data and information management capabilities to ensure that the information is trusted, cleansed, and able to aid in sound decision making.

▶ **Information governance**
Information governance focuses on the management and governance of information as a strategic asset. Once a company benefits from data management for business processing and analytical processing, the evolution is to an overall data management strategy that sees information as a critical asset and manages it holistically as intellectual property.

We discuss each of these scenarios in more detail next.

1.2.1 Operational EIM

Operational EIM covers the use of EIM in the operation and execution of business processes and tasks that happen throughout the day. It has very broad applications, from ensuring that material replenishment data is set correctly, to customer data quality management, to migrating new data from a merger, to ensuring that all contracts and documents are available for the business process, to removing data that is no longer required.

EIM solutions from SAP provide trusted data to drive and deliver best practice business processes. This value includes the ability to holistically manage data within business processes, ensuring the quality and ability to reuse the data.

Here are a few examples of operational uses of EIM:

▶ **Compliance and regulations in the financial industry**
The financial industry has requirements for financial risk-related data analysis. All data must meet quality levels and industry standards, and all associated

content (e.g., documents and invoices) must be correctly associated to financial contracts.

▶ **Data management of key master data, such as well management in the oil and gas industry**
Oil and gas companies have thousands of wells, with well information stored in many different types of systems. The overall production versus the cost of the well is only known through the synthesis and linking of the data across the enterprise.

▶ **Suspect tracking in public safety organizations**
Federal, local, and state agencies must share information on criminal activity and suspect tracking. Information management ensures that each new suspect is compared to others to confirm that it is a unique suspect. Data quality rules can ensure that the most up-to-date information is available for suspect tracking.

▶ **Data management, conversion, and migration due to mergers, acquisitions, and global implementations across all industries**
Information management lowers the risk of business and application disruption during mergers, acquisitions, and new application implementations.

▶ **Harmonized master data across industries**
Harmonized master data across disparate applications enables a single view of master data across the enterprise.

▶ **Retaining and deleting information in the pharmaceutical industry**
During the development of new medicines, all documents and government standards must be adhered to through various stages of research, development, trial, and release. When the compliance period has ended, information should be removed unless it is required for a legal hold.

▶ **Fraud detection in telecommunication and other industries**
Telecommunications, media, high tech, and utilities share similar requirements for capturing, addressing, and mitigating fraudulent activity. Large volumes of data and real-time transactions place these industries at increased risk, as perpetrators can be "on and gone" before they are caught using traditional time-consuming software reporting methods provided by vendors today. Information management enables the filtering of diverse data to determine where the company is losing money across a broad spectrum of applications and business processes.

▶ **Plant maintenance compliance and data assessment**
Ensuring that the virtual plant aligns with the physical plant, information management ensures that maintenance plans and documents are associated with each asset, asset tags are accurate, functional location information is complete, and all asset document and maintenance guides are available on the plant floor.

▶ **Data quality and data assessment in the retail industry**
The retail industry requires high data quality; for instance, retailers must know article data throughout all stores where the articles are sold. For retailers, data quality and assessment is an ongoing business process; it includes, for example, tracking articles that have not been maintained in required stores, articles missing valid sales price conditions, articles missing required procurement data, and articles with duplicate EAN codes.

Notice that many of these examples are focused on ensuring that information is managed, available, reliable, and serves the operational business process; the list can go on and on.

Chapter 5 provides more detailed real-world and practical scenarios for EIM.

1.2.2 Analytical EIM

EIM has a long history in business intelligence and analytics. If you look at some definitions of EIM online, you will see statements that EIM drives decision-making analytics. Many of the operational use cases mentioned above also fit into operational reporting and have some reuse for strategic reporting and analytics as well. Some examples of EIM for business intelligence and analytics include:

▶ **Analysis of supplier spend**
Analysis of who are the top suppliers, how much they spend, and payment and credit issues can only be done if supplier records are transparent and harmonized, cleansed, and de-duplicated. When making decisions related to the supply network, the supplier data must be accurate and trusted.

▶ **True cost assessment of manufacturing goods in the manufacturing industry**
Analyze total costs for making and delivering products. Crossing multiple business domains, data must be cleansed, duplicates removed, and correlations created to ensure that analysis provides accurate information.

▸ **Bring together timely, accurate, and actionable data to provide insights into the factors impacting sales and customer behavior**
Silos of data sources and applications, limited business user access, and dependence on IT to create reports limits the business' ability to gain insights on sales and customer behavior. Information management brings together the data and provides data lineage and analysis so the users can create reports and know where the data is coming from.

▸ **Text mining to understand opinion and sentiment**
Text and rich media content accessible on the web or on social media sites contain a lot of information that can be analyzed and used for sentiment analysis to get a better understanding of consumer opinions about a product or idea.

1.2.3 Information Governance

The third use case for EIM is the management and governance of information as a strategic asset, normally referred to as *information governance*. Information governance is a discipline that oversees the management of your enterprise's information. It expands upon the idea of *data governance* to include some more ambiguous aspects of governance, including the lifecycle of information, accountability, monitoring of the governance process, and managing the information's return on investment (ROI).

Information governance enables a repeatable, governed process to manage key data and information. Governance is the linchpin of EIM that empowers business users to own and manage data as a strategic asset, governs data in the business process to optimize operational performance and ensure compliance, and establishes trust in structured and unstructured information by ensuring data quality throughout its lifecycle.

Governance will be a common thread throughout the book and will be covered in more detail in Chapter 2.

1.3 Common Drivers for EIM

All organizations today create and use information. But do organizations use information just to support a narrow aspect of the business operations, or is information used strategically? Is information used to grow the business? To take market share from competitors? Improve organizational efficiencies? Better serve customers or constituents? The more optimally information can be used for its original purpose, and extended to new uses, the more valuable it becomes. Mundane data or documents can become weapons in gaining and sustaining competitive advantage when used in decision making and supporting critical processes. Information can even become a strategic weapon if an organization manages enterprise assets such as capital. Treating information as an organizational asset recognizes that it moves from a single-purpose use to something that must be managed for multiple uses.

Common business problems that require an EIM strategy often may not have the words *information, enterprise, management, data,* or *governance* in them. The business issues driving initiatives for EIM include but are not limited to trucks going out at the wrong weight, deliveries to the wrong location, hazardous products not in compliance with government standards, customer satisfaction issues, incorrect billing, misunderstood supplier networks, services that don't align with customer demand, lack of compliance with a government mandate that impacts payments or revenue, and so on. Many process issues are the result of a lack of an information management strategy—from poor-quality data to master data not being updated correctly, to not having the documents required for order processing, to financial documents not aligned with sales documents, to different parts of the organization using similar terms in different ways.

Adoption of enterprise information management capabilities is normally driven by a few fundamental needs—responding to a growing set of compliance requirements, improved operational efficiency, and the strategic application of information to better manage your organization and gain competitive advantage. Next we discuss specific examples of issues as drivers of EIM adoption.

1.3.1 Operational Efficiency as a Driver of EIM

Operational efficiency includes many moving parts to ensure the company has an improved operational margin. From the perspective of EIM, operational efficiency includes the provisioning and preparation of data so it can be used to keep the business running well. The following are typical operational efficiency scenarios and the role of EIM.

Improving Payment Processing

The time taken to collect payments and the improvement of payment processing is critical in all industries, and this is a process that is heavily impacted by the quality of the data. One example is the healthcare industry; in healthcare it is critical to ensure that hospitals collect what they should from government agencies such as Medicare and Medicaid in the United States. Effectively provisioning data from disparate systems ensures data compliance with U.S. laws for Medicare and Medicaid and enables hospitals to receive their payments, having an impact in the millions of dollars.

Ensuring a Successful ERP Go-Live

An SAP customer was implementing a new SAP system and had to migrate data from many non-SAP data sources. The customer was concerned about the large volumes of data to migrate from both the parent company and a variety of subsidiaries. It was critical that the entire business not be on hold during the migration, and the data from the migration had to be loaded accurately and safely. The requirement from the customer was a single, integrated application providing a high degree of visibility that could be easily rolled out to multiple subsidiaries, eliminating hours of custom coding to load data into the SAP system. SAP's EIM solutions were used to extract data from third-party applications and support smooth transfer to a new environment. This automated approach saved valuable resources and expedited data migration processes, resulting in a smooth—and on-time—go-live, reducing the overall cost of the implementation.

Consolidating Systems to Improve Information Management and Reduce IT Spend

An SAP customer ran 80% of its business with several SAP systems and wanted to reduce IT costs and improve transparency of information across the systems. The company had 8 SAP systems when only 3 were needed and over 400 non-SAP systems, most of which could be retired. EIM's role in this included the assessment, alignment, migration, and retirement of data and legacy systems and ensuring that the three remaining SAP systems had accurate and timely information.

Speaking the Same Language to Increase Operational Efficiency

Another SAP customer had issues where no one spoke the same language. For example, the term *margin* covered different realities depending on the department and employees concerned. To set things right, the company specified four objectives for itself: to centralize its data in a common environment, to secure the data, to make the data more reliable, especially for management access, and to standardize its vocabulary for indicators. EIM accelerates employee access to information and, as a result, saved significantly on the amount of time required to perform routine tasks. Teams made enormous gains in responsiveness. Where it previously took one week for data to be available after accounts were closed, the operation is now instantaneous.

1.3.2 Information as an Organizational Asset

All organizations have assets: capital, employees, materials, brands, and physical and intellectual property that are all managed carefully. Information is similar, as it, too, is an asset that must be managed and protected. With the right EIM strategy, information can be leveraged and used as an organizational asset. We'll now discuss some specific examples of how actual companies use information as an organizational asset.

Improving Patient Care and Payer Response

An SAP customer is a large hospital conglomerate focused on first-class patient care and creating innovative ways to improve care. First-class patient care requires the management of information in large volumes and with daunting complexity. EIM was used to extract, transform, integrate, cleanse, load, and correlate patient records from many diverse systems for analysis by doctors and line managers. The cleansed and aligned data enabled line managers to improve operational efficiency (including aligning information across multiple hospitals). The project extended the use of information such that doctors now have the ability to "slice and dice" information as needed on patient groups and to provide recommended treatments and wellness programs based on trends, including readmittance trends, long-term performance of different treatments, and so on. The other focus of the project was to ensure a high quality level of data provided to and by patients. The improved data quality improved patient service, which led to improved payments by payers, resulting in the collection of several million outstanding dollars.

Growing Past "Tribal Knowledge" to "Enterprise Information"

A large SAP customer had a wealth of information that was vitally needed across departmental lines, but the information—documents, spreadsheets, manuals—was locked up in information silos. Shared—or nonshared—hard drives, separate portals, and multiple content repositories held the data, with no central search or access capability. This resulted in "tribal knowledge"; the different departments could usually find the information that their employees created, but this information was not effectively shared with other departments. By implementing a strategic enterprise content management and global search capability, the customer was able to create a single enterprise information store that all employees could search and use regardless of department.

Improving Data Quality for Customer Interactions

Another SAP customer had a goal to create a 360-degree view of customer data for sales, marketing, and service. EIM was used to consolidate heterogeneous data into a single database, integrate structures and processes across sales, marketing, and service, as well as ensure a systematic information exchange between field sales and sales support. Improved customer data quality strengthened dialog with these customers and systematized customer-related processes across sales, marketing, and service. The data quality improvement and improved transparency drove a new structured quotation process. The new process provides time savings and fewer errors when creating quotations.

1.3.3 Compliance as a Driver of EIM

As governmental regulations and controls increase, and the cost of legal issues due to data issues rises, compliance plays a key role in most industries. Every company and its network of suppliers that produce a durable good that ends up in a shopping cart have compliance requirements. Other organizations, such as utilities, government agencies, security, and financial service providers, are also subject to regulatory and compliance issues. In addition to industries, countries have import and export regulations that impact the ability to do business globally.

Next we discuss some general examples of compliance issues that indicate a need for an information management strategy.

Keeping Data Too Long

For regulatory compliance, companies must ensure that they keep retention-relevant data for a minimum period of time, as defined by retention laws. They must also ensure that certain data is purged from the system. For example, data privacy laws mandate the destruction of person-related data after a specified period of time. In Germany, companies must delete data from rejected job applicants in their HR systems not earlier than 6 months, but not later than 12 months, after the applicant was rejected. Failing to comply with these regulations may result in large fines for companies. Another example is a pharmaceutical company that must keep information related to a new clinical trial for a number of years. Once that time has passed, the information should be deleted. Not deleting sensitive information after the required retention period increases the risk from potential lawsuits.

Building According to Specs

Remember the Mars probe? Launched in 1999, the Mars Climate Orbiter was designed to gather amazing data to help scientists better understand the universe. However, none of that amazing data was gathered from the $125 million venture. Why? Because groups working across the globe failed to operate under similar units of measure. Specifically, the American units of measurement used in construction had to be converted to metric units for operation. Core information management principles could have helped alleviate this risk by documenting the data definitions and outlining use of that data throughout the data's lifecycle.

Maintaining Industry Standards for Data

Some external standards apply to entire industries. For example, global standards (GS1 standards) aim to help companies exchange information in the same format, thereby increasing the efficiency and visibility of supply and demand chains globally.[2] To participate, however, you not only need to understand the relevant GS1 standard, but you must also fully understand your data, the data model, and current data quality levels. Without this baseline understanding, your use of GS1 would be flawed at best, and you would miss golden optimization opportunities.

1.4   Impact of Big Data on EIM

It is well documented that the volume of data created in organizations is large and growing at a velocity that is unprecedented. It is now commonplace to have organizational data stores measured in terabytes or even petabytes. Although, as of 2009, the entire Internet was estimated to contain close to only 500 exabytes, it is not hard to imagine that organizations will soon routinely deal with data stores comprising multiple exabytes; indeed, can the day be far off when organizations deal with more than a zettabyte (equivalent to a billion terabytes) of internal data?

---

2   Source: *http://www.GS1.org/about/overview*

There are many reasons for the unparalleled growth in data stores: social media, compliance and regulatory requirements, transactional data, sensory data (such as data from real-time shop floor sensors), multimedia content, mobile devices, RFID-enabled devices, the "internet of things" (connected devices), the never-ending quest to improve organizational effectiveness, and the list goes on. The fact is that data creation has become a by-product of nearly all individual and organizational activities.

Moreover, the reason data is preserved and reused is that it has value well beyond its original use. We dare to say that the value of the data created to automate business processes may in some cases be greater than the process itself. Today the market has christened the phenomena of organizations' desire to harness the great torrent of data, as well as the velocity, variety, and variability of information known as *big data*. Figure 1.6 is a representation of the volume, velocity, variety, and variability of data. It remains to be seen if the term *big data* will stick. However, as long as organizations can create value through data, the continued growth and importance of data will be immutable. Fortunately, advancements in computational power, storage capacity, information access and management, and analytics are progressing at an equally impressive rate. Two such advancements are Hadoop and SAP HANA (to be discussed further in Chapter 3). The combination of massively greater amounts of data with the tools and talent to analyze it promises to launch the next wave of innovation and productivity and even spawn new business models.

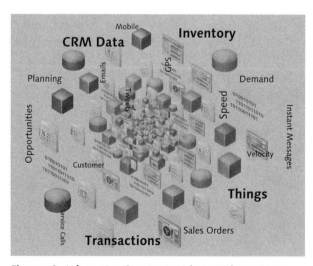

Figure 1.6 Information Growing in Volume, Velocity, Variety, and Variability

One example of new innovation provided by the ability to manage and analyze big data is in the healthcare industry, specifically related to the area of cancer treatment. The human genome contains 6 billion DNA base pairs; as the genome sequence for each patient will be decrypted in the near future, these billions of data points must be managed. Add to that documentation and features such as speech recognition, and you will end up with 20 terabytes per patient.

The velocity of data collection is building daily, and you must manage and make sense of your data on the fly. You need to remain flexible through instability and change. You cannot underestimate the pace of innovation, and you do not want to be playing catch-up with your competitors. If planning and implementing a coherent data management strategy seems daunting when your organization owns a few terabytes of data, how difficult will it be when you own thousands of terabytes?

Some examples of big data and its impact on EIM include:

▶ **Real-time analysis**
Using columnar databases (discussed in Chapter 3) and in-memory computing, analysis of what once took three days now takes three minutes. For the analysis to be that fast, the provisioning, verification, and cleansing of data must be done prior to executing the hard-core analysis algorithms. EIM plays a crucial role in the very early provisioning of data for instant analysis.

▶ **Healthcare**
What if your doctor could compare your unique health profile with millions of patients and identify the best treatment for you while you are in the exam room? EIM ensures that millions of patient records have met certain quality standards and are compared to compliant data points so that the doctor's view of the data can be trusted.

▶ **Retail**
What if you knew your customers so well you could offer them a favored style before their current article wears out? EIM ensures that the retail agency has updated customer information and is also able to turn social media and other unstructured information into new data points about the customer.

▶ **Supply chain**
What if a supplier stopped shipment between a factory in Taiwan and a location in Toledo, but your global supply chain could auto-adjust to prevent manufacturing delays, so customers get what they want when they want it? How would that impact customers' loyalty? EIM can detect the stopped shipment, correlate

with other events, and ensure that the supply chain process has the correct information to adjust the shipment.

▶ **Insurance**
What if your house burned down and the insurance company had a virtual view of everything you own? They could provide full reimbursement in a fraction of the time it now takes. How would that impact customer loyalty? EIM's role in this is to manage the pictures and documents as well as ensure that customer data is accurate.

SAP's focus on big data will enable companies to run their business better with the right software to manage information for competitive advantage. SAP will always remain focused on enabling customers to solve business problems and enable innovation.

The best way to realize the promise of big data, today and in the future, is to develop and adopt an enterprise information management strategy. This strategy should cover your entire enterprise to take advantage of the benefits of sharing information and aggregating data across your organization. Typical topics that must be considered for an effective EIM strategy include interoperable data models, architectures for analytical and transactional data, integration architecture, analytical architecture, and information security and compliance. The goal is to have data that is sharable and can be leveraged over time within and across business units. The deployment of SAP solutions for EIM within a defined EIM strategy is a key starting point. The alternative is to have massive amounts of disintegrated and unreliable data analyzed fast.

"Garbage in, garbage out" is one of the oldest adages in information processing; when the volume of data reaches the big data stage, getting productive use of poorly managed information becomes the equivalent of searching for a priceless antique in a landfill.

1.5   SAP's Strategy for EIM

The role of EIM solutions for SAP is to orchestrate, cleanse, and manage data, information, and content. This includes information residing in and moving between on-premise, on-device, and on-demand sources.

Figure 1.7 shows SAP's EIM solutions as the logical layer between information sources and applications. Notice that the bottom part of the figure shows the various sources of information, including structured data, unstructured data, and diverse data sources. The sources can be application databases, data warehouses, unstructured text from blog entries, email, raw text, and so on. SAP's EIM solution portfolio provides information capabilities to interface with almost any database and with almost any application. These applications include both SAP applications such as the SAP Business Suite and SAP BusinessObjects analytical applications (such as those that run on SAP HANA), as well as non-SAP or custom applications, and other data sources such as flat files or Excel spreadsheets.

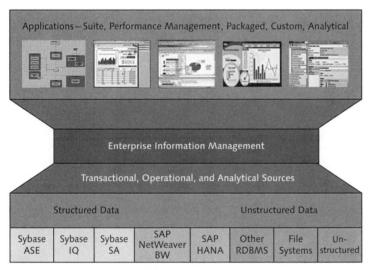

Figure 1.7 EIM in SAP's Portfolio

SAP's solutions for EIM are broad and deep in functionality, including capabilities to support data management, information governance, master data management, enterprise content management, and system decommissioning.

You might have seen presentations on SAP's company strategy to help the world run better by, in part, providing the best business applications on premise, on demand, and on device, with orchestration of processes across all applications. SAP's solutions for EIM provisions information across business applications, delivering integrated, accurate, and timely information—both structured and unstructured—to your entire enterprise. SAP's investment in EIM is strong and will continue to grow as the requirement to provision data across many applications and databases grows. An overview of SAP's solutions for EIM will be provided in Chapter 4.

1.6 Typical User Roles in EIM

Throughout the book, various user roles will be mentioned. The exact definition of EIM-related user roles varies by company; this section presents the common roles of people involved in EIM and the definitions assumed for this book. All these roles collaborate together for best results:

▶ **Data owner**
A data owner role is accountable for the overall quality of a master data area. A master data domain such as customer may have various cross-departmental contributors, but one individual will own a given master data area.

▶ **Business process owner**
A business process owner role is accountable for developing and implementing a strategy for a business area. The role is accountable for identifying improvements, driving standardization, and monitoring/measuring the process.

▶ **Business process manager**
A business process manager role is responsible for developing various business processes as per the strategy developed by the business process owner. The role is responsible for identifying improvements, driving standardization, and monitoring/measuring the process.

▶ **Data steward**
A data steward understands data management practices and has domain knowledge for data and its impact on various business processes and business drivers. A data steward understands and develops policies and rules for data quality, text analytics, and information governance.

▶ **Global data manager/manager of master data**
The global data manager manages the data governance program across IT and the business units. He may also manage the data stewards, development teams, and migration activities.

▶ **Data analyst/IT analyst/business data analyst**
The analyst performs data profiling and quality assessment, defines validation rules and data quality scorecards, determines cleansing requirements, and analyzes metadata impact and lineage.

1.7   Example Company: NeedsEIM, Inc.

In this section (first mentioned in Section 1.1.1), we describe the fictional scenario that we will refer to throughout the book. It depicts a company that needs an information strategy for its complex supplier network. This company is called NeedsEIM, Inc.

NeedsEIM, Inc. is a Fortune 500 company specializing in the manufacture of retail durable goods. It has outsourced the manufacturing to different contract manufacturers but still has to deal with a vast supplier network in procuring finished goods, raw materials, and services to support the enterprise.

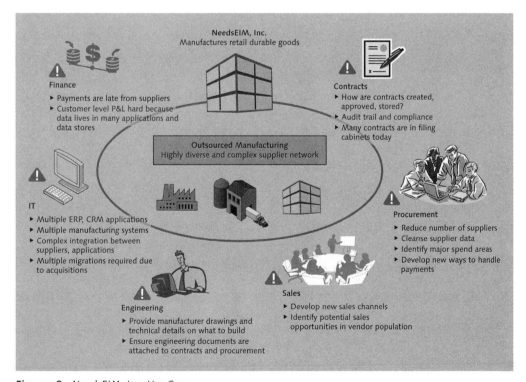

Figure 1.8   NeedsEIM, Inc. Use Case

NeedsEIM, Inc. has several business challenges, described below and shown in Figure 1.8.

1.7.1 CFO Issues

Legal issues around vendor contracts have caused major disruptions in the past. The chief financial officer wants to get a handle on how contracts are created, approved, and stored so that the required audit trail and documentation is available in a timely manner.

1.7.2 Purchasing Issues

The vice president of purchasing has issued a different mandate: to decrease the number of suppliers, identify major spend areas, and develop new ways to handle payments to suppliers. There is a cost associated with paying a supplier through a credit card versus bank account ACH transaction versus check. The goal is to optimize the mix so that the payment costs are efficiently managed.

1.7.3 Sales Issues

The sales director is interested in developing new channels and identifying potential sales opportunities in the vendor population. Current processes are manual and time-consuming, consisting of spreadsheet analysis that compares all customers with vendors. Inconsistent data makes it hard to conduct any reliable and repeatable analysis. The sales director also faces a similar problem on contract management, where all documents are currently in filing cabinets, and any disputes or questions require staff poring over paper documents. In addition, it is hard to do any customer-level profit and loss analysis given the state of data. Multiple ERP, procurement, customer relationship management (CRM), and manufacturing systems make it that much harder to rationalize and do any type of analysis that can be actionable.

1.7.4 Engineering and Contracts Issues

The engineering department has received escalations of the products not being built to the correct specifications provided by engineering. The contracts and engineering departments are trying to both ensure that the legal contracts with the manufacturers have the correct drawings and technical details, and that all changes go through contracts back to the manufacturer.

1.7.5 Information Management Challenges Facing NeedsEIM, Inc.

NeedsEIM, Inc. is typical of a company with a diverse supplier network and out-sourced manufacturing. None of the issues discussed above make it immediately obvious that the answer is a need for better information management, but, as you examine the problems, it becomes clear. Notice, most importantly, that most of the issues are cross-departmental: The different organizations need information provided by another organization, or the organizations need to ensure that they are providing and making decisions based on the same information. Thus, while no one is screaming for an information management strategy, an information strategy is the building block to addressing the business concerns of NeedsEIM, Inc. Key information management challenges facing NeedsEIM, Inc. include:

▸ Identifying and managing customer, supplier, and analysis of master data.

▸ Need for audit trail and workflow for contracts and unstructured data.

▸ Ability to link unstructured data to master data.

▸ Integration between disparate systems.

Throughout the book, NeedsEIM, Inc. will be referred to when we look at specific capabilities of EIM and how they can help address business issues.

1.8 Summary

In this chapter, we have presented many real-world problems that can be addressed with enterprise information management. It is likely that you or your company are already addressing these challenges, but with disparate tools and hand-coded scripts and manual procedures. This is an expensive and unsustainable model for managing an ever-increasing volume of business-critical information. We are advocating that you, and all companies, understand and harmonize your treatment of information, because you can't keep up with hundreds of ad-hoc approaches. As EIM is adopted, you can free your people to use information to solve big strategic problems instead of fighting daily data fires.

This chapter has looked at the key drivers for having an enterprise information management strategy and introduced NeedsEIM, Inc., which is the fictional company used as an example throughout the book. Subsequent chapters will examine information governance, EIM and SAP HANA, examples of EIM and how it is used today, and key parts of SAP's solutions for EIM. We will also provide concrete examples for getting you started using EIM.

By bringing together the right people, processes, policies, and metrics, an information governance discipline will ensure trusted, consistent, and clear information throughout your organization.

2 Introducing Information Governance

Information governance is the practice of overseeing the management of your enterprise's information. It provides oversight to ensure successful execution of your information initiatives and involves the management of people, technology, and processes based on policies, standards, and metrics, including the ongoing oversight necessary to manage information risks.

> **Information Governance versus Data Governance**
>
> The terms *information governance* and *data governance* are sometimes used interchangeably. SAP uses *information governance* because it is a broader term that indicates how the practice must expand beyond master data to include rich content (documents and PDFs), archiving and retention policies, and the business process context of that information.

By following the approaches outlined in this chapter, you'll learn how to establish an effective information governance program, so an information governance team can deliver information-driven projects both on-time and without excessive rework. *And* these new-found skills can be reused for the next information project, which reduces cost.

The chapter begins by introducing information governance and then discusses the following topics:

► How to evaluate your existing information governance needs and resources, including establishing a plan for maturing your information governance policies.

► How to optimize existing infrastructure and resources to maximize the value of information governance.

► How to establish an information governance process by following a few key examples (creating a new reseller, supplier registration, and data migration).

▶ How to round out your information governance processes with key practices of identifying the impact of missing data, gathering metrics and key performance indicators (KPIs), and establishing a before-and-after view of your organization.

2.1 Introduction to Information Governance

Information governance touches all aspects of EIM, from information discovery to data integration to enterprise content management to retention and archiving policies. Figure 2.1 shows some of the key information-heavy use scenarios (scenarios where information provides critical elements, such as business analytics) where you should apply information governance principles.

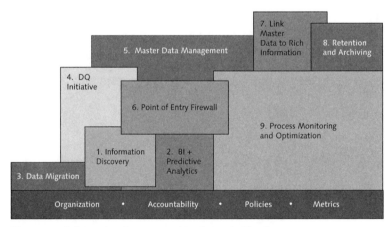

Figure 2.1 Information Governance Use Scenario Phasing

By now, most chief information officers (CIOs) have heard the phrase "data as a strategic asset" or "enterprise data assets." On the surface, this sounds really important. But how many organizations know what it means to tactically execute on information as a strategic asset? Most corporations are just scratching the surface of which practices to put in place to support data as an enterprise asset. Whether you are part of management or of an IT department, it is important to move beyond this basic understanding and begin employing practical applications of the idea. If your company has any of the following characteristics, then providing governance around how information is managed or used is key to mitigating risks (operational and legal) and optimizing value:

- Legal requirements
- Regulatory and standards compliance
- Information-driven projects such as business process engineering, predictive analytics, and strategic initiatives

Several aspects of information can be governed:

- **People**
  - Informational ownership and accountability
  - Information access (who, when, where, what)
- **Processes**
  - Data handling (creating, updating, deleting)
  - Information storing (archiving, security)
- **Metrics**
  - Data quality levels
  - Reporting (who, when, what)
- **Policies and standards**
  - Data definitions
  - Allowable values
  - Information architecture

It is important not to underestimate how business processes rely on good information. To make this concept clear, let's consider an example from the airline industry.

Information as a Strategic Asset from the Airline Industry

Recently, Southwest Airlines had an issue with a Boeing 737-300. The Boeing experienced a ripped fuselage shortly after take-off. Southwest then voluntarily cancelled at least 600 flights in the week following the emergency landing.

After much analysis, the Federal Aviation Administration (FAA) issued an emergency directive requiring electromagnetic inspections of Boeing 737-300, -400, and -500 airplanes with a specific number of takeoff-and-landing cycles—more than 30,000 planes. The goal of these inspections was to proactively find signs of excessive wear.

Imagine the information governance that both the FAA, Boeing, and individual airlines must have in place. First, the companies had to (very quickly) identify the causal issue, based on detailed maintenance logs, manufacturer data, and even the specific manufacturing processes involved. Next, the companies had to (just as quickly) do some predictive analytics to find where similar problems may be lurking to stop a disaster before it occurs. These predictive analytics had to be run across the individual airlines and take into account multiple parameters: manufacturer, manufacturing process, model numbers, inspection logs, and more. As if that wasn't enough, Southwest Airlines alone had to cancel flights, notify passengers, move aircraft around, and rebook at least 600 flights.

To track all of this information and react quickly, these organizations had to, in advance, clearly identify critical data elements that they needed to track (maintenance logs, manufacturing processes, etc.). They also had to document their information policies: how long to keep information, how to analyze information in maintenance logs, service-level agreements (SLAs) for notifying passengers of flight changes, and so on.

The business processes above rely on clean, consistent information. If a model number is not stored according the defined data standard, quick access to that aircraft would not happen. In this case, the risk of *not* applying information governance principles is very clear and unacceptably high.

Information governance is a sustained activity that can be applied to one project, can be started with one data domain, and should be extended to the enterprise.

2.2   Evaluating and Developing Your Information Governance Needs and Resources

Now that you know what information governance is and how it can help, you can determine the shape of information governance at your company. In this section, we will discuss the process of evaluating and developing your information governance needs and resources.

2.2.1   Evaluating Information Governance

Wait! Claim Success Immediately!

Yes, that's right. Before you even begin, you should recognize that you do have some information governance policies in place. Your business has information. Somehow you are shipping product to…someone. Someone is creating that information. Someone is updating that information. Guess what? Those are information policies. Write them down. Document the policies—informal though they may be—that your company is practicing right now. Assemble them in a central place and then publicize a few of the surprising policies you discovered. You haven't fixed any problems yet, but just gathering the policies in-practice is a huge step forward for information governance.

When getting started with an information governance policy, there are several key questions to be answered. Which information elements are absolutely critical? Which business processes depend on those information elements being of high quality? What does "high quality" mean to each individual business process? Which elements must be dealt with first? Who owns understanding the ramifications of poor governance and driving the information governance program forward? Does the business have an accurate assessment of current quality levels? Could the business quickly use predictive analytic techniques to proactively avoid large problems? Does the chief financial officer (CFO) have confidence enough to sign-off—on the threat of imprisonment or fines—that all the required regulations and organizational policies are being met while capturing and sharing this information? Above all, to get started with an information governance policy, a company must understand how quality, timely information is critical to business function, value, and risk reduction.

Because information governance is most successful when practiced on an individual project (and thereafter sustained as an ongoing culture), there cannot be a single best practice that fits most organizations. Instead, you need to evaluate your company along the below dimensions and develop a plan that works best for your needs:

▸ **Culture dimension** (Figure 2.2)
   How much change can your organization tolerate? Do you have lines of business or divisions that are used to working independently? Is the company process driven or action oriented?

Figure 2.2   Culture Dimension of Information Governance

The farther your company falls to the left (independence), the more you'll need to focus on applying specific data standards on critical data elements. Do not immediately start a project to optimize information for order to cash, for instance. The kinds of sweeping change that information for business process optimization would require will be more than your organization can tolerate. The farther your company moves to the right (collaboration), the more you can focus on fit-for-use standards—and cleansing—for impactful business processes.

▶ **Enterprise information management maturity dimension** (Figure 2.3)
Do you have any centers of excellence running around information (business intelligence, data quality, master data, etc.)? Do you operate in a shared services model? Do you have enterprise information architects that guide individual project decisions? Do you have a strategic information plan?

Figure 2.3 EIM Maturity Dimension of Information Governance

The farther your company falls to the left (individual projects), the more you'll need to focus on localized value first. Do not immediately start a project to manage vendor information globally, for instance. The farther your company moves to the right (information strategy), the more you can use executive sponsorship and more centralized decision making in your initial information governance efforts.

▶ **Management sponsorship dimension** (Figure 2.4)
Who feels the most pain as a result of poor information? Do you have a senior executive (one with organizational clout) who understands the power of information? Would an executive sponsor be able to align all of the individual stakeholders to common goals and success metrics?

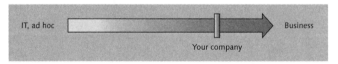

Figure 2.4 Management Sponsorship Dimension of Information Governance

The farther your company falls to the left (IT, ad hoc), the more you'll need to focus on easy-to-interpret information projects, such as automated cleaning of address information according to governmental standards. Although the business would certainly need to understand the kind of cleansing happening with their data, the extent of business/IT collaboration is limited because external bodies have already made many of the fit-for-use decisions. The farther your company moves to the right (business), the more you can focus on projects where fit-for-use is very open to interpretation (for example, classifying and attaining a single view of vendor information).

▶ **Data domains and process dimension** (Figure 2.5)
Which business process or data domains are causing the most trouble in your organization? Which information is strategic? Which information is critical? Which information is shared across multiple business processes?

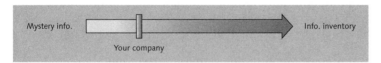

Figure 2.5 Data Domains Dimension of Information Governance

The farther your company falls to the left (mystery information), the more you'll need to focus on finding, identifying, and tagging the information that has high business value for your chosen project. Without this first step, your fledgling information governance team will have no way to prove value or impact. In addition, your group will not be able to accurately target their work for high value or estimate the amount of work necessary to complete the project. The farther your company moves to the right (information inventory), the more you can use established baselines to set realistic, high-visibility metrics for your information stakeholders.

With answers to these questions in hand, you will be able to domesticate your wild information. Business leaders and IT leaders can now collaborate on a working definition of information governance that is tailored to your company. SAP's services organization can also help you with this process via our Strategic Information Management group's Information Governance Maturity Assessment (*http://www.sap.com/services/portfolio/business-transformation/index.epx*).

After you tailor your governance approach to your company's quirks, you will be ready to start talking resources. Although it may be tempting to start evaluating technology resources, the best first step is to figure out people resources; for example, people who modify information frequently and who decide what should be archived.

One great way to discover these hidden assets is with surveys. Send a quick web survey out that asks employees if they touch, enrich, or manage information. Then have the employees clarify which information they touch, and what general actions they perform on that information (create, read, update, and delete). The survey results will show you the breadth of your information governance problem and will give you some idea of the direction you need to go.

Assessing Resources

One global company discovered that they had 92 people managing information, most certainly inconsistently. With this information (including the details of which information elements were touched and how), they were able to make a clear plan to centralize and standardize operations down to 19 employees.

Once you understand what people resources you have, you can decide what additional resources you need (for example, business data analysts, data quality specialists, data stewards, global data managers, and business data modelers). Only after you have employees in place (even if only part-time) and have gained some experience actively managing the information, can you begin to develop decent requirements for technology that will help you scale your efforts.

After you have the employees and your executive sponsor in place, you need to define the scope of your first project. Keep in mind that managers and executives have the most to gain from high-quality data, so do not under-sell your initiative. When choosing a project, make sure to consider which information elements are the most critical to govern. What does good governance look like for those key information elements? Then start working on documenting ownership and policies and standardizing important processes (for example, can VENDOR CREATE use most of the same input form as CUSTOMER CREATE?). These activities can be as light or as heavy as you define in the tailoring step.

2.2.2   Developing Information Governance

You have defined a process and established both a rough organization and some basic tool requirements. Now, you need make sure this information governance policy matures with time. Keep the following steps in mind:

1. Define a data strategy that supports the business strategy and goals.

2. Identify the critical data elements that support those business goals.

3. Quantify how managing those data elements increases value.

4. Establish a current baseline for those critical elements.

5. Create an improvement plan.

6. Align business and IT behind enterprise data standards, policies, and processes.

7. Create data standards and processes supporting end-to-end (E2E) business processes instead of ad-hoc projects.

8. Achieve greater control over and visibility of the data.

9. Understand and manage full the data lifecycle (creation/acquisition to retirement/destruction).

10. Quantify results.

11. Do it again.

12. Manage the change cycle.

Keep in mind that any new critical projects can likely derail this project. Be prepared for these changes by using basic project management and tracking tools for your initial information governance project. (This is where starting out information governance as a smaller project really helps.) Use these tools to document owners, policies that the groups decided on, criticality, metadata inventory, and more. If you document/track wisely, you'll be able to pick up the project right where you left off. Also, you'll be able to easily extend some of the decisions you made to the *next* information governance project.

For most companies, the key is to start with a small, tactical project. Track a few simple metrics along the way. Then widely publicize the great results you attained (in terms of business value). For details, see Section 2.5.2.

2.3   Optimizing Existing Infrastructure and Resources

Companies need a systematic way of looking at the entire information landscape. Your company probably has a rough idea of that clear, orderly picture you would draw if you were starting from scratch. But because you have been managing information in an ad hoc manner for a while, you desperately need a system to help you figure out where to start.

Here are some of the criteria to factor into your plan:

► **Assessment/discovery**
First, make sure your picture of your information landscape is accurate. Do you know how the business processes feed each other? Do you know which business intelligence (BI) and analytics systems depend on which data stores? Do you know when/how often you are getting data from external sources?

► **Nicely contained**
One place to start might be where a system can be nicely contained. Not too many far-afield applications or processes depend on the information. In this way, a small, well-informed team can design, test, and deploy the new system.

► **High value**
Your company may have a board-level initiative around customer information. If so, you could be nicely attached to executive sponsorship and funding. However, even in customer information, you would have multiple projects to choose from. Choose a project that can show hard return on investment (ROI) through metrics you can reasonably track. Don't tie yourself to a metric of increased customer satisfaction if you have no way to refresh that metric until long after your project is done—and no way to trace increased customer satisfaction back to better information. It's tempting. Don't do it. Focus on value you can *get* and value you can somehow track back to better information.

► **Remove an external service**
Often, companies use external service bureaus for part of list processing—either in preparation for mailing or in purchased-list merging. Replacing these external providers with in-house processing is a natural, low-risk project. These projects are nicely contained, for one. Second, the cost is well defined, because you are paying the service provider. Third, somewhere you already have design specifications that you passed off to the service provider. So you have a jump start.

► **Strategic impact**
Do not pick an area that will undergo a lot of technical change in the next six months—major, disruptive technical change. If you're looking to start major changes such as SAP HANA or mobility in a specific area, do not spend your time implementing a technical solution where there will be major requirement/infrastructure changes. In some small set of cases, if you can implement quickly, then you may get automatically included in the disruptive project. It's up to you. That's more of a political decision.

As always, make sure you understand the roadmap and direction from your major technology partners. Without that information, you may box yourself in.

If your company has been good—solving information problems along the way—it may seem like you've made the problem of strategic information governance harder for yourself. And in some ways, you have. However, in the most difficult aspects of a project, your path is easier:

▶ You have people who understand information.

▶ You have design documents and requirements—somewhere.

▶ You have a pretty good understanding of where you can do better.

▶ You have competency in a myriad of tools.

▶ You have a company that expects you to be able to solve information problems—and that understands that information problems *must* be solved.

Use these things to your advantage when setting up your first information governance process.

2.4   Establishing an Information Governance Process: Examples

Now you have a good handle on what information governance is and why you need to apply those principles to all of your information-heavy projects. But how can you go about setting up your first information governance process? First, recognize that there are two main types of information governance:

▶ **Preventative**
Information governance enforces compliance before substandard information even enters your productive systems. For example, information may be cleansed and validated before it achieves *live* status in your business applications (such as SAP ERP, for example).

▶ **Reactive**
Information governance enforces compliance after information has made its way into your productive systems. For example, check for redundant information across different information silos.

To explore reactive information governance, let's look at an example where a homeowner in Omaha, NE, received an erroneous water utilities bill for $13,499.02. The bill claimed that her residence used 4.5 million gallons of water in a month. Some possible causes for this localized billing error are:

▶ The homeowner's bill was mistakenly merged with other bills, creating a larger cumulative total.

▶ The technician who read the homeowner's water meter mistakenly entered how many gallons she used.

Following good information governance principles, you'd start by performing solid root cause analysis. What could you do to prevent problems like this from occurring again?

▶ Require a review of merged records, where the types of records are different (residential and business, for example).

▶ Provide last month's reading to the technician at point-of-entry. Question the technician if the difference is greater than 50%.

▶ If you can't provide point-of-entry information or validation to the technician, at least run validations before the bills go out. Catch records where the difference in usage is more than 50%, and double-check the readings.

You can do these things by hand, manually scanning rows and rows of data. Better yet, use tools like SAP Data Services (hereafter Data Services), SAP Information Steward (hereafter Information Steward), and SAP NetWeaver Business Process Management (BPM) to automate this information governance workflow. (We will discuss SAP's solutions for EIM in more detail in Chapter 4.) Or use Transaction EL27, which checks for implausible meter readings.

To finish the story, the utilities department did admit that the bill was wrong. A new one was sent in the mail. This example illustrates reactive information governance because an external event (in this case, a very public one) triggered an evaluation of the policies and processes governing information.

Now imagine this same story, but apply preventative information governance. In that case, you would follow these steps:

1. Upon creation of the billing business process, evaluate which key information elements support that process, such as meter reading.

2. Define what a good meter reading looks like: format, data type, completeness, freshness, and ownership.

3. Establish the policies outlined above and build automation that enforces that policies at point-of-entry.

4. Monitor compliance to the established policies to pinpoint information problems before an erroneous bill goes to a customer.

Notice that you can easily move from reactive information governance to preventative information governance—and in many cases, you can use the crisis of reactive information governance to gain support for a preventative information governance program.

In the next section, we provide some examples of how some companies got started with setting up an information governance policy.

2.4.1 Example 1: Creating a New Reseller

For this example, think about becoming a new customer of NeedsEIM, Inc. (a manufacturer of retail durable goods who sells primarily to resellers of their equipment, introduced in Chapter 1). New customers/resellers require in-depth evaluation. NeedsEIM, Inc. will be sending hundreds of thousands of dollars of inventory to these resellers, which tells you about the resellers expectations.

Because of the price, the resellers will have high expectations for personal service. Often the customer/reseller record may be created while sitting with the sales person or by calling the company directly (perhaps based on a referral from another company). Therefore, it is a good idea to set up a policy and procedures for how to handle this case. The steps below are one example of how the process might work:

1. The reseller identifies key suppliers and then calls account management to create a new customer record.

2. The account representative verifies reseller information.

3. The account lead verifies if the reseller is related to any other resellers the company already has: subsidiary, different division, parent corporation, and so on.

4. Account information is dispersed to the operational systems (customer and supplier relationship management systems, such as SAP Customer Relationship Management [CRM], SAP Supplier Relationship Management [SRM], logistics, engineering systems, and more).

5. Each operational system adds the account information necessary to complete the customer/reseller from their perspective. This completion cycle is predictable, repeatable, and well known. It follows a workflow that notifies users when

it is their turn to add or approve information. Some of this information may include engineering drawings, aggregations, contracts, and more. The actual contract may not be stored with the master record, but a link to the transactional and associated metadata will be.

6. Each operation system feeds some of the new elements they added back to the customer/reseller definition of master data.

7. When enriching the master record with the data from separate operational systems, sometimes the user finds conflicts. They must resolve these conflicts by working through a conflict resolution process. This resolution process is predictable, repeatable, and well known. It follows a workflow that notifies users when it is their turn to review or approve conflicts.

8. Every month, refresh the company/reseller information (such as Dun and Bradstreet data) to make sure changes are captured.

9. Every month, refresh the address data to make sure changes are captured.

10. Push company/reseller information (such as Dun and Bradstreet data) hierarchy number changes and address changes to the operational and reporting systems.

This is a heavyweight process because creating a new business to work with has both high impact and low frequency. Mistakes caused by bad information are extremely expensive, so it's a good example of where an information governance policy should be established and followed.

2.4.2 Example 2: Supplier Registration

As a starting point, although not inclusive of all of the aspects and technologies of information governance, you could build a cross-system supplier self-service registration and approval process. This example takes some of the concepts in the example discussed in Section 2.4.1, and applies them to a similar scenario. In addition, this example provides a bit more technical tooling to build on what you've learned so far. (The SAP solutions mentioned here will be discussed in more detail in Chapter 4.) The steps in this process might be as follows:

1. A supplier registers via a website and enters some initial data such as company name, street, city, and postal code. These global attributes are stored in SAP NetWeaver Master Data Management (MDM) for further distribution to non-SAP systems.

2. When the master data specialist approves the supplier, a change request is automatically generated in SAP Master Data Governance (hereafter SAP MDG).

3. A workflow in SAP MDG ensures that all SAP ERP–specific attributes are maintained.

4. After final approval in SAP MDG the new supplier is activated and distributed.

5. After activation a notification is sent to the original requester.

For this example, assume that the following systems are part of this process (the systems can do much more than what is outlined below):

▶ SAP MDG: Maintain and distribute SAP ERP-specific attributes

▶ Data Services: Clean address information and check for existing duplicates

▶ SAP Extended Enterprise Content Management (ECM) by OpenText: Attach relevant supplier contracts

▶ SAP NetWeaver MDM: Maintain and distribute global attributes

▶ SAP NetWeaver Process Orchestration: Process runtime, workflows, and user interfaces, work lists, web service consumption and provisioning, business rules, application integration

This example process implements integrated master data maintenance. The process starts with the request by a supplier, which goes to a business user. That business user continues with processing and commenting by different expert users and stakeholders and finishes with approval or rejection by authorized experts.

Depending on the business use, different types of change requests are offered. In this example, the change request is a create (meaning the change is creating a new record, not an edit to an already-existing record). However, you could reuse much of this process for change, block, or set flag for deletion. This reuse ensures that the correct information is maintained in the change request. The following list describes the process for creating, reviewing, and approving the new supplier's information:

1. The business user submits a request for creation, in response to a call from the prospective supplier.

2. The master data specialist reviews the change request.

3. The business user completes the new supplier information, including cleansing and enriching the data, as well as checking for existing duplicates.

4. The master data specialist works with the knowledge worker to reference the correct supplier contract.

5. The master data specialist approves the create request.

The business value of this process is both fulfilled compliance requirements and improved information quality.

In our example, we assume that the process was implemented using SAP NetWeaver Process Orchestration for the design and execution of the cross-system process. The example also leverages the out-of-the-box governance process in SAP MDG for maintenance of SAP ERP-specific attributes. The process is highlighted in Figure 2.6.

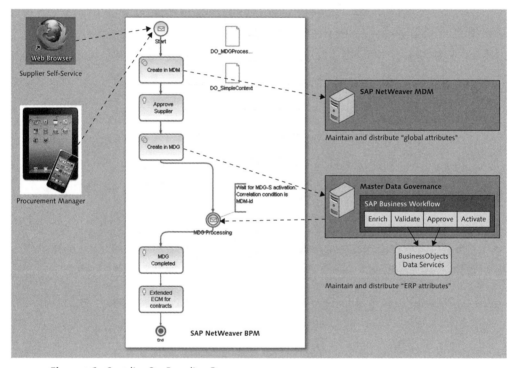

Figure 2.6 Supplier On-Boarding Process

The flow from a technical perspective is as follows:

1. The initial supplier registration web page triggers the start web service of the SAP NetWeaver BPM process.

2. The global attributes from the registration web page are used to create a new supplier record in SAP NetWeaver MDM.

3. In this human interaction step, a new supplier is being approved.

4. SAP NetWeaver Process Orchestration calls an SAP MDG service to create a change request with the initial supplier data. This also triggers SAP Business Workflow in SAP MDG.

5. SAP MDG triggers a web service call to Data Services to validate and automatically correct the address for the supplier. An additional web service call to Data Services uses matching to check if the supplier already exists in the MDG repository.

6. SAP MDG sends a message to SAP NetWeaver Process Orchestration so the flow can start.

7. SAP NetWeaver Process Orchestration uses the change request ID from SAP MDG to send an email to the original requestor. The email contains a link to the SAP Business Workflow log. Using this link, the original requestor can monitor the status of the change request in SAP MDG.

8. After sending an email, the SAP NetWeaver Process Orchestration process waits again for a message from SAP MDG. This time SAP MDG sends a message at the end of the SAP Business Workflow process after the supplier has been finally approved and activated. The message includes the final ID of the business partner in the primary persistence.

9. The last step in the SAP NetWeaver Process Orchestration process informs the original requestor that the new business partner has been created and activated.

10. SAP MDG sends an email request to the knowledge worker to attach the appropriate contract documents from SAP Extended ECM to the master record.

This example of governance processes applied to the process of creating a supplier helps you understand how you can connect SAP software solutions to automate much of your information governance processes. These software solutions will be more thoroughly introduced in Chapter 4, and then discussed in detail thoughout the book.

2.4.3 Example 3: Data Migration

Data migration projects are a good opportunity to start governance projects. One example is from a company that migrated from 4.6C to SAP ERP Central Component (ECC 6.0). Due to the 2009 financial crisis, executive management pushed the company to be a "break away" company, by leveraging industry best practices, and using as much standard processes as possible. The decision was to bring 60 countries online on the same day. The company was trying to minimize sequential go-live activities and reduce the amount of temporary interfaces between the old and new systems. The goal of the project was to use 90% standard SAP processes and 10% differentiating processes. Through a massive amount of coordination and hard work by the entire corporation, the organization was able to go live with the new system within 15 months.

Due to the complexity of this endeavor, there were risks from the master data management side. There were significant delays halfway into the project. To reduce the delays, management decided to move from cleansing 100% of the data to only cleansing critical fields. However, the project team performed the nominal checks needed to convert data from 4.6C to SAP ECC. After go-live, the organization had considerable global data issues, and the quality of customer data was degraded. In the worst case, certain sites were not able to ship for a few days, causing a task force to step in and identify all issues tied to the customer master. The task force manually addressed the issues.

This task force helped show the need for data quality. After surviving go-live issues, the company took a more holistic approach to enterprise information management with one key action: IT formed a data team to support the need for improved data quality. The new data team would take the existing SAP NetWeaver Business Warehouse (BW)/reporting team and add Data Services and information governance to complete the new organization. This allowed the data team to become a complete center of excellence in extraction, transformation, and loading (ETL) for the SAP ERP system, as well as SAP NetWeaver BW. Also, this team led the corporate discussion of data quality and formed an information governance council for the first time in the company's history.

Figure 2.7 shows the team's model of how communication flows from the top down and bottom up. The information governance committee works as the glue holding together process and data quality. Such a committee should be formed with middle to upper managers and become the strategic thinkers. When the committee approves certain processes and initiatives, these should be pushed down to global data stewards and IT/data management teams. For any issues not resolved by the information governance committee, the committee chair would need to discuss them with an executive advisor board, which includes VP and senior director-level members.

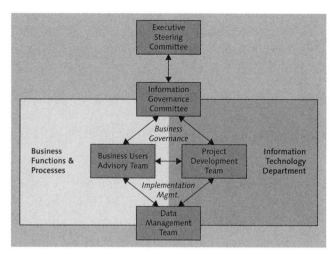

Figure 2.7 Organization for Information Governance

The information governance team quickly realized that although they were strong, forming the team is not enough. They immediately moved to formalizing team responsibilities and defining team interaction. The information governance committee also established a clear definition of success, including how to communicate that success.

Each team (executive advisory board, information governance committee and data stewards/IT support team) has different roles in information governance. In general, responsibilities are divided as follows:

▶ The executive board is primarily responsible for company culture.

▶ The information governance committee is primarily responsible for strategic approaches.

▶ The data stewards/IT are primarily responsible for tactical execution.

The leader of the data team created a strategic three to five-year plan and vision. This plan included topics such as data health metrics, master data strategy, and a rollout of an information governance program (customer, material, and vendor data cleansing, and data quality projects).

Since this was the first time the group had approached an information governance project, the data team leader used many resources to help design, build, and implement this strategic vision. Also, after building the first prototype, the leader worked with SAP experts in the EIM space to validate his work. After several iterations, the information governance strategy, plan, and package was presented to upper management and approved.

Takeaway

Go beyond building a roadmap. You need to also build a framework or structured methodology to help support sustainable growth. Part of an information governance framework should include (but not limit itself to) business process, definition, system, implementation, communication, and enforcement.

Table 2.1 shows the information governance framework that was derived from the example discussed in this section. It includes the definition, update, and enforcement of policies, and it ensures transparency so that everyone knows their role in information governance.

Category/Step	Data Governance Process
Business process	▸ Identify processes to match data set for cleansing rules ▸ Establish decisions and accountability
Define	▸ Define business rules from business users and IT ▸ Define data ▸ Specify data quality requirements ▸ Leverage stewardship with business users and IT
System	▸ Manager reporting, metrics, auto-cleansing functions ▸ Deploy governance tools
Implement	▸ Rollout business user roles ▸ Monthly cleaning ▸ De-duplication reports
Data/communication	▸ Global data owner/IT data manager to coordinate cleanup with regional owners ▸ Stakeholder communication ▸ Measuring and reporting value
Enforce	▸ Data governance committee and regional data owners to enforce policies ▸ Align policies, requirements, and controls ▸ Involves global and regional data stewards from business user groups

Table 2.1 Example Information Governance Framework

2.5   Rounding Out Your Information Governance Process

As you get started with your first information governance process, in addition to the organization, tools, and processes to enforce compliance, you also want to ensure that you measure your success and also keep in mind the impact of data that you don't have but need. Often, these steps are forgotten; however, you must incorporate these aspects of information governance to be able to show success. To show the success of your initiative, you need to take a picture of where you are now, define what success looks like, and take of picture at the end of your efforts. And don't forget to look for information that has gone missing, too.

2.5.1   The Impact of Missing Data

Too often all of our information governance efforts are focused on shaping, cleansing, and moving the most visible information. Definitely, that work needs to be done; however, keep in mind that missing information can significantly compromise your information governance success. This section not only highlights the impact of missing information, but shows you how to spotlight areas where missing information negatively impacts your organization.

According to research from Vanson Bourne, one-third of large companies in the UK say they have lost customers and business because their data was missing.[1] According to 500 IT managers and CIOs in the UK:

▶ 88% of businesses saw data as a strategic asset to their business.

▶ A third of large organizations in the UK admit to having lost a customer or new business due to missing data.

▶ Half of the respondents (52%) said their biggest frustration was the complexity around managing multiple data sources.

You can make a few assumptions from these results:

▶ If businesses knew their data was missing or incomplete, they would do something about it.

▶ If businesses could somehow tie missing data to real business processes or sales losses, they would get real resources to do something about it.

---

1   Source: Savvas, Anthony. "Firms admit losing customers as a result of missing data," (July 19, 2011) *CIO*, *http://www.cio.co.uk/news/3292136/firms-admit-losing-customers-as-a-result-of-missing-data/?olo=rss*

▸ When pieces of data—meaningful to a single business process—are spread across multiple data sources, it's too hard to tell if data is missing or incomplete.

Think of a cooking analogy: Before cooking you usually check about two cupboards for all of the ingredients. Imagine if you had to check five cupboards, and some ingredients were split across cupboards. You are much more likely to miss identifying an incomplete ingredient. Depending on the ingredient, you could compromise an entire meal. Information and business processes are much more complex.

When applied to information, how do you fix this problem? You need a solution with the following capabilities:

▸ Access to multiple data sources at once

▸ Ability to associate a field to a business process

▸ Ability to check for nulls or blanks in a critical data field

▸ Ability to check for nulls or blanks when conditions arise across multiple data fields from multiple sources

▸ Ability to check for incomplete (or shorter than expected) data in a critical data fields

▸ Ability to check for incomplete data when conditions arise across multiple data fields from multiple data sources

▸ Ability to notice incomplete data before a transaction tries to complete

▸ Ability to require complete data at point-of-entry

You don't have to lose customers or new business because of missing data or incomplete data. At least start by identifying *where* you have critical, missing data.

2.5.2 Gathering Metrics and KPIs to Show Success

Establishing your first information governance process should feel like a great success. However, you undoubtedly need to show that the work (and resources) applied to the project had solid impact. Therefore, it's important to gather metrics and KPIs to show success.

Keep in mind that you have two key audiences that want this proof:

▸ **Executives**
This audience wants to hear about increased business value, decreased cost,

increased revenue, decreased risk, or quantifiable optimizations. Normally, this group also wants a more visual display of dashboards. For this group, gather *offensive KPIs*. Offensive KPIs show high-level value.

▶ **Cross-functional**

This audience suspects that the business is running slower because of all of this new process. This group needs to hear about *service-level agreement* (SLA) compliance—including reverse SLAs. For this group, show detailed statistics on the quality and timeliness of data. At a high level, these metrics are categorized as *defensive metrics*. Defensive metrics help show—in excruciating detail—how specific lines of business, departments, or even individuals are supporting or hindering the information governance value.

SLAs are especially critical. Essentially, they define the expectations of the information provided to the data stewards or knowledge workers. Establish two kinds of SLAs when you start your information governance project.

▶ **Normal SLA**

How quickly the data stewards or knowledge workers will complete their work in creating, updating, or flagging information for deletion. You should have different SLAs for each domain (material, customer, supplier, etc.). Depending on your company, there will be different expectations for the timeliness of each of these domains. For example, perhaps pricing change requests have a one-month turnaround time, but a supplier has a 24-hour turn around time.

▶ **Reverse SLA**

How good and complete the information is that's coming from the business users—including timeliness. Instead of quantifying how well your information governance team is meeting expectations, this SLA measures how well the organization is complying with the agreed-upon information governance policies. Without this reverse SLA, you'll frequently hear that *90% of the problems are with master data*. For example, determine how many rush requests you are getting for each domain and publish those results back to the business units. If 70% of your rush requests are coming from pricing (which must be established six months in advance), then your group can work collaboratively with pricing to solve this problem.

Determine these metrics and KPIs as you are defining your information policies. In this way, you can capture expectations and constraints as your working group is thinking deeply about what quality enterprise information actually means.

The KPIs generally fall into two camps:

▶ **Generic estimates of the cost of quality information**
For this type, the business goes through a detailed process to assign a cost for each major type of error. The executive steering committee may decide that the cost of an incorrect address is $100 (for example). Then you can gather metrics that say how much bad addresses are costing your business.

▶ **Specific costs for the specific errors found**
For this type, use the open nature of your system landscape to tie specific values together. Instead of giving a generic cost estimate, you are giving the exact cost of the exact information that does not meet policy. For example, you can determine which master supplier records do not have a credit score. You can then look into the SAP ERP system to see how many open orders you have with that supplier. Add this to the other supplier records with significant errors, and you can publish a supplier-inventory-orders-at-risk number.

As with the rest of your information governance program activities, you can gather and publish these KPIs and metrics without sophisticated new tools. Some companies just use common email inboxes and manual logging of issues in spreadsheets. Perhaps this manual way helps you get the conversation going on acceptable metrics and KPIs.

However, you'll need to scale your efforts so you are not spending time on manual methods of aggregating information and building one-off dashboards. To this end, SAP products can be helpful. The following products help you automate not only the metrics around your data, but the visualization of those metrics for appropriate audiences. Automation means you'll spend less time assembling data anecdotes and more time discussing the resulting business value. We will discuss these products in more detail in Chapter 4 and throughout the course of the book.

▶ **Information Steward**
Establish drillable scorecards on each domain of information, letting the user go from a high-level score of "supplier is yellow" to which specific records are not passing the threshold.

▶ **Data Services**
Move metric- and KPI-associated information into a data mart that the reporting system can access. Data Services also provides the quality metrics for numbers of duplicates, numbers of clean, shippable addresses, and so on.

▶ **SAP NetWeaver Process Orchestration and SAP Business Workflow**
Provide details on how well the business processes are performing against their own SLAs. You can correlate these details to the quality of information for those specific business processes.

▶ **SAP BusinessObjects Business Intelligence**
Provide multiple methods to visualize the metric and KPI information to your different audiences, including dashboards for your executives.

Sometimes the differences between offensive KPIs and defensive metrics or SLAs are difficult to visualize. And yet you must understand the difference so you are reporting the right level of information to the appropriate audience. To help with that visualization, Figure 2.8 shows an example of a visualization that illustrates both defensive metrics and offensive KPIs.

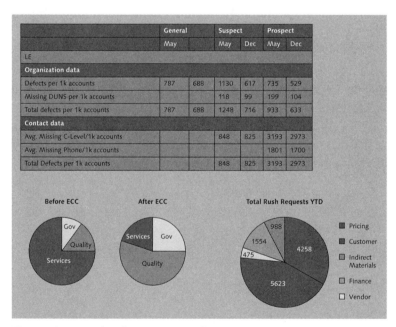

	General		Suspect		Prospect	
	May		May	Dec	May	Dec
LE						
Organization data						
Defects per 1k accounts	787	688	1130	617	735	529
Missing DUNS per 1k accounts			118	99	199	104
Total defects per 1k accounts	787	688	1248	716	933	633
Contact data						
Avg. Missing C-Level/1k accounts			848	825	3193	2973
Avg. Missing Phone/1k accounts					1801	1700
Total Defects per 1k accounts			848	825	3193	2973

Figure 2.8 Examples of SLA Metrics and KPIs

Even without reading the numbers, the sheer detail and presentation of the numbers in Figure 2.8 make it clear that this report is for someone who cares deeply about the fine details of information readiness. The rush request pie chart in the figure shows defensive metrics while also nicely illustrating the concept of reverse SLAs. The ECC pie charts highlight resource movement and whether those resource reassignments have met corporate targets after an initial SAP ERP implementation, which involved significant business process reengineering. These pie charts represent offensive KPIs to use with executives.

In conclusion, when evaluating the kinds of metrics and reports that you would provide to internal stakeholders, follow the advice summarized here:

▶ For executives, provide highly visual, business-value-based graphics (offensive KPIs).

▶ For cross-functional stakeholders, provide detailed information on SLA compliance, resourcing changes, and information quality. This information needs to be available both in simple charts as well as detailed data sheets.

2.5.3 Establish a Before-and-After View

Finally, know that to establish ongoing information governance resources—which is the best practice—you'll need to publish some kind of before-and-after view. To do this, you need to know what before looks like.

The only way to know what before looks like is to establish a baseline before you start any of your information governance work. Remember the use scenario phasing figure (Figure 2.1)? Hopefully it is now clear that information discovery is an important phase. Information discovery includes cataloging what you already have and the basic information quality level of the critical information assets.

Without this step, you cannot show the benefits of all of your work. It may seem like unnecessary busy-work when you spot a problem and are intent on fixing the critical problems. But you must do it.

2.6   Summary

This chapter has provided some concrete and real examples on what information governance looks like, what you need to do to get started with your first governance process, and how governance is a discipline that impacts users, organizations, and software. Information governance is a discipline that oversees the management of your enterprise's information. By bringing together the right people, processes, policies, and metrics, information governance delivers trusted, consistent, and clear information throughout your organization.

The 2000s saw the rise of "big data," a term coined by analysts to describe the massive amounts of information that businesses and other institutions began to store and process. This chapter discusses the enabling technological developments to deal with big data, including SAP HANA, Hadoop, and SAP's EIM solutions.

3 Big Data with SAP HANA and Hadoop

When discussing SAP's solutions for enterprise information management, including EIM with big data, it is imperative that SAP HANA be included in the conversation. This chapter will provide a brief introduction to SAP HANA and then discuss its impact on SAP's EIM strategy. Additionally, this chapter will introduce Hadoop as it relates to big data, SAP HANA, and EIM.

3.1 SAP HANA

SAP HANA is SAP's new platform for real-time analytics and applications. SAP's in-memory computing technology enables real-time computing by bringing together online transaction processing applications and online analytical processing applications. Combining the advances in hardware technology with in-memory computing empowers the entire business, from shop floor to boardroom, by giving real-time business processes instantaneous access to data. The alliance of these two technologies can eliminate today's information lag for your business.

SAP HANA was developed in response to SAP customers' requirements to deal with soaring data volumes and the need for speed when analyzing large amounts of data. As a result of society's requirement to get access to information *now*, to make sense of information *now*, and to make decisions *now*, businesses and employees must have quick access and the ability to analyze information quickly to make decisions. SAP HANA gives companies immediate insight into large volumes of operational data by placing real-time decision making in the hands of the business user.

In this section you will learn about the basics of SAP HANA, how it works, its use for analytics and business intelligence, and its use as an application platform.

3.1.1 Basics of SAP HANA

SAP HANA is a flexible, multipurpose, data-source-agnostic, in-memory appliance. It combines SAP software components that have been optimized on hardware from SAP partners. The software's core foundation is based on SAP's in-memory technology, allowing it to process massive quantities of real-time transactional data in the main memory of the server. The solution also enables a host of application scenarios based on real-time analysis of large data volumes at performance levels that are not possible in traditional systems.

At its core, SAP HANA uses an in-memory technique to store your data that is particularly suited for handling very large amounts of tabular or relational data with unprecedented performance. Common databases store tabular data row-wise; for example, all data describing an address is located next to each other in memory. As long as your requirements are to access a single address, your application will run quickly, as all the required data is stored contiguously. However, consider a situation where your application requires a count of how many of the addresses stored relate to a particular country, city, or zip code. In this case it would have to scan through the full table, select each row, and check for the country or city that is required. As all mass storage devices—for example, hard disks—access data stored in full blocks that can be quite large in comparison to the data of interest (e.g., 512 Bytes for a hard disk), it is likely that a mass storage device has to read one or more rows just to check for a couple of characters; for example, checking for Brazil or San Francisco.

Tables of business data often contain many data fields, or columns, that are rarely used. This includes data relating to other tables or data fields controlling how other fields are to be used. SAP HANA allows you to read around unwanted data by organizing tables in an efficient columnar manner. In addition to a common row-oriented storage schema, a column-oriented data storage layout can be used. This means your application does not have to wait for the database to fetch data that it does not need, as all the data in a table column is stored in an adjacent manner. So, in the example of the address table, scanning through the country or city column is much faster than in a row-oriented storage layout.

But what if your database system already caches all data in RAM, in fast accessible main memory close to the CPU? Would column-oriented memory layout still speed access up? Measurements conducted at SAP and at the Hasso Plattner Institute[1] have

---

1 *http://epic.hpi.uni-potsdam.de/Home/InMemoryDataMgmt*

proven that reorganizing the data in memory column-wise brings a tremendous speed increase when accessing a subset of the data in each table row. As SAP HANA caches all data in memory, hard disks are rarely used. Hard disks are still needed to record changes to the database for permanent persistence, for backup in case of disaster recovery, and for auditing purposes. SAP HANA keeps the number of changes to your dataset as small as possible by recording every change as delta to your original dataset. Data is not modified in place but is inserted or appended to a table column. This provides several advantages, not just speed of access. As all of the old data is retained, your applications can effectively "time-travel" through data, providing views of the data as it has changed over time.

3.1.2 How SAP HANA Works

SAP HANA starts by loading data from your operational systems (this is where SAP's solutions for EIM get involved, but that will be discussed in more detail in Section 3.2. Once the transactional data is captured, SAP HANA's in-memory computing engine processes it in the server's main memory. Through a data access layer, the processed data is then made available to SAP BusinessObjects Business Intelligence (hereafter BI) platform solutions and other purpose-built applications for various data consumption scenarios.

Figure 3.1 shows the major architecture components of SAP HANA. An introduction to each major component is provided next.

Figure 3.1 SAP HANA Architecture

In-Memory Computing Engine

The in-memory computing engine is what you hear first and most about SAP HANA. It is the columnar data storage discussed above that enables super fast access to large amounts of data.

Calculation and Planning Engine

The calculation and planning engine determines the best way to break up larger queries into operations that can be performed in parallel. The operations are passed to the database optimizer that will determine the best plan for accessing the data (algebraic transformations and cost-based optimizations based on database statistics).

Modeling Studio

SAP HANA offers an easy-to-use modeling experience to further increase the autonomy of business users. Using semantically enriched views that turn raw operational data into understandable, relevant information, business users can create new analytic models in a web-based modeling environment, without help from IT. Unlike other analytic applications, all data models built in SAP HANA are purely virtual and calculate results based on underlying operational data.

The modeling studio includes both an information composer tool for business users to load data directly into SAP HANA from CSV and Excel files, as well as the full SAP HANA modeling studio for modeling new data models, analytics, and calculation views.

Real-Time Replication Services

Real-time replication services replicate data into SAP HANA. For example, when a sales order is created in SAP ERP, it should immediately be replicated into SAP HANA. This is done using SAP Landscape Transformation. It allows real-time and scheduled data replication, replicating only relevant data into the SAP HANA database. SAP Landscape Transformation supports replication back to release SAP R/3 4.6C.

SAP Data Services

SAP Data Services (hereafter Data Services) can also be used to replicate data into SAP HANA in batch mode. Data Services is used any time data cleansing, matching, merging, or other complex transformations are required prior to the replication.

Additionally, Data Services is used to replicate all third-party data into SAP HANA. (We will discuss more about the basic functions of Data Services in Chapter 7, and then go into more detail throughout the book.)

3.1.3   SAP HANA for Analytics and Business Intelligence

The first use case for SAP HANA is analytics and business intelligence. This is particularly true for large amounts of data that are required to execute specific reports and analysis. SAP HANA is compelling for analytics and business intelligence because it provides the following functions faster than the traditional SAP NetWeaver Business Warehouse (BW): reporting and analysis (query 10-100 times faster), decreased data latency (data loads 5-10 times faster), and accelerated integrated planning (calculations 5 to 10 times faster).

The first applications being developed for SAP HANA focus on analytical and business intelligence, in order to take advantage of SAP HANA's ability to analyze large amounts of data quickly.

3.1.4   SAP HANA as an Application Platform

SAP HANA is not only a database, but also an application platform. Over time you will see more applications running on SAP HANA. SAP HANA provides a new foundation for a new category of applications (e.g., planning and simulation) to significantly outperform current applications in that category. The SAP HANA applications available today include multiple Rapid Deployment Solutions and SAP NetWeaver BW 7.3. In other words, the database for SAP NetWeaver BW is now SAP HANA. This solution is called *SAP NetWeaver BW, powered by SAP HANA Database*.

Over time, many more SAP HANA applications will be available. In addition to the SAP HANA applications, there are also Rapid Deployment Solutions (RDS) available on SAP HANA. They allow for easier, faster, and more predictable consumption of SAP software. An RDS gets you as close as it gets to "ready-to-run" for a given business problem and bundles SAP's standard products with best practice preconfiguration, services and enablement content at a fixed price. Existing RDS for SAP HANA include:

▶ SAP ERP rapid-deployment solution for profitability analysis with SAP HANA

▶ SAP ERP rapid-deployment solution for operational reporting with SAP HANA

- ▶ SAP ERP rapid-deployment solution for customer segmentation with SAP HANA

- ▶ SAP rapid-deployment solution for sales pipeline analysis with SAP HANA

- ▶ SAP Bank Analyzer rapid-deployment solution for financial reporting with SAP HANA

- ▶ SAP ERP rapid-deployment solution for accelerated finance and controlling with SAP HANA

New RDS solutions for SAP HANA are released quarterly. For the latest list go to *http://service.sap.com/solutionpackages* and select IN-MEMORY COMPUTING.

3.2   SAP HANA and EIM

As a database and application platform, SAP HANA does not fall into SAP's EIM family of solutions. However, it is tightly coupled with enterprise information management. After all, what is the use of fast access to data if the data itself isn't good?

EIM's role with SAP HANA is to ensure that all data loaded into SAP HANA is correctly provisioned and ready for use in SAP HANA applications. This is especially important when loading data from diverse systems into SAP HANA. Normally you do not want to just load the data without first assessing data quality levels, duplicates between the different systems, and other cleansing options that are discussed in Part II of this book.

To ensure that the cleansed data arrives in SAP HANA, some of the EIM capabilities are delivered with SAP HANA. For example, when a customer purchases SAP HANA, the Data Services Data Integrator is included for loading data into SAP HANA. The following sections provide more details on loading data into SAP HANA using Data Services. It also discusses future plans for managing master data with SAP HANA, as well as Rapid Marts on SAP HANA.

> **Note**
>
> An overview of Data Services will be offered in Chapter 7, and then discussed in more detail throughout the book. The discussion in this section is purely focused on how the product relates to SAP HANA. For more details about the product itself, keep reading!

3.2.1 Using SAP Data Services to Load Data into SAP HANA

This section provides a high-level overview of loading data into SAP HANA. For more practical instructions, refer to Chapter 7, where we discuss Data Service's connection to data sources. Because SAP HANA is considered another data source in Data Services, the discussion in Chapter 7 also applies to SAP HANA, and no additional special configuration or development is required.

Data Services enables very complex transformations (hierarchy, history preservation, cleansing, address, matching, etc.) using multiple source tables mapped to one output table. For now, you should understand that Data Services enables you to:

▶ Create a connection to an SAP target system.

▶ Import SAP metadata.

▶ Create jobs in Data Services to load data.

▶ Execute the jobs and preview the data in SAP HANA.

This is shown in Figure 3.2.

Figure 3.2 Data Services to Load SAP HANA

Figure 3.2 shows Data Services and SAP HANA. Notice the dotted arrow connecting the repository in Data Services to the SAP HANA Studio. The repository in Data Services and the SAP HANA Studio first exchange metadata about the data to be loaded. Jobs are then created in Data Services and used to load SAP HANA.

These jobs can contain data from SAP application systems, an SAP NetWeaver BW system, or any other source system. (More details on Data Services, including the repository, the jobs, and the Data Services designer, can be found in Chapter 7.)

3.2.2 EIM Solutions and SAP HANA

For all of SAP's EIM solutions that use a database or data warehouse, SAP HANA will be a verified target. For example, Rapid Marts now runs on SAP HANA. SAP NetWeaver Information Lifecycle Management (ILM) uses reports for auditing on SAP NetWeaver BW. With SAP NetWeaver BW supporting SAP HANA as a target database, so will SAP NetWeaver ILM. Future releases of master data management capabilities will leverage SAP HANA as the platform to enable a single view of master data across master data central governance, consolidation, and high velocity integration. As EIM solutions expand to support SAP HANA use cases, they will retain the major strengths of EIM, including stewardship and governance of information, data quality, data integration, and support for new technologies such as Hadoop (discussed in the next section).

To provide a holistic look at SAP HANA, EIM, and the management of complex data, we also must pay a bit more attention to the big data concept mentioned in Chapter 1.

3.3   Big Data and Hadoop

Chapter 1 discussed the market term *big data* to describe the growth in volume and complexity of information that must be managed today. This section discusses big data in relation to Hadoop, one of the most interesting and promising new technologies related to big data. By the end of this chapter, you will have a basic understanding of how Hadoop compares to other available technologies and how to future-proof your EIM strategy.

3.3.1   The Rise of Parallel Processing Architectures

New tools, techniques, and strategies have been developed to manage ever-growing data volumes. There are two ways to scale a system so it can handle a larger workload: *scaling up*, which uses faster, more capable hardware and *scaling out*, which adds more independent hardware. For example, adding RAM to a server is scaling up, while adding another server is scaling out. In the 2000s, it became clear that scaling out was the winning approach to scaling.

One reason scaling out won the day is that microprocessors stopped getting faster. In 2002, CPU clock speed reached its maximum and has stayed at that level ever since. At the same time, Moore's Law, which holds that the number of transistors on a chip doubles every 18-24 months, still applies. The result is that computing power has increased by having more CPU cores on a chip, but the CPU cores are not getting faster. Even though our computers are getting ever more capable, they do so by dividing the processing among cores.

In practical terms, this means computers can handle tasks faster only if the tasks can be parallelized to run among the various cores. Even better is when multiple machines can run completely independently. Additional technology catalysts, such as ever decreasing memory and storage costs, make such parallel processing solutions even more attractive. Parallelization is fairly easy to do with web servers, but traditionally is complex for databases for various reasons that we discuss next.

3.3.2 NoSQL: A New Kind of Database

Taking advantage of the scalability offered by parallelization requires a new kind of datastore. These new solutions are called *NoSQL datastores* because they are non-relational and therefore cannot support full SQL semantics. The idea is that if you throw out the relations between pieces of data, then it's much easier to spread the data over multiple machines and therefore scale out. There is a range of NoSQL solutions with slightly different capabilities, depending on the exact trade-offs made in their design. Hadoop, which we will discuss later, is one of these solutions.

To understand how the NoSQL solutions scale so well, we need to think about the two types of traditional database, OLTP (online transactional processing) and OLAP (online analytical processing). The OLTP, or operational database, is great for trans-actions and relational data, but those same useful characteristics make it difficult to scale out because each table may refer to many other tables, and retrieving a piece of information for an application may involve lots of intertwined tables. The infor-mation about an entity—say, a sales order—might live in several tables (product, customer, etc.), and those tables all need to be accessed to fulfill a request. OLAP databases scale out more effectively than OLTP databases because of optimizations such as aggregations that remove many of the size and speed roadblocks, but they still bog down at very large scales. This is largely due to the underlying relational database that makes it tricky to spread data evenly across machines.

It is unlikely that NoSQL datastores will actually replace traditional databases. However, NoSQL datastores eliminate or at least minimize the relational aspect of relationship databases. Each piece of data stored has no specific relationship to any other piece of data stored. These systems are highly effective for certain applications such as crawling the web or analyzing log files, where each piece of data is logically independent of the others and where the ability to process large data volumes is more important than transactional integrity. Imagine storing a private copy of, say, one million web pages. Each one would have a unique identifier (the URL), a body, and perhaps a few other bits of information. It would be relatively easy to spread that information across many independent nodes because no document has any particular relation to any other.

Most NoSQL datastores do not support schemas at all. Instead, each piece of data stored is unstructured from the datastore's perspective—simply a bunch of characters with no particular meaning and no relation to any other piece of data. The program that uses the data stored in them needs to make sense of what is retrieved. Clearly, this makes such solutions more difficult to work with in the EIM context. You may find that a programmer or data analyst with programming skills is needed to work with a NoSQL datastore. Also note that most EIM tools are designed to leverage SQL interfaces and to rely on the schema to define the semantics and structure of the data. If you plan to employ a NoSQL datastore, make sure you understand the implications and tools available for information management purposes.

3.3.3　Hadoop Primer

So far we have concentrated on the general conditions that have given rise to Hadoop. In this section we will define Hadoop, explain briefly how it works, and describe some key technologies that have been built on top of it. This is not intended to be a comprehensive discussion, but rather a simple, high-level overview that will help you understand what Hadoop can and can't do. We encourage you to seek out more information sources online for this fast-developing space.

Introduction to Hadoop

Hadoop is free and open source Java-based software that enables *distributed, scalable, reliable* computing on clusters of inexpensive servers. Let's consider each of those characteristics separately.

Distributed

Hadoop runs on a coordinated group of machines known as a cluster so that large amounts of RAM, storage, and CPU power can be brought to bear on big data sets. The Hadoop framework provides a high degree of automation for the core operations involved in running a distributed computing solution, such as partitioning, scheduling, dispatch, execution, communication, failure handling, monitoring, reporting, and more.

A Hadoop cluster has several *worker nodes* and one *master mode*, which acts as the overall coordinator for the cluster. When some piece of data is added to a Hadoop cluster, the master node decides which worker nodes (by default, three) will get that block of data. The master then keeps track of which workers have which data, so that programming jobs or "tasks" can be run against those data. When a task arrives at the master node, the master dispatches it to the worker nodes with the needed blocks of data, which then signal the master node once task execution is complete. Thus, programmers who use Hadoop don't have to concern themselves with the details of the location of data on which they want to perform operations.

Reliable

The Hadoop software is fault-tolerant, meaning it expects and handles hardware and software failures. This is important because with the large number of computers, individual data items, and processing steps involved in most big data use cases, failures are inevitable. Handling such failures with as little human intervention as possible, and separating cleanly the work of operations and computer programmers, is a core design goal of Hadoop. Large complex computer systems that grow past a certain point begin to consume engineering resources just to stay operational, at which point new features or other optimizations become impossible.

One way Hadoop provides reliability is by automatically replicating data to physically different machines. If the master node detects that a worker node is out of service, the master node automatically instructs another worker node to create a copy of the data that was on the expired worker node. Furthermore, it instructs the new worker node to pick up any outstanding tasks that the worker node has not completed, all without human operators or programmers having to think about it.

Scalable

Hadoop is designed for a massive scale of processors, memory, and local attached storage. It is well known that Hadoop has been shown to scale up to 4,000 machines.

To give you an idea of the size of the problems that Hadoop can tackle, consider that several businesses sprang up in the late 2000s that store a complete copy of the Internet on Hadoop clusters, which they also use to process that data.

Hadoop Common: HDFS and Map Reduce

Any Hadoop installation involves the pieces discussed in this section: HDFS and map reduce. Those two taken together are known as Hadoop Common. They are the core technologies that fulfill Hadoop's design goals of being distributed, scalable, and reliable.

HDFS, or Hadoop Distributed File System, is the code responsible for storing data across potentially thousands of machines and retrieving it when needed. Behind the scenes, HDFS keeps track of where each piece of data is and ensures replication and data integrity. Because HDFS does all the work, programmers can use it almost as easily as they can use the file system on a single machine.

Map reduce is a programming model that allows programmers to use the processing and storage power offered by the Hadoop cluster. The idea behind map reduce is to apply a "divide and conquer" approach to processing data. It has two explicit phases: map and reduce. In the map phase, a simple program is run over lots of independent pieces of data. Then, in the reduce phase, the results of the map phase are gathered from each independent worker and programmatically combined into a single result set.

> **Map Reduce**
>
> The term *map reduce* can refer to both a parallel programming model in general and to the specific component in Hadoop that implements that programming model. Several other technologies, including Sybase IQ and the proprietary Google BigTable, have their own implementations of map reduce.

Let's consider an example to help understand how map reduce works. Imagine that the guests at a dinner party are asked to find all the instances of "white whale" in the book *Moby Dick*. This problem can be done in a map reduce paradigm. The map function would tear up the book into chapters, hand them around to each guest, and instruct them to write down every line number where the phrase is found. The reduce function would take all of the results from each guest and put them together into a single, ordered list of the line numbers where the word appears. The end result is an index of every occurrence of the phrase "white whale" in the whole book. It's not a difficult leap to go from there to understanding how such an approach could be used to build an index of the World Wide Web.

Before we conclude this section, it's important to point out that Hadoop is not just a place for storing data, but also provides a mechanism for processing the data stored in it. That is, it closely combines not only the data storage and access, but also the programming and computation. This is unlike most other relational and nonrelational databases, which are primarily mechanisms for data storage and management: they retrieve data requested by a program, perhaps performing some operations in the form of stored procedures before doing so. If intensive processing of that data is required, it is typically done in the application; that is, outside the database. By contrast, Hadoop combines the massive data storage and processing power offered by many machines and puts an easy programming interface on top. The end result is that instead of having to remove data from the database to process it, the processing can be done right where the data is stored. This *in situ* processing allows many steps to be chained together—or, for recursive algorithms, the same step to be run over and over without moving the data over the network.

Allied Hadoop Technologies

Hadoop is an open source project that has a very active community contributing not only bug fixes but also a considerable number of modules that provide additional capabilities to the Hadoop core. The Hadoop technology family is shown in Figure 3.3 and discussed in more detail in this section.

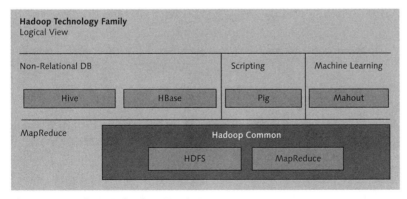

Figure 3.3 Hadoop Technology Family

Hive: SQL on Hadoop

Probably the most useful Hadoop project for the enterprise, *Hive* is a data warehouse that provides an SQL interface on top of the Hadoop cluster, allowing programmers to interact with the Hadoop cluster like a gigantic database. Hive supports an extensive but incomplete set of SQL semantics. This has the advantage of allowing programmers and data analysts to analyze and slice and dice data using tools that are familiar to them, rather than having to write map reduce jobs for even simple tasks.

Because all operations are done as map reduce jobs behind the scenes, there is a rather large minimum processing time for any query due to job initialization and parallelization. Therefore, Hive is almost exclusively used for batch mode processing.

HBase: NoSQL Data Store

HBase is a column-oriented, schema-less, distributed database modeled after Google's BigTable. It offers random, "real-time" read-write access to data. It is a NoSQL-type datastore as opposed to an RDBMS (relational database management system), so it lacks many of the features and data management capabilities of traditional databases. Unlike many other NoSQL distributed data stores, HBase offers strong consistency, meaning it can be used well for things like high speed counter aggregation (e.g., how many times has an ad been displayed on the web?).

At first glance, HBase seems like it would be extremely useful to the enterprise, but it really only makes sense with very large data sets involving either billions of rows or massive binary datasets such as photograph or video sharing sites might have; otherwise HBase performs worse than similar technologies because of high initialization costs. Note also that the programming, management, and operations for HBase are quite specialized and can be tricky to achieve near real-time performance. In most cases, an enterprise would be better served using SAP HANA.

Pig: Scripting

Pig is a platform for manipulating and analyzing large data sets in Hadoop. It's primarily intended for data analysts, who can use its scripting language for manipulating and transforming data. Why do analysts have to program to work with data in Hadoop? Data stored in Hadoop is not self-describing; that is, it is schema-less and data may be untyped. Hadoop data also tends to be unstructured and may change over time. Because of this, analysts make sense out of the data using programs, which can be understood, reused, and tweaked by others. The result is that a greater than usual burden of understanding the data falls on the data analyst. Familiar tools for data analysts, including those based on SQL, either cannot be used at all—or, if Hive is available, can be used to the extent that the tools support it. Pig helps fill this tool gap, but it has a significant learning curve.

> **Note**
>
> Both Hive and Pig will be supported by Data Services. This is discussed in Chapter 7.

Mahout: Machine Learning

Mahout is a set of machine learning libraries for Hadoop that can leverage big data sets to provide recommendations, clustering, classification, and itemsets. Examples of machine learning include grouping related news stories or suggesting products that shoppers might want to buy. If you have a core business-differentiating service that runs in Hadoop, it may be worth leveraging machine learning techniques to process that data more quickly and effectively. Otherwise, you may find that the built-in machine learning capabilities in the SAP HANA Predictive Analytics Library offers easier management and faster performance.

Now that you understand Hadoop concepts, let's apply them to common business requirements.

3.3.4   Hadoop: Enterprise Use Cases

In this section we will consider the most likely cases in which Hadoop might be used in an enterprise.

Hadoop for Pre-Processing Raw Data

The most common use of Hadoop today is to store and process unstructured data such as log files stored in plain text, thereby turning them into structured information that can be read into a database or enterprise data warehouse for further analysis or consumption. This is also likely to be the number-one enterprise use case.

Although the term *log files* suggests highly technical information that's only of interest to a systems administrator, log files are actually used for storing business information as well. For example, an e-commerce site may store its web access logs that show which IP addresses requested which resources on the site. With proper processing, those log files can be turned into information on which products were viewed, how long web visitors stayed on each page, and so on.

Hadoop tends to be useful for batch-style, exploratory data processing in which analysts sift through large volumes of data to find new patterns and relationships that were not envisioned at the time the data was collected. There are two reasons why Hadoop is good for this.

First, processing raw information is computationally intensive. It's done by analyzing huge files line by line and organizing the information into a totally different form. Hadoop has this processing power right in the storage tier and can handle even highly recursive algorithms. By contrast, to process log files in a database, you first need to read the information into a program, then process it, and write each processed unit back into the database. In the past this was precisely what people did, but as mentioned above, the larger such a system gets, the more prone it is to unexpected failures and the harder it is to keep running.

Second, unstructured information by definition doesn't follow a schema. Its format is unpredictable and may change over time. Hadoop's processing imposes meaning on this data *post hoc*, meaning analysts decide what information they want to pull out when the analysis is needed, instead of being stuck with whatever was specified when the application was built.

This doesn't mean Hadoop should be used for all unstructured information handling. Unstructured data such as emails, documents, and presentations tend to be stored in disparate systems throughout an enterprise and are better handled by EIM. They are unlikely to be processed in Hadoop in an enterprise setting, especially if good information governance practices are followed.

Extended Archive Solution

Some enterprises leverage Hadoop as an online archive for storing and analyzing nearline data. That is, instead of backing up to tape or deleting old data, they offload it from their enterprise data warehouse to Hadoop for cost-effective online data storage. Unlike tape, which is almost exclusively used for disaster recovery, Hadoop makes it possible to query the data if it's needed, although it is slower than pulling it from an enterprise data warehouse or active database. This can also be done at low cost if the enterprise is large enough to take advantage of economies of scale. Obviously, the extended archive solution only makes sense if information doesn't need to be retired in accordance with information lifecycle management (ILM) policies.

Advanced Scenarios

There is a wide variety of scenarios in which complex information processing is needed. This includes machine learning use cases such as the ones mentioned in the Mahout section earlier in this chapter, as well as more specialized uses such as video or image processing. Some real-world examples of this include using Hadoop for credit ratings, fraud detection, and risk assessment. In today's enterprise, such advanced scenarios are typically only seen when the Hadoop cluster provides a business differentiator or mission-critical service; for example, computer vision algorithms applied to satellite maps by a mapping company or genome sequencing by a biomedical research firm.

The good news for the enterprise information manager who might be faced with an advanced Hadoop scenario is that qualified staff will almost certainly be available for a mission-critical scenario as part of the overall IT investment. These individuals need to be consulted to provide data for analytics. Typically this data would be obtained using Pig or custom map reduce jobs and then pulled in batch mode into an enterprise data warehouse, SAP HANA, or some other database. SAP recommends using Data Services for this purpose.

Hadoop in the Enterprise: The Bottom Line

As of the writing of this book, Hadoop use in the enterprise is in its infancy. There is a lot of competition among Hadoop companies to provide services to this as yet small market. The enterprise information manager needs to navigate the sea of vendor claims to understand the true costs and benefits. This section outlines some basic factors to keep in mind when considering Hadoop.

Hadoop is well suited for very large data storage and processing needs. It is a proven technology that has been used productively for many years by companies such as Yahoo, Facebook, and eBay. It can scale up to thousands of machines with a high degree of automation. Hadoop clusters are highly reliable and easy to operate (compared to alternatives). Hadoop also provides great flexibility. It is open source, so changes can be made as needed, such as organization-specific customizations or bugs fixes. Because Hadoop runs on commodity hardware and the software is free and open source, users can avoid vendor lock-in, driving down costs further.

However, all of those advantages do not mean Hadoop is a must-have for the enterprise. At the time of this writing, Hadoop is mostly limited to Internet businesses, researchers, and intelligence organizations that use it to run high-value, business-differentiating services. These services store huge data volumes and require so much processing power that they are simply not feasible with other currently available technologies. There are several reasons why Hadoop has not become ubiquitous in the enterprise.

First, although it is free and open source, Hadoop can be expensive to run, primarily because of the capital outlay that is necessary to establish the Hadoop cluster and the accompanying trained and qualified personnel. Hadoop needs to surpass a certain minimum size in terms of data volume and processing needs before it begins to outperform alternative solutions. Because Hadoop is not efficient at small scales, it tends to only be used with lots of machines: no fewer than five but more likely tens or hundreds. The other cost driver is personnel. Hadoop requires highly skilled engineering, operations, and analysis resources. Because the technologies involved are still young, it can be difficult and costly to hire qualified people. Over time, this will likely change as Hadoop becomes more widespread.

The second factor limiting the spread of Hadoop is the immaturity of available tools. There are few reporting and analytics tools that interoperate well with Hadoop, and those that exist are less capable and user friendly than their traditional counterparts. This is true even if the Hadoop cluster uses Hive or Pig; Hadoop doesn't fully support SQL semantics.

Third, Hadoop does not currently support the type of role-based access that most enterprises rely on. Governance and security of data stored in Hadoop is not as well understood as data stored in SQL. Typically, if someone has access to a Hadoop cluster, they have access to all the data stored there. For the types of data traditionally stored in Hadoop—such as news stories, videos, or ad impression counters—this has not been a problem, but it is something to keep in mind when considering Hadoop for the enterprise.

Finally, it must be remembered that Hadoop is best for batch processing. Real-time processing is possible for certain use cases but is challenging at best and realistically beyond the reach of most enterprises. Table 3.1 depicts the strengths and weaknesses of Hadoop. See the next section for a discussion of Hadoop and SAP HANA, where this topic is covered in more detail.

Strengths	Weaknesses
▸ Huge data volumes	▸ Requires skilled engineering, operations, and analysis resources
▸ Unstructured data handling	
▸ Batch processing	▸ Hiring qualified talent
▸ Reliable	▸ Less mature than SQL
▸ Scalable	▸ Governance
▸ Lowest cost	▸ Real-time is challenging
▸ Open source	▸ Not efficient at small scales
▸ No hardware lock-in	
▸ Excellent paid support available	

Table 3.1 Hadoop Strengths and Weaknesses

3.4   SAP HANA and Hadoop

In enterprises, there are many scenarios where SAP HANA is likely to be a better solution than Hadoop for big data needs. In this section we will discuss why this is so and consider why in some cases Hadoop may be a useful extension to SAP HANA's capabilities.

3.4.1   The V's: Volume, Variety, Velocity

Analysts have used the term *the V's* to refer to big data: volume (how much data?), variety (how uniform is the data?), and velocity (how quickly does the data arrive and how quickly do you need to process it?). The V's provide a simple framework for comparing Hadoop and SAP HANA. On volume, clearly Hadoop can handle more data, but SAP HANA can scale up to handle most big data use cases that an enterprise is likely to encounter. More accurately put, Hadoop only makes sense when you are faced with many terabytes of data, whereas SAP HANA is also useful at smaller data volumes. Hadoop has the edge when it comes to handling a variety of data formats, including unstructured and nonrelational data. On velocity, SAP HANA is the clear winner, and for that reason, enterprise users may want to consider reading data processed in a Hadoop cluster into a SAP HANA box for faster consumption.

3.4.2 SAP HANA: Designed for Enterprises

Unlike Hadoop, SAP HANA was designed for enterprise use and is therefore easier to integrate with most organizations' available tools, personnel, and practices. Managing SAP HANA will be familiar to a database administrator; managing Hadoop requires a specialized skill set. Specialized programming knowledge is also required to write map reduce jobs, which are almost always used on Hadoop even if the primary usage is via the SQL-like interface of Hive. Even the skills required by data analysts using Hadoop tend to be quite different from what is typically found in the enterprise.

3.4.3 Hadoop as an SAP HANA Extension

Hadoop may be a useful complement to SAP HANA when complex information processing is needed; typically, when unstructured data needs to be turned into structured data. It can also be a good fit if data sets are too large to fit into SAP HANA RAM, discs, or require too many CPU cores for processing the information—any of which would happen with, for example, petabytes of data. Using this design pattern, processed data can be read out of the Hadoop cluster into SAP HANA or an enterprise data warehouse for further usage.

You will know if you have a good candidate use case due to extreme data size, but there are other cases that might not be so easily identified. First, complex information processing on large data sets can often result in a situation where significant custom coding is needed for job scheduling to prevent users of the system from clashing over resources and to prevent stalled jobs. Complex information processing in the form of highly recursive algorithms, algorithms that rewrite data regularly, or algorithms that can't easily be expressed as SQL may also be good candidates for use in Hadoop.

Hadoop can also be useful to keep information available at a lower cost; for example, offloading information that doesn't justify the expense of constant real-time availability.

3.5 EIM and Hadoop

While the uses of EIM and Hadoop have already been mentioned in this chapter, this section will focus on extraction, transformation, and loading (ETL) and Hadoop as well as issues of governance and information lifecycle management with Hadoop.

3.5.1   ETL—Data Services and the Information Design Tool

Very soon SAP will provide support for Hadoop using Data Services. Data Services is the single most important technology in SAP's solutions for EIM portfolio when it comes to Hadoop interoperability because it is the primary technology component responsible for ETL (transferring data from one system into another, and possibly massaging it along the way). Rather than trying to access Hadoop clusters directly for reporting and analysis, most enterprises will want to use Data Services to extract data from Hadoop in batch mode and store it in an enterprise data warehouse. From the data warehouse, analysts can access the data using familiar tools such as in the SAP BusinessObjects BI platform, or define universes using the Information Design Tool. Because Hadoop has high latency in retrieving data, it's unlikely that analytics tools would run well if they fetched their data directly from the Hadoop cluster.

3.5.2   Unsupported: Information Governance and Information Lifecycle Management

As will be described in more detail in Chapter 4, SAP's solutions for EIM include SAP NetWeaver Information Lifecycle Management (ILM) and technologies to support information governance. Hadoop lacks the basic technology hooks that would enable a program to enforce governance on data stored in a Hadoop cluster. Also, the use case is not quite right. You would not expect to find operational data of the type that is normally governed (e.g., master data domains such as customer data). This leaves uncertainty about what type of governance might be needed in this environment. Until these issues are cleared up, Hadoop as part of information governance is unlikely.

SAP NetWeaver ILM is also not likely to support Hadoop. SAP NetWeaver ILM performs the important function of obsoleting data that is no longer needed to reduce information overload and to mitigate legal risks. But again, this is not a likely Hadoop cluster use case. One the one hand, the types of data likely to be stored in a Hadoop cluster would not have a high probability of legal risk (as opposed to, say, company email or operational data). On the other hand, Hadoop is often inexpensive enough that organizations find it is more costly to identify which data needs to be purged than to simply add new machines to the Hadoop cluster. Besides, Hadoop tends to be used in cases where the business is deriving a core business advantage from having access to as much data as possible—more data than their competition—so they are unlikely to want to give any up.

3.6   Summary

It is too early to say with complete confidence what impact Hadoop will have in the enterprise space. Today it is the domain of specialists, but there are a number of venture capital-backed companies that are looking to break into the enterprise by solving many of the issues outlined in this chapter. SAP is closely monitoring developments around Hadoop and already provides support for the most common Hadoop use cases that an enterprise information manager is likely to encounter. As you consider the changes in technology that may affect your enterprise and its EIM strategy in the future, you can be confident that SAP will continue to provide additional interoperability where it makes sense and is technically feasible.

This chapter has provided insight into SAP HANA, Hadoop, and how they fit in with your enterprise information management strategy. Now that this and the previous two chapters have given you a big picture idea of the concepts and ideas behind EIM, you are ready to dive into the details: The next chapter provides specific information about SAP's solutions for EIM.

This chapter introduces you to SAP's solutions for EIM, allowing you to judge which products are of the most interest to you. Based on what you learn in this chapter, you can determine which chapters in Part II you should read first and where you need to start learning more.

4 SAP's Solutions for Enterprise Information Management

SAP's solutions for EIM have both great breadth and depth, spanning the full capabilities for managing information from its acquisition, through active use, until retirement and destruction. This chapter discusses all of the currently available products and solutions SAP offers for EIM. The portfolio will continue to grow as SAP continues to make investments in this area.

Chapter 1 discussed EIM in SAP's overall portfolio; Figure 4.1 shows the same portfolio view but also lists the EIM products, which are explored further in this chapter.

Figure 4.1 SAP's Solutions for EIM

Figure 4.1 shows SAP's solutions for EIM in schematic form. At the top of the graphic are applications that depend on the data that the SAP solutions manage; at the bottom are the data sources and the types of data, which both feed the information management products and are managed by them. The middle of the graphic is dominated by the set of enterprise information management solutions offered by SAP, all beneath a box labeled "Information Governance." (Information governance is not a product, but a discipline that is supported by multiple products. It is discussed in more detail in Chapter 3.) The following products are included in SAP's solutions for EIM:

- **SAP Data Services**
  Hereafter referred to as Data Services, this is a product that has combined SAP Data Integrator and SAP Data Quality Management into one, even though the solutions can still be delivered independently if needed. However, most customers require both products, so this book will focus on Data Services and refer to Data Integrator as the data integration capabilities delivered with Data Services. SAP Data Quality Management will be referred to as the data quality capabilities delivered with Data Services. A third major capability built into Data Services is called text data processing.

- **SAP Information Steward**
  Hereafter referred to as Information Steward.

- **SAP NetWeaver Master Data Management**
  Hereafter referred to as SAP NetWeaver MDM.

- **SAP Master Data Governance**
  Hereafter referred to as SAP MDG.

- **SAP NetWeaver Information Lifecycle Management**
  Hereafter referred to as SAP NetWeaver ILM.

- **Enterprise Content Management (ECM) by OpenText**
  ECM by OpenText is a group of related products. ECM products included in SAP's solutions for EIM are:
  - SAP Archiving by OpenText
  - SAP Document Access by OpenText (includes SAP Archiving by OpenText)
  - SAP Extended Enterprise Content Management by OpenText (hereafter referred to as SAP Extended ECM). SAP Extended ECM includes both SAP Document Access by OpenText and SAP Archiving by OpenText.

▶ SAP Invoice Management by OpenText

▶ SAP Document Presentment by OpenText

While there are many OpenText products included with SAP's solutions for EIM, this book will focus on SAP Extended ECM and its components: SAP Document Access by OpenText and SAP Archiving by OpenText.

▶ **Sybase Replication Server (hereafter referred to as Replication Server)**
Replication Server supports the enterprise data management environment by replicating and synchronizing databases such as Sybase Adaptive Server Enterprise (ASE), Oracle, Microsoft SQL Server, and IBM DB2 Universal Database (UDB) database transactions.

▶ **Sybase Power Builder (hereafter referred to as Power Builder)**
Power Builder is a modeling tool that offers a model-driven approach to improve business intelligence and information architecture. Enterprise architects use it to bring together many of the moving parts that make up the enterprise: systems, applications, business processes, and requirements.

In addition to the software products mentioned above, there is a solution called data migration that is built on top of existing EIM products. It is not listed in Figure 4.1 because it is not standalone software, but a solution built on Data Services.

This chapter will provide a brief introduction to SAP's capabilities for EIM, whether they be software products (such as Data Services, Information Steward, SAP MDG, etc.), solutions built on software products (such as data migration), or disciplines (such as information governance). Part II of the book will provide greater details on some of the capabilities; however, due to the extent of the capabilities, not all of them will be covered in depth.

> **Note**
>
> We do not focus on Sybase solutions in this book. For more information on Replication Server and Power Builder go to *http://www.sybase.com*.

Chapter 1 discussed the use of EIM for on-boarding, active use, and off-boarding of information. The following is a list of SAP's EIM capabilities for each area, all of which will be discussed in more detail in this chapter:

▶ **On-boarding**
Includes Data Services, Information Steward, SAP NetWeaver ILM, SAP NetWeaver

MDM, and SAP MDG as well as the use of data migration and the on-boarding of content with SAP Extended ECM.

▶ **Active use**
Includes Data Services, Information Steward, SAP NetWeaver MDM, SAP MDG, SAP Document Access by OpenText, and SAP Extended ECM.

▶ **Off-boarding**
Includes Data Services, SAP Document Access by OpenText, SAP Extended ECM, and SAP NetWeaver ILM.

4.1 SAP Data Services as a Data Foundation

Data Services is the primary tool to extract, transform, and load data from one or more source systems into one or more target systems; Data Services lets you improve, integrate, transform, and deliver trusted data to critical business processes across the enterprise for both SAP and non-SAP systems. Data Services can be used in almost any scenario that requires you to move, enrich, transform, or cleanse data, and in this regard functions as the technology foundation for a coherent enterprise information management strategy. The following sections provide an overview of the capabilities delivered with Data Services.

4.1.1 Basics of SAP Data Services

Data Services is used for data migration, systems migration, data synchronization, application data cleansing, loading data warehouses and data marts, and for query, reporting, analysis, and dashboard data provisioning. The three major capabilities of Data Services are data cleansing, data validation, and text data processing. The core of Data Services is the data services engine (see Figure 4.2, which shows Data Services' capabilities and typical uses). As mentioned previously, Data Services combines two products: Data Integrator for extraction, transformation, and loading (ETL) and SAP Data Quality Management for data validation and data cleansing. The third major capability of Data Services is text data processing and is referred to simply as *text data processing*.

The left side of Figure 4.2 shows the data sources supported by Data Services. Data Services can access data from a wide variety of applications and file sources and can consume almost every type of data—structured, semi-structured, and unstructured—from those sources. Data Services can be called in batch mode (for example, to extract and deliver data for reporting in the data warehouses) or via client applications such as SAP ERP, SAP Customer Relationship Management (CRM), or custom applications to perform data transformation and cleansing in real time.

Notice in the figure that Data Services shares a common technology layer with the SAP BusinessObjects Business Intelligence (BI) platform. This allows for common user provisioning; advanced user management; password and security policies; use of external authentication mechanisms such as Active Directory, lightweight directory access protocol (LDAP), or SAP NetWeaver Identity Management; and granular access control.

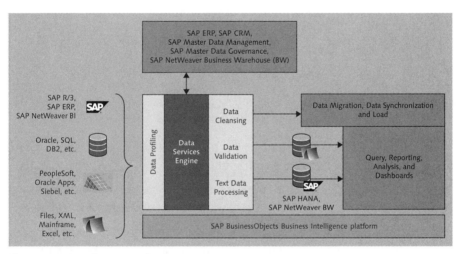

Figure 4.2 Data Services Architecture

You can see in Figure 4.2 how Data Services can access many types of systems and applications and can work with many kinds of data and how that data can be profiled. The connectivity options and profiling capabilities of Data Services are described below.

Connectivity Options for SAP Data Services

Data Services supports many connectivity options for structured and unstructured data. These include SAP applications, databases, other vendor applications, and pure files (Excel, mainframe, etc.). Details of the connectivity options are discussed in Chapter 7.

Data Profiling in SAP Data Services

Data profiling is the practice of determining the overall quality of data and finding data anomalies. While Information Steward is the primary tool for data profiling, technical data profiling can be done directly in Data Services; you can go beyond simple viewing of the data to conduct an analysis of your data. You can build better jobs in Data Services by understanding the following types of information:

► Frequency distribution

► Distinct values

► Null values

► Minimum/maximum values

► Data patterns (e.g., Xxx Xxxx99, 99-Xxx)

► Comparison of values between data sets

► Drill-down to view specific records

The profiling in Data Services allows you to quickly assess the source data to discover problems and anomalies, such as:

► Twenty-one percent of the employees in the Human Resources source system do not have a country associated with their ID.

► There are four genders entered: 60% are male, 30% are female, and the other 10% are either "unknown" or have a question mark in the gender field.

► Benefits are available for all new employees after one month of service, but 35% of three-month employees still have no benefit ID assigned to their HR records.

You can also quickly detect patterns, distinct values, and null values for zip codes, product codes, sales items, and other key data fields to better understand your data.

4.1.2   SAP Data Services Integration with SAP Applications

Data Services provides seamless integration with SAP applications as an integration and data quality tool. Specific examples include SAP CRM, SAP ERP, SAP NetWeaver MDM, SAP MDG, SAP NetWeaver Business Warehouse (BW), and SAP HANA. Data Services is used as a service to the applications, called only to perform a specific function when needed. It can also be used to load data into the applications. Next we discuss a few examples in a bit more detail.

SAP Data Services for SAP Data Quality Management with SAP ERP, SAP Customer Relationship Management, and SAP NetWeaver Master Data Management

Figure 4.3 shows common uses of Data Services with the SAP Business Suite. One common use of Data Services with the SAP Business Suite is the deep integration with Business Address Services (BAS). BAS is an SAP NetWeaver capability embedded in the ABAP application server. BAS provides flexible dialog integration for standard functions such as creating, changing, displaying, and finding addresses. It is a reusable component across the SAP Business Suite that is used heavily in SAP ERP (such as SAP ERP Central Component [ECC] 6.0) and SAP CRM. With Data Services integration to BAS, as addresses are updated, the data quality capabilities in Data Services are used to correct the addresses and check for duplicates. Figure 4.3 shows Data Services integration with BAS.

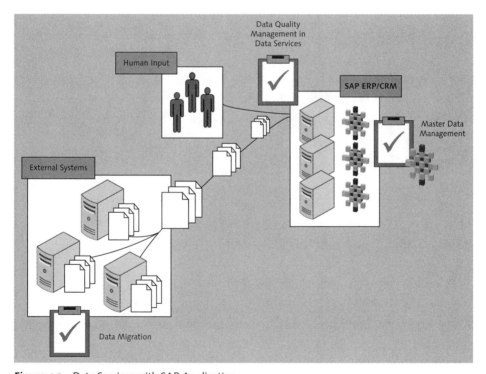

Figure 4.3 Data Services with SAP Applications

In Figure 4.3, notice that Data Services is used for data migration to the SAP Business Suite. SAP provides a robust data migration solution for mapping and validating source data against the SAP target system using Data Services. Data Services is used to migrate each application object (for example, materials, sales orders, cost centers, etc.). For each object, the data is cleansed, validated against the required configuration in the SAP target system, and loaded into the SAP system. Reports are provided using SAP BusinessObjects Web Intelligence so users can monitor, remediate, and govern the data migration project.

Additional integration with Data Services for SAP applications includes integration with SAP NetWeaver MDM and SAP MDG. SAP NetWeaver MDM uses Data Services for loading data as well as cleansing names and addresses, de-duplication and automatic consolidation, and data validation. Data Services provides real-time cleansing, matching, and consolidation activities for SAP MDG, providing re-usability between SAP NetWeaver MDM and SAP MDG. Figure 4.4 shows Data Services integration with SAP MDG.

Figure 4.4 Data Services Integration with SAP MDG, SAP ERP, and SAP CRM

Next we will discuss how Data Services is used with SAP HANA, SAP NetWeaver BW, and the SAP BusinessObjects BI platform.

SAP Data Services for SAP HANA, SAP NetWeaver Business Warehouse, and the SAP BusinessObjects Business Intelligence Platform

A key strength of Data Services is its easy integration with data warehouses and databases for analytics. This is true for Data Services integration with SAP NetWeaver BW, SAP HANA, and the entire SAP BusinessObjects BI platform.

Data Services is the preferred tool for loading non-SAP data into SAP HANA. In fact, the data integration capabilities of Data Services are included with SAP HANA. Additionally, SAP is making major improvements for a seamless user interface between Data Services and SAP HANA. This is explained in more detail in Chapter 3 and Chapter 7. Figure 4.5 shows the integration of Data Services with SAP NetWeaver BW and SAP HANA.

Figure 4.5 Data Services Integration with SAP NetWeaver BW and SAP HANA

Data Services can also be used for loading data into SAP NetWeaver BW. Existing SAP NetWeaver BW customers can now easily apply data quality transformations when loading data into SAP NetWeaver BW. They can use one tool to define all extraction, validation, and cleansing rules to load all data (SAP and non-SAP) into SAP NetWeaver BW. This is important to understand because everyone faces data quality issues, and you don't want to re-implement your ETL jobs to add data quality. Non-SAP NetWeaver BW customers can get *native* access to the SAP Business Suite, including delta changes, without going through SAP NetWeaver BW.

In addition to integration with databases and data warehouses, Data Services also works natively with the SAP BusinessObjects BI platform. Data Services is used for the provisioning of data for reports, dashboards, ad hoc queries, OLAP (online analytical processing) analyses, and data exploration. Data Services provides access and integration of disparate data from virtually any data source, structured or unstructured. This data can be built up in a data warehouse or data mart to provide historical trending and analysis for more accurate decision making. Data Services also enables the understanding of information context (data lineage) to help you make more confident decisions. The integration with the SAP BusinessObjects BI platform is standard functionality that comes out-of-the-box.

4.1.3 SAP Data Services Integration with Non-SAP Applications

Data Services has a much longer history of integration with non-SAP applications than it does with SAP applications. It started as a pure ETL tool that moved data from any source to any source. It has grown into a full-scale data foundation that includes extraction, transformation, loading, data quality, and text data processing, with deep integration into SAP applications while maintaining the ability to integrate into any application. In your enterprise there could be few or many non-SAP systems where integration, data quality, and data validation are required. Data Services is well equipped for the requirement of moving and transforming data between diverse non-SAP systems. Figure 4.2, showed the connectivity options for Data Services, ranging from Microsoft Excel spreadsheets to Oracle applications to mainframe connectivity. Refer back to Figure 4.3: You can also see the reference to data migration, data synchronization, and data loading. In this book, we will focus on data migration to SAP target applications when we discuss data migration. When migrating to SAP applications, the target canonical data formats, field requirements, and so on, are delivered by SAP. However, Data Services can easily be used to migrate to a new home-grown application or some other niche application as well; in this case, however, you need to define the target structure.

Figure 4.3 also showed that external systems and human input are linked to the data quality capabilities in Data Services. This is very common for Data Services integration with non-SAP applications. One very specific example is the SAP Data Quality Management SDK (software development kit). SAP has many software partners who develop their own software but use part of SAP's solution within their solution. The SAP Data Quality Management SDK provides developers with a lightweight integration method to integrate the robust capabilities of the data cleansing and validation capabilities directly in their own custom applications.

Non-SAP integration with Data Services includes loading third-party data in SAP HANA and SAP NetWeaver BW, as well as extracting data to go in other data marts, data warehouses (such as Sybase IQ), and applications.

Data Services' native capabilities for dealing with both SAP and non-SAP data provide great flexibility so that Data Services can be embedded in SAP and non-SAP applications and used across the SAP family of solutions where data cleansing, validation, and integration are critical for the application.

4.1.4 Data Cleansing and Data Validation with SAP Data Services

SAP Data Quality Management is a key capability in Data Services and will be covered in detail in Chapter 8. Data quality capabilities include address cleansing, data standardization, data validation, data correction, data enrichment, and matching. Figure 4.6 shows an example of the entire data quality process.

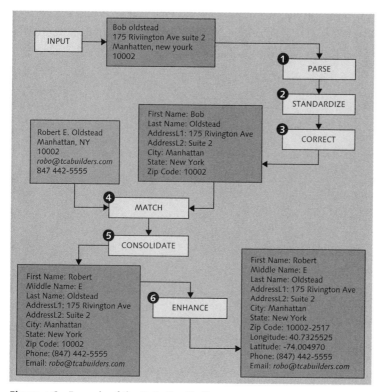

Figure 4.6 Example of the Data Quality Process

To begin, the input record is parsed into its component parts and standardized. Figure 4.6 shows the following example:

- First Name: Bob
- Last Name: oldstead
- Address1: 175 Riivington Ave
- Address2: Suite 2
- City: Manhatten
- State: new yourk
- Zip Code: 10002

Errors in the record are corrected; for instance, "Oldstead" is capitalized, and the street name, city, and state are edited. After this step, the record looks like this:

- First Name: Bob
- Last Name: Oldstead
- Address1: 175 Rivington Ave
- Address2: Suite 2
- City: Manhattan
- State: New York
- Zip Code: 10002

Data Services then searches for a matching record in the target application and finds the following match:

- Name: Robert E. Oldstead
- City, State: Manhattan, NY
- Zip Code: 10002
- Email: *robo@tcabuilders.com*
- Phone: 847 442-5555

The two records are consolidated:

- First Name: Robert
- Last Name: Oldstead
- Address1: 175 Rivington Ave
- Address2: Suite 2
- City: Manhattan
- State: New York
- Zip Code: 10002
- Phone: (847) 442-5555
- Email: *robo@tcabuilders.com*

Finally, the record is enhanced with a normalized zip code and geographical coordinates to provide a complete record:

- First Name: Robert

- Last Name: Oldstead

- Address1: 175 Rivington Ave

- Address2: Suite 2

- City: Manhattan

- State: New York

- Zip Code: 10002-2517

- Longitude: 40.7325525

- Latitude: -74.004970

- Phone: (847) 442-5555

- Email: *robo@tcabuilders.com*

While this example focused on cleansing a customer record, the data quality process can be applied to business partners, material products, services, and many other types of data that need parsing, standardization, and data cleansing.

4.1.5 Text Data Processing in SAP Data Services

The text data processing (TDP) feature in Data Services unlocks unstructured text sources. With advanced linguistic and semantic capabilities, TDP knows the elements of human language, how these elements differ from language to language, and how their dependencies express the underlying salient information. It understands the meaning and context of information, not just the words themselves. Through core natural-language processing of the entity extraction transform, TDP extracts key information—the "who, what, where, when, and how" in text—revealing important relations and events occurring between these entities. Ultimately, it gives structure to unstructured text sources and disregards the noise, allowing for business analytics and reporting. The following are some common use cases for text data processing:

- **Electronic discovery law**
  Discovery is a pretrial phase in a lawsuit in which each party makes information available to the other. TDP accelerates the process of analyzing documents for evidence.

▶ **Brand monitoring**

A company wants to know what people are saying about its products and brands. Are they creating buzz? Is that buzz positive or negative, and how does it change over time?

▶ **Employee morale**

Sentiment analysis of collaboration spaces and employee surveys can detect employee problems and feedback.

▶ **Customer service**

Companies can optimize call centers by routing questions to the right person.

The following are several business examples of how text data processing is used today.

▶ **Media company**

- ▶ Problem: Records containing artist names, songs, and movie titles are stored in legacy repositories where they can't be queried, analyzed, or aggregated.

- ▶ Goal: Integrate legacy records into a warehouse for a single source of truth for reporting.

- ▶ Solution: Text data processing identifies artist names, titles, dates, and so on. Data quality normalizes names and titles. Integrated, trusted data is loaded into a data warehouse.

▶ **Law enforcement**

- ▶ Problem: Agents need to link the common characteristics of crime scenes with suspects. Databases are incomplete, and important clues may be lost in the volumes of textual information in field notes, case documents, IM logs, emails, and so on.

- ▶ Goal: Integrate content from unstructured sources into agency databases so it is available for investigations. Via analytical application, the agent queries for suspects, things, organizations, and locations, as well as links or co-occurrences between these.

- ▶ Solution: Text data processing extracts person names, objects, locations, and other data of interest using public sector extraction rules. The extracted entities are cleansed and normalized by data quality. Human review of the output occurs prior to database commit.

> **Optional Function for Law Enforcement**
>
> When joining results into the repository, the match function looks for similar persons, addresses, or other attributes that may resolve identities.

▶ **Maintenance and repairs**

    ▶ Problem: A company doesn't know what repair issues are most common or why. Managers are under pressure to reduce maintenance-related costs. Technicians do not always select correct values in a database.

    ▶ Goal: Analyze field technicians' repair logs and profile maintenance issues to drive predictive analytics for future maintenance problems. Identify root causes of costly warranty repairs and report back to engineering. Complete blank fields in structured data based on comments.

    ▶ Solution: Text data processing recognizes concepts, part numbers, and problems. It matches cluster concepts, which reveal the most common issues. Models and part numbers can be normalized.

Text data processing extracts the text and clearly recognizes its meaning from a large number of words. One example is reporting on the most mentioned concepts. An output report created by analyzing comments about a car could result in the information in Table 4.1 (with drill-down capabilities to get more details).

Concept	Total Feedback	Negative Sentiments	Positive Sentiments	Requests
Handling	109	9	98	2
Maintenance	98	19	64	15
Brake	66	20	43	3
Cup holder	51	27	20	4
Interior	50	4	42	4
Mileage	37	4	30	3

Table 4.1 Car Sentiment Report

From the car sentiment report you can see that cup holder and brakes have the most negative sentiments and that handling has the most positive. This report can be used to drill down to collect feedback that can be used to support marketing and advertising or provide input into future designs of the car.

Text data processing is covered in more detail in Chapter 10.

4.2 SAP Information Steward

Information Steward delivers a single environment to discover, assess, define, and monitor the quality of your enterprise data. It is positioned as a key user interface for governance with the ability to monitor the quality of your data over time and centrally catalog the different data assets and business term definitions in your organization. The combination of these disciplines allows companies not only to identify bad data, but also to see where the data is coming from (and where it is used in downstream processes).

Information Steward provides an environment that enables you to do the following:

▶ *Discover* and understand enterprise data. This includes data profiling and meta-data management. Information Steward gives your company the means to discover its data assets, visually assess its quality, isolate issues, and understand the impact they are having on your critical business processes. And in doing so, it provides a starting point for both business and IT users to collaborate on and improve data quality. It is an essential starting point for any information governance initiative.

▶ *Define* the data quality requirements and data quality business rules, as well as the common business term glossary centrally in one application. Information Steward provides a means to define ownership and accountability of critical business data assets and the ability to relate them to business terms in a business glossary. This helps establish a common understanding of the data and its meaning for key stakeholders of a governance program. In addition, Information Steward provides users with the ability to define validations rules to further assess the quality of the data. And as data quality issues become apparent, both business and IT users are able to define cleansing packages to address them.

▶ *Monitor* data quality over time, provide data quality scorecards in business user applications, and resolve data quality issues over time. With Information Steward both business and IT users are empowered to monitor data quality throughout the enterprise via the use of standardized scorecards that are easy to access, intuitive to use, and allow the user to interactively drill down to the data sources that have failed to meet defined validation rules. In addition, business users can also access these same data quality scores in the environments they already work in. For example, an analyst viewing a report has the ability to see where the data in the report originated and the data quality score associated with the report sources.

In this section we will provide an overview of each major capability in Information Steward. Chapter 6 and Chapter 9 will provide more details on the profiling and data quality scorecards. In Information Steward there are four major areas:

▶ **Data profiling and data quality monitoring**
These are used to gain insight, assess data, and provide dashboards for monitoring data quality over time.

▶ **Metadata analysis**
Metadata analysis integrates and relates metadata from multiple systems in the company and allows transparency of the existing assets in the company and how they are related to each other.

▶ **Cleansing rules**
Cleansing rules enable the creation of specific rules for cleansing data according to company policies, industry standards, and so on.

▶ **Business term glossary**
A business term glossary provides a central glossary for organizations to store business terms or definitions that have been approved by the responsible business experts.

> **Tip**
>
> The term *metadata,* when used with respect to Information Steward, refers to technical metadata regarding the structure of the data. The National Information Standards Organization defines metadata as "structured information that describes, explains, locates, or otherwise makes it easier to retrieve, use or manage an information resource."

Each of these areas will be discussed next.

4.2.1 Data Profiling and Data Quality Monitoring

Data profiling and data quality monitoring are key capabilities of Information Steward. You can assess and monitor the data quality of a specific data domain for a specific purpose (for example, customer quality assessment, sales system migration, or master data quality monitoring).

By measuring data quality along the core processes in your organization, from the point of entry down to the place of consumption, you can easily identify which business process is processing good data. Ongoing data quality monitoring allows you to respond early to slight dips in your data quality level. With early detection you can set up the necessary cleansing activities or processes, rather than identify data quality issues after they have negatively impacted your core business processes.

Figure 4.7 shows an example of a data quality scorecard that provides a quality score along specific data quality dimensions.

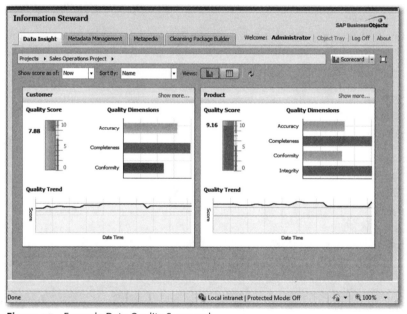

Figure 4.7 Example Data Quality Scorecard

The following are typical activities that are done for data profiling and data quality monitoring:

▶ **Adding tables to a project**
For example, in a project to assess supplier master data, you would include tables and files that should be analyzed to assess supplier master data.

▶ **Profiling the data**

You interactively execute data profiling steps to create statistical information on minimum values, maximum values, frequency distribution of values, pattern distribution of values, and so on. This is a first insight into the content of the data when the first outliers are identified. For example, with supplier master data, say you assess the data and notice that the pattern of the supplier name includes a high percentage of special characters. You can directly create validation rules from the profiling results area that the data steward later verifies and approves from a business perspective.

▶ **Setting up the data quality validation rules**

You might have a great set of already documented or identified requirements based on policies, industry standards, or external regulation that you can transfer into validation rules. A typical validation rule for supplier master data validates that the name of the supplier does not contain any characters other than letters or number and blanks.

▶ **Binding the validation rules to your data**

Since the central validation rules are generic and can be reused for multiple tables, they are bound to the multiple tables in your company after their approval by the data steward. For example, a definition for a valid telephone number format is done once centrally by the data steward but is then bound to your employee, customer, and supplier data tables.

▶ **Executing the rule tasks**

Apply the defined validation rules to the existing data in the tables, files, or applications that you have bound to your project to calculate the number of failed records for each rule.

▶ **Analyzing or reviewing the current data quality level from different perspectives**

From a technical perspective you can view the quality of the data based on specific tables or applications; for example, data quality in the completeness of sales orders tables for the sales application. Alternatively, the data quality level can be viewed from the perspective of a business user or data steward who is responsible for a specific data domain such as supplier master data. In this case, you are only interested in the overall score of your key data domain; in other words, drill down from the data quality scorecard domain (such as supplier, product, or customer) to the data quality dimensions, to the individual rules set up for your data domain, and down to the individual tables where your data is stored.

▶ **Scheduling rule tasks for ongoing monitoring**
Since data quality measurement is not a singular activity, you can set up scheduled execution of your rule tasks using the internal scheduling capability.

Specific details of how to create a data quality dashboard are covered in Chapter 9.

4.2.2 Metadata Analysis

Metadata analysis enables users to know what data assets exist in the company and the relationships between those data assets. For example, in the business intelligence suite, users can track the source data used for a report, and they can see how a change in a source will impact a report. For example if you delete a column in one of your source systems, this might have a significant impact on your reports; it could result in missing data and erroneous calculations. Metadata analysis empowers users to do the following:

▶ Understand the entire business intelligence environment

▶ Trace a data lineage from a report to sources

▶ Identify a change impact from a source to reports and users

▶ Manage metadata from various data sources, data integration technologies, and business intelligence systems

▶ Lower the total cost of ownership by tracking usage and promote reuse of data and reports

▶ Improve decision making and regulatory compliance

▶ Provide root-cause and impact analysis of bad data in the system landscape

Metadata analysis consolidates metadata from various sources, stores it in a central metadata repository, and analyzes the dependencies and relationships between the different data assets. This consolidated and related metadata enables auditing, usage, change impact, and data lineage analysis. Metadata can be supplemented with custom attributes and annotations to add further information to the collected metadata to provide a full picture and understanding of the existing data assets. Figure 4.8 shows the integration with the central repository. The universe creation in the figure refers to the universe capability in the SAP BusinessObjects BI platform.

Figure 4.8 Consolidate, Integrate, and Audit Your Metadata

One of the most common use cases of the metadata management capabilities in Information Steward is the direct integration of the data lineage capabilities into the launch pad in the SAP BusinessObjects BI platform. In the launch pad, users can choose to view the lineage of a report they are working on. The lineage offers a graphical representation of what data from which sources a report uses and how the data is flowing into the report. In addition to knowing how much they can trust the data in the tables, users can also see the results of a data quality assessment on the source or data warehouse staging area tables. Leveraging the metadata analysis with the data quality assessment provides credibility to the report.

Another example of metadata analysis is to support data quality root-cause analysis and impact analysis. While you are reviewing the data quality results you can drill into the failed data. When you drill down you can directly call the metadata management functionality to see where the data in the assessed column is coming from. This enables you to evaluate the source of the error as well as where the data is used in downstream reports. The linkage goes all the way to the business terms and linkage to the business process. This allows you to drill down from your business process name to the associated tables and contextualize the quality score for the table and the individual columns.

4.2.3 Cleansing Rules

Information Steward also provides a capability called the cleansing package builder. This enables the creation of custom cleansing rules that Data Services uses as a transformation step to cleanse and standardize your data. You can create custom parsing and standardization rules that can be used with the data cleanse transform in Data Services. (Note: Chapter 8 covers the data cleanse transform.)

Custom cleansing rules can be created to parse and standardize account numbers, product codes, product descriptions, purchase dates, part numbers, SKUs, dates, names, social security numbers, and so on.

The cleansing package builder was created to empower the data steward or subject matter expert to develop a custom data cleansing solution, allowing the user to easily and quickly develop new data cleansing solutions for data domains not provided out-of-the-box (for example, product data in the pharmaceutical industry) and to customize the cleansing packages delivered by SAP.

The data steward defines how the data should be classified simply based on the desired output. Once the desired output is created, the cleansing package builder automatically creates the data dictionary, rules, and patterns that make up a cleansing package, which is then consumed by Data Services data cleanse transforms. The following example shows the input and output after using a custom cleansing rule developed using the cleansing package builder:

> *Glove ultra grip profit 2.3 large black synthetic leather elastic with Velcro Mechanix Wear.*

After the cleansing step executes, the parsed and standardized output would look like the information shown in Table 4.2.

Parsed Text Output	Standardized Text Output
Product Category	Glove
Size	Large
Material	Synthetic Leather
Trademark	Pro-Fit 2.3 Series
Cuff Style	Elastic Velcro
Palm Type	Ultra-Grip
Color	Black
Vendor	Mechanix Wear
Standard Description	Glove—Synthetic Leather, Black, size: Large, Cuff Style: Elastic Velcro, Ultra-Grip, Mechanix Wear

Table 4.2 Parsed and Standardized Output from the Data Cleanse Transform

In the cleansing package builder, the data steward can set up how to create a standard for parsed values, a standard description, and any punctuation. For example, the input includes the phrase "profit 2.3," but after the cleansing package executes, the description for the trademark attribute is "Pro-Fit 2.3 Series." You can also see that the standard description has appended multiple attributes together and added additional punctuation. Ultimately, the data steward can control how the data looks based on business requirements. The cleansing package builder can be used to create custom cleansing rules for specific industry standards such as GS1 (Global Standards 1) and UNSPSC (United Nations Standard Products and Services Code). It can be used to create company-specific cleansing rules so that data is uniformly cleansed according to company policies and compliance requirements in diverse application systems.

4.2.4 Business Glossary

If you ask five employees in your company what the term *revenue* means to them, you might get at least three different definitions. But for analysis and decision making, it is essential that everyone in the company be on the same page when talking about the same terms or policies. Information Steward provides *Metapedia* as a central location for the definition, maintenance, and approval of business terms; its goal is to promote proactive information governance with common understanding and agreement on business terms and concepts.

The application range for Metapedia is broad: from descriptive explanations of terms (like in a simple dictionary) to central storage of calculation formulas, to technical terms, to business process descriptions associated with tables and data assets in business processes. Metapedia also enables business users to understand data attributes used in business intelligence reporting environments with business user-oriented descriptions. In Metapedia, you can organize business terms into categories or hierarchies that align with business subject matter or lines of business.

Metapedia's searching capabilities let you search for not only the terms that have been created, but also synonyms that have been assigned to them. From the search results you can easily trace the associated objects or their details into the categories and hierarchies the terms are linked to. In this way, Metapedia terms can be associated and linked to other technical objects in your Information Steward system. This is used to extend the central data assets repository with business terms. For example, you can define business names in Metapedia and assign them to the technical column names in your metadata management. If a business user searches for a business term such as *telephone number,* he can get a list of all table columns associated with that business term in the system landscape, including telephone number information, even if the column is labeled "PHNNR."

Metapedia is a helpful component to bridge the gap between IT and the business user, providing a common understanding of what information is available where in the company.

4.3 SAP NetWeaver Master Data Management and SAP Master Data Governance

Managing master data is critical to an enterprise-wide information management strategy. Every company, every line of business, is impacted by master data. From financial close, to product development, to order management, to help desk support, to supplier management, every organization is impacted by master data—especially when the master data is wrong, unclear, redundant, or conflicting. SAP's solutions for EIM include an integrated suite for managing and governing master data. These solutions include previously discussed capabilities, such as Data Services and Information Steward. Additionally, two other key capabilities for managing and governing master data include SAP NetWeaver MDM and SAP MDG. The focus of SAP NetWeaver MDM is to consolidate and harmonize master data in application- and system-agnostic contexts (for example, in analytical scenarios, to ensure trustworthy data for enterprise reporting). SAP NetWeaver MDM supports all domains for master data consolidation, harmonization, and stewardship, covering business initiatives such as mergers and acquisitions, divestitures, and supply chain optimization.

SAP MDG provides centralized master data creation, maintenance, and governance for the SAP Business Suite and beyond. In the standard version, this is pre-built for selected data domains, such as the financial, material, supplier, and customer domains. It can be extended for additional domains. SAP MDG is focused on operational master data management. It is a natural extension of the business processes running in the SAP Business Suite, adding prebuilt master data creation, change, and distribution processes and stewardship.

4.3.1 SAP NetWeaver Master Data Management

SAP NetWeaver MDM enables you to manage master data across multiple domains and multiple systems. It is primarily used for master data consolidation and master data harmonization; both are described below.

Master Data Consolidation

Master data consolidation aggregates master data across SAP and non-SAP systems into a centralized master data repository. Once data is consolidated, you can search for data across linked systems, identify identical or similar objects across systems, and provide key mapping for reliable companywide analytics and reporting.

Master Data Harmonization

Master data harmonization first consolidates the master data from heterogeneous systems and then harmonizes the data to meet global quality standards. It ensures high-quality master data by distributing harmonized data that is globally relevant using distribution mechanisms. Subscribing applications can enrich master data with locally relevant information.

For more details on SAP NetWeaver MDM see *SAP NetWeaver Master Data Management* (Heilig et al., SAP PRESS, 2007).

4.3.2 SAP Master Data Governance

SAP MDG provides centralized governance for selected master data domains based on SAP's standard data models and is extensible to custom-defined models. It performs native integration with the SAP Business Suite, using existing business logic and customer-specific configuration, for validation of master data while it is being created. In addition, SAP MDG integrates with Data Services for data quality and enrichment. It uses the data quality engine mentioned previously to inform the user about duplicate data sets. It also uses Data Services' rich address enrichment features to support users in entering correct addresses for their business partners.

SAP MDG uses SAP Business Workflow for the governance process and allows you to design your own workflows for the central master data creation or maintenance process. These workflows typically involve multiple people adding their expertise to complex master data (for example, one person edits a material's classification information and another adds units of measurement and their conversions). The workflows also include workflow steps for approval of the changed data.

Until the approval, inactive data is kept in a staging area, separate from productive master data, and it is only after approval that the data is posted to the master data tables in the SAP system and distributed to systems that subscribe to these master data changes. Through this process, SAP MDG delivers consistent definition, authorization, and replication to corporate systems such as SAP Business Suite and non-SAP systems. By tracking all changes and approvals, SAP MDG supports compliance and a complete audit trail.

SAP MDG provides master data maintenance capabilities through a role-based, domain-specific user interface. In addition to central maintenance of master data in the SAP Business Suite, data from external sources is supported. For example, you can upload data into SAP MDG via a file or services and then further process (or enrich) the data in SAP MDG. SAP MDG provides governance for specific master data areas. The primary areas are discussed below.

SAP Master Data Governance for Financial Master Data

SAP MDG provides governance processes for a broad set of financial master data, including charts of accounts, general ledger accounts, companies and conglomerate companies, consolidation units, profit centers and cost centers including their hierarchies, and cost elements and cost element hierarchies.

SAP Master Data Governance for Supplier and Customer Master Data

SAP MDG supports the governance of customer master data creation and changes. The focus of the first release is generic business partner attributes, general customer data, and address information. For both customers and suppliers, SAP MDG supports the search, display, change, and creation of single master data sets as well as mass processing or changes to hierarchies.

Figure 4.9 is an example of the master data governance process for supplier data. A requestor enters the initial supplier data and submits the master data record for approval. A specialist can review the request and either return it to the requestor for additional information, reject the request, or approve the request. If additional data is required to enrich the record—for instance, purchasing data—then a domain specialist can perform this data enrichment. Once the record is complete and has received final approval, it is created in the SAP ERP system and, if applicable, distributed to other systems that share the data. Prebuilt workflows are used to control the creation process at every step.

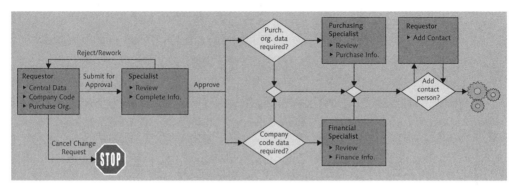

Figure 4.9 Example of SAP MDG Process for Supplier

SAP Master Data Governance for Material Master Data

SAP MDG allows for central creation and change processes for material master data. The focus is on identifying and describing attributes of the material master data, including basic data and classification. Again, you can search, display, change, and create a single material master data element, perform mass processing, and upload files.

In addition to the governance processes provided, users can also create customized governance processes. Business process experts can define enhancements and checks (for example, by enriching parts of data through assigning an enrichment spot, skipping unnecessary checks, or ensuring that validations occur by assigning checks). They can also set field properties for entity types and attributes by specifying which fields are relevant and which relevant fields are required through field properties. They can assign a different user interface in addition to the standard interface configured for the data model. All this allows a maximum of flexibility on the change request step level.

In addition to this flexibility at design time, power users or even end users can easily adapt the user interface to their specific needs at runtime. For example, they can rearrange the screen layout or set default values on selected fields for their most often-used screens. All this is based on the new user interface design paradigm that has been adopted across SAP MDG's master data domains.

SAP Master Data Governance Integration with SAP Data Services and SAP Information Steward

Native integration between Data Services, SAP MDG, and Information Steward is critical to ensuring ongoing data quality, data remediation, duplicate prevention, validations, and data enrichment. Combined, these three applications provide a holistic solution for governing master data in the SAP Business Suite.

SAP MDG focuses on comprehensive master data governance ready for use in SAP applications, through ready-to-run governance processes for specific master data domains. In addition, the SAP MDG application foundation allows for custom-defined master data objects, processes, and user interfaces. SAP MDG provides prebuilt validation against SAP business logic and customers' configuration settings and can distribute master data to SAP and non-SAP applications.

Further details of SAP MDG are covered in Chapter 12.

4.4   SAP Solutions for Enterprise Content Management

Enterprise content management (ECM) is a broad area that includes the capturing, managing, preservation, and delivery of content and documents to organizations and business processes. ECM focuses on unstructured information. Some consider ECM to be a completely separate discipline from EIM, but SAP takes a different view; documents and other content are critical information assets that must be managed in a holistic information management strategy. ECM covers a wide range of technologies and use cases, extending EIM to unstructured content that is critical to the business. ECM delivers solutions that focus on the following business pain points:

▶ Inability or excessive effort to find and reuse relevant content

▶ Exponential growth of unstructured content

▶ Content fragmentation across applications and content silos

▶ "Tribal knowledge" vs. enterprise information

▶ Need for long-term preservation and legal compliance

▶ Cost reduction and increased process efficiency via digitization of paper documents

These pain points reduce business efficiency as it relates to content and increase legal and compliance risk. *Reduced business efficiency* includes the inability to find what is needed to complete a business process. For example, before you sign a contract with a new vendor, a specific spreadsheet or email needs a final review, but where is it? Perhaps it is in an application that the user can't access or in a file share for which the user has no permissions, or the content has been fragmented and parts are stored among several applications. There could also be paper documents that are difficult to tie to a digital process.

Increased legal and compliance risk includes content that was not kept for the legally required duration (for example, someone got rid of an old file without realizing that some documents for a legal hold were inadvertently deleted as well), or content was kept longer than legally required. Additionally, regulation requires auditable content lifecycle records.

Table 4.3 depicts a list of concepts and activities typically considered to belong to the ECM solution space. SAP provides solutions for each of the ECM components listed in the table.

ECM Process	Key Features
Document Management	▶ Basic content handling capabilities such as retrieval, storage, versioning, and check-in/check-out ▶ Metadata handling ▶ Security handling ▶ Audit trails
Input Management	▶ Capture manually created or scanned information (office documents, forms, or rich media) ▶ Capture application-created information (XML, financial applications, or e-forms) ▶ Recognize printed or written information (optical character recognition, barcode, or hand-printed character recognition)
Output Management	▶ Assemble documents from text fragments, data, or a clause library (based on simple rules or complete business logic) ▶ Make transformation (conversion, syndication, and compression)

Table 4.3 Scope of Enterprise Content Management Solutions Provided by SAP

ECM Process	Key Features
Output Management (Cont.)	▸ Perform security (digital rights management, watermark, and digital signatures) ▸ Distribute (Internet, intranet, email, fax, CD/DVD, or paper)
Records Management	▸ Manage enterprise information as a business record ▸ Perform file plan classification (automatically and interactively) ▸ Fulfill compliant standards (such as U.S. Department of Defense 5015.2 certification and International Standard Organization 15489 standard) ▸ Map classifications to retention rules and support of disposition management
Web Content Management	▸ Create web content (manage content with template support) ▸ Include documents or social media/collaboration capabilities in web content ▸ Manage web content lifecycle and publish content to different channels
Digital Asset Management	▸ Support consuming, annotating, cataloging, storage, and retrieval of digital assets (photographs, videos, and music) ▸ Manage metadata for digital assets, copyrights, and distribution rights
Email Management	▸ Email classification ▸ Integrate emails into business processes or records

Table 4.3 Scope of Enterprise Content Management Solutions Provided by SAP (Cont.)

SAP's ECM solutions provide end-to-end support for processing unstructured content, including activities such as capturing, managing, storing, preserving, sharing, and distributing content. Capabilities for managing unstructured content in SAP's ECM solutions include:

▸ **Content creation and capture**
This produces new content with editing capabilities and handling of inbound information as content (for example, content provided via email or scanning).

▶ **Content discovery, sharing, and collection**
This covers all activities around finding and searching content and browsing through existing content repositories. Created content has to be shared and published. A typical example of sharing content is to create web content and publish the information in an intranet. Collaboration capabilities are crucial to working jointly on content.

▶ **Content governance and compliance**
This is required to freeze content (for example, via generating stable outputs in PDF) or to treat content as a record, which means fulfilling predefined compliance rules for the content. An example of a compliance standard is the U.S. Department of Defense (DoD) 5015.2 certification.

▶ **Content archiving and destruction**
This process ensures a proper, total cost of ownership-minimizing end of life for content.

This section discusses the actual SAP products that are associated with the tasks of ECM. We begin by offering an overview of all the ECM solutions, and then dive into a more specific discussion of the most commonly used solutions: SAP Extended Enterprise Content Management by OpenText, SAP Document Access by OpenText, and SAP Archiving by OpenText.

4.4.1 Overview of SAP's ECM Solutions

To deliver on the full breadth of functionality and to offer an enterprise grade ECM offering, SAP's extended and full-fledged ECM offerings include both SAP solutions and solutions provided by OpenText as solution extensions. The OpenText products have been tested to conform to the SAP product standards, can be purchased from SAP, and are maintained via SAP standard support mechanisms.

The following is a list of ECM solutions, divided into SAP solutions provided by OpenText and SAP solutions provided by SAP.

SAP's ECM Solutions Provided by OpenText

▶ **SAP Document Presentment by OpenText**
Automates document generation and personalization. Examples include billing statements, campaign execution, and customer-focused marketing messages.

▶ **SAP Digital Asset Management by OpenText**
Provides optimized management of rich media assets, as well as the ability to integrate media into marketing communications. For example, images for a new washing machine that might be used on the web, for mobile devices, or printed on a brochure. These washing machine images could be part of a marketing campaign for new washing machines, with all images managed by brand and model.

▶ **SAP Invoice Management by OpenText (including optical character recognition)**
Minimizes capture effort and human intervention and streamlines accounts payable processes (for example, scanning invoices to create the invoice document in the SAP system).

▶ **SAP Travel Receipt Management by OpenText**
Automates receipt handling and streamlines the expense management process.

▶ **SAP Employee Management by OpenText**
HR file administration; enables self-service scenarios such as a requests to see personnel files.

▶ **SAP Portal Content Management by OpenText**
Manages version control, sharing, and collaboration of documents in SAP NetWeaver Portal.

▶ **SAP Portal Site Management by OpenText**
Manages web content in a company's SAP NetWeaver Portal installation.

▶ **SAP Archiving by OpenText**
Storage of information, including scan and viewer technology. For example, it stores scanned images of invoices in the archive and links them to the invoice in the SAP ERP system.

▶ **SAP Document Access by OpenText (includes SAP Archiving by OpenText)**
Offers 360-degree information access with SAP GUI context, meaning that from within SAP GUI, users can get a complete view of all content associated with a transaction, master data, or business process. For example, when you look at a plant asset, such as a machine, all manuals and pictures associated with a physical asset on the plant floor are available in the SAP asset transaction. This includes

the ability to check in and check out documents, get authorization and access rights, and search for documents.

▶ **SAP Extended ECM by OpenText (includes SAP Archiving by OpenText, SAP Document Access, and SAP Portal Content Management by OpenText)**
Connects unstructured content with SAP business processes—including document and records management, collaboration, archiving, scanning, information retrieval—that interconnect with SAP software and support core business processes. For example, you can associate a picture, resume, or performance review with an employee.

Figure 4.10 shows several of SAP's ECM solutions provided by OpenText.

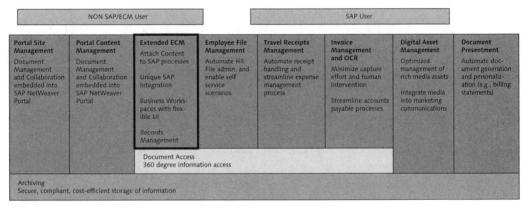

Figure 4.10 SAP's ECM Solutions Provided by OpenText

In Figure 4.10 notice that the bottom horizontal solution is archiving. All OpenText solutions use the archiving layer for secure, compliant, and cost-effective storage of all content. Notice Document Access above the archiving layer. Document Access is available in the SAP GUI to view content related to a business object; for example, a customer. Also notice at the top that all content is available to SAP and non-SAP users with security access to the content.

SAP's ECM Solutions Provided by SAP

In addition to the solution extensions provided by OpenText, SAP offers a range of products that provide content management capabilities:

▶ **SAP Product Lifecycle Management (PLM) Document Management System and SAP Easy Document Management**

Supports the scenarios delivered with SAP Product Lifecycle Management, including integration with computer-aided design tools (which, for example, lets you store CAD files of a new engine in the SAP system and automatically create and update material master data in the SAP system based on the information maintained in CAD tools).

▶ **SAP cFolders**

Supports seamless collaboration on documents and material master data with external parties such as suppliers. This can be done without giving them access to your corporate system within the firewall.

▶ **SAP NetWeaver Folders Management**

Allows customers to build intuitive, structured views of diverse application data to boost business user productivity and support workflows on these folders and cases (for example, to manage dispute cases or change cases).

▶ **CRM Content Management in SAP CRM**

Attachment service that allows users to attach documents to any CRM object (for example, a lead within the SAP CRM web interface).

▶ **Email Response System (ERMS) capability in SAP CRM**

Manages automatic replies to emails (for example, a notification that your email was received and the recipient will get back to you as soon as possible).

▶ **SAP Enterprise Workspace for SAP NetWeaver Portal**

Supports easy creation of collaboration spaces, workgroups, and teams via SAP NetWeaver Portal.

▶ **Knowledge Management in SAP NetWeaver Portal**

Supports basis document management functionality in the SAP NetWeaver Portal frontend.

▶ **SAP NetWeaver Information Lifecycle Management (ILM)**

Manages retention and retirement of content associated with SAP via SAP ArchiveLink business processes in system decommissioning and retention management scenarios.

▶ **SAP StreamWork**

Content capability in the cloud for collaboration on documents and projects (for example, writing an EIM book by collaborating with SAP and non-SAP authors).

▶ **SAP NetWeaver Enterprise Search**
Has search capabilities for structured and unstructured content.

▶ **SAP Content Server**
Content server delivered by SAP and supporting SAP ArchiveLink to support document storage.

4.4.2 SAP Extended Enterprise Content Management by OpenText

SAP Extended ECM is a full ECM suite (including document management, collaboration, capture, workflow, content access, records management, and archiving) and combines content management capabilities with deep SAP integration to provide content-enriched SAP business processes. It provides a new paradigm where content is managed *within* the business processes instead of *outside* the business processes. This is shown in Figure 4.11.

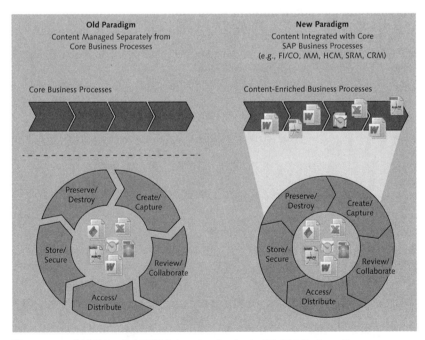

Figure 4.11 SAP Extended ECM Integrates Content with SAP Business Processes

Figure 4.11 depicts the integration of content and the business process with the content-enriched business processes on the right side of the figure. The integration between SAP systems and SAP Extended ECM is described next.

Deep Integration with SAP

The deep integration of SAP Extended ECM with other SAP systems includes work spaces that natively extend SAP processes. SAP Extended ECM is seamlessly integrated inside SAP applications such as the SAP Business Suite and SAP NetWeaver Portal to enable SAP users to easily access content. In addition to accessing content in SAP's native user interfaces, content can be accessed from an SAP Extended ECM web user interface, Microsoft Outlook, and Microsoft Windows Explorer. The support for many user interfaces allows for sharing of content between different stakeholders in an organization, independent from what applications the content originates or what a user's preferred user interface may be.

The deep connection with SAP extends beyond the user interface to data, structures, roles, and permissions. Basically everything customers have already standardized around SAP processes can be leveraged for ECM use cases. The impact is that SAP and ECM are always in sync. As shown in Figure 4.12, the SAP Business Suite is integrated not only in the frontend, but also in the backend by data referencing and data, user, and authorization synchronization, which supports single sign-on.

Figure 4.12 SAP Extended ECM Integration with SAP Business Suite

In Figure 4.12, notice the constant synchronization of data references between SAP Extended ECM and the SAP Business Suite. Metadata synchronization, user synchronization, and access controls are driven from the SAP Business Suite to SAP Extended ECM, meaning that the security setup in your SAP system is inherited and applied to SAP Extended ECM. Also notice the variety of user interfaces in the figure. The content can be accessed from SAP GUI, SAP NetWeaver Portal, an SAP Extended ECM user interface, Microsoft Outlook, Lotus Notes, web browsers, and Windows Explorer (not included in the figure).

Examples of Content-Rich SAP Business Processes

SAP Extended ECM's deep integration provides very content-rich SAP business processes in the SAP Business Suite. Some examples of those content-enriched processes are project management, product lifecycle management, procurement, quality management, case and claims management, asset management, and customer relationship management. In each of these examples the process is enriched due to the content.

One specific example is SAP Enterprise Asset Management, which is used heavily in SAP Plant Maintenance for processes such as equipment failure analysis, shutdown turnaround, and general change management. In this example, SAP Extended ECM leverages and extends SAP Enterprise Asset Management for plant maintenance, providing content management and collaboration capabilities in every step related to the analysis and reporting the results to various stakeholders. The following is the process in SAP Plant Maintenance:

1. **Create maintenance notification**
   When the maintenance notification is created, a work space is created in SAP Extended ECM that includes the notification documents. The work space allows you to add additional content for sharing.

2. **Create work orders**
   As the work order is created to investigate the problem, a failure analysis process is triggered in SAP Extended ECM. SAP Extended ECM collects failure data, scope, photographs, analysis, email correspondence with suppliers, and a final report for review.

3. **Schedule and fix**
   As the technician is assigned and works on documents, all photos, manuals, and

correspondence — that is, all content required for the repair — is provided via SAP Extended ECM.

4. **Completion**

The root cause analysis can require updates to maintenance plans, equipment repair, and so on. All information is captured in the final analysis report managed by SAP Extended ECM.

Figure 4.13 shows an example of the content integrated in asset management.

Figure 4.13 Example of Content Integrated in Asset Management

Figure 4.13 shows a workspace in SAP Plant Maintenance where the user can access all content regarding a specific piece of equipment. In the example it is an electric pump. The user can access the manuals, inspection reports, pictures, drawings, warranties, and so on required to maintain and fix the electric pump. (Note: Workspaces will be discussed in more detail in Chapter 14.)

4.4.3 SAP Document Access by OpenText and Archiving by OpenText

SAP Document Access by OpenText and SAP Archiving by OpenText are two key capabilities included in SAP Extended ECM that enable great flexibility when managing unstructured content. These capabilities are used heavily in both SAP Extended

ECM and SAP NetWeaver ILM (covered in Section 4.5). SAP Document Access by OpenText and SAP Archiving by OpenText are discussed in more detail next.

SAP Document Access by OpenText

SAP Document Access is powerful enterprise content management software that integrates fully with your SAP applications. It allows you to store, manage, and retrieve documents across SAP transactions or applications such as SAP ERP or SAP CRM. Content can also originate from various sources such as host systems, legacy software, or customer-specific applications. SAP Document Access provides three key features:

▶ **Ease of use**
Enables even occasional users to quickly retrieve content by working with the intuitive, customizable navigation based on folder structures.

▶ **Ready access**
Offers 360-degree views of SAP documents and SAP online and archived data.

▶ **Web interface**
In addition to the SAP GUI interface, the web interface provides a convenient web user interface that can be integrated into a customer portal or in the SAP NetWeaver Portal component.

An example of using SAP Document Access is providing front office employees with a complete view of all customer interactions (for example, customer messages, emails, and letters written to the company), all brought together in one place so the employee can quickly gain insight into the customer's request.

SAP Archiving by OpenText

SAP Archiving by OpenText securely stores all types of documents and links them to SAP transactions via SAP ArchiveLink. SAP Archiving by OpenText also minimizes your database growth and improves performance, resulting in a lower total cost of ownership for your SAP software. Combined with SAP NetWeaver ILM, the archiving function lets you address the compliance requirements associated with electronic document retention regulations from government agencies (such as the U.S. Securities and Exchange Commission and the U.S. Food and Drug Administration) and mandates (such as the Sarbanes-Oxley Act and Germany's Principles of Due Operation of Electronic Bookkeeping Systems and Principles of Data Access and Auditing of Digital Documents).

> ### What Is Archiving?
>
> The term *archive* has two meanings:
>
> ► The relocation and removal of content from your systems (for example, removing all closed purchase orders over 10 years old and relocating them to a storage system).
>
> ► Associating content with data in your system (for example, scanning invoices or emails associated with a vendor).
>
> SAP Archiving by OpenText helps with both processes.

As you can see, ECM is a very large area. Chapter 14 focuses on SAP Extended ECM and how to get started using SAP Extended ECM in SAP ERP.

4.5 SAP NetWeaver Information Lifecycle Management

Information has a predictable lifecycle. It is created, lives, and changes in databases, repositories, and software solutions. It is archived and eventually destroyed. A comprehensive strategy for information lifecycle management (ILM) focuses on maintaining a balance between total cost of ownership, risk, and legal compliance. It specifies steps to define, document, and introduce ways to better manage the information that exists across the organization. The ILM process includes knowing and categorizing your data, defining policies that govern what you do with the data, and setting up your system in such a way that you can apply these policies to your data. You then implement your information management strategy with the help of technology. The added value of ILM compared to more conventional information management strategies is automation and completeness.

Several factors have converged to bring about a major change in the way companies manage data. For example, awareness of the unforeseen events that could occur—such as natural disasters, terrorist attacks, or financial meltdowns—has set in motion new efforts to protect consumer identity and privacy. This awareness has led to an explosion in legal requirements. There are currently thousands of regulations worldwide pertaining to the handling of electronic data, and that number continues to grow. Another factor that is becoming increasingly urgent is the management of legacy systems in both SAP software and non-SAP software landscapes. Not only are the aged systems generating ongoing and unnecessary costs through the consumption of electricity and the need for administration and maintenance effort, but they pose a significant legal risk. The data they hold must be accessible and ready to be presented at relatively short notice (for example, to an auditor in the event of a tax audit). However, as knowledge about the old systems gradually fades from the company and the old hardware is physically removed, it is difficult to predict whether that data will be accessible when needed. The management and retention of information has become so important that traditional data management approaches are no longer sufficient. An effective ILM strategy is an essential part of an enterprise's overall strategy for dealing with the challenges of cost, compliance, and risk. SAP has developed an approach to ILM that meets the complex information management needs of today's organizations.

SAP NetWeaver ILM comprises the policies, processes, practices, and tools used to align the business value of information with the most appropriate and cost-effective IT infrastructure from the time information is created through its final destruction. The complete, flexible, and automated approach to ILM advanced by SAP gives you the support you need to adapt to constantly changing regulations. It helps you accomplish the following steps:

▶ Identify and categorize your data

▶ Define policies that govern what you do with data

▶ Leverage application and storage technology in such a way that you can apply these policies to your data

▶ Implement your information management strategy

▶ Shut down your legacy systems in a legally compliant manner

Figure 4.14 shows the evolution from data archiving to retention management to systems decommissioning. This evolution is discussed in more detail next.

SAP Archiving by OpenText versus SAP Data Archiving

SAP Archiving by OpenText is a product used for the storage of content. For example, it is used to store scanned invoices in an SAP ERP system. SAP Archiving by OpenText is also used for the storage of those scanned invoices after they are retired from the SAP system. This product was discussed in Section 4.4.3, and is not the focus of this section.

In this section, we talk about *SAP Data Archiving*. This refers to the *relocation* of business-complete data from the SAP application database to the *storage system*. The archived data can be accessed from the original system at any time for read-only activities, such as reporting, for example, the archiving of closed invoices older than 18 months.

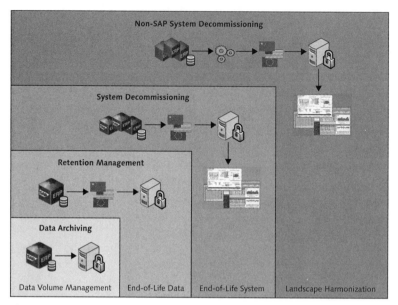

Figure 4.14 Evolution of Data Archiving

SAP NetWeaver ILM has evolved from a simple data archiving solution to a comprehensive solution for determining how long and in what ways data should be kept and used and the means for decommissioning SAP and non-SAP systems. It works with Data Services and SAP Archiving by OpenText for a complete ILM solution. SAP Data Archiving has been around for many years and lets you archive selected business objects from business-complete processes, relocating them from the database to an external storage system. Examples include closed purchasing documents, order history, and technical items such as IDocs and workflow work items. SAP Data Archiving has evolved into retention management, enabling you to proactively monitor how long you need to keep data in your system and placing legal holds as required on selected data. The further expansion of SAP NetWeaver ILM includes decommissioning of SAP and non-SAP systems that are no longer required.

SAP NetWeaver ILM provides three major use cases and scenarios for use:

▶ **SAP Data Archiving**
Again, this data archiving should not be confused with SAP Archiving by OpenText. It is a product that enables you to associate images, such as scanned invoices, with SAP business objects. *SAP Data Archiving* is a core component of SAP

NetWeaver ILM that enables you to move business-complete data (transactional and master data) that is no longer required in everyday business from the database into long-term, less expensive storage. The data is still available to meet regulatory or other legal requirements when it is stored in the archive.

▸ **Retention management**
SAP tools and technologies for SAP NetWeaver ILM provide retention policy management functions that support the complete information lifecycle from creation to retention to destruction. They enable you to enter different rules and policies reflecting various criteria, including where data is stored, the duration of data retention, and when data can be destroyed. The policies, usually based on external legal requirements or internal service-level agreements, can be applied to both structured and unstructured data stored on all types of media. Based on the rules, the data is automatically archived into the correct storage area and receives an expiration date. SAP NetWeaver ILM-aware storage integration means your storage systems understand and can act on the stored data based on rules you define. At the end of the lifecycle, an automated destruction function permanently destroys the archived data when the expiration date has been reached. SAP NetWeaver ILM includes functions that support legal-hold management and automated electronic discovery.

▸ **System decommissioning**
SAP NetWeaver ILM provides a complete approach to shutting down legacy systems and bringing the data from both SAP and non-SAP software into a central SAP NetWeaver ILM retention warehouse. In the retention warehouse, the data is stored with the relevant expiration dates in SAP NetWeaver ILM-aware storage and can be viewed with different reporting options even after the original system has been shut down. Functions of SAP NetWeaver BW as well as local reporting functions are used to extend the SAP NetWeaver ILM retention warehouse with centralized auditing and reporting functions. Included are functions that enable you to create snapshots of master and customizing data and provide on-demand analysis of archived data.

The major SAP NetWeaver ILM components that support these use scenarios are retention management and system decommissioning capabilities within SAP NetWeaver ILM, which are discussed next. Both these components integrate natively with SAP Archiving by OpenText and SAP Document Access.

4.5.1 Retention Management

Retention management provides a range of dedicated tools and functions to help you adequately control the retention of your data along its entire lifecycle. This holds true for structured information, such as a sales documents posted in the SAP application, as well as for unstructured information such as scanned invoices. Once a policy is set up and activated in the SAP NetWeaver ILM policy engine, data is protected against destruction until its expiration date has been reached. Retention management is based on SAP Data Archiving technology, so you do not have to start from scratch if you are already using SAP Data Archiving. You can use retention management functions directly within your SAP ERP application as of SAP ERP enhancement pack 4 or higher. Retention management includes the follow capabilities:

▶ Archiving data from open and completed business processes

▶ Storing archived information on an SAP NetWeaver ILM-certified server (to guarantee nonchangeability of the information and protect from premature destruction)

▶ Determining and managing retention rules

▶ Inclusion of retention rules for stored information so the destruction is timely and in adherence with the retention periods required by law

▶ Using stored information to create reports for tax auditing and product liability

▶ Retrieving information for legal cases and defining legal holds

▶ Destroying stored information after the retention period has expired, assuming there is no legal hold

More details on these capabilities will be provided in Chapter 13.

4.5.2   System Decommissioning

System decommissioning enables you to consolidate multiple large legacy systems into a small single instance and retain on-demand access to data from legacy systems as well as respond to tax audits and create reports. The legacy data is stored in the SAP NetWeaver ILM retention warehouse, which serves as a single repository for multiple systems. When the data is required for legal, audit, or tax purposes, it is exposed to a data warehouse such as SAP NetWeaver BW (and, in the future, SAP HANA) for flexible and modern reporting capability. The business knowledge and context is preserved during the decommissioning even as retention policies are being enforced. After moving retention-relevant data from the legacy system to the SAP NetWeaver ILM retention warehouse, you can shut down the legacy system for good.

In a typical decommissioning scenario, you have one or more systems that will be shut down and a dedicated retention warehouse system that will receive the data you want to retain from the original systems. The retention warehouse consists of three pieces:

▶ A dedicated SAP ERP application running only SAP NetWeaver ILM

▶ A dedicated implementation of SAP NetWeaver BW

▶ Third-party SAP NetWeaver ILM-certified storage hardware

In the retention warehouse, data from decommissioned systems is organized according to audit areas and covered by the retention policies you define and manage using the software. This means retention times and legal holds apply to the data maintained in the retention warehouse, just as they do for non-decommissioned (or live) systems.

The system that is to be shut down is first emptied of its data using standard and SAP NetWeaver ILM-enhanced archiving objects and programs. You can archive all the business-complete data and then use snapshot functionality to archive data from objects that are not yet business-complete, as well as any related master and context data. Figure 4.15 shows the decommissioning of several systems to a single SAP NetWeaver ILM system and related storage. Next, we discuss a typical system decommissioning scenario and some of the required steps.

Figure 4.15 Decommissioning Systems Using SAP NetWeaver ILM

A Typical System Decommissioning Scenario

For a decommissioning project, there are multiple steps that can be roughly grouped into two categories: steps for the legacy system and steps for the retention warehouse in SAP NetWeaver ILM.

► **Steps for the legacy system**

  ► Analyze the system

  ► Enable the legacy system for archiving

  ► Prepare the legacy system for shutdown

  ► Extract data from the legacy system

  ► Conduct testing and quality assurance

► **Steps for the retention warehouse**

  ► Install an SAP ERP application with only SAP NetWeaver ILM and SAP NetWeaver BW, and connect to an SAP NetWeaver ILM-aware storage system

  ► Set up the retention warehouse

  ► Set up audit areas, policies, and rules

  ► Move archived data to the retention warehouse system

- ▶ Convert and store the archive files and apply rules

- ▶ Generate business warehouse queries using archived data or run a local reporting option

The following sections discuss several of the most important steps in more detail. You can find more details on SAP NetWeaver ILM in Chapter 13.

Analyze the Legacy System

It's not uncommon for IT departments to have only limited knowledge of their legacy systems, particularly with respect to the amount and types of data they contain. If you don't know what your legacy system "looks" like, you have the option of either moving everything over to the retention warehouse system or, once you run an analysis of your system, moving only the specific data you will need later for auditing and reporting.

Enable the Legacy System for Archiving

Once you have identified the data you need to retain and the tools you need to retain it, you can enable the legacy system for archiving. Since SAP NetWeaver ILM is delivered with SAP ERP, your older, legacy system has to receive the necessary SAP NetWeaver ILM functions. (SAP NetWeaver ILM natively supports legacy systems back to R/3 4.6c. For older releases additional consulting is required.) This includes enhancements for archiving objects, snapshot functionality, and the context data extractor. The context data extractor functionality is preconfigured for tax reporting and product liability reporting.

Extract Data from Legacy Systems

Once the legacy system and retention warehouse are prepared, you can extract the data from the legacy system. This includes enhanced data archiving functionality, such as the snapshot option (one of the archiving options), and the context data extractor functionality. After you have "emptied" the legacy system, moved data to the retention warehouse, and performed testing, you can shut the legacy system down.

SAP NetWeaver ILM provides a streamlined IT infrastructure and lowered costs through the safe and efficient decommissioning of redundant systems. It provides reduced risk by delivering full auditing and reporting functionality and rules-based enforcement of retention policies and preventing destruction of important data.

This enables greater legal compliance by automatically managing the retention of data from your SAP applications based on retention policies and rules you define.

Set Up the Retention Warehouse

After preparing your legacy system to be shut down, you can set up the retention warehouse to receive the data from the system you want to decommission. Your dedicated SAP ERP application should be set up and connected to a third-party storage system, which must be an SAP NetWeaver ILM-certified product. If you are using SAP Archiving by OpenText for your image and content storage, you can automatically use it for SAP NetWeaver ILM as well. (To find an SAP NetWeaver ILM-certified partner, visit *http:/www.sdn.sap.com/irj/sdn/interface-certifications*.) In addition, you need to connect SAP NetWeaver BW. SAP recommends that you use a dedicated business warehouse system for your data retention warehouse.

This section introduced SAP NetWeaver ILM. More details can be found in Chapter 13.

4.6   SAP Solutions for Data Migration

Migration projects are relevant for all types of companies, including those with SAP applications, non-SAP applications, and those who are upgrading—any company that needs to migrate data from one application to another. This includes companies that are:

▶ Acquiring or merging with other companies

▶ Expanding into new lines of business

▶ Initiating green IT projects to reduce hardware and environmental and monetary costs

▶ Harmonizing data and processes across organizational boundaries

▶ Conducting a global SAP rollout

Because of this, data migration is often a first entry point with EIM, and it serves as a compelling use case for starting data management and information governance initiatives across the enterprise.

Planning for a data migration project is a major task. Getting data cleansed, transformed, and loaded into a new application can seem daunting. Add to that task the following common questions:

▸ How much of my data and related content do I take?

▸ Is my data ready to be migrated?

▸ What do I do with the legacy application after the migration?

▸ How long do I need to keep the data in the new application?

▸ How do I handle contracts and documents related to my data?

Dealing with the source system, content, and how long to keep data are often discussion items that go to the back burner because of time constraints, resource constraints, political constraints, and the tactical pressure to get the base migration completed. By extending the conversation from data migration to systems migration, the questions of the source system, information retention, and content management can be addressed, feeding into an overall coherent information management strategy.

Next, data migration will be discussed in more detail, explaining SAP Best Practices and Rapid Deployment Solutions for rapid data migration, and then systems migration.

4.6.1 SAP Data Migration Software

SAP Data Migration uses many of the software components already discussed. This means the data migration solution uses Data Services and includes some SAP BusinessObjects Web Intelligence reports.

As discussed earlier, Data Services delivers data integration and data quality as part of its data foundation. With its native connectivity to many applications, it is the perfect software capability to drive data migration projects. Information Steward lets you get to know your source data very well, and has metadata capabilities to reconcile what was loaded in a migration cycle with the source data. The SAP BusinessObjects BI platform provides reports on migration progress. Using business intelligence capabilities, such as SAP BusinessObjects Web Intelligence, enables a business user to easily distinguish the good and bad data in an easy-to-read report. The six major steps of SAP Data Migration are shown in Figure 4.16.

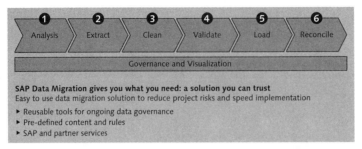

Figure 4.16 SAP Data Migration

The first step in SAP Data Migration is analysis, which includes data profiling and getting to know your data prior to migrating it to an SAP application. This includes the profiling capabilities delivered with Data Services that were discussed in Section 4.1.1, but also the more advanced data profiling capabilities provided with Information Steward. (Information Steward data profiling capabilities were mentioned in Section 4.2 and will be discussed in more detail in Chapter 6.)

Once you understand more about your source data, you can extract source data and place it in a staging area in Data Services. The extraction is based on the Data Services connectivity options mentioned above. After the data extraction occurs, data cleansing starts. This can be simple data cleansing such as checking for null values and correctly formatted zip codes, to very complex cleansing such as address cleansing, duplicate checking, and so on. A good example of data cleansing is provided in Chapter 8.

Once data has been cleansed, the validation phase begins with value mapping. *Value mapping* is when you map how specific values need to convert to other values for the new application. For example, consider a situation where the country in the source system is *United States*, and the country code in the new system is *US*. This would mean that the process of value mapping would map all records with the country code of *United States* to *US*. Value mapping is done with the Migration Services tool provided with the content for data migration. More details on the validation and value mapping are discussed in Chapter 11.

Once you know the data is good, then it is loaded into the SAP system. The load will happen based on the application's requirements for loading. For example, many core objects are loaded via IDocs, which are a proprietary format for loading data into SAP systems. Other options include loading via an industry-specific technique, for example, when loading utilities for banking data or loading via the

Legacy System Migration Workbench (LSMW) or other SAP NetWeaver loading mechanisms. Examples of SAP NetWeaver loading mechanisms include BAPIs, ALE (application link enabling), etc. Once the data has been loaded, a reconciliation is performed to check what was loaded versus what was planned to be loaded.

In Figure 4.16, notice that the data migration solution is based on reusable tools for ongoing data governance, predefined content and rules, and SAP and partner services. The reusable tools for ongoing data governance refer to Data Services, Information Steward, and the SAP BusinessObjects platform. The predefined content and rules will be discussed next, but before moving on to the migration content, we'll explain the SAP and partner services. Normally with a first migration project most companies choose to use an experienced consulting organization. The SAP consulting services organization includes a global team trained in EIM, including data migration. As well as SAP consulting services, SAP has several consulting partners who are also experts in Data Services and the predefined content and rules delivered for data migration. It is recommended that your first data migration project be done with SAP or a partner who has been trained using the migration content provided by SAP (discussed next).

4.6.2   Predefined Content and Rules for Data Migration

When migrating to SAP applications such as SAP ERP, SAP CRM, and SAP ERP Human Capital Management (HCM), as well as industry solutions such as utilities, banking, and so on, it is important to understand what data is expected in the SAP system. This includes understanding the required fields, how the data must be formatted, relationships between data objects, and so on. This knowledge is well known to SAP but unknown to the source system. To expedite the understanding of the SAP data structures, SAP has provided migration content that is available in Data Services. This means SAP has looked at the objects most commonly migrated (business partner, material, cost center, plant, etc.) and has created all required elements in Data Services, mapping to the SAP objects, and reports, in a bundle for data migration.

For data migration, over 100 objects are supported for migration to SAP applications and industry solutions related to SAP ERP, SAP CRM, SAP ERP HCM, utilities, and banking industries. More migration content for additional objects is released each year. The predefined migration content includes:

► **Data validation content**
This enables mapping of legacy source data to SAP data, including validation of key values. Specific examples of the migration content include:

- ► Business partner content such as customer and vendor masters.

- ► Logistics content such as material masters, bills of material, purchasing documents, and sales documents.

- ► Financial content such as receivables, payables, and cost elements.

- ► Sales content such as activities, leads, opportunities, and contracts.

► **Documentation**
There is a Quick Guide on how to install the content, order to load the data, and how to extend the content provided by SAP.

- ► A business process document for data migration provides a process flow and the sequence in which the objects need to be loaded into Data Services.

- ► An extension guide provides the information you need to extend and modify the content according to your specific needs.

In addition to migration content for many core objects, there is also content for data quality capabilities including address validation, duplication detection, and data remediation. Also included in the migration content is a structured approach for governance for data migration projects.

All the data migration content is provided by the SAP Best Practices and Rapid Deployment Solutions organization at SAP. This group creates preconfigured solutions that ease implementation and provide scenario-specific solutions out-of-the-box. This content includes everything from specific Data Services content to provided reports, to migration tools to map source data, to validation of SAP fields (for example, U.S.A. and United States must all migrate to the country code US in the target SAP system).

In addition to creating content for data migration, the Rapid Deployment Solutions organization creates other solutions for EIM as well as other components in the SAP system. For example, there is a Rapid Deployment Solution for integrating customer data on SAP NetWeaver MDM. Because new solutions are released quarterly, the best place to look for new solution packages is at *http://service.sap.com/solutionpackages*.

For more details on data migration, go to *http://service.sap.com/bp-datamigration*.

4.6.3 Systems Migration

Systems migration is the migration of data and associated document content from one or more existing stores of information to a new application deployment, including the retirement and decommissioning of legacy data stores. Information includes both data and rich content (text and binary documents, PDF, email, and pictures).

Systems migration includes the data, metadata, unstructured content, and information required to support application migration projects. Also included is the decommissioning of source systems that are no longer required, as well as the archiving of data no longer required in the existing system.

Systems migration combines the capabilities of Data Services, SAP NetWeaver ILM, and SAP Document Access to provide a holistic offering for migrating to new systems and decommissioning the systems no longer required. For more information on systems migration, see *http://wiki.sdn.sap.com/wiki/x/sAWcDQ*.

4.6.4 SAP Rapid Marts

SAP Rapid Marts (hereafter Rapid Marts) provide data extraction from SAP systems, put the data in a data mart (currently supported by various databases and SAP HANA and will be supported soon by Sybase IQ), and provide reporting content. Rapid Marts deliver departmental business intelligence solutions for key subject areas. In most cases, Rapid Marts serve as jump-start blueprints but require customization to meet the customer's requirements.

SAP's array of Rapid Marts is expanding, but it currently provides the following:

- **Finance**
  General Ledger, Accounts Receivable, Accounts Payable, Fixed Assets, and Cost Center

- **Manufacturing**
  Plant Maintenance, Production Planning, and Project Systems

- **Operations**
  Sales, Inventory, and Purchasing

- **Human capital management**
  Human Resources

New Rapid Marts are released each year. For more information on Rapid Marts see *http://www.sap.com/solutions/sapbusinessobjects/data-warehousing/rapid-marts/index.epx*.

4.7   Information Governance in SAP

We introduced the discipline of information governance in Chapter 2 of this book. In this section, we review the concept and then explain how SAP solutions can assist with information governance. It is important to understand that all information management must include governance from both product capabilities and across all processes that update critical information in your enterprise. Information governance is a discipline that provides oversight to ensure successful execution of your information initiatives. It involves the management of people, technology, and processes, as well as policies, standards, and metrics, including the ongoing oversight necessary to manage information risks.

Information governance can be applied to one project, can be started with one data domain, and should be extended to the enterprise. Information governance is a sustained activity.

How do you know if problems you are seeing in your company can be attributed to a lack of information governance? The first step is always to listen. Words such as *mergers, risk, compliance, migration, acquisition, shared services, security,* and *Sarbanes-Oxley* can all point to information governance.

Case Study: New Driver's License in Indiana

In Indiana, 58,600 residents lost confidence in state IT practices when, as Chris Sikich noted in a *USA Today* article, the Bureau of Motor Vehicles (BMV) sent out a notice for drivers to renew their driver's licenses. The notices were intended as a proactive measure, since the state is expecting a glut of renewals in 2012. Because 2.4 million people will need to renew their license, the state spent $247,450 to mail postcards to about 700,000 people with birthdays from January through August.

Of those 700,000 people, 58,600 (approximately 8.3%) received incorrect information. Though, for many recipients, addresses and last names were correct, first names were not. For example, Rod Humphrey received a notice for Brandon Humphrey. Rod just threw out the renewal notice, effectively subverting the proactive measure taken by the BMV. The consequences of this are twofold:

▶ The renewal notices are more likely to be ignored, and therefore the proactive renewal-avoidance process is less effective.

▶ The mailing cost of those postcards was wasted. At a cost of 35 cents per mail piece, the postal cost of the error was approximately $20,510.

The next section discusses scenarios for how to get started with information governance.

4.7.1   Information Governance Use Scenario Phasing

The Indiana driver's license case study indicates a data quality problem. However, many other kinds of use scenarios can spur you to start an information governance project. Figure 4.17 highlights common use scenarios that your company may be approaching. The size of the bubbles indicates the relative complexity of each of the use scenarios, paying particular attention to the organizational change management and business process changes required to succeed in the individual use scenarios.

Figure 4.17   Information Governance Use Scenario Phasing

Notice that the use scenarios overlap. For example, if you do the work for an information discovery project, you can reuse some of that work for your business intelligence and predictive analytics project. For a business intelligence and predictive analytics project, you need to know the location of the best information (and the quality of that information) from which to drive the decision making. Information discovery includes activities such as knowing where the information is kept as well as quality level base-lining.

The following list describes each of the use scenarios.

▶ **Information discovery**
Finding all of the critical information sources in your company, including discovering (and documenting) quality levels, freshness, and timeliness of those information sources.

▶ **Business intelligence and predictive analytics**
Using high-quality, fresh, and timely information to drive decision making throughout the enterprise.

▶ **Data migration**
Moving and integrating data as you move from one system to another (for example, moving data from a retiring system to a new version of SAP ERP), including aggregations and quality corrections.

▶ **Data quality initiative**
Establishing policies to answer questions such as "What is a customer? What is a material? How can we create a single view of a material? Who needs to create and approve these master records?"

▶ **Manage master data**
Creating single points of reference for master data records, including setting up review and approval workflows for creating, changing, and flagging records for deletion.

▶ **Point-of-entry firewall**
Proactively fixing and verifying information before it enters productive systems in a live state, including enrichment and verifying against third-party truth sources.

▶ **Link master data to rich information**
Correctly linking rich information (documents, PDFs, videos, etc.) to the master data that needs that information, requiring accurate identification and tagging of both rich information and master data.

▶ **Retention and archiving**
Establishing retention and archiving policies in compliance with both corporate policies and enforced compliance policies, including both enforcement and manifestation of the policies.

▶ **Process monitoring and optimization**
Actively monitoring how well both business processes and information governance processes are performing, including where key bottlenecks are forming and recommendations for optimizing both business processes and information governance processes.

Refer back to Chapter 2 for more on getting started with governance initiatives.

4.7.2   Technology Enablers for Information Governance

You can implement information governance without any new technology purchases. Many customers use standard software to facilitate their information governance project: email, departmental Microsoft SharePoint, and spreadsheets. You can do this. In fact, you *should* start information governance this way because it helps you gain experience and perspective, and grow your information network.

However, keep in mind human nature. You can establish all of the good policies and standards in the world, and people can agree on the inherent goodness of these policies and standards. But if these policies and standards are inordinately difficult to comply with, people will find a way to get around them.

How do you make your information governance program easy to comply with? Technology is a great force multiplier here. Figure 4.18 ties in the EIM technologies mentioned in this chapter with information governance.

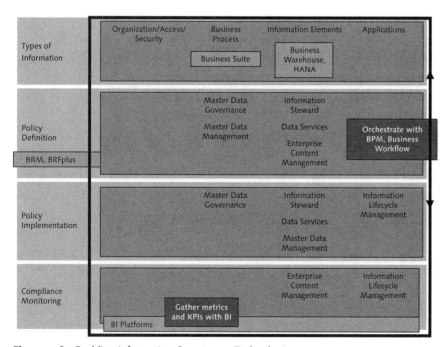

Figure 4.18   Enabling Information Governance Technologies

Figure 4.18 demonstrates that information governance does not only apply to master data. It applies to the organization, including governing user access and monitoring security. Information governance must be concerned with how the business processes use your enterprise information and where all of the data is stored. Finally, which systems access, use, and update the business processes and data elements that truly are enterprise assets?

For all of the above kinds of information (organization, business process, data elements, and systems), you have the following kinds of activities:

► **Policy definition**
What does "good" look like? How should this information behave? These policies are defined in plain language by the key business stakeholders. The following list mentions the major products where information policy definitions are created.

  ► *Information Steward:* This is the place for data stewards to define policies for master data.

  ► *SAP Extended ECM:* SAP Extended ECM supports the definition of retention policies determining how long documents should be retained and how access rights should be changed over the lifespan of content. SAP Extended ECM is also able to use SAP data from the SAP Business Suite to define retention periods.

  ► *SAP NetWeaver ILM:* SAP NetWeaver ILM supports the definition of retention policies determining how long data and associated documents should be retained. It is possible to synchronize (to create, update, and delete) SAP NetWeaver ILM retention policies via APIs with SAP Extended ECM retention policies.

► **Policy implementation**
How can you seamlessly implement and enforce the policies you defined—with as much collaboration and as little rewriting as possible? The following software and components can help:

  ► *Data Services:* This is the place for IT developers to design, move, aggregate, and understand master data, transactional data, and text data. Also, data stewards and IT developers can collaborate on core questions such as how to define a unique customer at the global level.

- ▶ *SAP NetWeaver MDM:* This is an environment for data stewards and IT developers to design and enforce master data storage, provisioning, and quality rules in analytical master data management scenarios.

- ▶ *SAP MDG:* Much like SAP NetWeaver MDM, this component takes advantage of the SAP ERP environment as a master data repository, business rule repository, and business workflow processing.

- ▶ *SAP Extended ECM:* Records management manages the retention and disposition of paper documents and digital content according to compliance requirements supporting international records management standards.

- ▶ *SAP NetWeaver ILM:* Establishes retention and policies for transactional data, master data, and rich content (such as documents), and enforces those policies.

▶ **Compliance monitoring**

How can you prove that you are complying with the information policies defined above? For a legal hold, can you prove that you are following industry standards when the audit department comes calling? The following software and components can help:

- ▶ *SAP BusinessObjects BI platform:* Here you can organize information and package it in a way that allows the business users to make decisions based on that information.

- ▶ *Information Steward and SAP MDG:* These enable you to monitor over time how well the data is complying with the business rules.

In addition to the software capabilities previously mentioned for policy definition, policy implementation, and compliance monitoring, SAP NetWeaver Business Process Management (BPM), SAP Business Workflow, Business Rules Framework Plus (BRFplus), and SAP NetWeaver Business Rules Management (BRM) are software components that have a cross-functional role in information governance. They can be used to support policy definition, implementation, and compliance monitoring.

As you can see, information governance requires a holistic look at policies, processes, and procedures to ensure that you are provisioning trusted, relevant, and reliable information for business processes.

4.8   NeedsEIM, Inc. and SAP's Solutions for EIM

Now that you understand the EIM solutions offered by SAP, let's take a high-level look at how these solutions may help NeedsEIM, Inc. (We will go into more detail about this in subsequent chapters of the book.)

Chapter 1 introduced NeedsEIM, Inc. and discussed its business challanges. SAP technologies that can help address them are shown in Figure 4.19. (Note that this is only one possible solution. Depending on your specific landscape, there are other alternate options that can provide similar resolutions for your business challenges.) Notice that the EIM components cover the cleansing and consolidation of information for both operational use in the applications and analytical use in the SAP BusinessObjects Business Intelligence (BI) suite. Using SAP NetWeaver Portal, SAP NetWeaver Business Process Management, and SAP Business Workflow, a master data creation and updating process can be designed that provides clear audit trails of approval. The record is stored in the MDM system, prior to which it goes through standardization, cleansing, and any enrichment processes using SAP Data Services. The data can now be syndicated to subscribing systems such as SAP ERP, SAP Customer Relationship Management (CRM), and so on. If there is any unstructured content that has to be managed and attached to a master data record (such as a W-4, company financials, or a vendor record), the attachment can be triggered as part of the approval workflow, and the documents can be stored in a content repository along with requisite metadata. A one-time migration of existing master data from various systems includes cleansing, matching, de-duplicating, and enriching, which can all be done using SAP Data Services and SAP Master Data Governance (MDG).

The issue of contracts may require a complex contract lifecycle management (CLM) solution or a combination of workflow and ECM solutions along with integration between systems. The analysis required to identify supplier spending may need a combination of information from a vendor master data governance process and an application that tracks spending. This data can be housed in an analytic database such as SAP NetWeaver Business Warehouse (BW) and/or SAP HANA for further analysis. A similar solution can be applied for customer-level profit and loss that would need all types of expense data collected from various applications such as SAP ERP Human Capital Management (HCM), SAP CRM, and SAP ERP along with revenue data from SAP ERP to arrive at the comprehensive profit and loss figure by customer.

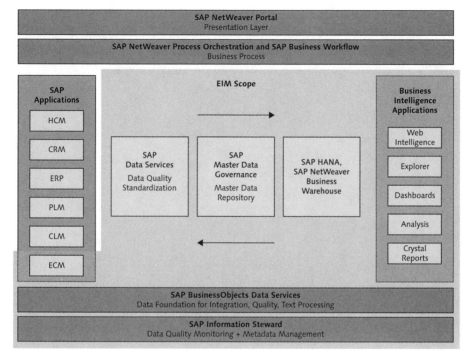

Figure 4.19 Sample Solution Architecture

As you move through Part II of the book, you will see how different capabilities within SAP's EIM portfolio can be used to address the major issues at NeedsEIM, Inc.

4.9 Summary

This chapter overviewed of all of SAP's solutions for EIM. It introduced Data Services for data integration, data quality, and text data processing. More details on Data Services can be found in Chapters 7, 8, and 10. You have seen how managing master data includes both SAP NetWeaver MDM and SAP MDG as an embedded master data solution. SAP MDG is discussed in more detail in Chapter 12. You now understand the breadth of ECM solutions offered by SAP and OpenText. SAP Extended ECM is the primary offering from OpenText and is discussed in more detail in Chapter 14. You understand that information is a risk if kept too long, so data archiving, retention policies, and systems decommissioning must be included in an information management strategy. Chapter 13 provides more details on SAP NetWeaver ILM.

In addition to details on the specific software capabilities, in Chapter 5 you will learn about real-world applications of EIM that are being used today. Chapter 5 is provided by named and unnamed customers who describe how they are using EIM and SAP's solutions for EIM to solve specific business problems.

This chapter shows SAP's EIM solutions in action and offers real-world experience and advice from actual customers of SAP.

5 Practical Examples of EIM

This chapter focuses on actual examples of how enterprise information management is being used today by different companies. While there are real-world example scenarios in many of the chapters throughout this book, the goal of this chapter is to provide broad-based examples of EIM use across different scenarios and organizations. Examples range from managing data migration projects, to master data projects, to developing an architecture for information management. This chapter is best read by thinking of each section as its own chapter since the topic for each section is different.

5.1 EIM Architecture Recommendations and Experiences by Procter and Gamble

An enterprise information architecture is ultimately intended to deliver the right content to the right end users. This means data that is in the right form, in the right level of quality, in the right level of granularity, and on the right timing.

To be successful in a business context, the architecture must be inclusive of classic architecture elements, most notably principles, guidelines, standards, inventories, and models, which give it focus and meaning within an enterprise. It must take into account the information-producing and information-consuming processes of the enterprise and all manners of interfaces. It must be supported by solid data governance, data stewardship, data maintenance, and logical and physical design. And throughout that set of considerations, information security must be a part of the equation.

To deliver a manageable and well-formed architecture, we typically create three leveled views:

▶ Conceptual—the user's view

▶ Logical—the designer's view

▶ Physical—the builder's view

This section will focus on the framework and elements that need to go into such an architecture. The purpose of the architecture is to guide decision making for IT projects such that systems can:

▶ **Increase end-user productivity**

  ▶ Eliminate time wasted looking for information

  ▶ Simplifying knowledge generation

  ▶ Increase time for analysis and decision making

  ▶ Reduce effort in data/information manual rework

▶ **Reduce total operating costs**

  ▶ Streamline the architecture, information lifecycle management, data marts

  ▶ Eliminate and consolidate databases

  ▶ Eliminate redundant data solutions

▶ **Increase speed to market**

  ▶ Establish reusable data assets for solutions and applications to deploy

  ▶ Establish a clearly defined set of rules for managing data that projects and organizations will use in their work

Next we discuss the details of an EIM architecture. This includes the principles grounded on accepted industry practices, the scope of what the architecture should include, the types of structured data included in the architecture, what is required for unstructured data, data standards, governance, typical lifecycle information, and the role of enterprise information architecture in the organization.

5.1.1   Principles of an EIM Architecture

An EIM architecture must be based on principles grounded in accepted industry practices. Principles guide decision making in areas where there *are* viable alternatives, and you want to guide the organization consistently. To help with the understanding and adoption of those principles, they are generally created as follows:

▶ The *principle*, which is a statement of choice

▶ The *rationale*, which provides the basis for making that choice

▶ The *implications*, which call out the major consequences of making this choice so that the organization is clear on what this means

Principles

Several principles may be involved in information management. One example of such a principle might be:

> *There is one comprehensive, integrated, information architecture, and it encompasses all shareable content, whether structured or unstructured. This includes text, image, video, and voice data.*

Rationale

Some examples of the rationale for an EIM architecture might be:

▶ The complexity introduced by the continued acceptance of multiple, local variations (for example, when each region has their own architecture), and/or solution-specific architectures is inconsistent with our corporate objectives of rapid response to business need, productivity break through, improved decision making, common solutions, simplification, and standardization.

▶ A single information architecture focuses resources on achieving meaningful results by reducing the opportunity for divergent project and technology efforts while reducing the complexity of support.

▶ A single information architecture enables the delivery of information that spans type (e.g., structured, text, image, etc.) using standard tools and techniques, as opposed to requiring each application to reinvent this increasingly needed functionality. Business users of our IT products and services and our own resources are consequently more productive.

Implications

Some examples of the implications of an EIM architecture might be:

▶ Application development teams, support staff, and business partners must define and be accustomed to work processes that allow them to effectively achieve their objectives while sharing the control and use of their resources on which they depend.

▶ Integration across data types (i.e., structured, text, image, etc.) will be driven by the business user's context—job, roles, and decision types. That experience will be designed following this single architecture.

It is suggested that you start with the first principle discussed above—one comprehensive integrated information architecture—and then add in the other handful of strategic choices that you need to make to deliver this "one architecture." Other principles may touch on the areas of:

▶ Data ownership

▶ Information as a shared asset

▶ The management of master data versus other types

▶ Lifecycle management

5.1.2 Scope of an EIM Enterprise Architecture

Data, *information*, and *content* should all be within the scope of information management. For the purposes of this discussion, these three terms are defined as follows:

▶ **Data**
Content that is captured via a system process but has had no human intervention.

▶ **Information**
Content that has had subsequent human thought processes applied to it.

▶ **Content**
Unstructured content, including documents, video, image, and audio content. The term *content* is used in this section to imply any unstructured data or information.

A truly inclusive and comprehensive enterprise information architecture encompasses the following content scope:

▶ Operational data stores, data warehouses, data marts (centrally or locally)

▶ Internal and external content (e.g., the Internet)

▶ Local, regional, and corporate content with abilities to integrate

▶ Dimensional data (e.g., reference or master data), hierarchies, and taxonomies

▶ Key performance indicators (KPIs) or "measures" data at atomic and aggregate levels

▶ Metadata

▶ Purchased data, aggregator subscriptions (e.g., wire feeds, RSS, etc.)

▶ Behavioral data, performance data, preferences, and subscriptions

▶ Unstructured content types, including voice, video, and multimedia

5.1.3   Structured Data

A simple architectural view of structured data classifies the data as one of the following three types:

▶ Reference data

▶ Transactional data

▶ Management reporting data (including analytics)

Each of these classes of data has particular characteristics that need to be properly accounted for in a well-designed information architecture. Consider characteristics such as time, data volume, performance characteristics, numbers of users, and read-to-write profile, and it becomes clear that special handling is required to meet the variety of use cases. Let's define each of these classes in a little more detail.

Reference Data

Reference data provides the dimensional basis for transactions or events. Those dimensions typically include time, location, geography, organization, and parties involved, and are often characterized as "nouns" (e.g., customer, consumer, supplier, legal entities). It often includes objects involved in the transaction (e.g., product, services, raw material). This class of data is usually the object of master data management.

Transactional Data

Transactional data typically describes an event (the change as a result of an operation; for example, creating an order, initiating shipments, etc.) and is often described with action-oriented nouns (e.g., order, shipment, invoice). Transactional data always has a time dimension and a numerical value and refers to one or more objects (i.e., reference data).

The use of transactional data, in an event-reporting context, is referred to as operational reporting. Operational reporting is concerned with the reporting of transactional data, often at the discrete transaction level (e.g., a *single* invoice) produced at the time of the actual event. Operational reporting takes a very short time horizon, from as short as a single event, and does not aggregate from multiple applications. It is generally produced from the transactional system, using this lowest level of data. That lowest level—an individual transaction—is often referred to as *atomic data*.

Management Reporting

Management reporting is concerned with reporting data over longer periods of time or over larger sets of data (e.g., aggregates and summaries) than operational reporting systems support. It consequently takes operational data and applies further processing against it. This may be in the form of aggregations, historical collections, or integrating multiple measure types (e.g., shipments and consumption). It is this subsequently processed data that is typically managed in the data warehouse environment. For our purposes we include analytics use cases in this same class, including operational analytics.

5.1.4 The Dual Database Approach

A longstanding cornerstone of this kind of data architecture is based on a dual database strategy. The dual database strategy sources standard, shareable data from the operational environment (i.e., transactional systems) to the data warehouse environment each supported by a common "reference" capability that maintains standard reference/master data used in both capture and access environments.

Transactions are entered, processed, and ultimately formatted and sent to the data warehouse. Data is stored in a data warehouse complex at an elemental level according to data subject, where it may be further aggregated and summarized and accessed via any business intelligence use cases. Reference data capability consists of master data, reference data, and metadata and is available to interact with and support both types of processing through interactive and callable interfaces.

This framework is predicated on the following:

▸ An environment for single-sourced data, thereby eliminating the productivity problems caused by multiple sources. This is fundamental to achieving a single basis for truth, and for many of our information systems, a single version of the truth.

▸ Reference data (including master data and metadata that encompasses a data dictionary as well) that is managed distinct from a single application, representing the union of our requirements for that reference subject area.

▸ A data dictionary to be used by all systems, thereby reducing if not eliminating the problem of data credibility caused by the lack of consistency in data definition and content.

Implementing this single data architecture throughout the enterprise provides common processes to follow, with consistent data as the product. From creation, maintenance, extract, transform, load, all the way to end-user consuming processes, you can measure, control, predict, and improve the performance of your data capabilities. With such an architecture you can reasonably expect to be able to access the data when needed, with assurance that it will be consistent and accurate.

Dual Database Strategy

With the advent of memory-based and solid-state appliances supporting a new class of data warehouse "appliances," some argue that the "dual database" strategy is dead. The following considerations cause us to propose that a dual strategy will remain viable in the short run:

▸ The scope of history held in the transactional environment may not meet the needs of what is retained separately in the data warehouse.

▸ As storage gets cheaper, the business desire to have more history online continues to grow. This further calls for a separate database for data warehousing, to preserve performance requirements in our operational databases. Therefore, we will generally move operational data into a distinct database for performing operational analytics.

▸ For management, availability, and recoverability, a single database may simply not make sense in many instances, requiring the isolation of workloads.

5.1.5 Typical Information Lifecycle

It is useful to consider the full lifecycle of information, its uses and characteristics, and an enterprise-wide strategy for how it needs to be managed. Taking this holistic view is uniquely within the purview of the enterprise information architect and, if neglected, can lead to detrimental and/or disastrous consequences for the enterprise. History and newspapers routinely recount the unfortunate choices companies have made that can be attributed to information stewardship neglect.

Figure 5.1 shows a very simple model, but certainly it is more complicated in real life. For example, development, quality assurance, and production instances may exist, but we are considering the simple cases for our purposes. The same principles would apply throughout a complete lifecycle of data warehouses.

Figure 5.1 Typical Information Lifecycle

Each area of Figure 5.1 is described below in more detail.

Transactional/Operational Data

Operational data is captured in what is referred to as the system of record, which is the system responsible for the initial creation of the data in the transactional system. It should be captured in a well-formed system that has the following characteristics:

- ▶ Data standards for the data it is creating
- ▶ Standard master data, which is managed independent of this application
- ▶ Clear ownership of all data in scope
- ▶ Data retention clearly specified, at a minimum at a database level, as well as at a "record" or document level
- ▶ Backup and recovery requirements
- ▶ Security classifications as defined by the enterprise
- ▶ Access requirements and controls consistent with enterprise definition

Operational Analytics

It is often desirable to be able to perform analysis on data that is in the transactional system, looking for trends, anomalies, or solutions to specific problems. While it may be possible to do this directly against the operational environment, there may be circumstances that introduce performance considerations requiring that a separate environment for operational analytics be set up.

When that occurs, a separate, data warehouse-like environment can be created to prevent the sorts of I/O contention that typically occur, while providing for longer retention of data in the operational analytics that the transactional system can support. Statistical analysis over long periods of time and correlation across transactions are typically run here.

ETL

ETL (extraction, transformation, and loading) is a set of processes executed in support of formal data warehouse preprocessing, and it is supported by formal tools designed for that specific purpose. Admittedly, enterprise application integration (EAI) tools may be used as a vehicle for feeding downstream data warehouses in a publish/subscribe fashion; however, we will present a traditional ETL approach to illustrate the flow of data.

Management Reporting and Analytics

In Figure 5.1, *management reporting and analytics* is a data warehouse providing management reporting and analytics capabilities by bringing data together from one or more operational systems. A data warehouse exists to provide the following kinds of capabilities:

▶ A longer time basis of data than the operational systems, for reporting beyond operational needs. For example, summaries by week, month, quarter, and year may be desirable.

▶ The ability to create multi-fact-type integration. Where the data scope of a transactional application may only cover a few transaction types, a data warehouse may source those transactions and provide an integrated view, enabling greater insight; for example, combining shipment, financials and market share.

▸ A shareable data asset that can meet the needs of many use cases and organizations beyond the scope of a single application; for example, a data service that provides customer information to be used by many applications.

▸ Scale, cost savings, and efficiencies over individual, redundant, point to point copies of data.

▸ A single source for reporting a single set of "official numbers."

Data Levels of the Data Warehouse

The well-formed data warehouse is based on atomic data, an integrated data layer, and then business views composed upon the integrated data layer. Let's look at these layers in more detail:

▸ **Atomic data**

Atomic data is the lowest level of data granularity, based on a single transaction, whose source is preserved as originally captured. A data warehouse that is composed of atomic data can be used to "roll-up" data along many different dimensional lines; it can be reorganized from the atomic level, and different views can be created. This lowest-level, fundamental ingredient is the foundation upon which your data warehouse architecture should be constructed.

▸ **Integrated data**

An integrated data layer is intended to serve the many needs of many divergent applications by providing multi-fact integration of many data types in a broadly shareable asset. It is this level of the data in the data warehouse that is the target for end-user and application access. This layer is typically centrally managed. Orders, shipments, services, inventory and account receivables (for example) can all be integrated.

▸ **Business views**

Creating value-added business views on top of the integrated data layer provides an instantly usable asset to project teams, superior to creating additional copies of the data and/or external data marts. The business views layer is composed of views (and potentially local data) that are owned by the various business areas and applications. It is typically not centrally managed. For example, you may have a subset of orders, shipments, and inventory based on a designated time duration critical from a planning perspective.

Summaries and Aggregations

The data warehouse provides capabilities to support management reporting and analytics. While it is the goal of data warehouse designers to do as much work on-the-fly as possible, it often becomes clear that the warehouse needs to deliver an answer to an end user within a committed time frame (i.e., a service-level agreement; for example, a three-second response time for less than 1000 rows of data). When that occurs, summaries of data are precalculated to improve query performance.

Caution should be observed when creating summaries/aggregates to avoid, when possible, the inclusion of dimension types that are likely to change. When you include such dimensions, your aggregates take on new maintenance overhead and may have to be recalculated. If your data warehouse contains many years of history, recalculating that history can be costly.

Sample Data

The data warehouse environment can quickly "accrete" large quantities of data, which has positive and negative consequences. Long-running jobs not only frustrate the job owner, but may negatively impact other users of the shared environment. Creating sample sets, statistically valid representative samples of a broader population, may allow you to deliver an analytics result without having to process the entire population of data. This can save time, money, and aggravation.

Analytics Considerations

There has never been more data available, and it is growing at an alarming rate. As sources grow (e.g., the Internet), as types of data grow (e.g., geolocation), and as value in mining the data grows, we must increasingly look at different use cases for the data. Analytics is increasingly one of these use cases.

Simply retaining more data is not sufficient. As good stewards we should strive to process it in practical, efficient ways. Considerations include:

- ▶ Can I use sample data?
- ▶ Do I need to employ aggregates?
- ▶ Can I leverage tiered storage?
- ▶ Can I leverage analytics that are part of the data warehouse platform (i.e., can I directly "play the data" where it lies)?

▶ Are the scalar functions of the database management system (DBMS) sufficient, are additional functions or extended procedure libraries available, or do I have to move the data to an analytics server?

These are just a few of the considerations that the enterprise information architect must contend with. But increasingly, it is highly advantageous if you can leverage the data warehouse for use cases beyond traditional reporting; for example, ad-hoc queries, exploratory analytics, etc.

Data Warehouse Governance Considerations

You will want to build the rules of engagement for your data warehouse environment. Considerations should include a landscape strategy that defines how and where your databases will be located, sourcing strategies, staging, ETL, reference data design, fact data design by layers, and how applications interact with the centrally managed layers. You should also consider local data and its integration with other levels of data as well as overall governance of what can become a large, complex environment.

Archival

Archival strategies and storage tiers must be considered as part of the strategy. As you create your information management architecture, you assign retention limits and factor the cost and timings of retrieval needs into your tiered storage plans as part of a broader information lifecycle management strategy. Security considerations (e.g., security classifications by data subject area) should be identified and factored into the thinking.

5.1.6   Data Standards

Information management is predicated on having clear, effective, measurable data standards. We have defined data standards as being composed of three parts:

▶ **Business definition**

  ▶ Definition of the data element in terms of its business use

  ▶ Allowable values for a data element

  ▶ Rules governing uniqueness (i.e., no two instances have the same code) and exclusivity (i.e., an instance has only code)

  ▶ Rules governing assignment and reuse of codes

- ▶ **Organizational ownership and stewardship**

  - ▶ Business owner: Person and role accountable for developing and maintaining this data standard

  - ▶ Business process for creating and maintaining the data

  - ▶ Data administrator: Person and role accountable for the business process of maintaining data

  - ▶ Business unit scope: Business units to which this standard applies

- ▶ **Technical definition**

  - ▶ Official source system that produces the data

  - ▶ Number of instances

  - ▶ Canonical data structure agreed on and maintained as an enterprise standard, including attributes/fields associated with this subject area as well as data type and length of data elements

  - ▶ Format: Is there a specific format for storing or reporting this data? (For example, a date must include CCYYMMDD, a monetary amount must have three decimal places, and so on.)

  - ▶ Optional/mandatory (field by field)

  - ▶ Structure

5.1.7 Unstructured Data

Unstructured data includes documents, images, audio, video, and social content. It is the unstructured nature of this class of data or content that makes it much more difficult to find and beneficially apply in an enterprise. Consequently, metadata and accompanying metadata standards are required to give unstructured data the corresponding context that makes it findable and usable. We will examine the role of metadata more closely in subsequent sections.

To properly manage unstructured content, it is necessary to look at the continuum of processes that interact with the content, cradle to grave. Following this approach, we can zoom in on needs at particular steps along the way. Figure 5.2 depicts the overall lifecycle.

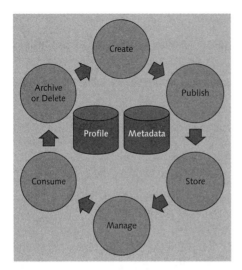

Figure 5.2 Unstructured Content Lifecycle

Create

In this step, content may be authored locally or in a shared authoring tool. Information management must be considered with the business processes and the kinds of content produced by those processes so that the appropriate metadata designs may be employed as that content is published.

Publish

Publishing is the act of formally releasing the content from the authoring/creation environment into a shareable environment. It is in this process that metadata can be beneficially applied; applying a few standard tags to assist in finding desired content may require one minute by the publishers, but without such tags, end users may spend many minutes searching for that exact content. The investment in applying tags in the publishing process can more than pay for itself and shows consideration for the content consumer's time.

Store

For completeness, we include this step of physically storing the content. Actual physical storage may trigger the automatic activities that can be considered as management processes.

Manage

Management processes applied on the stored content may include, but are not limited to, the following activities:

▸ Applying default retention rules

▸ Automated tagging

▸ Indexing of the content

▸ Triggering routing/approvals

▸ Applying analytics (e.g., tag clouds, usage, etc.)

▸ Managing site content—ensuring that the content meets quality standards, metadata and content standards, and security standards; versioning is appropriately applied; and so on

▸ Enterprise content management (discussed in Chapter 4 and Chapter 14)

Consume

For completeness, we include the step of consumption, defined as the act of end users physically accessing the content. This can occur via an enterprise search, direct navigation, routing, subscription, application search, and so on. Given the many ways that physical access (consumption) may occur, it should become clear that the architecture standards and management processes are essential to facilitating efficient consumption.

Archive/Delete

All content should have retention limits established when published. Those dates should be used to ensure that documents and content stores are moved to archival storage and/or deleted.

5.1.8   Governance

Governance is the capability that enables consistency of decision making through defined decision rights, in accordance with aligned policies and procedures. Organizations evolve in their ability to govern. The corporate culture plays a major role in how strong a first-generation governance model can be and how it will evolve. For example, if governance policies are too broad and too quickly deployed, adoption is very low. A balance of control, delivering stability and value, needs to be realized for the governance to become part of daily work.

Different organizations and their unique cultures, drivers, and strategies may dictate a different approach to governance. One size probably does not fit all in this realm, so the approach described here should not be taken as prescriptive, but instead should provide insight to one company's journey that you may be able to learn from.

Scope and Intent of Governance

At Procter and Gamble the scope and intent of governance started with the dual database strategy in the late 1980s with a focus on managing the master data centrally, independent of the consuming applications, and enforcing a standard definition of keys in the core subject areas such as material, product, customer, and vendor. This evolved in the late 1990s to managing master data across all major platforms, including product lifecycle management, SAP ERP, and reporting/analytics. This was pursued as part of the journey to deliver a single version of the truth. Some of the lessons of that journey are defined below.

Harmonization of Keys and Single Version of the Truth

The first step in creating a single version of the truth in data is to have a standard definition, unique identification, and official sources from which to provide the information. In our first steps, business functions and country IT organizations separated their master data from the applications. The journey into data management began with a separation of duties for control purposes and managing data as an asset. The first value realized was globally and uniquely identifying key assets such as product, material, vendor, and customer.

Integrated Application Platforms

As the IT architecture evolved, integrated platforms were developed for managing the major application components supporting the supply chain. Thus was born the early stages of product lifecycle management, SAP ERP, and an integrated reporting and analytics capability. At this stage, central management of the primary key and basic data was insufficient. Governance was expanded to any master data that needed to be shared between transactional and/or reporting functionality. Successful governance of the global data with reliable data distribution laid the foundation for a central organization to deliver data to thousands of downstream systems with high reliability in a manner that supported the transactions from those applications to be sent to a common data warehouse for analytics.

End to End Process Management

As productivity and efficiency requirements continued to increase, the platform management was insufficient. End to end work processes needed to be addressed, and the silos of the platforms needed to be broken down. The application architecture and individual data owners were no longer sufficient to enable the required data governance.

Application Architecture Evolves to Data Governance

The dual database architecture provided a foundation for data management that served Procter and Gamble for 20 years, growing from a country and regionally organized company to a globally managed one. As the complexity of the global operations grew and the need to respond more quickly to changing business conditions grew, the application architecture was insufficient, and a business-led data governance capability was required.

Consequently, C-level sponsorship initiated a project to design and implement a new organizational capability delivering global data governance to enable an end to end supply chain capable of keeping pace with the rapidly changing requirements for data. The new organization is bringing executive-level governance to master data work processes and the quality requirements of the data. Data steward roles are being formalized with an expectation of leading business transformation to drive clarity of responsibility and designing system automation (workflow, validation rules, etc.).

Data Quality as Defined by the Consuming Business Process

As data governance is being defined, one of the overarching goals you can expect is to increase the quality of the data. However, without an agreed upon definition of quality, it is impossible to measure. The critical component of defining quality requirements is for all consuming processes to document their requirements. Not all requirements will necessarily be met, but without the complete list of requirements the data providers cannot report the effectiveness of their governance in a context that reflects business value.

An industry study of this space typically shows that the components of data quality include:

- ▶ **Timeliness**
  Is the data available when the consuming processes require it?

- ▶ **Completeness**
  Is the data complete when consuming processes require it?

- ▶ **Consistency**
  Are related data elements logically consistent with each other? For example, does the individual item weight of an item in a case containing 12 items equal item weight times count (e.g., 12). If not, there is an error in the relationship between these fields.

- ▶ **Accuracy**
  Accuracy can be challenging to measure, as it often requires physical audits. A key element of accuracy for numerical data is the allowed tolerance. There may be tolerances for accuracy that vary by data item. Some may have zero tolerance, and others might have a tolerance range, for example, ±4%.

Data Quality Measures

Measuring governance and data quality is an evolving capability, just as is overall governance. First-generation measures are often activity-based. A metric may be deployed to track the effort it takes to keep operations at the current level. But with time, it may be determined that activity is not a measure of actual business needs, nor of the value, nor of the quality of the data being delivered.

Quality measurement often evolves to focus on timeliness, completeness, consistency, and accuracy. With this focus and additional scope, business impact may be inferred. Correlations to improvement in data quality can be linked to efficiency improvements in the business process. This "virtuous cycle" should drive greater data quality.

It may also be seen that there are linkages of quality metrics of the data with incident management, and data outages may be identified as root causes of specific business process performance or specific incidents. When such examples surface, make sure to factor in the true cost of poor data quality as being the business impact as well as the cost of the organizational capacity to resolve the errors.

Information Security

While it is not the intent of this section to cover the breadth and depth of information security, we would be remiss to not at least touch on some of the essential elements, which are presented here independent of how a firm may organize around information governance and information security.

Information security should be a policy-driven approach to governance, covering information assurance, physical safety and security, and business continuity and disaster recovery. Such a policy is augmented by required standards and recommended guidelines, which specify in more detail how the requirements set forth in the policy are to be satisfied. Finally, operational units (IT and business) are expected to develop written procedures that enable security-related tasks to be performed in a defined, repeatable, and policy-compliant way.

The differences among policies, standards, guidelines, and procedures are outlined below:

▶ **Policies**
Policies are general statements of direction and purpose. They outline specific high-level requirements or rules that must be met, but do not specify how that is to be done. Policies are for the most part non-technical in nature, and are intended to remain relatively static over long periods of time.

▶ **Standards**
Standards are specific and, where applicable, technical documents containing directives and specifications for implementing the requirements and rules set forth by policies. Compliance with standards is mandatory; their requirements must be met by everyone (although some standards may have documented exception processes). Standards are generally written using the verb "must," and to the extent possible, apply in all situations.

▶ **Guidelines**
Guidelines are similar to standards, but advisory in nature. Guidelines represent suggestions for best practices, and while implementing these suggestions is not required, doing so is strongly recommended. Guidelines are generally written using the verb "should," and frequently apply to very specific situations.

▶ **Procedures**
Procedures provide detailed instructions (usually step-by-step) for performing activities that are governed by the policies, standards, and guidelines. Procedures are generally developed by each individual unit that is required to comply with

a particular policy, and reflect the individual unit's particular business environment.

5.1.9   Role of the Enterprise Information Architecture Organization

The enterprise information architecture organization is responsible for delivering the following kinds of capabilities to the enterprise:

▶ The big picture. From a planning or strategic perspective, what does the information landscape look like? This can take the form of an enterprise data model and will find many uses as projects try to navigate this space.

▶ Roadmaps for the current state and future state assessments of the information capability, as well as roadmaps for driving improvements.

▶ Artifacts for the information domain, such as models, standards, designs, roadmaps, assessments, metrics, and so on.

▶ Impact analysis. When change is needed that spans organizations and geographies, the enterprise information architecture organization may be the only ones with the appropriate skills, scope, and vantage point.

▶ Metrics that indicate that the coverage of artifacts have been defined as required.

This section discussed information management architecture recommendations starting with a definition of principles for your architecture, the scope, the types of structured data, and the dual database approach. It discussed a typical information lifecycle for structured and unstructured data, data standards, governance, and the role of the enterprise information architecture organization. The next section provides recommendations for managing data migration projects.

5.2   Managing Data Migration Projects to Support Mergers and Acquisitions

Companies that are successful with merger and acquisition migration activity excel at managing their ability to map legacy data into the current business process and have a sustainable method for managing their data load activity. The secrets to this success include the ability to:

▶ Understand and build a specific scope of what needs to be loaded.

▶ Manage business rules and how incoming data is transformed.

▶ Create flexible and sustainable ETL programs using SAP Data Services (hereafter Data Services).

▶ Create a roadmap document that can be used to manage and govern the entire data load process from cradle to grave and be able to report to leadership on status.

Without doing this, major business processes could be impacted; for example, you cannot ship or receive goods. You could also have quality issues that are reflected in incorrect billing and payments, as well as poor customer service.

In this section, we discuss tips for scoping your data migration project, an example migration process flow, and the options for enriching data during a migration project.

5.2.1 Scoping for a Data Migration Project

The first step to a successful data migration project is to understand the scope of your data requirement. You need to work with many groups; for example, finance, controlling, plant maintenance, sales, supply chain, materials management, customer service, and so on, to understand what they need for a successful implementation. In the finance area you might need to load elements such as accounts receivables and accounts payable open items, assets, bank master records, and so on. Also, you need to consider subcategories within the same data object; for example, a customer master record where some fields are in SAP ERP and other fields are in SAP Customer Relationship Management (CRM). While the use of customer data in SAP CRM and SAP ERP maybe be different, it is important for the migration to look holistically at all attributes required for the customer. Cross-functional meetings are the best place to detect and discuss the cross-use of data elements for the same object. One way to ensure that you capture the correct data requirement is by using a data plan. This is not the only way to do it, but the following outlines a data plan and how it can be used to ensure that data requirements are captured for a data migration project. The data plan is an Excel spreadsheet that captures the following information:

▶ **Priority**
Priority of load. For example, master data comes before transactional data.

▶ **Team**
Which specific team is responsible for the load (i.e., purchasing/supplier relationship management [SRM]).

- ▶ **Data type**
  Master data versus transactional data.

- ▶ **Conversion description**
  Object detail (i.e., accounts payable).

- ▶ **Source**
  Source of data you are extracting.

- ▶ **SAP load date**
  Estimated load.

- ▶ **Estimated hours to load**
  Estimated hours of runtime.

- ▶ **Load order**
  Overall job sequence to help with planning.

An example data migration spreadsheet is available for download from this book's page at *http://www.sap-press.com*. The second tab in the data plan spreadsheet covers the data details. The data details provide the following nine subcategories that help manage the entire process holistically:

- ▶ **Source data**
  Database size and record count; used for production load.

- ▶ **Data mapping**
  Number of fields to be mapped, business owner, percentage complete.

- ▶ **Business rules**
  Number of fields to be mapped, business owner, percentage complete.

- ▶ **Data cleaning**
  Number of records cleaned per object, percentage complete.

- ▶ **Development/programming**
  Program name, tool (e.g., Data Services, ABAP).

- ▶ **Data extract**
  Date, extract option (e.g., Data Services), number of records extracted, number of rejected records, number of extracted versus total count.

- ▶ **Data extracts/loads into development system (unit testing)**
  Load date, number of records loaded, percentage of records loaded versus total count extracted.

▶ **Data extracts/loads into quality system**
For advanced unit testing and integration testing: load date, number of records loaded, percentage of records loaded versus total count extracted.

▶ **Data extracts/loads into production system**
Load date, number of records loaded, percentage of records loaded versus total count extracted.

5.2.2 Data Migration Process Flow

When preparing for a data migration project, it may be helpful to break the conversion into two phases: data cleansing and data loading. The data cleansing phase prepares you and your organization for cleaning and de-duplication of data. Once the data is cleansed, it is loaded. Figure 5.3 shows an example data migration process flow.

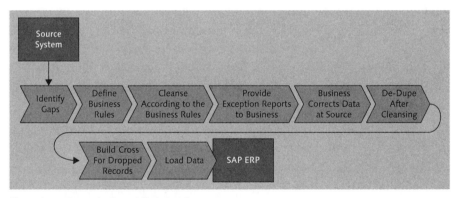

Figure 5.3 Example Data Migration Process

When loading SAP customer master data, you can take the approach of creating a super table that holds many field attributes that are contained within the sales view. Because the sales view of the customer master holds many SAP tables, it is good to have one staging table that is logically defined. If you use the SAP-delivered content for data migration *(http://service.sap.com/bp-datamigration)*, there is already content provided for validating the fields. The SAP-provided migration content is discussed in Chapter 11.

Next we discuss more details of the process flow shown in Figure 5.3. This includes identifying what data you want to cleanse, defining the business rules, cleansing, providing errors and exceptions to the business users, correcting the data, de-duplicating, building a cross-reference (or key mapping), and finally transferring all cleansed data to the target system.

Identify What Business Objects Need to be Cleansed

Identifying your cleansing objects may be one of the most important steps in your process. It is vitally important to identify what to clean and the scope for data governance. You will want to start with something small; for example, you should look at cleaning a small part of a larger master data element or related master data areas, as in the sales view of the customer master. This allows you to begin crafting your approach of data quality and to provide your company with a visible win and promote the process of a reusable data quality project. Also, it is very important to have buy-in with the IT and business leaders on the scope of work and other follow-on projects.

SAP Information Steward (hereafter Information Steward) can be used to help you determine which objects you really need to cleanse. Data profiling of key objects will provide quick insight on the major data quality issues that require attention. Information Steward for data profiling is discussed in more detail in Chapter 6.

Define Business Rules

Once you have decided on the scope of work, you should move into the specific business rules. This step is as important as defining your scope of work. You should take three specific steps in this area.

First, conduct workshops with all parts of the company that have a responsibility in the area you want to clean. For example, if you are developing rules for the materials resource planning (MRP) view of the material master record, you should make sure people involved in your initial workshop are from production planning, purchasing, logistics/warehousing, and inventory management. Also, you need to make sure you align the proper IT counterpart in this workshop.

Second, it is good to have a data architect who can document all requirements and another person to lead discussions in each workshop. It is *critical* to have open dialog in the workshop and to allow all users to communicate all possible business rules. Allow the synergies of the collective group to help brainstorm and provide the best input possible.

Third, when you have all possible business rules provided by the team, these rules can be created in Information Steward. Creation of business rules is discussed in more detail in Chapter 6. Having these rules in Information Steward ensures reuse and the ability to clean data on an ongoing basis.

Cleanse According to the Business Rules

During your cleansing of the data per business rules, it is important to be holistic. When implementing a field to clean, you should make sure the field being cleaned has a standard definition globally, and the rule being applied should be considered a "global cleansing method" throughout your enterprise. When you start to design cleansing rules differently across countries and organizations, you add complexity and additional management needed to maintain your data governance organization. The cleansing is done using the cleansing transformations provided by Data Services. A detailed example of data cleansing and validation is provided in Chapter 8.

Provide Exception Reports to Business

Depending on how often you decide to clean your data, you need to work together with your business leaders to develop the correct time for each cleaning cycle. Typically, if you are cleaning customer master information on a global level, most companies look at processing the cleansing jobs once per month or bimonthly. The cleansing jobs separate good from bad data. The good data is staged and isolated to ensure that no further handling is needed. The bad data is separated into two areas. The first subdivision of bad data is corrected based on the specific business rule. The second portion of bad data is sent on an "exception report" that key users in the business community need to review and then report on to their management and/or IT leadership for further correction and processing. The main reason for the data split is to support the business rules. Users back in the business definition phase determined that certain rules can be simply updated with the correct data and other bad data needs to be analyzed further, as it is exceptional. Part of the users' job is to review each exception and update the spreadsheet or system if it needs to be updated or to ignore the exception. If an exception is to be ignored, then you need to design the system to flag this item to not be considered in the future.

Correct Data at the Source

In some cases bad data needs to be corrected in the source application where the business rules are being checked. You need to take into consideration the replication of jobs systems. There are several ways to update your data. First, you can have local users update bad data from the exception reporting. Second, you can leverage Data Services to make updates in the source system to fix the bad data. You can also use a workflow or use SAP Master Data Governance (MDG) for key master data changes. SAP MDG is a good fit if your project is going to launch a centralized master data project. SAP MDG is discussed in Chapter 12.

Duplication after Cleansing

When identifying duplication and cleaning your system, most people focus on cleaning the specific duplicate record, such as sold-to or ship-to customer. This is fine, but you need to also look at the entire system if you want to clean in a holistic manner. For example, if you want to clean and remove duplicate sold-to customer numbers, you also need to look at all objects within your target system that link to the customer number. You need to consider things such as customer part numbers, customer info records, customer pricing records, customer hierarchies, all forms of sales documents (sales orders, sales contracts, sales schedule agreements), customer discount records, price lists, and so on. Timing is also important. For example, do you wait until your last delivery is shipped and then block customer B, or do you place a hard block on customer B and back all open orders and start with customer A? It is best to devise an action plan and sequence for proper de-duplication efforts. This action is not to be minimized, as you will need a strong focus and commitment to make sure all steps per each duplicate record are cleansed and removed if required.

Build Cross-References for Dropped Records

Part of a successful de-duplication effort is the ability to record your dropped records. It is important to have your system maintain a historical master list of current and duplicate records. Some companies look at the ETL system maintaining a master file or database (i.e., staging table) that lists the object going through the duplication process and understand which one is the current versus duplicate record. For example, if you have five customer numbers for John Doe, you need to label which one is current and which ones are duplications. Then you use this information to point the duplicate records to the current one within your SAP ERP system. This process of keeping a master list applies until your SAP ERP system has holistically removed the reference of the duplicated customer number.

If you are using an application such as SAP MDG, you can build the cross-references using key mapping. This is discussed in Chapter 12.

Transfer the Cleansed Data for Migration to the Target System

As cleansed data is transferred to your target system, you should start to develop monthly KPIs or "health of the data" metrics for IT and the business units to measure and build accountability. For example, each month you process customer or material master cleansing, you should be able to gather the following data: number or records extracted, number of records in bad files, number of records sent to good files, number of records corrected from bad files, number of records not corrected due to loading issues. This type of data will help you transform simple data into powerful information. With this information you can tell per sales organization if you have recurring data corrections every month. Perhaps you have 50 errors and then 50 corrections for the same business rule every month. This may be due to the same customer service representative making the same mistake, and you are simply running the cleansing jobs over and over. You do not gain anything with this data governance initiative if you are not looking at these types of KPIs. However, if you pay attention to these types of issues, you can proceed with data mining and find you have a training issue that needs to be addressed. Historically, this data has been collected using spreadsheets, but Information Steward can be used for data quality trending over time.

5.2.3 Enrich the Data Using Dun and Bradstreet (D&B) with Data Services

In addition to the typical data migration process flow described in the previous section, data migration projects may also include data enrichment. While data enrichment is discussed in more detail in Chapter 8, it is worth mentioning that many companies use a DUNS (data universal numbering system) number to enrich SAP's customer hierarchy approach. (A DUNS number is a unique identifier assigned to each business by Dun and Bradstreet.) The use of the DUNS numbers with the customer hierarchy helps manage and report on DUNS numbers and their relationship to the parent customers (i.e., sold-to and ship-to) within the customer database. A common practice is to have Dun and Bradstreet provide a DUNS number in conjunction with SAP's customer hierarchy approach. Then a business intelligence (BI) reporting layer is created to publish real-time reporting to show customers across different sales organizations and product divisions. This allows your company to have product market managers to take an active role in making decisions on information from your core ERP system and use a tool, such as D&B for customer account management.

This section has provided recommendations and hints for successful data migration projects. Next we discuss the evolution of Data Services at National Vision.

5.3   Evolution of SAP Data Services at National Vision

National Vision's use of Data Services evolved over a period of time and is continuing to change with business requirements. When reflecting back over the various projects that extended the use of Data Services, the evolution has (so far) included five phases. This section will discuss each of those phases, explaining how EIM solutions were used to address specific business challenges.

5.3.1   Phase 1: The Enterprise Data Warehouse

Data Services was first introduced at National Vision as the main tool selected to build an enterprise data warehouse. The business challenge being addressed was the requirement to bring together timely, accurate, and actionable data to provide insights into the factors impacting retail sales and customer behavior. The following were the key issues the project contended with:

► Silos of data sources and applications (ERP system, human resources system, store point of sale system, e-commerce system, etc.).

► Limited business user access to information needed to make informed decisions.

► Business users had to wait for IT programmers to create or make changes to mainframe-generated reports. Additionally, business users worked mainly in a Windows environment, and the mainframe interface made it difficult for them to interact with reports.

► Inconsistent definition of key metrics; for instance, the definition of "sales revenue" varied among store brands and channels.

The solutions chosen to address these problems were the Data Integrator capabilities of Data Services and the SAP BusinessObjects Business Intelligence (BI) platform. Using the ETL functions in Data Services, an enterprise data warehouse was created and loaded nightly, consolidating data from disparate sources. This was then exposed through business intelligence to provide improved transparency in the flow of data from the source to the reports for the end users. Figure 5.4 shows how Data Services was utilized to load the data warehouse. Data flowed from applications to the enterprise data warehouse to the SAP BusinessObjects BI platform.

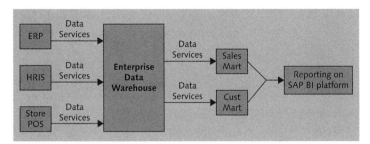

Figure 5.4 Data Services to Load Data Warehouse

Data Services was used to extract data from over 20 applications, such as an ERP system, HRIS (human resources information system), and store POS (store point of sale) system. Once the data was extracted to the enterprise data warehouse, Data Services was again employed to create subject area data marts optimized for reporting. Examples included data marts for customer data, employee data, sales data, and order detail data. The data marts focused on subject area, but benefited multiple functional departments.

5.3.2 Phase 2: Enterprise Information Architecture—Consolidating Source Data

The next business challenge addressed arose from the realization that many applications require and utilize the same data. The lack of sharing data between applications resulted in duplicate and manual data entry, inefficient processes, and data not kept in sync between applications. Table 5.1 shows an example.

ERP	HRIS	Store POS
Customer data	Store data	Customer data
Sales data	Employee data	Sales data
Store data		Employee data
Product data		Product data

Table 5.1 Same Data Required in Multiple Applications

Much of the same data is stored in and consumed by multiple siloed applications. However, up to this point, the stored data that was shared between the ERP and HRIS systems had not been rationalized or compared. The same was true for employee data, product data, and to some extent, the customer data.

The solution was to extend the use of Data Services beyond just loading the data warehouse. Data Services was engaged to identify a single origin for each data subject, determining which system "owns" the data, then operated as the conduit to push the data to other systems that consume the information. Reusable data flows and transforms (explained in Chapter 7) were created, and the data flows became more focused on each data object (data flows for customer data, for product data, for employee data, etc.).

In the example of the employee data, the HRIS system owned the data, and Data Services was used to replicate it, as shown in Figure 5.5. This figure shows the HRIS system in the middle, where all employee data is maintained and updated. It is then pushed to consumers of employee data, such as the enterprise data warehouse, ERP, training systems, and the store POS system.

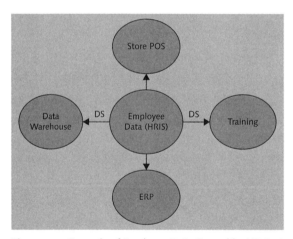

Figure 5.5 Example of Employee Data Owned by HR System and Replicated

Data management evolved through a process of identifying the best source systems and having departments take ownership of the data. The other systems became the recipient systems. This entire process emerged into a master data and governance discipline.

In addition to the governance and master data discipline that transpired from this (albeit sometimes painful) process, this solution also provided better data quality due to less manual data entry and less effort on keeping data in sync between the applications.

5.3.3   Phase 3: Data Quality and the Customer Hub

The third phase in our evolution was the creation of a global view of the customer across original data sources to meet the challenge of measuring retention, lifetime value, and the purchase cycle. This phase was important in addressing the following issues:

▶ Since many physical stores and the online channels originated customer data, it was stored in hundreds of separate databases.

▶ There was little consistency in customer data entry; it was only as good as entered.

▶ Customer address information was out of date as a result of relocations.

▶ The source system analysis and data profiling on new data sources was manual.

The solution was to use the data quality capabilities within Data Services. The employment of data quality enabled the following:

▶ Customer data from all sources moves through address cleansing and standardization transforms in Data Services, utilizing the U.S. Postal Service database, which is updated monthly via subscription. (Chapter 8 covers the details of how this works in Data Services.)

▶ National changes of address (NCOA) are now applied monthly, and addresses are kept updated.

▶ Updated customer records go through a matching routine in Data Services to determine duplicates. (Chapter 8 covers matching capabilities.)

▶ All de-duped customers are grouped and assigned a global customer ID, populating the *customer hub* database.

▶ Geocoded, cleansed customer records, and the global customer ID are pushed from this hub to various applications, such as campaign management, a geospatial application, and the enterprise data warehouse.

Figure 5.6 shows an example of how this works. In this example, William Smith is a customer entered in a specific store *and* Bill Smith originates from the web channel. Data Services realizes both records refer to the same customer and harmonizes them to be William Smith, which is then replicated to the customer hub that owns the customer data. The de-duped customer data is then replicated to multiple applications.

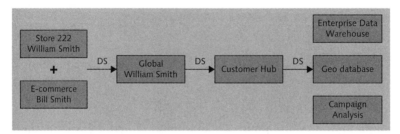

Figure 5.6   Data Services to Cleanse and Remove Duplicates Before Replicating to Multiple Target Systems

Another example of improved data quality relates to the telephone number. This data is important in a business-to-consumer (retail) scenario where you need to call the customer to let them know their order is ready or to follow up their store visit with a customer satisfaction survey. Prior to this phase, the customer phone number was stored in over 125 patterns. After this phase, the phone number across many systems was stored in one pattern, improving data quality and customer service. Data quality supported the project with:

▶ Cleansed and parsed customer data, including the ability to use existing dictionaries to cleanse data and the ability to create a customized dictionary.

▶ Standardized names (e.g., Bob, Robert).

▶ Standardized different entities such as email, telephone numbers, and dates.

▶ Standardized and validated address data using built-in transforms and the government's address database.

▶ Geocoded customers based on address, appending latitude and longitude for each customer for placement on maps.

▶ Universal data cleansing that allowed non-customer data matching by utilizing rule-based parsing and rule editing architecture to achieve better results.

▶ The flexibility to create its own transform with nonproprietary Python code. (Chapter 7 discusses transforms.)

During this data quality process, it was critical that we match the customer records to remove duplicates. Why go to the trouble of matching data? The easy answers are: in-storage savings by eliminating redundant data, and in-time savings from moving data around between the applications. However, the major benefit of matching data remains the ability to identify and understand all interactions of a customer. Being able to measure the true value and lifecycle of a particular customer or household can potentially change how you interact with that customer. For example, a direct mail or email campaign may contain different messages or targeted offers based on the global customer's previous purchase activity. If that unmatched customer exists as multiple customers, the purchase history would be incomplete, likely resulting in the wrong offer and multiple mailings. For vendors or product-related matching, there are significant savings in consolidating the purchasing of related products and knowing where and what you are spending with each vendor.

5.3.4 Phase 4: Application Integration and Data Migration

The first business challenge addressed in the application integration and data migration phase was to integrate an acquired company's application output, especially from a different point of sale system, into the main company's applications, such as an ERP system, until the systems could be replaced.

The solution was to use Data Services to routinely extract data from the legacy point of sales system; cleanse, transform, and validate the data; and then load it into the ERP system on a daily basis. This was a complex integration project, but was accomplished within three months with the help of Data Services and a now experienced team, ensuring that the acquired stores' products were replenished on a timely basis, and their employees and customers were properly serviced. This project added event-triggered jobs in Data Services.

Later, when legacy systems, such as point of sale and financial/accounting systems from the parent company were being replaced, the new business challenge became the migration of historical, financial, and customer data into the new applications, from the old versions of each.

The solution was to again use Data Services to extract, transform, map, cleanse, remove duplications, and load historical data into new applications. Batch processing or using web service options within Data Services enabled communication and integration between applications. Data Services was used to consume XML messages, perform data cleansing and data standardization, and then output an XML hierarchy. The ability to reuse transforms from earlier projects greatly simplified development.

5.3.5 Phase 5: Next Steps with Data Services

In the case study discussed here, the next plans for Data Services are to cleanse and de-duplicate data at the source, when data is being entered into the system. Additional extensions will target the use of real-time loads to the data warehouse and to include the text data processing capabilities that bring in unstructured data to better understand customer behavior and sentiment.

This section discussed the evolution of Data Services from use as an ETL tool to load a data warehouse, to a data platform to manage and ensure the quality of data globally. Next we will discuss recommendations for a master data program.

5.4 Recommendations for a Master Data Program

Companies start managing their master data for a variety of reasons ranging from increased accuracy and reliability in business intelligence to operational improvements such as reduced shipping errors. They also start their journey at various levels of maturity. Whatever may be the end benefit, most have to follow a similar sequence of steps to achieve their specific goals. To be successful with managing master data, the following must be defined:

► Common enterprise vision and goals
► Master data strategy
► Roadmap and operational phases
► Business process redesign and change management
► Governance
► Technology selection

In this section, we discuss each of these concepts.

5.4.1 Common Enterprise Vision and Goals

A statement about an enterprise's vision and goals is an articulation of why master data management is important to the enterprise and the end state vision. Typically this is driven by vision/goal setting workshops that includes multiple business stakeholders; alternatively, it can be created by a smaller operating team that shares it with the larger organization for approval. Having this vision defined and supported by the necessary top management roles is essential for the program's success. Short-term goals that translate the vision into achievable milestones provide concreteness to the sometimes more abstract vision. For example, if the vision is to "transform enterprise data, business processes, and organization into assets that will provide business value," the shorter-term goals could include specific targets such as "Consolidate customer master data for the ERP and CRM systems by end of the second quarter of next year."

5.4.2 Master Data Strategy

For the purposes of this section, the master data strategy specifies the approaches, standards, and methodology for achieving the common enterprise vision. To continue with the example of achieving the vision of "transform enterprise data, business processes, and organization into assets that will provide business value," the approach could be regional, local, or global; the standards could be around data and business process; and the methodology could involve starting with one domain or multiple domains. So one variation of a strategy could be "global centralized management of customer master data by standardizing creation and updating processes and data elements."

5.4.3 Roadmap and Operational Phases

In this planning phase the strategy is made operational with specific scopes, milestones, and deliverables. This could be based on low-hanging fruit, or the most value that can be delivered to the organization within a given time frame. Whatever the approach, the end result is an operational plan with time-bound deliverables. The operational phase could involve various tasks such as data discovery, business process inventory, new process definition, data quality remediation, and so on. The operational phase is tied to specific systems, data domains, and delivery dates. Master data scenarios typically involve consolidation, harmonization, or centralization. The roadmap and operational phases could outline specific scenarios or styles for individual domains.

5.4.4 Business Process Redesign and Change Management

For ongoing maintenance and upkeep of master data, a certain amount of redesign is typically required with the master data management processes (create, read, update, delete/archive). The usual change management guidelines apply here with periodic communication of changes, training, and executive support. Data quality and process metrics are useful in enforcing these changes. For example, if master data was allowed to be created in various applications prior to a change that resulted in a centralized approach, the users have to be trained to follow the new process and understand the revised service-level agreements, the required data elements, and data quality checks/standardizations built into the process.

5.4.5 Governance

Governance is the glue that holds together the various components of a master data management program. Business driven and enforced, data governance helps organizations in an enterprise come up with processes to manage, measure, and control the quality of master data. Successful master data management programs are all backed by strong business-driven data governance efforts. Depending on the organization profile, data to be managed, and applications landscape, the governance organization can be centralized or decentralized. In most enterprises, the governance function is enforced by a combination of bottom-up effort driven by data stewards and analysts and supported by a top-down data governance council that acts as a final arbiter of data issues and an enforcer of enterprise standards and business processes. Since governance is management and business driven, to a large part, this is dependent on the organizational culture. Since a governance program is an important prerequisite for a successful master data program, starting and nurturing a governance initiative is an important task by itself that needs to be managed with due diligence.

5.4.6 Technology Selection

Technology selection is purposefully presented toward the end of the section, as the previous items are relevant and important to guide this task. While there is no one tool that will do all the required tasks, a combination of tools and technologies is now definitely available in the marketplace to help manage master data. Based on the vision, goals, and master data strategy and a combination of other factors, such as the existing solution and tool landscape and approved technology portfolio, this can be a complex task.

Following these steps will help the enterprise achieve its master data vision. The benefits can vary, but include:

▸ Operational efficiencies such as improved shipping and billing processes that ensure the right products are sent efficiently to the right customers, suppliers are paid on schedule using the right payment instruments, and the right products are included in the catalog for the correct set of customers or partners.

▸ Analytic improvements such as the ability to create true profit and loss reports by customer and/or product, identify true spend by suppliers across all the material/product categories, and rationalize the supplier base periodically to have the right mix required to support the enterprise.

Apart from these improvements, a structure that is in place for governing and managing master data can be used to effectively work with business scenarios including mergers and acquisitions, new product introduction, compliance initiatives, and so on.

Next we discuss recommendations on using SAP NetWeaver Process Orchestration; specifically, SAP NetWeaver Process Integration and SAP Data Services.

5.5 Recommendations for Using SAP NetWeaver Process Integration and SAP Data Services

In this section we will discuss the use of SAP NetWeaver Process Integration (a component of SAP NetWeaver Process Orchestration) and the use of Data Services for data integration. This section is intended for companies that have both SAP NetWeaver Process Integration (hereafter SAP NetWeaver PI) and Data Services. This section assumes knowledge of SAP NetWeaver PI and will not introduce this tool. If you do not already have SAP NetWeaver PI, you might want to skip this section.

5.5.1 A Common Data Integration Problem

When integrating data between multiple systems, the integration can include several layers and integration points. When something goes wrong with an integration process, a common problem that occurs in the enterprise is that people always want to "shoot the messenger." From an integration standpoint, this means the blame for poor performance or reliability issues is focused at the middleware. Of course, the middleware is sometimes to blame, but it is important to separate fact from fiction. A case in point is drawn from the timeframe after SAP NetWeaver PI was launched within a large company. SAP NetWeaver PI had a large role in the middleware; it abstracted services from SAP to be available to the rest of the enterprise (for example, get purchase order data, get customer information). Over time, the number of interfaces rose quickly. Data flowing in and out of the SAP backend was going through a messaging chain that included SAP NetWeaver PI.

A chorus of "SAP NetWeaver PI has a performance problem" or "SAP NetWeaver PI is broken" was growing. Further analysis showed that as projects were developing SAP NetWeaver PI interfaces between enterprise systems, they were using them not only for near-real-time data feeds, but also for very large data moves with short durations. Messaging chains through SAP NetWeaver PI and other enterprise web services that worked fine for incremental data transfers collapsed under the load of a huge data moves. Examples of these types of data moves were large product updates or wide-ranging price updates.

5.5.2 A Data Integration Analogy

As the company tried to explain the differences between ETL processes and incremental near-real-time processes, it became clear that the message was not sinking in across teams of developers, architects, and managers. The architects came up with an analogy that helped people understand this difference. It became known as the "concrete and sugar" analogy. Basically, it uses the example of a construction truck moving large numbers of concrete bags compared to a sedan used to move bags of sugar. The truck is a heavy-duty flatbed vehicle with a large bed for transporting material. It has a large diesel motor, a heavy-duty suspension, and big tires. The car is a standard passenger car with a medium-sized motor and has enclosed space for protecting passengers and carrying small items.

Both the truck and the car can move either concrete or sugar (the messaging layer doesn't care about the content), but the volumes that can be moved efficiently are not interchangeable. Trucks are like the large ETL systems. They excel at transforming and moving very large batches. Cars are like middleware that excels at moving smaller volumes repeated many times. The truck is most efficient at moving large numbers of large bags. But it can also carry small bags. It is designed to move a lot of material, but not at a very fast pace. The passenger car can move a couple of bags of concrete or several bags of sugar. It is designed for fast trips carrying small loads. It can even handle a burst of activity and carry a lot of bags of sugar.

You wouldn't say the car has "performance problems" because it can't move a ton of concrete, and you couldn't efficiently use a large construction truck for your regular trips to a grocery store to pick up a few small bags of sugar. Both the car and the truck are best utilized for the type of use case for which they were designed. If you move a couple of bags with the truck, it will work but won't be efficient. And it will take a while (won't be "real time"). If you try to move too much concrete at once, you will either slow down the passenger car or you will break it.

We found that using this analogy helped the developers, architects, and managers better understand the correct usage of SAP NetWeaver PI and Data Services. Next we will provide some guidelines in more detail on choosing the right software capability for the integration requirements.

5.5.3 Creating Prescriptive Guidance to Help Choose the Proper Tool

As the conversations on which tools to use continued, one thing that became apparent was that there was still a mindset in the enterprise that thought in terms of executing updates in large batches. But the enterprise architecture in many companies is moving toward smaller, incremental updates in a near-real-time (NRT) fashion. The collision of these two mindsets is where enterprise integration teams hear cries of performance problems and unreliability. As they work with project teams and clearly delineate the line between ETL and NRT, they need to create prescriptive guidance for the use cases and can thereby ease a lot of the problems. Figure 5.7 shows the convergence of ETL and NRT, with data synchronization on one end and multistep processing on the other end.

Figure 5.7 ETL and Messaging Spectrum

The following are some use cases where you would choose one method over the other or a blend of the two:

▶ **ETL**
The same data needs to be in two or more systems; for example, data migration projects to seed new applications.

▶ **ETL and messaging**
A transaction needs to be completed across systems. This can also be called a composite application.

▶ **Messaging**
A business process where several transactions occur in steps through a predefined sequence across two or more systems and you need to guarantee delivery.

The advantages of ETL lie in use cases that involve processing large amounts of data, use ETL tools already in place, and use complex transformations including data quality, cleansing, validation, de-duplication, enrichment, as well as point-to-point movement of data.

The advantages of messaging lie in uses cases that involve processing a high number of transactions over time, use messaging tools already in place, require little data augmentation but need message transformations, and involve one-to-many and many-to-many data movement.

Another way to look at the overlap between SAP NetWeaver PI and Data Services is by creating a radar map. This type of map plots the fit of each capability along the spokes of a circular radar graph and gives a good visual representation of the strengths of each tool as well as the areas of overlap. SAP has created a radar map for positioning Data Services and SAP NetWeaver Process Integration; it is part of a larger positioning presentation that you can find on the SAP Community Network (SCN).[1]

5.5.4 Complex Examples in the Enterprise

It's not that simple in all cases. If a project team has developed middleware interfaces for data feeds, they of course want to reuse those for the occasional big batch product/price updates mentioned previously. They would ask, "Why should we create a process/tool for the batch updates when we have a perfectly usable interface in place?" This question requires more analysis. An example use case is one where SAP data was being fed near-real-time through SAP NetWeaver PI to another legacy transformation engine and then through a web service that loaded into another database.

---

1   *http://www.sdn.sap.com/irj/scn/go/portal/prtroot/docs/library/uuid/10fbac70-c381-2d10-afbe-c3902a69
4eaf?QuickLink=index&overridelayout=true*

This chain performed very well with incremental feeds but was overwhelmed in the web service layer during large batch loads. As the endpoint overloaded, the problems backed up through the messaging chain, and the integration team ended up with "PI has performance problems" messages in their inboxes from the angry project team.

In reality, SAP NetWeaver PI had so much capacity in the environment that as the source system was pushing large updates out, SAP NetWeaver PI was overwhelming the downstream chain. This use case was not one where the project team had the time or the resources or the need to build an ETL solution for these infrequent data pushes. The solution that the integration architecture team came up with was called "throttle at the source." Through benchmarking, they determined the volume at which the weakest link in the integration chain would break. Using this information, they worked with project teams to determine a throttle rate for the source system that would allow data to flow smoothly and efficiently given the existing capacity of the enterprise systems. This increased the time required to complete the total data movement, but there were some dials that could be controlled on this throttle to minimize the total time.

Throttling the rate at which messages are sent from the source system can be seen in the example of price updates, where a large number of products need to have prices updated in one or more systems. Instead of pushing out product prices as quickly as the system can, it can be controlled so that only x number of price updates per hour are sent from the source system for instance. Any mechanism that can control the rate at which messages or updates are sent into the enterprise can be used as an effective throttle.

Other ways to minimize the impact on the systems in the enterprise are as follows:

▶ Move the pushes to off hours when the systems have more available capacity and do not collide with known peak messaging times.

▶ Sometimes systems can also be segmented such that hardware can be dedicated in the short term to service the data push without impacting other critical interfaces. SAP NetWeaver PI, for instance, has the ability to segment queues that are used.

▶ Move interfaces to asynchronous processing. The middleware layer can help with reliability and can make the system less susceptible to failures by using asynchronous processing instead of the more fragile synchronous processing.

5.5.5 When All Else Fails...

In spite of the best architecture efforts, there will still be occasional big batches that are pushed through unexpectedly and that could break somewhere in the integration chain. That is where the final defense needs to be architecting robust systems that degrade gracefully and where there are better monitors in place to proactively detect the problems as early as possible so that there is time to react and protect critical interfaces.

What is graceful degradation? It can be seen in a complex system that instead of reaching complete failure as errors occur continues to limp along and process messages as system monitors are alerting support personnel of the problems so they get the system back up to full capacity. A complex system that uses asynchronous messaging along with hardware and software segmentation greatly improves the chances for graceful degradation during system problems and improves the probability of a happy ending.

5.6 Ensuring a Successful Enterprise Content Management Project by Belgian Railways

This section will discuss SAP Extended Enterprise Content Management by OpenText (hereafter SAP Extended ECM) and its use by Belgian Railways, including how the business case was built and key success factors for the project.

5.6.1 Building the Business Case

The business case for SAP Extended ECM focused on the overall return on investment. A high-level calculation was used that, perhaps surprisingly, considered not document volumes, but rather the number of employees. Because most employees handled paper documents at some point during the day, by determining the cost to handle a paper document, a general conclusion was reached. The following high-level calculation was used without any consideration for document volumes but based on the number of employees:

▶ Handling cost of one document is approximately 15 EUR.

▶ Each employee handles at least one document a day and works at least 200 days a year. The average cost is theoretically about 3,000 EUR per employee per year.

- For 10,000 users, this cost is *theoretically* about 30,000,000 EUR a year.
- By combing measures to drastically reduce the use of paper and using SAP Extended ECM, this cost can be reduced by at least 50%.

A detailed budget planning was presented to the board of directors to raise the funds from the government needed for a four-year roadmap, along with the arguments for each of the following corporate objectives defined by the government:

- Cost optimization driven by paper-reduction strategy and lower TCO for a unique central repository
- Enhanced customer services by offering faster response to customer complaints, faster customer contract handling, punctuality of rail services, and standardization of communication
- Improved punctuality of rail services due to valid information (legal procedures, enhanced training materials, weather conditions) to the train conductors; troubleshooting wizard
- Uncompromising safety through accessibility and accuracy of technical drawings and work procedures, better train maintenance operations and audit/traceability, controlled and validated information to train conductors, enhanced training materials, skills management

Our goal with SAP Extended ECM was to not only create a benchmark in terms of document management but also to add value by enabling content-enriched business processes with new views and perspectives on data and documents.

The following are examples of what has been or is planned to be implemented at Belgian Railways.

Drawing Management for the Maintenance of Rolling Stock

Drawing management is a business activity focusing on the creation, editing, and publishing of 2D/3D designs related to any train part. These designs are provided by third parties or self-made. In the past, drawing management was prone to inconsistencies, duplicates, obsolescence, and inaccuracy due to the use of many decentralized file servers and legacy databases with local versions of drawings. Operational activities were planned and managed in the SAP Business Suite, while the related technical documents such as plans and drawings were managed in collateral environments.

This did not facilitate the integration and planning of operational activities within the company, and this was often the source of the purchase or production of huge amounts of wrong spare parts, with significant money loss.

Today, there is only one repository containing all released 2D/3D designs integrated with bills of materials used in purchases and production. These drawings are managed with drawing management software, and metadata is maintained and synchronized with SAP Extended ECM once a drawing is released. All previous versions are kept to provide traceability and auditability. Tools have been provided to migrate all legacy databases and perform mass upload from third-party drawings needed from time to time. Once a material has been connected to a mark within a drawing, any new version of the drawing is visible from the material, bill of material, and so on. When a document is used in a purchase requisition or in a production order via a material, a snapshot is generated to keep the version used at that time after a last approval from the drawing office to ensure its validity. These documents are also regulated with watermarks to visually inform users about their status.

The immediate benefits include the availability of documents in their latest version (the only version of the truth), a better integration between SAP processes and documents, improved search capabilities, and accurate purchase and production of spare parts leading to more safety on the rail and cost optimization.

Purchasing Transparency

Fraud detection is critical in the public sector, and it starts with the public tenders for the purchase of goods and/or services. The end-to-end business process needs to be auditable, not only in terms of data and approvals/signatures but also in terms of documents. Purchasers deal with all vendors, from the request for quotation until the invoice. All posted mail documents, emails, and files used need to be classified correctly, need to be secured by using legal holds, and need to be fully integrated with the SAP Business Suite and attached to every business process step (business object), automatically if possible.

When a purchase order is created, it goes through a release strategy with workflow to gather digital signatures from the selected hierarchy printed on the released document. SAP Extended ECM enables every printout of a changed purchase order to generate a new version stored in SAP Extended ECM for better traceability and auditability.

Customer Complaints Handling

Customer complaints are treated by a call center using SAP Customer Relationship Management integrated with web, email, and telephone support. Claim forms on paper are sent to the call center and are scanned. All these documents are linked to activities and stored on the SAP CRM system, leading to capacity and performance issues.

All these documents will be migrated to SAP Extended ECM, using its optical character recognition (OCR) capabilities to automate the processing of a claim form. The new process will provide privacy compliance of customer data to comply with governmental legislation and prescriptions. A business workspace (explained in Chapter 14) will be added to SAP CRM's customer interaction center to provide call center personnel with enhanced document management capabilities.

Intelligent Driver Assistant

Intelligent Driver Assistant is a program that will provide the train driver with legal information on a ruggedized tablet replacing a 20-kg backpack full of paper he has to carry every day to perform daily duties. This business transformation has been initiated by the unions having concerns about the impact of the backpack on the train driver's health and safety.

All documents are managed by SAP Extended ECM, providing version management, approvals for publishing, distribution for offline use, and reading confirmation as the train driver needs to know the latest rules, regulations, and requirements prior to the start of his duty with a specific train on a specific train track. The use of the ruggedized tablet will be extended with applications such as a troubleshooting wizard, time and activity registration, a holiday request e-form, a logbook, a weather channel (on train track conditions) to apply safety measures, an energy performance monitor, access to a corporate web portal, and so on.

Revision and Modernization of Rolling Stock

Revision and modernization are two types of maintenance managed by projects, as they involve many sequential and parallel activities with the highest level of quality and within tight schedules. To speed up and ease these activities, the technical worker will access all data and documents related to his activities with a tablet or a kiosk in the field. The accuracy of data and documents is critical to avoid safety breaches and can only be ensured by high-quality data and the latest released version of all related documents. Documents are linked to every project component such as functional location, equipment, bill of material, or material. The authoring and publishing of documents is managed by different offices outside the SAP GUI, the structure is managed by the project team via the SAP GUI, and the consumption is done via SAP NetWeaver Portal. When a document is linked to a project component, a snapshot is generated to keep the version used at that time. The same snapshot principle is used for traceability and auditability with SAP Plant Maintenance (PM) notifications and orders. You can use task lists and tasks (master data) where the link to documents is dynamic, providing version management.

Wagon Maintenance Services Compliance with Governmental Legislation

The Belgian Railways Wagon Maintenance Services (WMS) is an entity of maintenance shops with central coordinating services for maintaining train cars not only for Belgian Railways but also for other railways. A web portal provides all other railways companies with accurate information about any maintenance activities, coming from the SAP Business Suite. All documents related to these activities will soon also be available via this portal using SAP Portal Content Management by OpenText (discussed in Chapter 4).

The entity in charge of maintenance needs to comply with the following requirements:

▶ **It manages the maintenance logbooks and ensures correct implementation.**
This is done for each vehicle that is registered in the National Register of Vehicles as an entity in charge of maintenance. The correct implementation is ensured by checking that the vehicle is maintained in accordance with its maintenance backlog and requirements force, including the Technical Specifications Interoperability (TSI).

▶ **It provides traceability of maintenance operations.**
Traceability is performed on each vehicle by managing and keeping up to date the maintenance reports for each vehicle.

▶ **It analyzes the lessons learned.**
These include the data from maintenance, accidents, or incidents to update the owner's maintenance logbook adequately.

▶ **It informs the owner.**
It informs the owner of all restrictions and specific operation conditions of the cars.

▶ **It contracts liability insurance.**

Insurance covers sufficient financial risks arising from its activities.

Moreover, we need to keep track of 40 years of maintenance logs together with their related documents. This will dramatically increase the storage volume.

Therefore, we used SAP NetWeaver Information Lifecycle Management to define proactive data and document archiving strategies with volume management and (legal) retention management capabilities.

Projects and Resource Portfolio Management

The Belgian Railways IT department is managing, implementing, and supporting many SAP and non-SAP projects. To ensure an efficient follow-up, all documents related to resource management, project planning, project implementation, and project support will be managed by SAP Extended ECM using business workspaces (explained in Chapter 14). This way, documents are accessible not only from a project perspective, but also from a business partner perspective or from a support perspective; for example, they are linked to support tickets created in SAP Solution Manager. The storage of documents with SAP Resource and Portfolio Management (RPM) and cProjects is also done with SAP Extended ECM for a global unification, more functionalities, and better accessibility. Figure 5.8 shows how this works.

Figure 5.8 Projects and Resource Portfolio Management

Figure 5.8 shows the storing, organizing, and classifying of all project implementation documents, such as blueprints, technical specifications, training materials, project documentation, and SAP Solution Manager tickets. This will also contribute to better business process management when users need to search for relevant information; for example, if they need to locate all contracts related to a particular project. The filing and search capabilities offered by SAP Extended ECM bring significant value with business workspaces' deep integration with the SAP Business Suite. The workspaces provide team and project rooms, collaboration spaces, forums, and wikis.

Vendor Invoice Management

Prior to SAP Invoice Management by OpenText, purchasing, invoice reception, and accountancy were done at several work locations in Belgium. At that time, there were many lost invoices, double payments, lost discounts, and late payments (above 60 days and sometime up to 1 year). It was not possible to have accurate accruals, and closings were extremely difficult. There was no visibility into costs or vendor performance, as there was no integrated and optimized purchase-to-pay process with clear action at the source to prevent errors.

Then we went live with SAP Invoice Management by OpenText, along with the purchase-to-pay process optimization within the SAP Business Suite. The benefits are paper reduction, central processing within an integrated system, no more backlog, a 67% reduction in time to execute the business process, quality accruals, work distribution, traceability, on-time payments, more effective reporting, cost transparency, and easy closings with high quality.

Our goal is to migrate all scanned invoices to SAP Extended ECM, enabling full text search on all appendices that might contain critical business information. Today, only the invoice financials are optically recognized for efficient processing and to limit license fees per page read. If a purchaser or accounts payable clerk needs to find legal details related to the contract or purchase order within the appendices, he has to go to the MIRO transaction (invoice verification) and read the scanned document attached until he finds the relevant information. Along with the migration, we will provide a business workspace to access documents from a vendor perspective that will grant access to any document within a virtual folder structure generated from purchase requisitions, requests for quotations, contracts, purchase orders, and invoices related to a single vendor. All appendices will go through basic optical character recognition (OCR) to provide full-text indexing and full-text search capabilities. This migration will add more value to the existing vendor invoice management process.

5.6.2 Key Success Factors for Your SAP Extended Enterprise Content Management by OpenText Project

The following outlines key success factors for a successful SAP Extended ECM implementation.

Building a Roadmap

To build a successful roadmap, you first need to select business processes that are already standardized in your SAP Business Suite for which you have the highest number of users and the highest volume of documents, such as SAP Plant Maintenance or SAP Enterprise Asset Management. In parallel, you should select some document processes like the one used in legal services or corporate communication to reach different types of audiences.

Another approach consists of interviewing every business unit, department, plant, and so on to collect information regarding all the document types and associated procedures they are dealing with on a daily basis. The result of these interviews should guide you in trying to standardize their processes.

Project Team Setup

The ideal project team would consist of business analysts, SAP experts, OpenText experts, ECM experts, change management consultants, a system administrator, and a project manager with a strong track record of business process improvement projects.

The ECM experts need to support the role of business analysts to successfully describe the document processes and the way to classify documents at the enterprise level using best practices. The ECM experts set up the governance model to ensure consistency and integrity with the continuous addition of new document types.

The OpenText experts translate the business requirements formulated in the various business blueprints into technical specifications for the configuration of the platform. The OpenText experts need to be consulted at any stage of the blueprint phase to ensure the feasibility of the realization phase and to ensure that standard features are being used.

Change Management

Change management is always a challenge, but it is an even bigger challenge with content management, as you will face the paper syndrome — resistance to change as people try to keep their paper processes as they are today. You may face resistance while converting, cleansing, and migrating your legacy systems and fileservers to the platform, as you will force the use of a unified classification and unique naming conventions for metadata and its possible values. For example, different units or departments working on the same set of data and documents have different ways to classify data and have different naming conventions. A specific example is drawings (2D/3D designs) provided by the drawing office used for purchasing for maintenance operations and for production.

You might also meet user disappointment at the go-live stage in some cases. For example, SAP Invoice Management by OpenText means no more paper invoices. Vendor invoices with their scanned images are distributed through the organization via SAP Business Workflow. This is a big change for people used to an In bin and Out bin from which they could see the work done at the end of the day.

You will also face people printing documents for approval without using the defined workflows. Don't forget to perform your paper reduction strategy by removing printers and copiers from time to time and replacing them with controlled mail/fax rooms.

You will need strong sponsorship and patience to articulate the change even if empowered from the top. However, the different user interface options fully integrated with SAP Extended ECM will help you achieve good user adoption by selecting the right user interface for the right audience: An accounts payable clerk uses the SAP GUI to perform invoice verification, a purchaser uses Microsoft Outlook to manage all vendor correspondence in a purchase process, a technical worker accesses documents in plant maintenance orders using SAP NetWeaver Portal, a customer facing personnel dispatches all customer complaints from a business workspace in the SAP CRM Customer Interaction Center, a legal expert manages records using Microsoft Windows Explorer, and so on. (User interface options with SAP Extended ECM are covered in Chapter 14.)

In the first stage of your roadmap, you will need to limit the rollout to basic functionalities such as version management and workflow to avoid uncontrolled resistance. People have to abandon the paper culture before you give them functionalities such as forums, collaboration spaces, and wikis.

Governance

You need to set up governance that controls the cohesion and consistency at functional and technical levels. It defines a set of guidelines for the correct use of the platform. Governance spans from governing the portfolio and project prioritization through governance on operational issues, from the updating of models through the help desk experience. The goals of the governance program included reducing administrative overhead, ensuring conformity to regulations, and ensuring a single platform for a single version of the truth.

Once SAP Extended ECM was implemented, its document controls were used to govern content approvals, check in/out, version control, and other document maintenance tasks.

Additionally, governance had to extend to governing the content itself. This included:

- Types of information
- Communication channels
- Establishing what document is the working copy
- Naming requirements
- Multilingualism
- Content templates

There is also governance on configuration such as the folder structure (for example, not more than three levels that will be freely defined) and information metadata.

The governance program increased predictability and the quality of results, reflecting business terminology, creation of name standardization and clarity of reuse of naming, and coordination within a larger architecture as an element of communication between platforms and ensuring correct access for multiple target groups.

The governance guidelines for the architecture included standardization of integration, standardized functionality, and use of standard user interfaces. Included were guidelines for operations; for example, all master data must come from SAP, and global master data must be managed centrally. The governance board was defined at a strategic level, and the governance team was defined at an operational level.

This section has introduced SAP Extended ECM including specific use cases and the value of using SAP Extended ECM. More information on the details of SAP Extended ECM, including business workspaces, is covered in Chapter 14.

> **Note**
>
> You can connect with others involved in enterprise content management by joining the ECM LinkedIn community: *http://www.linkedin.com/groups?gid=3874677*.

Next we discuss recommendations for creating an archiving strategy.

5.7   Recommendations for Creating an Archiving Strategy

Archiving data is usually the last thing anyone thinks about during an SAP implementation. All of the focus early in an SAP project is usually directed at business process chains, such as sales or procurement processing, and not much attention is paid to retention policies or retirement of data. However, data archiving is just as important as any other process in an SAP system. Eventually all of those documents and transactions are going to have to be removed from the database. Executing well-defined data archiving projects should be an important part of your overall enterprise information management strategy.

5.7.1   What Drives a Company into Starting a Data Archiving Project?

There are several reasons companies execute data archiving projects. These reasons have changed: It started with *disk drive costs* in the 1990s and then moved to *system performance* gained by the removal of data no longer required. As time progressed, SAP provided support for the *Euro* as well as support for *UNICODE*. The Euro and UNICODE upgrades required converting a lot of data from all of those previous transactions that still resided in the database. Data archiving was used to reduce the amount of data in the database that needed to be converted and shorten the *system down time*.

Legal compliance and *records management requirements* are also major drivers for data archiving. Many companies have records retention policies that specify a life span for business transactions and other data. These policies mandate that expired data be removed from the database and destroyed. As many SAP implementations are now maturing past the retention policies, this is becoming a very common reason for initiating a data archiving project.

> **Note**
>
> SAP NetWeaver Information Lifecycle Management (hereafter SAP NetWeaver ILM) supports both retention policy management and archiving. SAP NetWeaver ILM is discussed in Chapter 13.

We are approaching a new era with SAP HANA. Starting with business warehouses, SAP HANA will transform the performance of those systems, and it will be important to start your migration with a lean system and not retain data that is unnecessary to your business units. You will want to include archiving in your overall SAP HANA strategy.

While the reasons just discussed are examples of a real need to archive, the best time to start your archiving project is when you are first implementing the system. At this time you have the resources engaged to define an entire archiving strategy. If you didn't do that, don't feel bad. You are not alone. Most archiving projects are started well after the deployment teams have dispersed.

Next we discuss recommendations for getting started with an archiving project.

5.7.2 Who Initiates a Data Archiving Project?

Archiving projects are rarely initiated by the business. The business experts want as much data as possible in the system. Data is value—that's their motive.

The legal department may initiate an archiving project to eliminate risk. If your organization has been live on SAP long enough that documents or transactions are approaching the expiration date per your records retention schedule (you do have one, don't you?), the legal department may approach the IT department and query about your archiving policy. You will want to be ready for this conversation. So, why would legal worry about archiving so much? Many companies have been sued for a variety of reasons—say, for instance, unfair business transactions. The courts have ordered that the defendant (in this case, your company) must turn over all records pertaining to the case. If you have a retention schedule of say, seven years, and you have not archived any data in the twelve years since your SAP system has been live, you could be forced into turning over much more data than you would have had to if you expunged your records per your retention schedule.

Database administrators are usually the first to inquire about archiving data from the database. They are on the front line and are the first to see the impact of a database that is too large. They look at data archiving from a strictly technical sense. The database administrator's motivations are directly opposite the business units. They use tools such as transaction codes to analyze the size of the tables in the database. They use this as one of the inputs to monitor the health of the database.

Your SAP development teams may also initiate an archiving project because they have been educated by webcasts or user group seminars such as ASUG or DSAG, or maybe they've read some consulting company white papers on archiving SAP best practices. Or it may be a line item or subproject in a conversion or upgrade initiative.

The important take away from this conversation is that you *need* an archiving strategy in your systems roadmap. Be sure to have that 30-second elevator speech ready when your CIO pops the question about your archiving strategy.

5.7.3 Project Sponsorship

As with any project, you will need sponsorship; a data archiving project requires a very strong sponsor. It's not one of those glamorous projects like customer relationship management, supplier relationship management, or any of the other enhance capabilities projects, but it is just as important because it has all of the key project components—risk, expense, and scope. Each of these will be explained next.

Risk

All projects have risk, but an archiving project carries a little more than most projects you may have done in the past. A well-managed data archiving project manages risk at every project milestone. You will want to evaluate the risk and put a mitigation plan in place for each major milestone in your project plan. For instance, during the project initiation phase, you may notice that there isn't a lot of participation in the project. Don't underestimate the impact on your project when team members don't show up for meetings or think this project is a minor distraction in their day. This is where you need that strong sponsor mentioned above. All team members should be fully engaged.

Another risk is the impact you will be imposing on the business units. After all, you are changing the way they access and use their data. Depending upon your retrieval and/or display plans, you may have to do some significant retraining. There may also be data that will no longer be included in reports. You will need to plan for this training in your change management portion of the project.

Expense

An archiving project can be as expensive as you make it. Depending on the reason you have initiated the project, this is a highly variable figure. If you are planning extensive archiving, then you will most certainly benefit by utilizing consultants to help you along the way. You may need to procure a storage platform for your archive files, whether that resides physically in your data center or, more recently, in the cloud. Depending on your retrieval/display requirements, you may or may not need an external content server. Archiving to a file system is completely supported within SAP but usually not implemented in common practice. Most companies utilize an external content server, especially when implementing SAP NetWeaver Information Lifecycle Management.

You will want to make sure that you have done your homework during the planning stages of the project and ensure that you manage your project budget accordingly. Of course, the scope of the project will be the key variable that will impact the cost of the project.

Scope

So you've decided to start the inevitable archiving project. What's next?

The section above stated many reasons you may choose to, or need to, execute an archiving project. The reason will be a major determining factor on how your project will be structured. For instance, there are two methodologies for setting the timeline of a project: left to right and right to left.

▶ **Left to right planning**
When setting the schedule of a project, classic project management tells us to carefully plan each step, determine the availability of the required resources, determine the required amount of time needed for each task, sequence the steps and add any dependencies, and finally derive the end date of the project from the resulting Gantt chart. This is often called left to right planning, as the time-line is a direct result of the careful analysis of each step as well as the input received from the expert resources you've consulted for each task.

▶ **Right to left planning**
This is when you are forced into an end date as a result of an uncontrolled dead-line. In this method, you start with an end date and then work your way back to the left until you get to the present day. Here's an example of this with respect to archiving: It was back in 1997, and we were approaching a top limit of our database just two short years after our go-live. If we didn't immediately reduce the size of the database by archiving, the SAP system we just rolled out was going to come to a complete halt because of a size limitation of the database. Another example might be if you are going to archive because you are planning an upgrade, and that upgrade project requires a lot of data conversion. If you

can reduce the amount of data to be converted, you can reduce the system downtime during the data conversion step. Right to left planning can work, but you better do your homework first. There are a lot of opportunities for that unexpected pitfall that will set you back.

So again, why are you doing your archiving project? There are other factors that are part of your project planning as a result of the reason for archiving data. If you are archiving because of a performance problem, then you must first analyze where the problem exists. Are your business users in the sales department complaining about customer programs running slow because of all those billing documents? Are you a retail shop and your material movement documents are slowing you down? (SAP retail systems can generate a tremendous amount of data, and archiving should be considered during your initial blueprinting.) These kinds of questions will help you determine the resources you'll require to bring your project to a successful end.

Resourcing Your Project

To staff your project you will need people from the applications that are most impacted (for example, when archiving financial information), but who else will you require to be an active part of the team?

Some choices are obvious: system administrator, database administrator, business expert for the application areas, legal department, tax specialist, project manager, and data warehouse expert. Other recommended project team members may not be as obvious: training, communication, and documentation specialists. These team members are also needed to ensure that users understand the changes that will impact them after the data has been archived. Reports will look different, transactions may look different, and the end users need to understand how they will be impacted by the archiving project.

5.8 Summary

This chapter has provided many real-world examples of using SAP's EIM solutions for specific business needs, and has discussed recommendations for getting started as well as the benefits of EIM.

Now that you have a basic understanding of the concepts of EIM, the EIM solutions offered by SAP, and some real-world examples, Part II of the book covers more details on the specific technical components of EIM in SAP.

PART II
Working with SAP's Enterprise Information Management Solutions

If you really want to understand your data and how well it is supporting your business, you need to understand the details of the data, where it's stored, and factually determine how good or bad it really is.

6   Getting to Know Your Data with SAP Information Steward

When starting a project to assess critical business data, you start with an *as-is* analysis and then define what you want to achieve. You need to start by determining what data should be included in the project. You obviously won't be profiling all your data. What data is most important to you? Examples of where to start include assessing the quality of your plant assets, examining customer data from a recent acquisition, and examining sales order data to determine why shipments are chronically late.

In this chapter we will focus on the data quality profiling and assessment capabilities of SAP Information Steward (hereafter Information Steward) and how they support information governance. Information Steward can be leveraged to support the following three components of an information governance program:

▶ **Discover**
Discover and understand your enterprise data by using data profiling and metadata management capabilities as well as creating a central catalog all of your data assets.

▶ **Define**
Define the data quality requirements as validation rules or cleansing rules to document and implement the quality targets that you want to reach. Set up and maintain your organization's central business term glossary to ensure that everyone in the organization has the same understanding of key terms and definitions.

▶ **Monitor**
Apply the validation rules to the data to measure the current state of data quality once, and apply the same validation rules on an ongoing schedule to monitor your data over time and monitor how your data quality level changes.

Information Steward has four major capabilities:

- **Data insight**
  For data profiling and data quality monitoring.

- **Metadata management**
  For metadata analysis.

- **Cleansing package builder**
  For the creation of cleansing rules.

- **Metapedia**
  For a business term taxonomy.

This chapter will discuss data insight projects and metadata management, starting with metadata management to catalog your data assets and their relationships. Then you will learn how to profile your data by creating data insight projects. Finally, you will learn how to use validation rules to monitor and assess the quality of your data.

6.1 Cataloging Data Assets and Their Relationships

One of the initial activities required to learn about your data is the central documentation and collection of all the technical metadata of your existing data assets. The goal of a metadata management repository is to consolidate technical metadata from individual data sources and applications into one central location. Getting metadata information together and linking information about the table structure — for example, names and columns as well as additional information about data mapping or movement information from extraction, transformation, and loading (ETL) tools — enables you to identify similar redundant data objects existing in different databases or applications. By linking physical data objects with the data mapping information, it is also possible to track how data is moved from different sources to target systems. This analysis provides data lineage, answering questions such as "From what source system is the data within my data warehouse coming?" A metadata management repository also enables impact analysis, answering questions such as "What reports are using the data from my operational source system?" This analysis improves trust and confidence in the system landscape.

To integrate metadata information from several solutions, you must first set up the required metadata integrators and the necessary connection parameters to access the source systems and execute the metadata integration collection. *Metadata integrators* read metadata from multiple systems. They read the table headers, columns, ETL jobs, and other technical information about the data in your landscape. This is an important first step to learning what data is stored where and how many different names you use for the same data.

In this section, we give step-by-step instructions to set up a metadata integrator source and to execute and/or schedule a metadata integration job.

6.1.1 Configuring a Metadata Integrator Source

Follow the steps below to configure a metadata integrator source:

1. Log on to the SAP BusinessObjects Business Intelligence (BI) Central Management Console (hereafter CMC) and go to the Information Steward section.

2. Add a new integrator source by clicking on the MANAGE button.

3. Define all the necessary connection options for NEW INTEGRATOR SOURCE. Depending on the integrator type that you choose from the dropdown menu, the layout and requested parameters change.

4. Test the connection to the metadata source by clicking on the TEST CONNECTION button.

5. Click on the SAVE button to save and close the new metadata integrator source definition.

In Figure 6.1, a connection is made to a sales warehouse by selecting SAP BUSINESS-OBJECTS ENTERPRISE in the INTEGRATOR TYPE field. The integrator types connect to the database directly. Other integrator types include SAP NetWeaver Business Warehouse (BW), SAP Data Services (hereafter Data Services), and a relational database integrator. When connecting to SAP application systems, the relational database integrator is used.

In addition to the integrator types provided by SAP, there is also a third-party metadata integrator (SAP Information Steward Multi-Source Integrator by MITI Add-on) that allows you to connect over 50 applications, including data modeling tools and other ETL tools.

Figure 6.1 Creating a New Metadata Integrator Source

After setting up connections for all systems, the system administrator can review the list of all defined integrator sources by following the menu path INFORMATION STEWARD • METADATA MANAGEMENT • INTEGRATOR SOURCES in the CMC.

Central Management Console

The CMC is a web-based tool that offers a single interface for day-to-day administrative tasks, including user management, content management, and server management. The CMC is used by the SAP BusinessObjects platform as well as Data Services and Information Steward. It will be discussed in more detail in Chapter 7.

The next activity is to either execute each integrator source once or set up an appropriate schedule for executing ongoing metadata integration tasks. The execution will collect and consolidate all technical metadata descriptions. The integration tasks collect the following information:

▸ **Database system information**
Includes the description of the table names, field names, and data types. Note: This includes information from an SAP application database.

▸ **Data modeling**
Includes the description of the relationship between different models.

▸ **Data movement and ETL systems**
Includes the description of the data movement jobs from target to source sys-

tems. This information is available when connecting to Data Services as a metadata integrator source.

▶ **Business intelligence and data warehouse systems**
Includes the description of queries and reports.

The metadata integration tasks include all information in its central repository. Relationships between the different metadata objects are automatically determined by Information Steward's relationship service.

6.1.2 Executing or Scheduling Execution of Metadata Integration

Follow the steps below to execute metadata integration:

1. Highlight one of the integrator sources from the INTEGRATOR SOURCE LIST in the CMC.

2. Choose RUN NOW from the ACTIONS dropdown list to run the metadata integrator immediately.

3. Choose SCHEDULE from the ACTIONS dropdown list to open the scheduler configuration window.

Figure 6.2 shows an example of the results of this job.

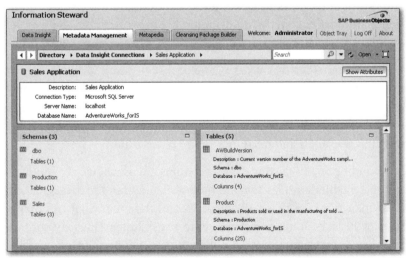

Figure 6.2 Data Catalog for Data Insight Connection Database Sales Application in Metadata Management

Figure 6.2 shows the METADATA MANAGEMENT tab of Information Steward. In the results for the job, you can see there are three database schemas and five tables. You can see the number of columns for each of the tables. You can also drill down into each level to see column names and other information such as field attributes.

The consolidated and enriched metadata information allows the data analyst or business user to review, search, and browse the complete metadata catalog, including all data objects as well as related information on descriptions, synonyms, or associated business terms. Another perspective allows the user to view the data lineage or impact analysis representation in either tabular or graphical form to see how information is moving from source to target systems within the system landscape. Data lineage and impact analysis are discussed in more detail in Chapter 9.

In the next section you will learn how to get started with data profiling for key data domains.

6.2 Profiling Data

Dealing with data in an unknown environment can be a challenging, if not daunting, task. Even if you have documentation for the metadata of the different data assets, including the schema, table names, and column names, you shouldn't rely on the headlines of the columns and expect to find exactly the content that the headline implies. You definitely need to drill into the table columns and analyze what information is really stored in those fields.

Information Steward provides easy access to helpful statistical information about the data that is stored in any database system, application, or file. Using not only statistical information but also a user-friendly user interface to drill down into details, even down to the individual rows, the data analyst gains insight about what the content behind the labels and headlines in the tables *really* is.

Executing data profiling on the existing databases, applications, or files of a company is essential to find the hidden rules that are only visible within the data itself. An example of a hidden rule is the discovery that 95% of the time when an order is placed for the Northeast region, the order is set to a rush order. This may not be a documented policy or instruction but a discovery made while analyzing the data. It could be that if 95% of the time a pattern emerges, it should also happen the other 5% of the time, so a new rule is needed to document the unspoken policy.

Data profiling is a fast way to identify suspicious data or outliers that should be used to establish further data quality rules based on the finding of the data profiling. This can be used to enforce service-level agreements within a governance project (governance projects with service level agreements are discussed in Chapter 2). Data profiling can also be used to assess data quality requirements from external regulations or already documented internal data quality requirements.

This chapter focuses primarily on data insight projects in Information Steward and how they are used to define separate projects for different functional areas in a company, ensuring users access to only the projects they have been assigned.

Data profiling first requires you to create a data insight project for data profiling. Then within the project you select the source system for the profiling and drill down to select the specific tables and files that should be included in your data insight project. You start by gaining some statistical information on the data content, executing some basic profiling, and then you focus on relationships between fields and columns.

6.2.1 Configuration and Setup of Connections and Projects

After the project team has identified what database tables, applications, or files should be used for initial data profiling activities, the IT administrator provides the access to those systems for Information Steward. Information Steward is able to connect directly to a large number of databases or applications; however, it is a system design question whether a company wants to execute the data profiling and data quality monitoring directly on their production system, or on a snapshot or staging area of the data.

For allowing the data analysts to access the necessary tables of files in their data insight projects, connections in the CMC are configured to the necessary application, database, or file directories. Besides giving the connection a unique name, further system parameters such as the database name and user credentials are set up, and the general access is tested.

Data profiling projects are called *data insight* projects in Information Steward. The following describes how to set up a connection for a data insight project. An administrator normally performs this task. This includes setting up the connection to the source system for the data insight project, creating the new project, and adding information on the data you want to profile; for example, the specific tables and/or files that should be included.

Setting Up a Connection for Data Insight Projects

When getting started with data insight projects you first need to set up a connection for the project. This is done using the following steps:

1. Log on to the CMC.

2. Go to the INFORMATION STEWARD section.

3. Follow the menu path MANAGE • NEW • CONNECTION.

4. Define all the necessary options for the new connection. Depending on the connection type you choose from the dropdown menu, the layout and requested parameters change.

5. Test the connection to the data source by clicking on the TEST CONNECTION button.

6. Save and close the create connection configuration window.

In addition to the different connections that provide access to the data, multiple individual data insight projects can be defined on an Information Steward installation. Projects are dashboards that are composed of several related score cards. A project, for example, can represent different application areas, different data domains, and different regions or business processes. Data analysts working with Information Steward are granted only specific user rights to their data insight project(s). This allows the system administrator to explicitly limit access to data insight projects to those users who are allowed to see the data.

Setting Up a Data Insight Project

Once the connections are done you set up the data insight project itself. This includes providing a project name and description.

1. In the CMC go to the INFORMATION STEWARD section.

2. Follow the menu path MANAGE • NEW • DATA INSIGHT PROJECT.

3. Enter a project name and project description in the NEW DATA INSIGHT PROJECT configuration window.

4. Save and close the NEW DATA INSIGHT PROJECT configuration window.

After the IT administrator has set up the basic technical configuration required for Information Steward, the data analysts are able to log on to a web browser-based user interface and start working on their data insight projects. The users can add files or tables from the technical connections to the file directories, database systems, or applications. Using the integrated metadata browsing capability, the data analyst will get an overview of all available files and tables, including tables from SAP applications and the technical names and business names or descriptions of the embedded tables.

Adding Tables or Files to a Data Insight Project

This example describes how to add tables or files to your new data insight project.

1. In the DATA INSIGHT tab, click on your project's workspace link.

2. Go to the WORKSPACE HOME tab.

3. Click on the ADD button and choose the type of data object (table or file) you want to add to your project.

4. In the BROWSE METADATA window, select the preconfigured database connection where you want to add tables.

5. Select the tables that you want to add from this connection. You can take a look at the data before adding it to the project by clicking on the VIEW DATA button, shown in Figure 6.3. Notice the selection of SALES APPLICATION and then the PERSON.ADDRESS table.

Figure 6.3 Browse Metadata Catalog to Add Tables to Your Data Insight Project

6. Click on the ADD TO PROJECT button to add all selected tables from this data source to your project.

7. Close the BROWSE METADATA window.

Once the tables are added, you can start to profile and collect information about the data content.

6.2.2 Getting Basic Statistical Information about the Data Content

The easiest way to get some initial insight into the content of a table or columns in a spreadsheet is by applying sorting or filtering capabilities. It is amazing to see how even some simple information like the smallest and biggest value of a column can give a data analyst hints about potential data quality issues. Take the case of NeedsEIM, Inc., which has issues with their supplier data. When examining the supplier email field, they quickly see +180062545, which looks like a telephone number. While this type of basic profiling can be done with a spreadsheet application, when it comes to the analysis of large data sets, more mature and sophisticated solutions are required to support data analysts in their interactive analysis.

You can set up a basic data profiling task for any of the files and tables that are added to a data insight project. Within basic data profiling, you not only can define details on the data sample size and the detail level of data profiling statistics, but also can determine if the basic profiling task should be executed immediately or be scheduled.

The next example describes how to define and execute a basic profiling task and review the results of a data profiling task.

Define and Execute a Basic Profiling Task

The following steps describe how to create a simple column profiling task.

1. Go to the WORKSPACE HOME tab in your data insight project.
2. Check the file, table, or view for the basic profiling.
3. Click on the PROFILE button and choose the COLUMNS option.
4. In the DEFINE COLUMN PROFILING TASK window, give this task a unique name and set the required options for the profiling task (described in more detail below and shown in Figure 6.4).

Figure 6.4 Defining and Immediately Executing a Column Profiling Task

5. Click on Validate Filter Condition if you have defined a filter condition to see if you used correct syntax.

6. Click on the Save and Run Now button to immediately execute the profiling task or click the Save button to save the task for later execution or scheduling.

After executing the basic profiling task, you can view results for every table profiled. The following list describes what is available with basic profiling:

▶ **Summary**
The summary column includes icons for data design information such as primary keys, sparsely populated columns, and so on, where the data analyst can get detailed information when he moves the mouse over the icon.

▶ **Properties**
The properties columns include metadata information for the individual columns, such as the description field and the data type.

▶ **Value (min, max, average, median)**
The value columns include information about the minimum and maximum values of the column as well as the average and median values for numeric values. Even if there are only two values for a column, like the minimum and maximum for a field, those two values can be a hint about existing internal data quality

problems that should be tracked further with a validation rule and ongoing assessment. Clicking on the hyperlinked numbers in the value columns opens a separate data review area that shows the corresponding data record sample. An example of what you can see could be colors for a particular article of clothing. You would easily be able to see how many color values, including articles that have no color assigned (null values in columns where there should be a value).

▶ **String length (min, max, average, median)**
The string length columns include information about the minimum and maximum string length stored in the column, as well as the average and median string length. The maximum string length information in particular can be very helpful together with the data type definition of the column.

If the maximum string length is equal to the field length definition, this might indicate a truncation problem; for example, if a user copies data from one data source to another, truncation could occur if the source field is longer than allowed in the target field. By clicking on the hyperlinked numbers in the string length columns, a separate data review area opens where the corresponding data record sample is shown.

▶ **Completeness (Null %, Blank %, Zero %)**
The completeness columns include detailed information about how many records of the data source include either technical null values or empty blank strings or zero in a numeric data field. You should look closely to see if any mandatory columns have null or empty values. By clicking on the hyperlinked numbers in the completeness columns, you can see the corresponding data record sample.

▶ **Distribution (Value, Pattern, Word)**
The distribution columns include information about the number of distinct values in the data source column. The VALUE column shows the number of distinct values for the complete data field, while the WORD column shows the number of distinct values for a string field content when the individual words within a long string are counted individually. The PATTERN column shows the number of distinct patterns in the column, where digits are represented by 9 and characters by A. You can get more details on the frequency distribution of the values, pattern, or words in a separate distribution list by clicking on the hyperlinked number.

Reviewing the Basic Profiling Results

This example describes how to view the results of the profiling task. Figure 6.5 shows the example results.

Figure 6.5 Basic Profiling Results—Frequency Distribution and Failed Record Sample Data

1. Go to the WORKSPACE HOME tab in your data insight project.

2. Click on the PROFILE RESULT tab.

3. Change the view to BASIC.

4. Expand the database connection entry in the tables column.

5. Expand the table entry where you want to review the basic profiling results.

6. Click on the hyperlinked numbers to either drill down to a frequency distribution overview or go directly to the records that are counted for this number.

   On the right side of the screen shown in Figure 6.5, Information Steward displays colors and the frequency distribution. For example, the most-used color is no color (set to null), and the second color in the list is black. This area is the frequency distribution. When you are in the frequency distribution area, you can click on the hyperlinked numbers to get to the corresponding records.

7. Reduce the number of columns, filter the number of records that are presented, or click on the EXPORT TO EXCEL button to save the records for external processing in a Microsoft Excel spreadsheet.

What kind of information might this reveal to users? To understand this, let's turn to our NeedsEIM, Inc. example. The NeedsEIM, Inc. data analyst is reviewing the data profiling basic results for the supplier master data table. In the region field, the results show that the minimum value is 1 and the maximum value is WY. Since the expected result is to have only two character region codes, this is an indicator that further analysis of the region field is needed; for example, reviewing the pattern distribution in the basic data profiling.

In the basic data profiling, it is discovered that the email address field of the supplier master data table is not always populated, and there are a small number of null values within this field. Additionally, it is discovered that there are several records with the same supplier names. Finally, the frequency distribution of the words shows that among the 25 most common words in the supplier name field are Limited, Lim., and Ltd., which are all legal forms of companies but should be standardized to one single representation.

The example we just discussed shows profiling within a single column. Next we discuss profiling cross-field and cross-column data relationships.

6.2.3 Identifying Cross-Field or Cross-Column Data Relationships

The basic profiling activity provides information on a single field or column content. For cross-column or cross-table profiling, extended functionalities are provided in the advanced profiling area. The next example discusses how to create an advanced profiling task. This will including defining an advanced profiling task as well as how to review the results.

Define and Execute an Advanced Profiling Task

Advanced profiling offers several options for profiling. The next steps describe how to create an advanced profiling task and the types of profiling available with advanced profiling.

1. Go to the WORKSPACE HOME tab in your data insight project.

2. Check the file, table, or view for extended profiling.

3. Click on the PROFILE button and choose the ADDRESS, DEPENDENCY, REDUNDANCY, or UNIQUENESS option (explained in more detail below).

4. In the DEFINE PROFILING TASK window, give this task a unique name and set the required options for the profiling task.

5. Click on the SAVE AND RUN NOW button to immediately execute the profiling task or click on the SAVE button to save the task for later execution or scheduling.

The following describes the types of profiling available:

▶ **Address profiling**
Address profiling allows validation against the backend address directories from Data Services' global address cleansing. For any data domain that includes address-relevant information, you can map the corresponding data fields and see a pie chart representation of how many addresses are already correct, how many are wrong but can be automatically corrected in a Data Services-based address cleansing job, and how many are wrong and cannot be corrected automatically.

▶ **Dependency profiling**
Dependency profiling identifies if there are business dependencies between two or more columns; for example, if there is a dependency between the locality name and the region name of an address or between a product name and a product class. With dependency profiling, you can review if a given value in one column only exists when a specific value in another column exists.

▶ **Redundancy profiling**
Redundancy profiling detects missing data that should be multiple tables; for example, expected redundancies between a table with customer data and a table with address data. Redundancy profiling detects where there are customers without addresses and addresses without customers.

▶ **Uniqueness profiling**
Uniqueness profiling detects if a primary key is sufficient to uniquely identify a record or if multiple fields are really needed to identify unique records. For example, in a product database, a primary key might be a product name, but if a uniqueness profile on product_name, product_color, and product_size indicates

that only 95% of records are unique, this means that 5% of products are redundant but have different primary keys.

After executing the advanced profiling task, you can find the results for every table selected for profiling. The next example shows how to view the results.

Reviewing the Advanced Profiling Results

The following steps describe how to see the results of an advanced profiling task:

1. Go to the WORKSPACE HOME tab in your data insight project.

2. Click on the PROFILE RESULT tab.

3. Change the view to ADVANCED.

4. Expand the database connection entry in the tables column. You can click on each profiled column to get to the next detail level showing the results of the advanced data profiling activity.

Figure 6.6 shows the result of advanced profiling.

Figure 6.6 Advanced Profiling Results—Address Profiling with Drill-Down to Automatically Correctable Address Records

Figure 6.6 indicates that most of the addresses are incorrect. The bottom part of the screen shows the addresses that will be valid if corrected. Not shown in the screenshot are the data quality codes that indicate the problem with the data.

When relating this to NeedsEIM, Inc., this graphic identifies that almost 4% of their addresses are not correct according to the official reference data, but most can be automatically corrected using the global address cleanse solution in Data Services. (Chapter 8 covers global address cleanse and other data quality functions.)

6.3   Monitoring and Assessing the Quality of Your Data

For ongoing monitoring and assessment of current data quality, it is essential to implement a solution that provides a repeatable way to apply business rules and requirements to your data assets. Getting permanent insight into the current data quality level as well as identifying early trends and changes enables you to react quickly to potential data quality issues.

Information Steward includes the ability to define *validation rules* that are managed and approved by data analysts, business users, or data stewards. Validation rules represent technical requirements or business rules that are essential for an organization's business execution.

Examples of a centrally defined and reusable validation rule include:

▶ Ensuring that required fields contain values and that those values are valid, such as a postal code that contains a four-digit extension.

▶ Checking to make sure a purchase order contains a valid product.

▶ Ensuring compliance with regulatory requirements or adhering to industry standards, such as having a 9- or 13-digit ISBN number for a book.

A validation rule consists of the following elements:

▶ **Unique name**
Each validation rule needs to have a unique name. Organizations might apply their own naming conventions to categorize or group their rules.

▶ **Description**
The rule description provides more detail about the core definition or content of the validation rule.

▶ **Category**
Each validation rule can be linked to a specific category name that is used for hierarchy, grouping, or use on the *data quality scorecard* setup. (Chapter 9 covers data quality scorecards in detail.)

▶ **Parameters**

A validation rule can have one or multiple input parameters dependent on the complexity of the business rule. If a parameter is used only for filtering or dependency condition checking and should not be assigned a score value, this needs to be configured in the validation rule editor.

▶ **Expression**

The validation rule expression represents the data quality requirements for the parameters. The rule definition editor includes a basic rule editor with a set of predefined validation function (e.g., IS NOT NULL) that allows easy setup of simple rule expressions. Additionally, there is an advanced rule editor with wizard-style support. Text editor capabilities are also an option to create the native scripting for any kind of complex validation rule expression. The transformation of the validation rule expression into the native Data Services scripting language is always shown in a preview window.

▶ **Submit for approval**

Every validation rule needs to be approved by a data steward or business expert before it can be used in enterprise-wide data insight projects. When the initial definition of the validation rule has been saved, the validation rule is in Edit status and can be submitted for approval.

The elements of a validation rule support an important Information Steward concept: Validation rules should represent an organization's requirements independent of the data assets to which they are applied. For example, a validation rule stating that all product names must follow a certain nomenclature is an organizational requirement. This rule can be applied to products and services of different types across different application systems. Another example is that all email fields cannot be null. This could be applied to customers, suppliers, contact persons,and so on.

After the responsible person approves the validation rules, the next step is to bind or link the generic validation rules to one or multiple data objects within the organization. Then the validation rules are executed based on the defined bindings on the data sources to calculate the individual quality score values.

In this section, you will learn how to define validation rules that meet business requirements for data quality. You will also learn how to link those roles to specific data sources (a term called *binding* in Information Steward) and how to execute the validation rules and view the results.

6.3.1   Defining Validation Rules Representing Business Requirements

Validation rules are the essential and central component for the ongoing monitoring and assessment of the data quality level in an organization. The sources for the validation rule expressions are manifold, and some of the examples discussed here will explain the two general ways of creating and defining a new validation rule. We will demonstrate how validation rules can be created either directly from the data profiling results based on the findings of the statistical analysis of the existing data assets, or from scratch, directly in the rules editor. Creating validation rules directly in the rules editor is important for rules based on external regulative requirements, common industry standards, or internal company policies. You will also learn how to test a validation rule.

Setting Up Validation Rules Based on Data Profiling Results

As discussed in Section 6.2, profiling results are a valuable source for interactively identifying outliers or data quality issues. This insight can then be used to set up the validation rules for ongoing data quality assessment. You can create validation rules directly from the data profiling results panel by following the steps below:

1. Figure 6.5 showed the results of a basic data profiling task. To create a validation rule, click on a hyperlinked number (e.g., the null percentage number).

2. Click on the CREATE RULE button.

3. In the validation RULE EDITOR, a new rule is created, including context-relevant information such as the input parameter $COLOR, the expression IS NOT NULL, and so on. This is shown in Figure 6.7.

4. Add the unique validation rule name, the data quality dimension, and the validation rule description. (Data quality dimensions will be discussed in Chapter 9.)

5. Save the rule after you have defined the expression and click on the VALIDATE button to validate the expression syntax.

In the example validation rule shown in Figure 6.7, notice that the rule is about the color; it should not be null. However, at this point, the rule is not tied to any specific application or table. This enables the rules to be based on business requirements and later be technically bound to the specific data element(s) for the rule.

By building the rule from the data profiling results, you can immediately transfer data profiling findings into potential data validation rules for ongoing data quality monitoring.

Figure 6.7 Example Validation Rule

Returning to the example of NeedsEIM, Inc., they have identified in the initial data profiling activity that the EMAIL_ADDRESS field is empty for some of their suppliers. From the PROFILING RESULT tab, they click on the hyperlinked number of null percentage values and then choose CREATE RULE to directly open the rule editor window that already includes the prepopulated name, description, parameter, and expression information.

Up to this point we have discussed the creation of validation rules based on data profiling results. Rules can also be created separately from the profiling results; for example, when creating a rule to enforce an industry format for an ISBN number. The steps are the same as described above; the only difference is that no data profiling is done before creating the validation rule, so you must provide parameters for the rule. Figure 6.8 shows the rules overview, where you can create a new rule or edit an existing rule separately from the profiling results.

Figure 6.8 Rule Overview

Creating a Validation Rule Directly in the Rule Editor

The following steps describe how to create a validation rule directly in the rule editor. This is required for industry rules or external policies you need to enforce in the data.

1. Go to the RULES tab in the DATA INSIGHT project tab. (Refer back to Figure 6.8.)
2. Click on the NEW button to open the rule editor.
3. Enter the name, quality dimension, and description information for the new validation rule. It will look like Figure 6.7.
4. Click on the ADD PARAMETER hyperlink to add a new parameter to the rule, define the parameter type, and add a description. Deselect the score box if the calculated score for a rule should not be attached to this parameter.
5. Create the rule expression based on the parameters defined. You can either use functions on the list of predefined functions (such as IS NOT NULL) for simple rule expressions or click on ADVANCED EDITOR to open a wizard-style editor, where you can define the expressions in a script language style.
6. Save the rule after you have defined the expression and click on the VALIDATE button to validate the expression syntax.

Testing a Validation Rule

During the definition of a validation rule, it is important to validate and test the correctness of the validation rule expression. This is especially true for complex validation rules. After saving a validation rule you can test the rule by executing the following steps:

1. Click on the TEST button in the RULE EDITOR window to open the TEST RULE window. (Shown in Figure 6.9.)
2. Each rule is represented as a column. You can add multiple test records in the TEST RULE window. If you want to test <Null> or <Blank> as test data, you can choose them from the dropdown in the field.
3. Click on the TEST button to execute the test run immediately.
4. The TEST RULE window shows the status (passed, failed, or filtered) of the entered samples of the test run.
5. Close the TEST RULE window by clicking on the CLOSE button.

Figure 6.9 Testing a Validation Rule

It is important to mention that the test values and status are stored with the validation rule, so that they are available for later testing after a validation rule update.

6.3.2 Binding Rules to Data Sources for Data Quality Assessment

In an enterprise, a validation rule is defined, managed, approved, and stored in the central repository. From this central repository, a validation rule is reused and linked in multiple projects and to multiple data sources. The linking of the rule to a data source is called *binding*. There are two ways to bind validation rules to data sources, both of which we describe next.

Manual Rule Binding

Manual rule binding is done for validation rules that have been defined from scratch and stored in the general RULES tab, or for rules where an existing rule is bound to an additional table. To manually bind a generic validation rule to a data source and its columns, execute the following steps:

1. Go to the RULES tab in the data insight project tab.

2. Highlight the rule that you want to bind to a table or a file and click on the BIND button to open the Rule Binding Editor.

3. Select the SOURCE dropdown list to choose the database table, view, or file to which you want to bind the rule. (Shown in Figure 6.10.)

4. Information Steward tries automatically to bind the similar columns form the source you have selected to the rule parameter. Check the suggestion and change the column name if necessary by choosing the right column name from the dropdown box.

5. A data quality score is between 0 and 10. You can determine what the thresholds are for green, yellow, and red indicators. For example, you could say everything below 5 is red. Here you can define the low and high threshold marks. The thresholds are used for showing traffic light color coding. Move the sliders to the values you want.

6. Save your new rule binding by clicking on the SAVE AND CLOSE button.

7. Review your new rule binding in the RULES tab.

Figure 6.10   Binding a Validation rule to a Data Source

Notice in Figure 6.10 that the rule is bound to a specific source; in this case, the sales application database and the product table. The column is selected for the variable $COLOR.

Rule Binding Based on Data Profiling Results

If a validation rule is defined directly from the data profiling result area and saved and closed, the rule is automatically bound to the new validation rule based on the context of the data profiling results. A status window is shown where you just need to confirm that it should be automatically bound. You can check the automatic binding by going to the RULES tab in your data insight project.

Returning to NeedsEIM, Inc., the data stewards centrally define a validation rule that validates the format of an email address field: "An email address needs to have a specific pattern." This validation rule is centrally stored and approved by the responsible data steward. As multiple data domains such as customer, supplier, and employees are stored with email address fields in the master database system, the validation rule is bound to the corresponding EMAIL_ADDRESS field in each of the three data sources.

6.3.3 Executing Rule Tasks and Viewing Results

In the previous section we described how the validation rules are created and how they are bound to the individual data sources. This represents the important task of transferring business knowledge and expertise as well as business requirements into technical rules and linking them to different data assets. The next step is to apply those validation rules to existing data and calculate the quality scores that represent how many records of a data source are compliant with or violate a specific validation rule.

Rule tasks can be executed interactively by a user or automatically executed using an integrated scheduler or an external scheduler. This supports the easy execution of the same set of validation rules on the same data sources over time to get historical trend information about data quality-level changes.

Next, we describe how to execute a rule task. Specifically, we explain how to execute a rule task, how to create and view a table-based data quality dashboard based on the rule, and how to create a rules data quality dashboard.

Executing a Rule Task

To calculate quality scores immediately or to create a rule task, execute the following steps:

1. Go to the WORKSPACE HOME tab in your data insight project.

2. Click on the RULE RESULT tab.

3. Check the file, table, or view for which you want to calculate the score.

4. Click on the CALCULATE SCORE button.

5. Complete the following parameters (shown in Figure 6.11):

   ▶ NAME
   Every rule task is assigned a unique default name, including the current creation date. This name should be changed to your own naming conventions.

   ▶ EMAIL NOTIFICATION
   An email address is used for notification if the score drops below the low threshold.

▶ SAVE ALL FAILED DATA TO

The failed record database allows you to store all failed records in an external database. This enables other external applications to directly access failed record information in their own system and integrate this into data cleansing or data remediation processes.

▶ TASK OPTIONS

Task options include the number of input records that should be used for the rule task execution, as well as for the optional input sampling rate. Additionally, you can set the size of the sample data.

6. When all parameters for the rule task have been defined, you can choose SAVE or SAVE AND RUN NOW.

7. Go to the TASK OVERVIEW tab in your WORKSPACE HOME tab and review the status and the execution of the rule task.

Figure 6.11 Defining a Validation Rule Task

For automatic ongoing measurement of the data quality scores, you can use the internal scheduler of the CMC. All defined task objects have a properties section that includes an option to schedule the execution of the task based on calendar schedules.

After successful execution of a rule task, the rule result panel is automatically updated with the most recent rule results and statistical information. This is shown in Figure 6.12.

Figure 6.12 Validation Rule Score Trend Chart and Failed Record Sample Data

Figure 6.12 shows a *table-based data quality dashboard* based on the customer email address validation rule. Here you can review in tabular form the quality score, the change from the last run, and the number of failed and successfully passed records for all data sources (table, view, or file). You can also drill down into the statistics for the fields in the sources down to the individual rules bound to the fields. Both the data quality score trend and the failed record sample data can be accessed from this scorecard.

Creating and Viewing a Table-Based Data Quality Dashboard

A table-based data quality dashboard is important if you want to get specific insight into the data quality of a specific table. The following steps describe how this is done:

1. Go to the WORKING SET tab in your data insight project and click on the RULE RESULT tab.

2. Expand the flat file location, sales application, or views group to view the individual data sources.

3. Expand the data sources to see the individual columns.

4. Expand the columns to see the bound validation rules.

5. Review the score and further details such as the change from last run and the number of failed and total records.

6. Click on the hyperlinked score value to drill down to individual trend charts and failed record sample data.

7. Click on the SHOW COLUMNS or FILTER CRITERIA button or on the individual headlines for sorting options to format the failed record sample data.

8. Click on the EXPORT TO EXCEL button to save your failed record sample data into a spreadsheet for external processing.

This dashboard supports users who are responsible for technical objects, such as a specific database system or files, and who want to get an insight into the overall data quality level of these technical assets.

Creating a Rules Data Quality Dashboard

In addition to the table-based data quality dashboard, there is also a rules data quality dashboard. The rules data quality dashboard is shown in Figure 6.13. Notice in Figure 6.13 the list of all the rules on the left and the data quality score for a selected rule on the right.

Figure 6.13 Overview of Validation Rules, Bound Data Sources, and Failed Record Sample Data

The rules data quality dashboard enables you to view all rules in a specific data insight project. The user can review in tabular form each defined validation rule and the quality scores for each individual rule binding to the different data sources.

The user can also see the trend of the quality score from the last rule task execution, and information on the low and high threshold definition. For each quality score, the failed record sample data can also be analyzed. This perspective supports users who are responsible for individual validation rules independent of the different data objects they are assigned to and want to gain insight into the data quality level of the different data stores based on their data quality requirements.

A rules data quality dashboard enables you to review the result of a rule execution in a dashboard. The following steps describe how to review the result of a rule execution:

1. Go to the RULE tab in your data insight project.

2. Select one of the validation rules from the rules list.

3. Review the individual binding of the validation rule to multiple data sources, the score, and failed and total record numbers.

4. Click on the SCORE value to drill down to the failed record sample data.

5. Click on the SHOW COLUMNS or FILTER CRITERIA button or on the individual headlines for sorting options to format the failed record sample data.

6. Click on the EXPORT TO EXCEL button to save your failed record sample data into a spreadsheet for external processing.

6.4 Summary

In this chapter you learned how to view, profile, and assess data quality for specific data domains or critical elements of a business process from within Information Steward. Information Steward can be used to support the business case for building a data governance organization, investing in master data management, or implementing additional data management procedures using business process management technologies. And by measuring data quality over time, Information Steward can provide evidence that investments in technologies, processes, and procedures are paying off, or indicate where more investment or adjustment is needed.

Now that you can assess your data, you are ready to start using Data Services to extract, transform, validate, and cleanse your data. In the next chapter you will learn about using Data Services for data integration.

This chapter introduces SAP Data Services as the data foundation for EIM. At its core, SAP Data Services provides a data integration platform to extract, transform, and load data in the enterprise, breaking down silos of information and provisioning information for analytical and operational uses.

7   Introducing SAP Data Services

Chapter 4 introduced SAP Data Services (hereafter Data Services) as the data foundation for EIM. Data Services includes data integration, data quality, and text data processing capabilities. Data Services allows you to integrate, transform, improve, and deliver trusted data to critical business processes across the enterprise for both SAP and non-SAP systems. It provides one development user interface, metadata repository, data connectivity layer, runtime environment, and the management console for administration activities.

In this chapter, we will offer a basic explanation of extraction, transformation, and loading (ETL), highlighting some of the high-level use cases supported by Data Services. The chapter starts by explaining typical data integration scenarios, and then discusses the Data Services architecture. Once you understand the architecture, you will learn about using the Data Services Designer to extract and load various data sources and targets. With this information in hand, you are ready to start creating your first job and learning about both basic and complex transformations, which are key to Data Services. To conclude the chapter, you will learn how to execute and debug a job, expose real-time services, and finally, how Data Services works with SAP HANA. Future chapters will build on the base established in this chapter, as Chapter 8 will cover data quality-specific capabilities, and Chapter 10 will focus on the text data processing capabilities in Data Services.

7.1 Data Integration Scenarios

In a perfect world, you would have a single software application that meets business needs, is easy to use, is fast, and stores all your information—current and past—in a single location. However, we must deal with the fact that most companies have many different software applications, from many different software vendors, which all hold different information from different points in time. This is why data integration is necessary.

NeedsEIM, Inc. introduced in Chapter 1 and Chapter 4, has several issues that can be addressed with the integration capabilities available in Data Services. Here are a few of them:

- **Integration between disparate systems**
  NeedsEIM, Inc. has many different ERP, CRM, and manufacturing systems, resulting in data fragmentation across the enterprise. Moving data between various types of systems can help pull this information together for operational and analytical use cases.

- **Master data management**
  NeedsEIM, Inc. is looking to improve its visibility into supplier spend and reduce the number of suppliers it deals with as well as get more visibility into customer profit and loss (P&L). To do this they need to consolidate all of their supplier and customer master data from their disparate systems into a single repository to understand the current state in order to start taking action. Data Services can help extract this data for cleansing and consolidation of this information into SAP's solutions for managing master data.

- **Data warehousing/analytics**
  NeedsEIM, Inc. is looking to better understand its supplier spend and customer profit and loss. Once they've harmonized their customer and supplier master data, they'll be able to pull in the related supplier invoices and customer P&L information to perform the needed analytics to make improvements in these areas.

- **Data migration/mergers and acquisitions**
  NeedsEIM, Inc. continues to grow its business through acquisition, and thus continuous data migration projects have been ongoing for the last few years to harmonize and move data from the acquired organizations' systems into the NeedsEIM, Inc. systems. SAP Data Migration software, discussed in Chapter 4,

uses Data Services and supports NeedsEIM, Inc.'s requirements for migration due to acquisitions.

The following provides a holistic list of use cases where data integration is commonly applied, including those covered above for NeedsEIM, Inc.:

▶ **Provisioning of data for operational use**

  ▶ Integration of data between applications; for example, upload of new products or sales orders from one system to another.

  ▶ Integration of harmonized master data (such as customer, supplier, and material master data) to provide a consistent view across the enterprise.

  ▶ Migration and conversion of data from legacy systems.

▶ **Provisioning of data for analytical use**

  ▶ Aggregation of data from operational systems and collection over time for business analysis in a data warehouse or SAP HANA.

  ▶ Provisioning of generic services for data, allowing organizations to provide a consistent means for accessing, transforming, and loading data in the enterprise that can be provisioned to various departments as a service.

> **Note**
>
> For some of the issues mentioned above, SAP provides additional comprehensive solutions (not mentioned in the book) that also utilize Data Services; for example, Spend Performance Management and Collaborative E-Care Management. You can find more information about them at *http://www.sap.com*.

7.2   SAP Data Services Platform Architecture

This section covers the basic architecture of Data Services along with the component, services, and user interfaces that make up this application.

Figure 7.1 provides a high-level view of the Data Services architecture. This figure includes closely related components for SAP Information Steward (hereafter Information Steward) and information platform services.

The three major components of the architecture that will be discussed in this section are the user interfaces/clients, the core server components, and the repositories. These discussions will explain what is shown in Figure 7.1.

Figure 7.1 Data Services Architecture

The various components of this architecture can, and are recommended, to be installed in most cases across different physical or virtual machines. This provides an architecture that allows for the most reliable system and the ability to scale as your needs grow.

Let's discuss what each of the major components of Data Services is so you better understand each of the elements of the architecture. We'll start with the user interface components, cover the core server components, and then finish with the repository components.

7.2.1　User Interface Tier

The user interface tier is shown in the top part of Figure 7.1. In the figure it is shown as CMC, DS Mgmt Console, IS UI, and Data Services designer. Each of these will be explained in more detail next.

SAP Data Services Designer

As indicated in Figure 7.1, the Data Services designer is used by the developer. The designer is a thick-client, graphical user interface, which runs on developers' desktop machines and allows them to create the graphical representations of how they want to extract, transform, map, and load data in their organization.

Don't be scared off by the term *developer*. The designer is a very easy to use interface, and in many cases there are analysts in organizations using this tool to do data transformation. However, it is most commonly used in the IT organization, and, as you will see next, Information Steward is the user interface focused on interaction with data management experts (such as data stewards, who may not be technical IT staff).

The designer provides a workspace where users can define the different sources and targets where data is stored. These source and target objects are placed onto a canvas where a data flow can be defined to perform various mappings and transformations to the data. The objects defined in the designer represent metadata that is stored in a repository. The job server uses this metadata definition of the data flow (also shown in Figure 7.1) to execute the data flow that was designed by the developer.

SAP Information Steward User Interface

The Information Steward user interface is depicted in Figure 7.1 as IS UI. Information Steward is a product that uses Data Services as a runtime engine. The user interface is a web-based user interface that is focused on providing various features around information governance and is specifically designed for the data steward or less technical individuals who are data domain experts. There are many different capabilities that are part of the Information Steward solution; we discuss these in Chapters 6 and 9.

SAP Data Services Management Console

The Data Services management console user interface is represented in Figure 7.1 as DS MGMT CONSOLE. The management console is a web-based user interface that provides the majority of the administration capabilities for Data Services, as well as some metadata and reporting capabilities. Notice that it is used by both the business user and IT analyst and the administrator. Below is a summary of capabilities that are part of this user interface:

- **Administration functions**

  - Scheduling, monitoring, and executing batch jobs

  - Configuring, starting, and stopping real-time services

  - Configuring job server, access server, and repository usage

  - Configuring and managing adapters

  - Publishing batch jobs and real-time services as web services

- **Metadata reporting**

  - IMPACT AND LINEAGE ANALYSIS: This functionality provides dependency information between objects within Data Services as well as the related source and target information. It allows a user to see what will be impacted by making a change, as well as where data is coming from and potential transformations applied to that data. (Note: Information Steward, discussed in Chapter 6, provides more comprehensive capabilities in this area.)

  - OPERATIONAL DASHBOARD: This functionality provides a graphical depiction of Data Services job execution statistics over time.

  - AUTO DOCUMENTATION: This functionality provides an easy way to generate documentation for all of the data integration objects created in Data Services. This capability captures critical information about each job from the metadata and provides a comprehensive summary that can easily be put into PDF or Microsoft Word format for easy sharing.

  - VALIDATION DASHBOARD: This functionality provides a graphical dashboard summarizing the quality of data based on validation rules applied within a data flow using the validation transform in Data Services. (Note: The validation transform will be discussed in more detail in Chapter 8.)

  - DATA QUALITY: This functionality generates reports for many of the data quality transformations in Data Services to provide a detailed view of your data's quality during processing.

Central Management Console (CMC)

The Central Management Console (hereafter CMC) is a user interface component of the information platform services that are part of the SAP BusinessObjects Business Intelligence platform. This user interface is where administrators create and maintain users, groups, and their rights for Data Services.

Other User Interfaces

The repository manager allows administrators to create, upgrade, and check versions of Data Services repositories. The server manager allows administrators to add, delete, or edit the configuration of job servers and access servers.

7.2.2   Server Tier

Figure 7.1 shows three categories of server tier components. Above those three components is the information platform services (IPS) bus. This will be explained in the next section, followed by the Data Services tier and repository tiers.

For the three categories of server tier components, discussed next, all are not required. You must always have the information platform services, and you can have both Data Services and Information Steward as additional tiers, or only Data Services. However, if you have Information Steward, then you must always have all three server tier components.

Information Platform Services (IPS) Server Tier

The information platform services (hereafter IPS) components are part of both Data Services and Information Steward. If you are familiar with the SAP BusinessObjects Business Intelligence platform, you will recognize IPS. IPS is a subset of functionality from the platform that is used to provide security and infrastructure capabilities for Data Services. If you are already using the SAP BusinessObjects BI platform (version 4.0 or higher), you can use that installation instead of the IPS component delivered with Data Services.

Data Services uses the Central Management Server (CMS) to manage the users and group security. The CMC user interface is used for configuration of these services.

SAP Data Services Server Tier

The Data Services server tier includes the server components delivered with Data Services for the execution of Data Services capabilities. These components include:

► **Job server**
The job server is responsible for starting the engines that execute the data integration jobs created with the Data Services designer. These engines perform the extraction, transformation, and loading of data in batch processes or process the data provided as part of a service call for real-time jobs that are managed by the access server.

► **Access server**
The access server acts as a message broker when real-time services are used. Various APIs including web services are used to send requests to Data Services, and the access server manages these requests and distributes them to the various engines for each service. The access server is also responsible for scaling up new engines to handle increased loads and distributing those requests across many engines.

► **Administration services**
Administrative services enable Data Services integration with Information Steward, IPS, and SAP NetWeaver Business Warehouse (BW).

Repository Tier

Data Services has a few types of repositories in its architecture that are managed by a relational database and contain tables with predefined system information, user-created objects, copies of source and target metadata, and transformation rules. There are two types of repositories:

► **Local repository**
There is a local repository for each developer using the Data Services designer. Each developer has his own instance of a local repository type to store the objects he creates. Normally there is also one local repository for test efforts and for the production environment.

► **Central repository**
The central repository is an optional repository that is used for more complex multi-user development environments. Its purpose is to act as a master repository for all objects across all developers. It provides a mechanism for locking an object while a developer is working on it as well as history tracking so users can revert to older versions of objects if necessary.

The information platform services repository contains the additional configuration information for all of the services running in the information platform services.

For Data Services, this is the security information about users, groups, and rights to the various Data Services repositories and features in the application.

7.3 SAP Data Services Designer Overview

This section provides a high-level overview of the Data Services designer. You will become familiar with all the major components provided in the designer.

The designer is made up of four major areas, as seen in Figure 7.2.

Figure 7.2 Four Areas in the Data Services Designer

The areas are the PROJECT AREA, WORKSPACE AREA, LOCAL OBJECT LIBRARY, and TOOL PALETTE. Each area is described in Table 7.1.

Area	Description
Project area (❶)	Provides a hierarchical view of selected projects and all objects within those projects (jobs, workflows, data flows, etc.).

Table 7.1 Major Areas of the Data Services Designer

Area	Description
Workspace (❷)	The open area where you drag and drop objects such as sources, targets, and transformations to operate on data.
Local Object Library (❸)	Provides access to objects created and stored in the repository such as jobs, workflows, data flows, and data source and target information. It also provides access to built-in system objects such as transformations.
Tool palette (❹)	Shortcuts on the right-hand side of the screen allow you to quickly add common objects such as data flows and workflows.

Table 7.1 Major Areas of the Data Services Designer (Cont.)

There are many object types in the Data Services designer. We'll cover just a subset of the main objects. You can always refer to the product documentation for far more detail about each available object.

Data Services contains two broad categories of object types:

▶ **Single use objects**
Single use objects are created for use in a job and can only be used in the context of that single job; for example, a script.

▶ **Reusable objects**
Reusable objects are created once and can be reused many times in different jobs. The majority of the objects in Data Services are reusable. This makes it easy to make a change in one place for an object definition and have it take effect in all places where it is used. This significantly reduces the work around standard definitions of rules, mappings, and transformations.

When objects are created in the designer, they are associated with each other in a logical manner, thus creating a hierarchy. Figure 7.3 shows a high-level set of relationships between the objects you can create with the designer. (Note: This is not comprehensive.)

The primary objects are the following:

▶ **Projects**
Projects are objects used to help organize all of the jobs you develop.

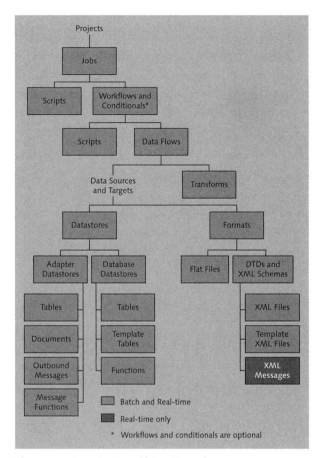

Figure 7.3 Data Services Object Hierarchy

► **Jobs**

Jobs are the one kind of object that is actually executed. It is a container that can contain many workflows, data flows, scripts, and control logic that are executed in serial and/or parallel. There are two types of jobs:

► *Batch jobs* are used to process large volumes of data. Data Services extracts data from one or more source systems and writes it to one or more target systems.

► *Real-time jobs* are used to expose real-time services. Their purpose is to accept requests to process data from other applications that come to Data Services via an API, web service call, or other transport mechanism—such as an SAP IDoc or Java Message Service (JMS), for example.

▶ **Workflow**
A *workflow* is a container where users can define control operations and decision making steps around the execution of data flows. A workflow exists inside a job. A typical use of a workflow in a BI project, for example, would be to control the execution of data flows that load a group of dimension tables and then another workflow to control the loading of fact tables.

▶ **Data flow**
The *data flow* is the work horse of Data Services. This is where developers define which source(s) to extract from, what transformations to perform, and which target(s) to write to.

▶ **Transforms**
Transforms are objects that perform complex operations on data being processed within a data flow. There are four categories of transforms in Data Services: platform transforms (most commonly used), data integrator transforms (usually used for the creation of data marts/warehouses), data quality transforms (for data quality operations), and text data processing transforms (for unstructured text).

▶ **Formats**
Formats describe the structure of a file-based source or target, such as a flat file, XML, COBOL Copybook, Microsoft Excel workbook, unstructured text document, or web log.

▶ **Datastores**
Datastores contain the information needed to access data in a database or application, such as connection information and configuration options. They also contain a copy of the metadata for the datastore to which they refer.

▶ **Functions**
Functions are reusable objects that execute a very specific operation on data. There are several built-in functions as well as the ability to write your own user-defined functions. Functions are discussed in more detail in Section 7.6.

This section provided an overview of the Data Services designer and the major components of the designer. Now you are ready to dive into more details for using the designer.

7.4   Creating Data Sources and Targets

One of the first steps in Data Services is to create connections to the source and target systems. This section describes the connections available as well as how to create a connection.

7.4.1   Connectivity Options for SAP Data Services

Data Services supports many connectivity options for structured and unstructured data. This ranges from SAP applications to databases, to other vendor applications, text files, Microsoft Excel, mainframe, and so on.

▶ **Databases**
SAP Sybase ASE and IQ, SAP HANA, Microsoft SQL Server, Informix, Teradata, ODBC, MySQL, Netezza, HP Neoview, Oracle, IBM DB2

▶ **Applications**
SAP, JD Edwards, Oracle, PeopleSoft, Siebel, Salesforce.com

▶ **Files/transports**
Delimited text, fixed-width text, XML, Cobol Copybooks ANSI 85, Excel, HTTP, JMS, web services (WSDL/SOAP, WS-Security)

▶ **Mainframe**
Attunity, ADABAS, ISAM, VSAM, Enscribe, IMS/DB, RMS

▶ **Unstructured data**
Any text file supported in 31 languages

Detailed information can be found on the SAP Product Availability Matrix at *http://service.sap.com/pam.*

Next you will learn how to create datastores to connect to a relational database as well as how to connect to a file source.

Connecting to a Datastore

Figure 7.4 shows an example of creating a new datastore. In this example a database datastore was chosen, but remember, there are many options, as described above.

Figure 7.4 Creating a Datastore to Connect to an RDBMS

The following steps describe how to create a datastore:

1. In the Local Object Library on the bottom left, click on the DATASTORES tab.

2. Right-click and select NEW.

3. Enter a datastore name. For this example we're using "MyFirstDatastore".

4. Select DATABASE for the DATASTORE TYPE.

5. For the DATABASE TYPE select the dropdown list and notice all the database options. Enter the details for connecting to the database.

Connecting to a File Source

In addition to databases, Data Services also supports connecting to file sources. Figure 7.5 shows the definition of a new file source. After you provide the file name it will show the column headers and data in the file (not shown in Figure 7.5).

Figure 7.5 Creating a File Format Definition

The steps below explain how to connect to a file source.

1. In the Local Object Library on the bottom left, click on the FILE FORMAT tab.

2. Expand the FLAT FILE node.

3. Right-click on FLAT FILE and select NEW.

4. Enter a format name. For this example we are using "MyInputFile".

> **Tip**
>
> If something changes in the structure of your datastore or format definition (such as new columns being added), you will need to change your definition. If your metadata is a datastore, you will need to re-import the metadata.

7.4.2 Connecting to SAP

When connecting to SAP, you have several options: connection to an SAP application such as SAP ERP or SAP CRM, connection to SAP NetWeaver BW, and connection to SAP HANA. Each of these will be described next.

Connecting to SAP ERP

Data Services provides multiple ways to connect to the SAP Business Suite applications for extracting and loading data. Below is a summary of those methods and a brief description of when to use each method:

▶ **Read tables via an ABAP program**
This method uses an ABAP data flow that generates an ABAP program. This should be used when extracting large volumes and performing transformations inside the SAP source (joins, lookups, and so on).

▶ **RFC_READ_TABLE**
This method is used when you simply drag a table from an SAP source into a regular data flow, not an ABAP data flow. Use this method when you are reading a single table and only a few rows are intended to be read.

▶ **RFC and BAPI**
Data Services provides a way to call a BAPI in the SAP system. The purpose of this is to reuse SAP logic already created inside your SAP system to extract

information, instead of reading from a table directly and re-creating the logic in Data Services. This should be used only when retrieving a small number of rows.

▶ **IDoc (Intermediate Document Type)**
IDocs can be received from SAP applications and sent to SAP applications from Data Services. SAP uses IDocs to send messages between applications, commonly for synchronization. Data Services can act like any other SAP system to send and receive these types of messages.

▶ **Extractors**
Extractors are designed for SAP NetWeaver BW to consume data from SAP applications such as SAP ERP. However, Data Services is also able to use them as a source. Extractors are delivered by SAP, but they do not exist for all information in SAP applications. They are tailored for data warehouse use cases and should only be used for large volumes. You can use extractors to easily get the data you want from an SAP system and then apply complex transformations such as data quality to that data.

You can find more information on these different methods in the product documents as well as on the SAP Community Network (SCN).

Connecting to SAP NetWeaver Business Warehouse

Data Services is integrated with SAP NetWeaver BW in many different ways. First, Data Services can be used to extract and load data with SAP NetWeaver BW. Data Services does the extractions and loads by using SAP NetWeaver BW's Open Hub service.

If you want to read from SAP NetWeaver BW first, some configuration is required in the SAP NetWeaver BW application before Data Services can access the information. You must execute the following steps to enable Data Services to read from SAP NetWeaver BW:

1. Configure an SAP NetWeaver BW Open Hub destination. This is essentially a table that acts as an interface between SAP NetWeaver BW and Data Services during extraction.

2. Configure an SAP NetWeaver BW process chain. A process chain is required to execute a SAP NetWeaver BW data transfer program (DTP) that is responsible for populating the Open Hub destination so Data Services can read the data.

3. Create the Data Services data flow. When the datastore is created for the SAP NetWeaver BW source, you'll be able to directly access the Open Hub destination just like a typical RDBMS table and can drag it onto a Data Services data flow as a source.

Figure 7.6 shows an example of how a data flow with SAP NetWeaver BW works.

Figure 7.6 Reading Data from SAP NetWeaver BW

When loading SAP NetWeaver BW, you can use Data Services as an external source to SAP NetWeaver BW. First the InfoSource and DataSource in SAP NetWeaver BW needs to be configured so that it can be loaded via Data Services. Once this is complete, Data Services will see this object, similar to a normal RDBMS table, and can used it as a target within a data flow. More details about these methods can be found in the product documentation or on the SAP Community Network (SCN).

In SAP NetWeaver BW 7.30, users of the SAP NetWeaver BW workbench can directly browse non-SAP sources. Any source Data Services supports can be viewed directly from the workbench. When the user selects the data they want to extract, the SAP NetWeaver BW workbench auto-generates very simple Data Services data flows and jobs that can then be immediately executed. The user of the SAP NetWeaver BW workbench can now easily access data from non-SAP applications using Data Services without having to launch the Data Services designer. Note that transformation logic cannot be defined from the SAP NetWeaver BW workbench. The Data Services designer still needs to be launched to create any complex transformation logic when using this method.

Connecting to SAP HANA

Data Services is delivered as part of SAP HANA and provides the primary data integration capabilities to extract data from various upstream systems into SAP HANA. In this case the SAP HANA database acts as another target for Data Services. Data Services and SAP HANA have been highly optimized to work together providing capabilities for high-performance loading of massive volumes of data. Section 7.10 provides a bit more detail on Data Services and SAP HANA.

7.4.3 Connecting to Hadoop

Chapter 3 discussed big data in terms of enterprise information management, SAP HANA, and Hadoop. As of the writing of this book, SAP is researching the option to support Hadoop in Data Services. A future release of Data Services will support reading from Hadoop (via Hive) as well as loading (via Pig). Coupling the Data Services capabilities of data integration, data quality, and text data processing with Hadoop and SAP HANA will provide the most comprehensive stack for big data processing and analysis.

7.5 Creating Your First Job

It's time to get down to business and create your first job. In this example you are going to create the most basic job and will build on what we learned in the last section, where you will create a file format and a datastore for a relational database. In this section you will create the data flow, add a source, add a query transform, add a target, do some mapping, and create the job.

7.5.1 Create the Data Flow

As previously mentioned, the data flow is the basic object type that does all the work. This data flow will read data from a flat file and load it into a relational database table. The example data flow you will create is shown in Figure 7.7. Execute the following steps to create the data flow.

1. Click on the DATA FLOWS tab in the Local Object Library.

2. Right-click in the white/open area on this tab and select the NEW menu item.

3. Select DATA FLOW.

4. Name the data flow "MyFirstDataflow".

5. Double-click on the data flow you just created to open it in the workspace.

Figure 7.7 Creation of a Data Flow

Now that you've created the data flow, it's time to add your source.

7.5.2   Add a Source to the Data Flow

Adding sources and targets to the data flow connects Data Services to your application, database, file, and so on using the list of connections previously discussed. In this example you will add a flat file as a data source.

Execute the following steps to add a source to a data flow.

1. Click on the FILE FORMAT tab in the Local Object Library.

2. Open the FLAT FILE node in the FILE FORMAT tab.

3. Drag the file format you created previously, MyInputFile, into your data flow in the workspace.

4. Select MAKE SOURCE in the popup dialog.

Now that you have added a source to the data flow, you will add a query transform.

7.5.3   Add a Query Transform to the Data Flow

The query transform has many uses in Data Services. It can be used to filter data, join data from multiple sources, perform functions on the data, and many other things. In this example, we will use the query transform to do basic field mapping to tell Data Services which columns from the flat file to populate in columns of the target relational database table.

Execute the following steps to add a query transform to a data flow:

1. Click on the TRANSFORMS tab in the Local Object Library.

2. Click on the PLATFORM node on this tab to open the list of transforms.

3. Drag the query transform onto the workspace somewhere to the right of the source object you already created.

4. Connect the source object to the query transform on your workspace. (You do this by clicking on the small output tab on the source object and dragging it to the query transform. You will see Data Services create a line connecting the two objects.)

Next you will add a target to the data flow.

7.5.4   Add a Target to the Data Flow

In this example, we have already created a table in the database being used as a target. When we created the datastore we imported the metadata for the tables we wanted to use as sources and targets. Therefore, we will use an existing table as a target. Execute the following steps to add a target to the data flow:

1. Click on the DATASTORE tab in the Local Object Library.

2. Click on the MYFIRSTDATASTORE node to expand it.

3. Click on the TABLES node to expand it.

4. Drag the table MYTARGETTABLE onto the data flow workspace somewhere to the right of the query transform that was added.

5. Select MAKE TARGET in the popup menu.

6. Connect the query transform to the target object.

Now it is time to return to the query transform and do some mapping.

7.5.5   Map the Source Data to the Target by Configuring the Query Transform

Next you need to map the source data to the target data. As you can imagine, the mapping can range from simple to very complex. The following is a simple mapping example:

1. Double-click on the query transform in the data flow workspace.

2. Drag and drop the source field to the desired target field to do a one-to-one mapping of the fields. You will then see the mapping editor shown in Figure 7.8.

Figure 7.8   Query Editor to Map Output Schema Fields to Input Fields

In Figure 7.8 notice that GIVENNAME from the SCHEMA IN MYINPUTFILE is mapped to GIVENNAME in the SCHEMA OUT QUERY. All fields in Figure 7.8 are mapped. This is indicated by the right-pointing arrow in front of each field.

3. Click the SAVE button in the menu bar at the top of the designer to save all your work.

Now that your data flow is created, it is time to finish with the creation of the job itself.

7.5.6   Create the Job and Add the Data Flow to the Job

Remember that the job is the object that is executed and will be the container object for the data flow we just created. The following steps describe how to create a job:

1. Click on the JOBS tab in the Local Object Library.

2. Click on the BATCH JOBS node to expand it.

3. Right-click on the BATCH JOBS node and select NEW.

4. Name the job "MyFirstBatchJob".

5. Double-click on this job to open it in the workspace.

Next, add a data flow:

1. Click on the DATAFLOWS tab in the Local Object Library.

2. Drag the data flow MyFirstDataflow to the job workspace.

3. Save the job by clicking the SAVE button in the toolbar.

That's it! You've completed your first job.

7.6 Basic Transformations Using the Query Transform and Functions

In this section you will learn how to do some basic transformation of data by using the query transform and the built-in functions in Data Services.

Data Services provides many functions for data transformation, and you can even create your own user-defined functions utilizing the built-in scripting language in combination with the built-in functions to perform whatever operations you would like.

Figure 7.9 is a screenshot of the built-in function categories in Data Services. You can see a sampling of some of the functions in the string functions category. The capabilities are broad, including trimming, matching patterns, conversions to ascii, and so on.

Figure 7.9 Function Wizard

In this next example we are going to perform a very basic transformation on the data in our flat file. In the source file there is a GENDER column. This column contains the full word MALE or FEMALE. However, in our target we want the value to be either M or F.

There are multiple ways this could be accomplished in Data Services, such as using some basic `if/then` statements, the `search_replace()` function, or the `lookup_ext()` function to look up the values in a database table. Since the `lookup_ext()` function is very commonly used, we will use that option for this example.

First, we will remove the current mapping for the gender column, and then we will add a lookup function.

To remove the current mapping for the GENDER column, follow these steps:

1. Double-click on the query transform in the data flow MYFIRSTDATAFLOW.

2. Right-click on the GENDER column representing the target's schema on the right side of the screen.

3. Select DELETE from the popup menu to delete the existing GENDER column.

4. In the SCHEMA OUT area, in the upper right-hand part of the screen, right-click on QUERY and select NEW FUNCTION CALL (shown in Figure 7.10).

Figure 7.10 Insert Lookup_ext() Function Call

The following steps add a gender lookup using a database table called GENDER-LOOKUP that was created for this example. See Figure 7.11 for the details of the lookup function.

1. Select the lookup function LOOKUP_EXT().

2. Click on the NEXT button.

3. At the top of the screen, browse to the lookup table by first selecting the data-store you created (called MYFIRSTDATASTORE), and then the GENDERLOOKUP table, which was created for demonstration purposes.

4. Next, in the CONDITION section, select GENDERLONG in the column COLUMN IN LOOKUP TABLE. Select = for the OP.(&) column (shown in Figure 7.11).

5. Enter "MyInputFile.Gender" in the EXPRESSION column. This tells Data Services that you want to select values where the GENDERLONG column is equal to the value of the GENDER column in your input flat file.

6. In the OUTPUT section, select the column in the lookup table that you want to return from the function call. In this case, you want the short version of the gender, so select the GENDERSHORT column under the COLUMN IN LOOKUP TABLE column of this section.

7. In the OUTPUT COLUMN NAME column enter the value "Gender".

8. Click on the FINISH button.

9. Select SAVE to save the data flow.

Figure 7.11 Details of the Gender Lookup Function

Now that you understand how to create a simple job with a query transform, we will introduce a few of the complex transforms.

7.7 Overview of Complex Transformations

Many other transformations are provided as part of Data Services. Many of them will be covered in detail in other sections of this book. This section provides a high-level description of some of the most commonly used platform transforms and the data integrator transforms.

7.7.1 Platform Transformations

Platform transformations are core to Data Services. This means that regardless of your scenario or use of Data Services, these are transforms that can always be used and apply to wide variety of data transformation requirements. The platform transformations include:

▶ **Query**
The query transform is the most commonly used transform in Data Services and provides several capabilities. The most common use is to express operations on data similar to a SQL statement for data stored in a database, but at a higher level of abstraction; for example, operations such as joins, ORDER-BY, and GROUP-BY. These operations are automatically converted by the Data Services optimizer at runtime to generate the proper SQL (if RDBMS) based on the sources. If sources other than an RDBMS are used, such as a file or an application interface, these operations may still be "pushed-down" to the source, or the data may be extracted and the operations performed in the Data Services engine.

Other common use cases include mapping data between different sets of fields, using functions to manipulate a column of data, manipulating hierarchical schemas such as XML, or calling out to a web service.

▶ **Case**
Case allows the user to distribute rows of data down different branches in a data flow. Case or decision logic to control the branching of rows is controlled by defining expressions in an expression table in the transform. For example, if you want to select only a subset of the rows you're processing to insert into a table, and the rest go to a flat file, you can use case to write the expression to identify those rows and route them accordingly.

275

► **SQL**

SQL allows a user to explicitly define a specific SQL statement to be executed and feed rows into a data flow as a source. This transform should only be used if for some reason complex operations cannot easily be accomplished using typical query transforms and datastore tables.

► **Merge**

Merge combines incoming rows with the transform from multiple branches or sources in a data flow, producing a single output dataset with the same schema as the input schemas; for example, merging customer information from two legacy systems. (Note: The input schemas must be normalized using the query transform to ensure that the schemas are identical prior to using merge.)

► **Map_Operation**

Data Services uses what is called an op-code to control the type of operation that should be done for each row when it is being pushed into a particular target. For example, when loading into an RDBMS, the op-code associated with each row of data is used by the loader to determine if a row should be inserted, updated, or deleted from the target. Some transforms automatically manipulate this hidden attribute, and in this case the Map_Operation transform can be used to explicitly set the op-code for the rows that pass through it.

► **Row_Generation**

Row_Generation is used to generate rows in a data flow. You can control how many rows will be generated. This transform is used for complex schema generation (such as XML) and to generate rows for creating time dimensions within a data warehouse.

► **Validation**

The validation transform enables you to define data validation rules and filter out rows with data that follow data validation standards. This is covered in Chapter 8.

► **User defined**

If Data Services doesn't provide a function or transformation that you need, you can create your own. The user-defined transform allows you to extend Data Services with custom transforms to perform any kind of transformation you need. This transform allows you to define custom input fields and output fields for mapping data in and out of the transform. The actual transformation logic is written using the Python scripting language, which is embedded in this transformation. You can create your own named transformation configurations (combination of field definitions and Python scripts) so other users can easily reuse your transform configuration in many different data flows.

7.7.2 Data Integrator Transforms

The group of transformations referred to as the data integrator transforms perform several operations. Many of them are very commonly used for creating data warehouses and others are used to manipulate data and enhance performance.

The three transforms that we will discuss are commonly used to easily manage the concept of slowly changing dimensions (SCDs) when building a star schema. Let's briefly discuss what we mean by this before jumping into the transform details. In a star schema there are dimension and fact tables. The dimension tables typically hold master data entities such as customers or products. When you are loading this type of information, there may be changes to the data, such as a customer moving to a new address or attributes of a product changing over time.

When this happens, you have to decide if you want to maintain the history of those changes over time (depending on whether they are important to the usefulness of your data). There are generally three basic ways of dealing with this, and they are referred to as type 1, 2, and 3 slowly changing dimensions:

▶ **Type 1 — no preservation of history**
Existing rows for a customer, for example, are overwritten with new information.

▶ **Type 2 — unlimited history preservation**
New rows are generated to represent the attributes of an entity at any given time. A surrogate key is used to reference the correct representation of the entity in other tables at any given time.

▶ **Type 3 — limited history preservation**
Typically only the current values and the last set of values for a given set of attributes are maintained. Columns instead of rows are used to store the prior value(s), and an effective date is used to signify when the change in values occurred.

Let's look at how Data Services makes it easy to handle history preservation. Three transforms are used in conjunction to accomplish this. In the examples below, the input table contains the new data coming through Data Services and being loaded into a data warehouse. The comparison table holds the existing data. The output table contains the output from the transformations based on the input table, comparison table, and transformation logic to preserve history.

The op-code column is the attribute for each row that Data Services generates in order for the loader in the data flow to know what it should do with the row, such as INSERT, UPDATE, or DELETE from the comparison table.

The three transforms used to accomplish this are table comparison, history preservation, and key generation.

Table Comparison

The table comparison transform compares the specified columns in the input with the comparison table to see if there are changes in the data (user defined). If there are, it flags the row with an op-code to update the existing row instead of inserting a new row by default. This transform can be used by itself in situations where history is not preserved.

In Figure 7.12, since the same customer was detected (by ID) but the address has changed, Joe and Sid are flagged for UPDATE, and Elvis is completely new, so he will be flagged for INSERT.

Figure 7.12 Table Comparison Output Results

History Preserving

When you want to preserve history, use this transform in conjunction with the table comparison transform. This ensures that the changed rows are inserted rather than updated to ensure tracking of all historical changes.

In Figure 7.13, we want to ensure that we track the history of changed addresses but not changes in names. Row IDs 10 and 20 will be converted from UPDATE to INSERT to preserve the history of the address change. But row 30 has only a change in name and so will remain an UPDATE since we do not track this type of history.

Input (from Table_Comparison):

ID	Name	Address	Op Code
10	Joe	11 Rehab Street	Update
20	Sid	13 Cadillac Dr.	Update
30	Charles	15 Yukon Lane	Update
50	Elvis	Graceland, Memphis	Insert

Output:

ID	Name	Address	Op Code
10	Joe	11 Rehab Street	Insert
20	Sid	13 Cadillac Dr.	Insert
30	Charles	15 Yukon Lane	Update
50	Elvis	Graceland, Memphis	Insert

Comparison table:

ID	Name	Address	Op Code
10	Joe	12 Halfway House	Normal
20	Sid	13 Deadhad Road	Normal
30	Charlie	15 Yukon Lane	Normal
40	Dolly	Goldrush Saloon	Normal

Figure 7.13 History Preserving Transform Output

Key Generation

This transform can be used following the history preserving transform to generate sequential key values for new rows, starting from the maximum existing key value in the target table where the INSERTs and UPDATEs are happening.

Figure 7.14 shows what a completed data flow may look like using these transformations together to find out which rows have changed, set up the INSERT and UPDATE operations to properly maintain history, and generate key values for any new rows.

Figure 7.14 Complete Slowly Changing Dimensions Data Flow Example

279

In addition to these, other transforms include date generation, effective date, flattening, pivot, and several others. For more information on transforms, see the online help at *http://help.sap.com*.

7.8   Executing and Debugging Your Job

Once a job is set up, it can be executed in many different ways, from batch to real-time to scheduled to ad-hoc. Jobs can be executed from the designer, management console, from the command line using a script, or from a web service. In the designer a job can be executed in debug mode.

The debugging capabilities allow you to set breakpoints anywhere in a data flow. When the job is executed in debug mode, the data flow stops running when the first row hits the breakpoint location (some point between transformations). The user is then able to click on a magnifying glass on any line between transforms to view the data that has travelled through that path. Data Services allows users to view the data in any two paths at a time so they can compare the data in those two points in a data flow. This is shown in Figure 7.15.

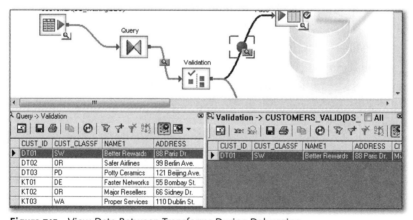

Figure 7.15   View Data Between Transforms During Debugging

Notice in Figure 7.15 that you see the data after the query step and prior to the validation step on the left side of the screenshot. On the right side is the first record after the validation step.

Breakpoints can be configured to be conditional. So instead of the breakpoint causing the execution to pause when the first row hits that point in the data flow, you can configure conditions. Only when a condition is met will the execution stop, and you can examine the data within the data flow. Figure 7.16 shows a conditional breakpoint.

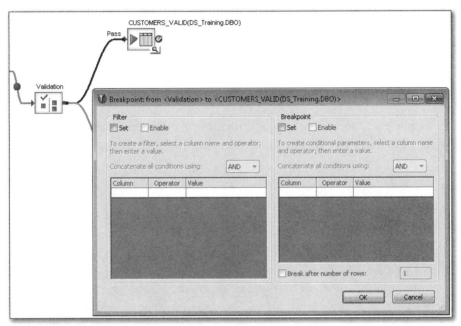

Figure 7.16 Set Up Conditional Breakpoints and Filters

In Figure 7.16, notice the option to filter based on a column, operator, and value.

For more information on debugging and administration, see the administrators guide available at *http://help.sap.com*. At the help site follow the menu path SAP BusinessObjects • Enterprise Information Management • Data Services.

7.9 Exposing a Real-Time Service

Data Services provides application programming interfaces (APIs) that allow many operations to be performed by other applications through the integration of these APIs. Usually, developers use the web service methodology to integrate with Data Services, but Java and C++ APIs are also provided for some of the more performance-intensive operations. The web service interface has many operations to perform activities, such as execute a batch job and retrieve operational metadata, logs, and current status for an executing batch job, as well as transactional integration and transforming of data.

This section discusses a use case that exposes a real-time service as a web service so that data transformations can be performed as a service. Other applications in the enterprise can then leverage these services. A common use case for this is data cleansing as a service. Many organizations expose services to perform data validation for master data; for example, address cleansing. Others may expose a service to perform matching against their master data to ensure that they are preventing duplicates.

Next we explain how to create a real-time job and a real-time service and expose the new service as a web service to be called from other applications.

7.9.1 Create a Real-Time Job

The first step is to create a job that is capable of being called as a service such that the consuming application is able to pass data to Data Services and Data Services is able to return data to the application. To do this, Data Services allows you to define an XML message source and an XML message target. These source and target objects are used in data flows that will be exposed as a real-time job. Whereas in batch jobs you typically use a database or file as the source and target, here you define an XML message structure.

A schema defines how the XML message structure should look, and must be defined first. The schema definition will be discussed next, followed by the data flow and the job.

Create a Schema

First go to the object library and the FORMATS tab. From here you can create schemas. This is done by defining a schema name and then importing an XML schema definition (XSD or DTD) that defines the structure. Figure 7.17 shows an example imported schema.

> **Notes for Creating Schemas**
>
> You should create a separate schema definition for your source and your target. Each should have its own unique namespace. Our recommendation is to always define a default namespace, target namespace, and specify the attributes *elementFormDefault* and *attributeFormDefault* for your schema.

Also, if you use the option in a query transform to create an XML schema, it will not automatically add a namespace and the above attributes, so you will need to manually add them to the XML schema file generated before importing the new schema into the designer.

Figure 7.17 Example of XML Schema Definitions

Notice in Figure 7.17 that XML schemas are another format type available in the Local Object Library. Next we describe the creation of the data flow.

Create a Data Flow

The next step is to create a data flow using the schemas: Simply drag the schema onto the designer as your XML message source and XML message target. From there the process is the same as creating any other data flow. Drag the desired transformations and perform the mappings. Figure 7.18 shows an example job created using XML schemas a source and target.

Figure 7.18 Example Data Flow for a Real-Time Job Using XML Schema Source/Target

Once this is done, you just need to create the job.

Create the Job

The final step is to create the job. Go to the Local Object Library and create a new real-time job. You can use the steps described in Section 7.5.6 for creating batch jobs, but select REAL-TIME. Then add the data flow you just created. It's that simple.

7.9.2 Create a Real-Time Service

Once you have completed the creation of a real-time job, it is the administrator's responsibility to expose this real-time job as a real-time service. A real-time service is an abstraction layer between the consuming applications and the Data Services job. Most organizations use naming conventions for the objects in their Data Services repository, and this process allows you to create a user-friendly name for the service instead of the job name.

The real-time service construct also allows the administrator to define settings to help ensure the quality of service and scale the solution. It's at this point that the administrator determines which job server instances the service will be provisioned on and determines settings such as request/response time-outs and how many service providers are required to handle typical loads and how to scale up automatically when peak loads occur.

To create the real-time service, execute the following steps, shown in Figure 7.19:

1. Log in to the management console.

2. Click on the ADMINISTRATOR icon.

3. Open the following tree: REAL-TIME • <ACCESS SERVER HOST:PORT> • REAL-TIME SERVICES.

4. Select the REAL-TIME SERVICES CONFIGURATION tab.

5. Click on the ADD button.

Figure 7.19 Select Configuration Tab to Create a New Real-Time Service

6. Set the service name.

7. Click on the BROWSE JOBS button to select a job to associate this service with.

8. Click on the hyperlink for the real-time job you created.

9. Click on the ADD button to add a job server as your service provider.

10. Click on the APPLY button (see Figure 7.20).

11. Click on the REAL-TIME SERVICES status tab at the top to view the list of available real-time services, which should include the new service just added.

12. Select the checkbox next to the real-time service you just created.

13. Click on the START button to start the service on the assigned job servers.

Figure 7.20 Detailed Configuration of a Real-Time Service

Now that you have a real-time service you can call this service using the Java or C++ Message Client libraries provided with Data Services. If you want to use web services instead of the Java or C++ APIs, see Section 7.9.3. To get more information about these please refer to the *Data Services Integrator's Guide* in the product documentation available at *http://help.sap.com*.

7.9.3 Expose the Real-Time Service as a Web Service

The final step is to expose the real-time service via the web service interface. Data Services supports the WSDL/SOAP standards for the web service interface. To expose this real-time service via a web service, execute the following steps:

1. After selecting the ADMINISTRATOR icon when logging in, select the WEB SERVICES hyperlink in the tree on the left-hand side.

2. Select the WEB SERVICES CONFIGURATION tab.

3. In the dropdown box, select ADD REAL-TIME SERVICE.

4. Click on the APPLY button.

5. Select the checkbox next to the real-time service you just created above.

6. Click on the ADD button.

7. Click on the WEB SERVICES hyperlink in the tree once again (or the bread crumb trail at the top of the page) to go back to the list of operations exposed as a web service.

8. You should see your new service in the list of web service operations.

9. Selecting the VIEW WSDL button launches a web browser with the WSDL file that a software developer can use to consume the web service. It contains all the metadata, including the schema for the source/target XML messages for the real-time job.

Figure 7.21 shows some examples of real-time services exposed as web service operations.

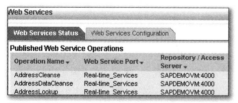

Figure 7.21 Web Service Listing of User-Defined Real-Time Services

A developer can now take the URL to the WSDL and import it into any development application to consume the web service for data transformation. There are two ways that the web service can be executed. The first is by an explicit web service operation named after the real-time service name defined during the creation of the service. With this method, the XML schemas are available in the WSDL so that the consuming application can more intelligently create code to automatically serialize and de-serialize the input XML message and output XML message. This brings a lot of simplicity to the consuming developer, as well as other tools such SAP NetWeaver Process Integration. Since the schemas are known, they can provide some automation.

The other method is to use the web service method `Run_Realtime_Service`. This method is more dynamic in the sense that you can use this one operation to execute any real-time service. The parameters for this operation are simply the name of the service, as defined when creating the service, and the XML string for the input conforming to the XML schema imported into the data flow.

7.10   SAP Data Services and SAP HANA

SAP HANA was introduced in Chapter 3 and discussed earlier as another source or target for Data Services. SAP HANA provides a flexible, data-source-agnostic, multipurpose appliance that has many deployment options. For example, customers can directly analyze large volumes of SAP ERP, SAP NetWeaver BW, or non-SAP data in "real real-time" without having to create any form of materialized views. This is possible because the software intelligently leverages the native multicore support and massively parallel processing capability of the appliance to provide a data–source-agnostic high-performance analytical engine.

Figure 7.22 was shown in Chapter 3 but now that you know much more about Data Services, it is worth showing again here.

Figure 7.22   Data Services and SAP HANA Example Architecture

Let's explore a very basic use case of SAP HANA and Data Services. Let's say you have information in your SAP ERP system and you want to analyze that information in SAP HANA. Maybe the information is your daily sales information so that you can quickly present the daily sales results to your executive team.

The steps to create and execute a simple Data Services job with a one-to-one transfer of data from the SAP ERP system to SAP HANA would include the following steps:

1. Create a new batch job in Data Services.

2. Create a new data flow containing the source table from the SAP ERP system, a query object with a basic one-to-one mapping, and the target table that already exists in HANA.

3. Execute the newly created Data Services job and preview the records with the SAP HANA studio.

Data Services is continually evolving, and you can expect continued updates to the user interface and continued improvements with native connectivity to other SAP applications.

7.11   Summary

In this chapter we started off discussing the different use cases for data integration, from data migration to business intelligence to master data management. Data Services provides a multitier architecture with different user interfaces for the different roles in the enterprise that may interact with this solution during data governance activities.

We covered the different user interfaces, with a primary focus on the Data Services designer for the technical user. You learned that there are many objects a developer can use to access data, transform that data, and load it into its ultimate target. You learned in detail how to create a job that extracted data from a flat file, performed a basic transformation (data lookup), and loaded that data into an RDBMS. Data Services is a powerful tool that not only provides batch processing capabilities, but also provides a way to expose data transformation as a web service to support your service-oriented architecture (SOA).

Data Services provides SAP's data management platform and supports many solutions from SAP. The next chapter will discuss the data quality capabilities within Data Services.

This chapter provides a practical example of the data quality capabilities included in SAP's solutions for EIM.

8   Managing Data Quality with SAP Data Services

Typically the focus of data quality issues is on core data entities such as materials, products, customers, business partners, and employees. These projects then extend to entities such as financial data and accounting objects. Business processes revolve around these entities, and transactional and historical information is related to them. Problems start with inaccurate information about these entities, such as missing or incorrect contact information for your customers or business partners, and problems compound when duplicate entities enter the picture. Ultimately, it becomes difficult to get a consolidated view of the data—how many customers you have, which products the customer owns, which products come from which suppliers, and so on—as the data quality problems continue to grow.

The data quality process takes action to guarantee clean and accurate data by automatically correcting your data based on reference data and data cleansing rules, enhancing your data with additional attributes and information, and finding duplicates and merging your records into one consolidated, best record. Figure 8.1 shows the data quality wheel that will be a guide for you throughout this chapter.

The goal of data quality is to have a single version of the truth. Whether performing a transactional or bulk data load into an SAP Customer Relationship Management (CRM) system, master data management, or an enterprise data warehouse, you want to have a consolidated view of the customer. Because most organizations put the customer first, we will as well, and focus on using data quality to create a single customer view throughout this chapter, with some content later that explains how data quality can be adapted to other domain types.

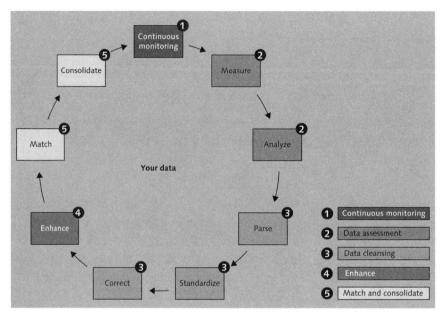

Figure 8.1 Data Quality Wheel

Tip

Before reading this chapter, please read Chapter 7. Chapter 7 introduces the basics of SAP Data Services (hereafter referred to as Data Services), including data flows and transforms, which are explained in more detail in this chapter.

In this chapter, we will explain how to maintain data quality using *transforms* in Data Services. The chapter will start with a discussion of data cleansing in Section 8.1. Next we discuss data enrichment (Section 8.2), which is what happens to data once it is cleansed. After that we discuss data matching (Section 8.3), which detects duplicates and can consolidate data records. These first three sections will walk you through each major step required to create a data flow, an example of which is shown in Figure 8.2. This example shows a data quality data flow created in Data Services using the transforms specific to data quality, including the *address cleanse*, *data cleanse* and *match* transforms, which will also be explained in these first three sections.

We will refer back to Figure 8.2 as we look at each transform in detail, so you might want to bookmark this page.

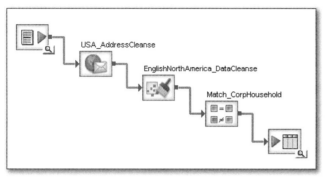

Figure 8.2 Example Data Quality Data Flow in Data Services

Finally, in the last section we will discuss other data quality capabilities; for example, embedding data quality capabilities inside SAP applications, data quality blueprints for getting started quickly with data quality, and extending data quality to be used for a variety of data types.

> **Note**
>
> For a complete list of data quality transforms, see Appendix A. (All appendices are available for download from the book's page at *www.sap-press.com*.)

8.1 Data Cleansing

General data cleansing starts with the *base transform*, which is used to configure a custom data cleanse transform. The base transform for general data cleansing capabilities is called the *data cleanse transform*. There are also several *sample data cleanse transform configurations* of the data cleanse transform shipped with Data Services; for example, EnglighNorthAmerica_DataCleanse, which is pre-configured to cleanse name, title, firm, date, email, and phone data using English-based data quality rules.

This section also discusses the address cleanse transform for more specialized address cleansing capabilities. Two base transforms are available for address cleansing, the *global address cleanse transform* and the *USA regulatory address cleanse transform*. In addition to the base transforms, there are several sample configurations, including the USA_AddressCleanse configured to cleanse address data in the United States (in a nonregulatory mode). Throughout this chapter, we will not be referring to specific base or custom transform configurations, but instead referring more generally to the data cleanse and address cleanse transforms.

Let's get started with cleansing data for NeedsEIM, Inc. using the first two transforms shown in Figure 8.2: the address cleanse and data cleanse transforms. The data cleansing process can be broken down into three steps: parsing, standardization, and correction. Validation is a fourth, optional step that is used to validate the data, and can be done before or after the core cleansing steps. Each of these will be examined closely in its own section.

8.1.1 Data Parsing

As the initial step, data parsing identifies and isolates data elements in data structures. Often, multiple data elements are collected and stored in a database grouped into single fields. Parsing identifies individual data elements and breaks them down into their component parts. It rearranges data elements in a single field or moves multiple data elements from a single data field to multiple discrete fields. Parsing is vital to the data cleansing effort, as it provides information about the type of data in each field, used later when correcting data as well as matching records. Figure 8.3 shows an example of data parsing with the input record and the output record after the data has been parsed.

Input Record	Output Record	
Mr. Dan R. Smith Jr. CPA Account Mgr. Jones Inc. Dept. of Accounting PO BOX 567 Biron, WI 5594	Prename	Mr.
	First Name	Dan
	Middle Name	R.
	Last Name	Smith
	Maturity Postname	Jr.
	Honorary Postname	CPA
	Title	Account Mgr.
	Firm	Jones Inc.
	Department	Dept. of Accounting
	Locality	Biron
	Region	WI
	Primary Number	567
	Postal Code	5594

Figure 8.3 Data Parsing Example

To get started with data parsing, you must first understand the makeup and format of the data in your source systems. Profiling can be very helpful in this process of getting to know your data (discussed in detail in Chapter 6) in terms of how the data is fielded, formatted, and populated. Figure 8.4 shows an example of how data is broken down for parsing.

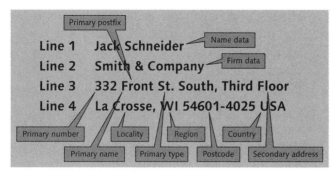

Figure 8.4 Basic Name and Address Components

Focusing on name and address information, Figure 8.4 highlights the basic data components, including:

▸ **Name line (lines 1–2)**

  ▸ Name: the contact name

  ▸ Firm: the company, business, or organization name

▸ **Address line components (line 3)**

  ▸ Primary range: the premises or street number (e.g., 332)

  ▸ Primary name: the street description, such as Front or Main

  ▸ Primary type: the abbreviated or nonabbreviated type of primary name, such as such as Street (St.) or Avenue (Ave.)

  ▸ Primary postfix: the abbreviated or nonabbreviated directional, such as south (S) or northwest (NW)

  ▸ Secondary address: the floor (e.g., third floor), unit, stairwell, or wing data

▸ **Last line components (line 4)**

  ▸ Locality: the city, town, or suburb, such as La Crosse or Chicago

  ▸ Region: the state (e.g., WI), province, territory, or region

  ▸ Postcode: the postal code, including primary (e.g., 54601) and secondary (e.g., 4025) postal codes

  ▸ Country: the country name, such as USA or Germany

These data components can be represented in a discrete, multiline, or multiline hybrid format. With a discrete format, data elements appear in the same field arrangement from record to record, meaning that a locality field will always contain city data, and a postcode field will always contain postcode data. In a multiline format, data is not consistently located in the same arrangement in all records. That is, data items "float" among fields, or data components may appear in different fields from one record to another. Multiline hybrid is a format that includes a combination of both discretely fielded and multiline formatted data in the same record. Figure 8.5 is an example of the discrete format.

Field	Record 1	Record 2	Record 3
Firm			Dupong S.A.
Address1	MikroElektronik GmbH	Nybroveg 120	225 rue de Bragance
Locality1	Baumschulgasse 25	Lyngby	Luxembourg
Region1	Weinheim		
Postcode	69469	2800	1449
Country	Germany	Denmark	Luxembourg

Figure 8.5 Discrete Format

Figure 8.6 shows an example of the multiline format. In this figure notice that both the first and last name are in a multiline field. Also notice the difference of use for multiline4. For record 1 it has an address, and for record 3 it has the name of a company.

Field	Record 1	Record 2	Record 3
Multiline1	Lance Robinson		Peter Grant
Multiline2	Information Services Plc	Gran Via de Carles S.A.	
Multiline3	Cornwall House	Ibarra Campilo	
Multiline4	56 Henley Road		United Car Rental Ltd.
Multiline5		48010 Bilbao	
Multiline6	London		
Multiline7	NW2Y 5DM		3150 S. Larkin Rd. Suite 10
Multiline8			Etobicoke, ON M9C4T9
Multiline9	United Kingdom	Spain	Canada

Figure 8.6 Multiline Format

Figure 8.7 shows an example of the hybrid multiline format.

Field	Record 1	Record 2	Record 3
Multiline1	Lance Robinson		
Multiline2	Information Services Plc	Gran Via de CarlesS.A.	Azko Chemicals
Multiline3	Cornwall House	Ibarra Campilo	
Multiline4	56 Henley Road		Moreelsepk 24
Multiline5			
Locality1		Bilboa	
Locality2	Harlow		
Region1	Essex		
Postal Code	CM19 5AE	48010	
Last line			3511 EP Utrecht
Country	United Kingdom	Spain	Netherland

Figure 8.7 Hybrid Multiline Format

While Figure 8.5 through Figure 8.7 show examples of address data, this concept extends beyond address data. You also should become familiar with how your other data components are being fielded and formatted. For example, do you have a discrete first name and last name field or a single name field? If you have a both first name and last name, how are middle names or initials handled (e.g., consistently at the end of the first name field, at the beginning of the last name field, or a combination of both)? Do you have multiple phone number or email fields, and are some more frequently populated than others? How consistently formatted are those fields? Ultimately, understanding the makeup and format of your data will help you later on when configuring various data cleanse operations.

Let's look at NeedsEIM, Inc.'s supplier data from one of their sources. The data, shown in Table 8.1, includes several discretely fielded data components (name, organization, city, region, postal code) along with multiline data (address1, address2, lastline). In addition, there are also nondiscrete data components represented as miscellaneous data fields with a mix of email, phone, date, and identification information (miscellaneous1, miscellaneous2).

	Record 1	Record 2
Name	Mr. Robert L King Jr	Chris C Henderson C.P.A
Organization	PRODIGY	LTD
Address1	208 South Akard Street	5000 BRDWAY ST S STE300
Address2	Suite 150	<Blank>
City	Dalas	Kansas City
Region	TX	Montana
Postalcode	75020	<Blank>
Country	<Blank>	US
Miscellaneous1	PROPERTY MGR	Jan 24 1984
Miscellaneous2	robertk@prodigy.net	800.223.1212 EXT 879

Table 8.1 Example Supplier Data for NeedsEIM, Inc.

To highlight the parsing capabilities in Data Services, we will now discuss the address cleansing transforms and the data cleanse quality transforms. The address cleansing can be done using either the global address cleanse or the U.S. regulatory address cleanse. In this example, we will use the global address cleanse transform.

Global Address Cleanse Transform

Look at Figure 8.2 again. In this example, you will learn how to parse data using the global address cleanse, which is the first transform shown in the example data flow in Figure 8.2. The global address cleanse transform enables you to parse data by mapping the input data to the transform's discrete and mutltiline input to do the data parsing. Follow the steps below:

1. Drag the GLOBAL ADDRESS CLEANSE transform to the canvas and connect the source data to the transform. The address cleanse transform will be used to parse the address fields from Table 8.1.

2. When you double-click on the transform, there are three major sections in the Transform Editor: SCHEMA IN, SCHEMA OUT, and a bottom configuration pane that includes INPUT, OUTPUT, and OPTIONS tabs (see Figure 8.10). The SCHEMA IN area relates the source data shown in Table 8.1.

3. Map the input schema columns to both discrete and multiline input fields that are recognized by the transform on the Transform Editor's INPUT tab. In Figure 8.8, ORGANIZATION, ADDRESS1, ADDRESS2, CITY, REGION, POSTALCODE, and COUNTRY are mapped to the address cleanse transform INPUT FIELD NAME in the leftmost column. The arrow icon indicates which fields are mapped.

Transform Input Field Name	Input Schema Column Name	Type
ADDRESS_LINE		varchar(256)
COUNTRY	COUNTRY	varchar(256)
FIRM	ORGANIZATION	varchar(256)
LASTLINE		varchar(256)
LOCALITY1	CITY	varchar(256)
LOCALITY2		varchar(256)
LOCALITY3		varchar(256)
MULTILINE1	ADDRESS1	varchar(256)
MULTILINE2	ADDRESS2	varchar(256)
MULTILINE3		varchar(256)
MULTILINE4		varchar(256)
MULTILINE5		varchar(256)
MULTILINE6		varchar(256)
MULTILINE7		varchar(256)
MULTILINE8		varchar(256)
MULTILINE9		varchar(256)
MULTILINE10		varchar(256)
MULTILINE11		varchar(256)
MULTILINE12		varchar(256)
POSTCODE	POSTALCODE	varchar(256)
REGION1	REGION	varchar(256)

Figure 8.8 Global Address Cleanse Transform Input Tab

4. On the OUTPUT tab, all the parsed output fields that are available to you are listed (Figure 8.9 shows just a sampling of the available fields). For example, notice that the address' primary number, name, prefix, postfix, type, and secondary information are all available as parsed, discrete output fields.

5. To build the SCHEMA OUT for the transform, select the parsed values to be generated by the transform from the OUTPUT tab, including the address line as a whole (the PRIMARY_SECONDARY_ADDRESS output field includes both primary and secondary address information) as well as the discretely parsed components, primary name and number, unit number, city, state, and primary and secondary postcode information.

Figure 8.9 Global Address Cleanse Transform Output Tab

6. To pass input fields (from the SCHEMA IN pane) through the transform, drag and drop the input fields from SCHEMA IN to SCHEMA OUT. *Pass through* refers to input fields that are unrelated to the current cleansing process (e.g., a customer ID that is unrelated to address cleansing) and fields for which you want to maintain the original content for later use. In our example, we are passing the contact name and miscellaneous fields through the address cleanse transform. These fields will be used later as input into the data cleanse transform.

> **Note**
>
> You can get help with the input or output fields that are available to you by viewing the embedded help. If help is not visible, mouse over the right-hand side of the Transform Editor to access it.

Figure 8.10 Global Address Cleanse Transform Editor

7. After the address cleanse step has executed, the parsed output will look like Table 8.2.

Pre-Parsed Data		
Address 1	208 South Akard Street	5000 BRADFORD ST S STE300
Address1	Suite 150	<Blank>
City	Dalas	Kansas City
Region	TX	Montana
Postalcode	75020	<Blank>
Parsed Data		
Primary Number	208	5000
Primary Name	Akard	BRADFORD
Primary Prefix	South	S
Primary Postfix	<Blank>	<Blank>
Primary Type	Street	ST
Unit Number	150	300

Table 8.2 Address Parsing Example

Unit Description	Suite	STE
Locality	Dalas	Kansas City
Region	TX	Montana
Postalcode	75020	<Blank>

Table 8.2 Address Parsing Example (Cont.)

Now that you have parsed the address data using the global address cleanse transform, you will see an example of parsing the nonaddress data using the *data cleanse transform*.

> **Note**
>
> Note that the data in Table 8.2 is parsed only. Standardization and correction as a part of the data cleansing process are covered in Sections 8.1.2 and 8.1.3.

Data Cleanse Transform

The *data cleanse* transform takes discrete or miscellaneous, multiline data and parses out date, email, firm or company, phone number, social security number, name, and title information into discrete fields. In addition, users also have the ability to define custom parsers to go beyond the recognized content types just listed, to be able to parse out and identify numbers (for example).

For each content type, *data cleanse* gives the user the option to further break the type down into smaller components. For example, name data can be parsed into first (given name 1), middle (given name 2), and last (family name) components along with prename and honorary (e.g., CPA) and maturity (e.g., Jr.) post-names. Email data can be further parsed into user, domain, and host. Name data is parsed differently depending on the cultural norm. For example, for Spanish, Portuguese, and Japanese names, it is considered a norm to have two last or family names. As such, *data cleanse* outputs to both a family name 1 and family name 2 output field. Appendix A (available for download from the book's page at *www.sap-press.com*) has an example of differences in name parsing logic to support various cultures and international data sets.

Refer back to Figure 8.2 for the next example, which builds on the second step in the data flow. When using the data cleanse transform, we are using the delivered variation of the transform, called ENGLISHNORTHAMERICA_DATACLEANSE.

The following steps describe how to use the data cleanse transform to parse data into discrete components such as first name, last name, title, organization, and so on:

1. Drag the DATA CLEANSE transform to the canvas and connect the GLOBAL ADDRESS CLEANSE transform to this transform. The data cleanse transform will be used to parse the nonaddress fields from Table 8.1.

2. On the INPUT tab, we will map the name, organization, and miscellaneous 1 and 2 data fields as input into DATA CLEANSE and pass through the parsed address components that were output from the preceding global address cleanse transform.

3. On the OUTPUT tab, the available parsed output fields are listed (Figure 8.11 shows just a sampling of the available fields). Select various parsed components, including PRENAME, HONORARY and MATURITY_POSTNAME, GIVEN_NAME1 (first name), GIVEN_NAME2 (middle name), FAMILY_NAME1 (last name), TITLE, PHONE, EMAIL, DATE, SSN (social security number), and FIRM (organization), for parsing.

Figure 8.11 Data Cleanse Transform Output Tab

4. To pass input fields (from the Schema In pane) through the transform, drag and drop the input fields from Schema In to Schema Out. In our example, we are passing the address-related fields from the Global Address Cleanse process through the Data Cleanse transform. This is shown in Figure 8.12.

Figure 8.12 Data Cleanse Transform Editor

After the data cleanse step has executed, the parsed output will look like Table 8.3.

Pre-Parsed Data		
Name	Mr. Robert L King Jr	Chris C Henderson C.P.A
Organization	PRODIGY	LTD
Miscellaneous 1	PROPERTY MGR	Jan 24 1984
Miscellaneous 2	robertk@prodigy.net	800.223.1212 EXT 879
Parsed Data		
Prename	Mr.	<Blank>
Given Name 1	Robert	Chris
Given Name 2	L.	C
Family Name	King	Hendersen
Maturity Postname	Jr	<Blank>
Honorary Postname	<Blank>	C.P.A
Organization	PRODIGY	LTD
Title	PROPERTY MGR	<Blank>
Phone	<Blank>	800.223.1212 EXT 879
Email	robertk@prodigy.net	<Blank>
Date	<Blank>	Jan 24 1984

Table 8.3 Name and Data Parsing Example

We mentioned earlier that data cleansing includes data parsing, data standardization, and data correction. Now that the data has been parsed, you will learn about data standardization next.

8.1.2 Data Standardization

After your data has been parsed, the next step is to ensure consistency across all of your records. This is necessary to prepare the data for validation, correction, and accurate record matching. Data standardization includes business rules concerning formats, abbreviations, acronyms, punctuation, greetings, casing, order, pattern matching, and so on. Each of these are examples of elements you can control to meet your business requirements. Figure 8.13 shows an example of data standardization.

Figure 8.13 Data Standardization Example

Take a look again at the data examples in Table 8.2 and Table 8.3. We can see that the data has been parsed into discrete components, but not always in a consistent, standardized manner. As examples:

▶ Primary Name, Primary Type, and Unit Description were output in mixed case as well as upper case (e.g., Akard and BRADFORD; Street and ST; Suite and STE).

▶ Primary Prefix, Primary Type, and Unit Description were output using the full as well as abbreviated forms (e.g., South and S; Street and ST; Suite and STE)

Looking at the OPTIONS tab of the global address cleanse Transform Editor, you can see several standardization options to control the way your address data is output (how your address data will look). Figure 8.14 shows just some of the standardization options that are available. There are options to control the capitalization, the style of the directional or primary type information (SHORT or abbreviated, LONG or spelled out, or PERSERVE as exists within your source data), the type of punctuation, the region and country style, and so on.

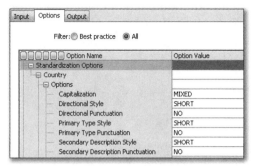

Figure 8.14 Global Address Cleanse Standardization Options

Similarly, on the address cleanse transform's OPTION tab, there are some similar standardization options for things such as capitalization and punctuation, but also some specific options for standardizing person, firm, phone number, dates, and so on (see Figure 8.15).

Figure 8.15 Data Cleanse Standardization Options

> **Note**
>
> You can get help with the available standardization options by viewing the embedded help. If help is not visible, mouse over the right-hand side of the Transform Editor to access it.

After you set up the standardization options on the address cleanse and data cleanse transforms in the OPTIONS tab, and after you adjust the data quality transform to select standardized output fields (instead of parsed-only data), the output changes to be more consistent, as shown in Table 8.4 and Table 8.5.

Pre-Parsed and Standardized Data		
Address 1	208 South Akard Street	5000 BRDWAY ST S STE300
Address 2	Suite 150	<Blank>
Parsed and Standardized Data		
Primary Number	208	5000
Primary Name	Akard	Brdway
Primary Prefix	S	S
Primary Postfix	<Blank>	<Blank>
Primary Type	St	St
Unit Number	150	300
Unit Description	Ste	Ste

Table 8.4 Address Standardization Example

Pre-Parsed and Standardized Data		
Name	Mr. Robert L King Jr	Chris C Henderson C.P.A
Organization	PRODIGY	LTD
Miscellaneous 1	PROPERTY MGR	Jan 24 1984
Miscellaneous 2	robertk@prodigy.net	800.223.1212 EXT 879
Parsed and Standardized Data		
Prename	Mr.	<Blank>
Given Name 1	Robert	Chris
Given Name 2	L.	C.
Family Name	King	Hendersen
Maturity Postname	Jr.	<Blank>
Honorary Postname	<Blank>	CPA
Firm	Prodigy Inc.	Limited

Table 8.5 Name and Data Standardization Example

Title	Property Manager	\<Blank\>
Phone	\<Blank\>	(800) 223-1212 Ext 879
Email	robertk@prodigy.net	\<Blank\>
Date	\<Blank\>	1/24/1984

Table 8.5 Name and Data Standardization Example (Cont.)

Notice the following changes shown in the previous tables:

▶ Capitalization is mixed-case throughout.

▶ The primary prefix and type information along with unit description is abbreviated.

▶ Phone and date information has been formatted.

▶ Punctuation is consistent throughout.

> **Note**
>
> To output *parsed data*, select output fields that have a FIELD_CLASS = PARSED on the data quality transform's OUTPUT tab.
>
> To output *parsed and standardized data* in the data cleanse transform, select output fields that have a FIELD_CLASS = STANDARDIZED on the transform's OUTPUT tab.
>
> To output *parsed and standardized data* in the address cleanse transform, select output fields that have a FIELD_CLASS = BEST on the transform's OUTPUT tab.

The other place where standardization rules are represented is in data cleansing packages. Cleansing packages are dictionaries that contain the rules that define how data will be parsed and standardized. Data Services offers out-of-the-box support for predefined cleansing packages for name, title, and firm parsing and standardization that can be utilized with the data cleanse transform. The name, title and firm cleansing packages are tuned to support various language nuances and cultural standards across the globe. As the name implies, these cleansing packages provide support to parse and standardize firm, or company, data as well as the names and titles of your contacts and customers. It will give NeedsEIM, Inc. a way to standardize supplier names on standard forms; for example, standardizing "Limited" instead of "LTD", as in Table 8.5. Standardizing supplier names will ultimately help NeedsEIM, Inc. get to that consolidated view of their suppliers, as it will allow accurate consolidation to occur.

Cleansing packages also contain powerful name, title, and firm alias information that serves as input into the matching process (discussed in Section 8.3) to overcome the challenge of different representations of the same data in a customer or supplier database. Think about trying to match "Mr. Dan R. Smith Jr., CPA" against another record in your database that represents that same person as "Daniel Smith Junior." Predefined cleansing packages for name, title, and firm allow you to output match standards to help overcome issues with identifying matching records due to alternative spellings (e.g., Catherine and Katherine or IBM and Intl Business Machines), nicknames (Pat and Patrick), and multiple scripts. Match standards are available for:

- Family_Name1 and Family_Name2 (supports alternative script type; for example, a Japanese family name represented in kanji as well as kana renditions)
- Firm and Firm Location
- Given Name 1 and Given Name 2
- Honorary Postname
- Maturity Postname
- Prename
- Title

Table 8.6 shows the match standards, or name aliases, that would be generated by the data cleanse transform for a first or given name of "Al."

Output Field	Value
GIVEN_NAME1	Al
GIVEN_NAME1_MATCH_STD1	Albert
GIVEN_NAME1_MATCH_STD2	Alexander
GIVEN_NAME1_MATCH_STD3	Alphonse
GIVEN_NAME1_MATCH_STD4	Alan
GIVEN_NAME1_MATCH_STD5	Alfred

Table 8.6 Match Standards Example

The matching standards will be discussed in the upcoming section on data matching (Section 8.3). Now that data has been parsed and standardized, it can be corrected, which is discussed next.

8.1.3 Data Correction

Let's finish up with the last step of the data cleansing process (see Figure 8.1)—data correction. Data with incorrect elements is known as *dirty* data. Cleansing dirty data involves verifying the data, correcting it, and adding missing elements such as directional or primary type information to an address. Depending on the data type, you can remove or correct dirty data using sophisticated algorithms and rules in conjunction with referential data. A data correction example is shown in Figure 8.16.

Input Record	Output Record	
Mark Kessler 117 - 138 St W Harlem NY 10030	**Name**	Mark Kessler
	Address	117 Odell Clark Pl
	Locality	New York
	Region	NY
	Postal Code	10030

Figure 8.16 Data Correction Example

The correction process leverages reference or "truth" data sets. For the address cleanse transform, these are referred to as *address directories*. There is an *all-world address directory* that supports last line (city, region, postal code, and country) parsing, standardization, and correction as well as *country-specific directories* for more precise address correction capabilities. For each country that you want country-specific support, you need a corresponding address directory that contains the detailed reference data necessary. With the country-specific address directories, reference data suppliers are picked carefully and in many cases are the local postal authorities. Country-specific directories give you finer-grain address assignment and accuracy with the ability to cleanse, in addition to last line information:

▶ Secondary information: unit, floor, or stairwell information

▶ Primary range: house number

▶ Primary name: street name

> **Note**
>
> The Data Services installation does *not* install address directories. Address directories are licensed on an annual subscription basis and are downloaded and installed separately from the product. They are updated monthly or quarterly, depending on the source.
>
> The location of your address directories is set using the REFERENCE FILES • DIRECTORY PATH parameter of the address cleanse transform's OPTIONS tab.

To realize data correction benefits, just adjust the address cleanse Transform Editor's OUTPUT tab to select corrected output fields (instead of parsed- and/or standardized-only data). Table 8.7 shows how the data components have been affected. After address correction, you can see several corrections that have taken place, including correction of street name, locality, or city name, and postcode, as well as the creation of the missing postal codes.

Pre-Cleansed Data		
Address 1	208 South Akard Street	5000 BRDWAY ST S STE300
Address 2	Suite 150	\<Blank\>
City	Dalas	Kansas City
Region	TX	Montana
Postalcode	75020	\<Blank\>
Cleansed Data		
Primary Address	208 S Akard St	5000 Broadway St
Secondary Address	Ste 150	Ste 300
Locality	Dallas	Kansas City
Region	TX	MO
Postcode 1	75202	64111
Postcode 2	4229	2413

Table 8.7 Address Correction Example

Note

To output *corrected data*, select output fields that have a FIELD_CLASS = CORRECT on the address cleanse transform's OUTPUT tab. These fields output the complete and correct value found in the address directories and are standardized according to any setting that you define in the standardization options group in the OPTIONS tab.

To output additional details about the type of correction that has occurred, use:

▶ **Information codes**
Available via the INFO_CODE GLOBAL ADDRESS CLEANSE output field; explain why an address was unassigned or uncorrected.

▶ **Status codes**
Available via the STATUS_CODE GLOBAL ADDRESS CLEANSE output field; represent the corrections made to the address during processing.

> ▶ **Quality codes**
> Available via the QUALITY_CODE GLOBAL ADDRESS CLEANSE output field; relay additional information about the quality of the address.

For more details about address cleansing, including unique capabilities of the U.S. regulatory address cleanse transform and global address cleansing capabilities, see Appendix A (available for download from the book's page at *www.sap-press.com*).

So far, you have learned how to cleanse data starting with data parsing, data standardization, and data correction. Once the data is cleansed, the next step is data validation.

8.1.4 Data Validation

Now that we have covered data cleansing, this is a good time to talk about data validation. You can use data validation up front, before data cleansing, to route only specific records to the data cleansing process—records where you have identified anomalies in the incoming data through the data assessment process. Alternatively, you can use data validation after correction has occurred to continue with only a subset of the parsed, standardized, and corrected records into the next phases of the data quality process: enrichment, matching, and consolidation. The validation transform in Data Services allows you to define rules that sort the good data from the bad. This can permit you to write the nonconforming data to a table or a file for subsequent review or route it to a set of transforms for continued or specialized processing.

For example, suppose your business rules dictate that all phone numbers in the United States should have the format (999) 999-9999. However, the profiling results show that records have varying formats, anything from 9999 to 9999999 to 999.999.9999. You can use a validation transform to identify rows containing the unwanted formatting. Then you can correct the data using the data cleanse transform to conform to your business rules and reload it. As another example, the address cleanse transform includes the ability to output various information, status, or quality codes that explain why an address was unassigned, represent corrections made, or relay additional information about the quality of the address. These codes can be used with the validation transform to route only the cleansed or quality addresses to the de-duplication process.

The following steps describe how to use the validation transform to validate a telephone number against a specific pattern:

1. Drag the VALIDATION transform to the canvas, connecting it to the previous data source or transform requiring data validation.

2. Double-click on the VALIDATION transform to open the Rule Editor. Set the name and description for the validation rule and select ACTION ON FAIL. Select the column to validate and the condition that must be met. In the example in Figure 8.17, we are creating a rule that validates that the format of a phone number matches the pattern (999) 999-9999. If the rule fails, records are routed to a separate failure output stream (see Figure 8.18).

Figure 8.17 Validation Transform Rule Editor

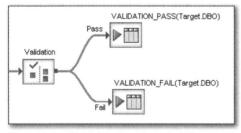

Figure 8.18 Validation Transform Dataflow

You now have a good idea of how data parsing, standardization, correction, and validation work in Data Services and the role they each play for data cleansing. Next we discuss the enrichment of data after it has been cleansed.

8.2   Data Enhancement

Returning to the data quality wheel (see Figure 8.1), let's take a look at data enhancement. Enhancement is the process of enriching your existing data set by appending additional data fields or attributes to it. This provides a more complete view of your data, which can be valuable for analysis, insight, and other business purposes. Enhancement options in Data Services include:

▶ Providing full international postal information

▶ Assigning longitude and latitude information to records

▶ Assigning geospatial information such as tax jurisdiction identifiers

▶ Assigning gender and prenames

▶ Using third-party referential data to enhance records

As discussed in the previous section on data cleansing (Section 8.1), the address correction process includes enhancing customer or supplier data with missing common address information, such as the street name, directional, city, state, or postcode. You can also append missing address information that is critical for mail delivery, such as a ZIP+4®, delivery point bar code (DPBC), or carrier routes that are available from the postal address directories. In addition, the U.S. regulatory address cleanse transform provides USPS®-certified options such as DPV (Delivery Point Validation), RDI (Residential Delivery Indicator), as well as interfaces with the USPS LACSLink™ (Locatable Address Conversion System), SuiteLink™, and NCOALink™ (National Change of Address) provide a wealth of data enrichment options for U.S. addresses. Appendix A (available for download from the book's page at *www.sap-press.com*) has more details on the U.S. regulatory address cleanse. Geospatial data is also available via the address cleanse transforms. Geospatial assignment of customer addresses can be useful for determining tax jurisdictions and insurance-rating territories and identifying insurance hazards. Data enhancement is accomplished by posting data from the data quality transforms via designated output fields.

From the data cleanse transform in Data Services, it is possible to output gender and prename information. Names in the SAP-supplied name, title, and firm cleansing packages have a gender associated with them (either ambiguous, strong male, strong female, weak male, or weak female). Gender can be output using the GENDER output field from the data cleanse transform. When the ASSIGN PRENAMES option is set to YES on the OPTIONS tab of the Transform Editor, the data cleanse populates the PRENAME output field with a prename (e.g., Mr. or Mrs.) when a strong male or female gender is assigned to a name.

Geocoding information, longitude and latitude, can be posted to records for business processes or policies (e.g., a marketing initiative) that are geographically based. The Data Services geocoder transform can enrich location data with varying degrees of precision:

▶ **Primary number exact**
The finest depth of assignment available, to the exact location.

▶ **Primary number**
The second most precise, with assignment to a primary address range (e.g., 100-500 Main St).

▶ **Postcode or locality level**
The most general output level, with assignment to a city, town, suburb, or postcode.

Adding location awareness to the analytical process helps many companies make better business decisions. For example, imagine a company is thinking about opening a new retail store. Some of the key factors to consider include:

▶ Number of new customers that can be targeted for the new store

▶ Proximity of competing businesses

▶ Distribution of complementary services (e.g., opening a fast food restaurant next to a large strip mall)

Consider an example in a mobile environment: Imagine being able to determine and track your customers' locations and then make them real-time offers based on location awareness. For NeedsEIM, Inc., knowing the location of all the suppliers can be critical when doing disaster planning. For example, if a natural disaster occurs and a supplier must suspend their business, you might want to know what other suppliers are in the same area and thus might be impacted. Additionally, you may need to quickly identify alternate suppliers outside the disaster zone. There is tremendous business value to having the tools to be able to take advantage of the context of location.

Along with longitude and latitude, the geocoder transform also supports point-of-interest (POI) geocoding, returning a list of all locations that meet the point-of-interest search criteria within a geographical area. This allows you to search for POIs (over 65 categories supported) within a radial range from or closest to a particular location. The geocoder transform also supports reverse geocoding, which identifies the closest mailing address (POI or residential) based on an input latitude and longitude. Going back to our previous example, POI geocoding and geospatial search capabilities help a business identify what other businesses, competitive and complementary, are already in a given area.

Like address cleansing, the geocoding enrichment process leverages reference data sets. These are referred to as *geo directories*. Geo directories are country specific. So for each country that you want geocoding support, you need a corresponding geo directory that contains the necessary detailed reference data.

> **Note**
>
> The Data Services installation does *not* install geo directories. Geo directories are licensed on an annual subscription basis and are downloaded and installed separately from the product. They are typically updated quarterly, depending on the country.
>
> The location of your geo directories is set in the REFERENCE FILES • DIRECTORY PATH parameter of the geocoder transform's OPTIONS tab.

Another form of data enrichment is demographic data. To append demographic information, you need a demographic database from a third-party data provider. When you obtain one, you can use the Data Services matching process to match your records to the demographic database and append the demographic information into your records.

8.3   Data Matching

We are almost around the wheel (see Figure 8.1), and the next step is a big one: match and consolidate. Matching and consolidation are essential for:

▶ Business intelligence initiatives where your goal is a single version of the truth.

▶ Migration of data from legacy systems or systems gained through acquisition.

▶ Leveraging third-party content such as do-not-mail, prison, or decreased consumer lists to avoid marketing to certain demographics.

For NeedsEIM, Inc., obtaining legal entity or corporate hierarchy information may prove very useful in the effort to get a consolidated view of their suppliers.

To start, look at Figure 8.19, which shows an example of matching.

Figure 8.19 Matching Example

Duplicate records often exist in one or more source systems. The goal of matching is to determine whether records refer to the same entity. This involves evaluating how well the individual fields, or attributes, of the records match each other. SAP Data Quality Management matching capabilities allow you to use various fields for comparisons, to compare records in multiple directions, and then join the intersections. SAP Data Quality Management employs powerful matching algorithms to account for data entry errors, character transposition, and other data inaccuracies to match records. Table 8.8 describes some of the typical use cases for matching.

Use Case	Description
Consumer householding	Duplicate detection based on person names and addresses at various levels, such as household, family, and individual. Can be used for targeted marketing campaigns.
Corporate householding	Duplicate detection based on organization names and addresses at various levels, such as firm, department, and individual. Can be used for partner or supplier consolidation when multiple contacts exist.

Table 8.8 Typical Match Use Cases

Use Case	Description
Identity resolution	Duplicate detection based on person names and addresses, and perhaps other attributes such as account numbers or identification numbers. Useful for fraud prevention. Duplicate prevention at point of entry. Used when adding a new entity to the master database to detect whether the record already exists. Used in SAP CRM and SAP ERP systems.
Direct marketing	Duplicate detection typically based on person names and addresses using customer lists and in batch mode. Used: ▶ To eliminate redundant communication or shipping costs ▶ To leverage purchased or rented customer lists ▶ To pull in additional third-party demographic information for targeted marketing ▶ With geocoding to match to a specific geographic proximity (e.g., within 50 miles of a particular retail store).
Master data management	Duplicate detection in existing master records or duplicate prevention when a new record or entity is added. Used to establish and maintain a single version of the truth.
Business intelligence	Duplicate detection when pulling multiple sources together to create a data warehouse for business intelligence initiatives. Used to establish and maintain a trusted, single version of the truth.

Table 8.8 Typical Match Use Cases (Cont.)

With data originating from different sources and systems and from different lines of the business with varying business processes and polices, identifying duplicates can be difficult. The example in Figure 8.19 shows the importance of data cleansing upstream of the matching process with all of the possible variations and inaccuracies that can exist in the data. We need to parse, standardize, and correct the information to improve the matching results.

NeedsEIM, Inc.'s finance department was finding it difficult to get at a customer-level profit and loss statement because the data lives in so many applications and datastores, and procurement wants to reduce the number of duplicate suppliers in their system to improve process efficiency. Now that the necessary data cleansing has occurred to parse, standardize, and correct the supplier data, it is time to tackle matching to identify duplicates and get to the consolidated view of major suppliers that finance and procurement is after.

Before we get into NeedsEIM, Inc.'s solution, let's spend some time covering some of the core concepts of matching. First, what is a duplicate? Records may look different, but for business purposes they are the same record. A duplicate is going to be different for different users, different data domains, and different business goals. Sometimes it just depends on who you ask and what type of data is under review; for example:

▶ For names, *William, Will,* and *Bill* are duplicates. But *Bill* and *Billiards* are not.

▶ For names, *Mary Jones-Smith* and *Mary Jones* are duplicates.

▶ For addresses, *First Street* and *1st St* are duplicates. But *First Street* and *Frost St* are not.

▶ For firms, *International Business Machines, IBM* and *intl bus mach* are all duplicates.

▶ For firms, *Midtown water and power* and *Midtown power and water* are duplicates, but *Midtown shipping* is not.

▶ For SSNs, *123-45-6789* and *122-45-6789* are not duplicates.

▶ For part descriptions, *40bar, 350Hp* and *350HP, 40bar* are duplicates. But *45bar, 350HP* is different.

Ultimately, you need to determine a matching strategy to decide what constitutes a duplicate and what type of results you want out of the matching process. Work with the business to determine the matching strategy for a data domain or data warehouse. Take a look at Table 8.9 for some examples of questions to consider.

Question	Example
What attributes does my data consist of?	Customer data, vendor data, international data, etc.
What fields or attributes are important in the comparison process?	Last name, firm, address, unique identifier, etc.

Table 8.9 Developing a Matching Strategy

Question	Example
What are the relative strengths and weaknesses of the data in the comparison fields?	The consumer address data may tend to be inaccurate or incomplete; however, email addresses are usually populated and accurate.
What end result do I want when the matching job is complete?	Depending on the use case (direct marketing versus master data management) the end result will be different—one record per family, per firm, etc.

Table 8.9 Developing a Matching Strategy (Cont.)

Tip
As mentioned a few times now, you will get better results if you cleanse your data before matching. If data attributes important to the comparison process are missing, and if you need to go to a third-party vendor to acquire that data, data enhancement may also improve matching results. Also, data profiling can help you answer some of these questions, especially to understand the relative strengths and weaknesses of the data.

Getting back to a technology perspective, there are many types of matching techniques and algorithms that can be applied to determine duplicates. The Data Services match transform performs rule-based similarity matching. Duplicate detection is based on *similarity scoring*, a scoring system that determines what percentage of the data or content is alike. A similarity score is derived using the edit distance method, calculating how many corrections are required to make two strings identical, and then determining the score based on the string length and corrections required.

In the example in Table 8.10, a similarity score of 100 means that match is 100% sure that the two records are the same (person). A similarity score of 80 means that match is 80% sure that the two records are the same. (Another way of interpreting a similarity score of 80 is that there is a 20% deviation between two records' measured content). This is a simple and straightforward matching example; however, many *match comparison options* are available with the match transform that can affect the similarity of the records and improve the flexibility and power of the matching capabilities. These match comparison options are explored in detail in Appendix A (available for download from the book's page at *www.sap-press.com*).

Record 1	Record 2	Similarity Score
Smith	Smith	100
Smith	Jones	20
Smith	Smitt	80

Table 8.10 Simple Similarity Score Example

Let's cover some of the basic aspects of matching using the match transform. A match transform in your Data Services data flow represents a *match set*. Each match set can have its own break groups, match criteria, and prioritization (concepts we will get to soon). A match set has three main purposes:

▶ To allow only select data into a given set of match criteria for possible comparison (for example, excluding blank SSNs, international addresses, and so on from the comparison process).

▶ To allow related match scenarios to be stacked, creating a multilevel match set.

▶ To allow multiple match sets to be considered for association in an associate match set.

A *match level* is an indicator of what type of matching will occur, such as on an individual, family, resident, firm, and so on. The purpose of the family match type is to determine whether two people should be considered members of the same family; the result of the match is one record per family. The purpose of the individual match type is to determine whether two records are for the same person; the result of the match is one record per individual. The same concept applies to a residence, firm, and person at a firm; the result is one record per each. There can be multiple levels of matching. Only records found in a match group at the first level are fed to the second level and so on.

Match criteria are the fields or attributes you want to match on. You can use match comparison options to specify business rules for matching on each of these fields or attributes, depending on the data type. *Match thresholds* allow you to control how close to exact the data needs to be for that data to be considered a match or a nonmatch.

Match groups are groups of records that the match transform has found to be matching, based on the criteria you have created. The *master record* is the first record in the match group. The master is sometimes referred to as the *surviving* or *highest-priority* record. You can control which record this is by using a group prioritization operation before the best record operation (data consolidation, or best record creation, is covered in Section 8.3.4). *Subordinate* records are all of the remaining records in a match group. This is sometimes referred to as the *nonsurviving* or *lower-priority* record from a master.

For each match criteria you define in your match set, there are three ways to prioritize the match criteria identified:

- ▶ **Rule-based matching method**
  All criteria for matching are given the same amount of importance (or weight). The method relies solely on the match and no-match scores to determine matching within a criteria. If any criteria fail to meet the specified no-match threshold, the records do not match.

- ▶ **Weighted scoring matching method**
  Relies on a total contribution score to determine matches, based on contribution values that have been set per criteria. Individual match criteria can be given higher weightings or contribution values to raise their priority in the match process.

- ▶ **Combination matching method**
  Combines rule-based and weight scoring methods. A no-match occurs when any criteria fails to exceed the no-match threshold. A match is determined only by comparing the total contribution score against the weighted match score.

Let's walk through an example of each method. After the matching, you will learn about consolidating data from the matching process.

> **Match Configuration**
>
> Match criteria and methods, including match and no-match thresholds, are set up using the Match Editor or optionally with the help of the Match Wizard. Section 8.3.3 describes a matching example for NeedsEIM, Inc.

8.3.1 Rule-Based Matching Method

In Figure 8.20 the first name, last name, and email have been identified as match criteria. Looking at record A and record B, with a similarity score of 100 and the match and no-match thresholds set, the first name is determined a match. The last name criteria similarity score of 80 is in the gray area (between the no-match and match threshold), so it will depend on the next criteria to determine whether the records are a match. Email is the last criteria and is a match with a similarity score of 91, so the records are a match.

Match Criteria	Record A	Record B	No-match threshold	Match threshold	Similarity score
First Name	Mary	Mary	82	95	100
Last Name	Smith	Smitt	74	95	80
Email	msmith@ abcdef.com	mary.smitt@ abcdef.com	79	80	91

Figure 8.20 Rule-Based Matching Method Example

8.3.2 Weighted Scoring Matching Method

The next technique is the weighted scoring method. Note that the no-match and match thresholds of -1 and 101 imply that these thresholds will not be used. Instead, a contribution value or weight for each match criteria is set. The contribution score for each match criteria is calculated as the similarity score multiplied by the contribution value. Then the contribution scores are added together to determine a total contribution value. In the example in Figure 8.21, the contribution scores of the first name, last name, and email are added together for a total contribution score of 91. If the weighted match score threshold set in the match transform is 90 or less, then all records with a contribution score higher than 90 will be considered a match. These records will be determined a match since the total contribution score is higher than 90.

Match Criteria	Record A	Record B	No-match threshold	Match threshold	Similarity score	Contribution value	Contribution score
First Name	Mary	Mary	-1	101	100	25%	25
Last Name	Smith	Smitt	-1	101	80	25%	20
Email	msmith@ abcdef.com	mary.smitt@ abcdef.com	-1	101	91	50%	46
						Total contribution score	91

Figure 8.21 Weighted Scoring Matching Method Example

8.3.3 Combination Matching Method

A combination of the previous two techniques can also be used. In the following example (Figure 8.22), a similarity score of 22 for the last name match criteria was below the no-match threshold, so records fail the match test. No further processing is required. In the second example (Figure 8.23), none of the match criteria fail to meet the no-match threshold. So the total contribution score of 91 determines whether or not the records are matches. Again, if the weighted match score threshold set in the match transform is 90 or less, then these records will be determined to be a match, since the total contribution score is higher.

Match Criteria	Record A	Record B	No-match threshold	Match threshold	Similarity score	Contribution value	Contribution score
First Name	Mary	Mary	59	101	100	25	25
Last Name	Smith	Hope	59	101	22	25	N/C
Email	msmith@ abcdef.com	mary.hope@ abcdef.com	49	101	N/C	50	N/C
						Total contribution score	N/C

Figure 8.22 Combination Matching Method Example 1

Match Criteria	Record A	Record B	No-match threshold	Match threshold	Similarity score	Contribution value	Contribution score
First Name	Mary	Mary	59	101	100	25	25
Last Name	Smith	Smitt	74	101	80	25	20
Email	msmith@ abcdef.com	mary.smith@ abcdef.com	79	101	91	50	46
						Total contribution score	91

Figure 8.23 Combination Matching Method Example 2

Another important concept in matching is a break group. A *break group* controls the number of comparisons required to complete the matching process. Break groups directly affect the performance of matching. When the number of comparisons is reduced, the time required to complete the matching process is also reduced. A typical break key in a customer scenario utilizes the postcode, and more specifically, the first three digits of the postcode.

Using this example, only records with the same first three digits of their postcode would be compared. This means John Smith who lives in Seattle (98406) would be compared to John Smith who lives in Tacoma (94816), but neither of these two would be compared to John Smith in Denver (80204). A break group consists of driver and passenger records. The first record serves as the driver. All remaining records in the break group serve as passengers and are compared against the driver to find matches. Once a passenger is found to match a driver, it is no longer used in the matching process. The next passenger in the break group that hasn't been found as a match is used as the second driver and is compared against any remaining nonmatched passenger records in the break group. The match process iterates through all records in a break group in this manner to identify matches. When finished with one break group, the process continues to the next break group and repeats the above iterations.

Match performance is improved when the break key creates many break groups with only a few data records in each break group. However, as more and more break groups are created, the risk of a missed match increases, because you are comparing fewer and fewer records and the matching process does not get the opportunity to match data records in different data collections. Match accuracy is improved when the break group compound results in a few data collections with many data records in each. Nevertheless, the disadvantage is that the matching process takes more time due to many comparisons in each data collection. Ultimately, you need to be careful to balance performance with results. The objective is to maximize the speed without compromising the accuracy of your matching process. You may need to use some degree of trial and error to find the right balance.

Needs EIM, Inc. and Data Matching

Getting back to NeedsEIM, Inc., it is time to take the next step toward that consolidated view of their suppliers by identifying duplicates in the supplier data. To match suppliers, the business owners have decided to take a first crack at de-duplication using match criteria focused on the organization and the contact's email address' domain host (e.g., "sap" in the case of *joex@sap.com*). The first thing we need to do is go back to the data cleanse transform and configure it to output the firm match standards and email domain host needed to support NeedsEIM, Inc.'s matching strategy. Match standards help you overcome matching problems related to alternative spellings or representations and acronyms. For example, HP is the match standard or alias for Hewlett Packard. If the data cleanse cleansing package does not have an alias entry for a given firm or organization, then the output field(s) are empty.

Referring back to Figure 8.2, the below example demonstrates the third step in the data quality data flow, using the Match Wizard and the Match Editor:

1. Double-click on the DATA CLEANSE transform to open the Transform Editor. Go to the OUTPUT tab to select the FIRM_MATCH_STD output fields for output to supply match standards for firms along with the EMAIL_DOMAIN_HOST parsed and standardized output component (see Figure 8.24).

PARENT_COMPONENT	FIELD_NAME	FIELD_CLASS
▶ DATE1	DATE	STANDARDIZED
▶ EMAIL1	EMAIL	STANDARDIZED
▶ EMAIL1	EMAIL_DOMAIN_HOST	STANDARDIZED
▶ FIRM1	FIRM	STANDARDIZED
▶ FIRM1	FIRM_MATCH_STD1	STANDARDIZED
▶ FIRM1	FIRM_MATCH_STD2	STANDARDIZED
▶ FIRM1	FIRM_MATCH_STD3	STANDARDIZED
▶ NORTH_AMERICAN_PHONE1	NORTH_AMERICAN_PHONE	STANDARDIZED
▶ PERSON1	FAMILY_NAME1	STANDARDIZED
▶ PERSON1	GIVEN_NAME1	STANDARDIZED
▶ PERSON1	GIVEN_NAME2	STANDARDIZED
▶ PERSON1	HONORARY_POSTNAME	STANDARDIZED
▶ PERSON1	MATURITY_POSTNAME	STANDARDIZED
▶ PERSON1	PRENAME	STANDARDIZED
▶ PERSON1	TITLE	STANDARDIZED

Filter: ○ Best practice ● In use ○ All
Input | Options | Output

Figure 8.24 Preparing the Data Cleanse for Matching

2. Use the Match Wizard in Data Services to get a jump start on configuring the match. Right-click on the DATA CLEANSE transform and select RUN MATCH WIZARD.

3. Start by selecting the corporate householding match strategy (Figure 8.25).

Figure 8.25 Match Wizard—Select Match Strategy

4. Select LOOK FOR CORPORATE-LEVEL MATCHES and then FIRM and EMAIL (Figure 8.26).

Figure 8.26 Match Wizard—Define Matching Levels

5. Set up the match criteria fields, mapping in the appropriate FIRM, FIRM_MATCH_
   STD, and EMAIL fields from the data cleanse (Figure 8.27). We are going to skip
   the break key definition (we will need to set it up later to tune the matching process).

Figure 8.27 Match Wizard—Select Criteria Fields

6. Click on FINISH. The result is a newly generated match transform with the basic
   match setup configured (Figure 8.28).

Figure 8.28 Data Quality Data Flow with Match Transform

7. Double-click on the MATCH transform that was generated to make some initial
   adjustments to our matching configuration. When opening the match transform,
   you will notice a few things that are different from the other data quality

transforms. In particular, the OPTIONS tab of the match transform is not editable. Match has a specialized Transform Editor. To access it, click on the EDIT OPTIONS button on the OPTIONS tab.

8. In the Match Editor, you can review the match criteria that the Match Wizard set up by selecting MATCH CRITERIA in the left pane (Figure 8.29).

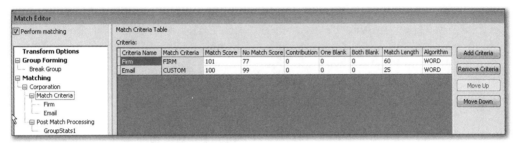

Figure 8.29 Match Editor Match Criteria Table

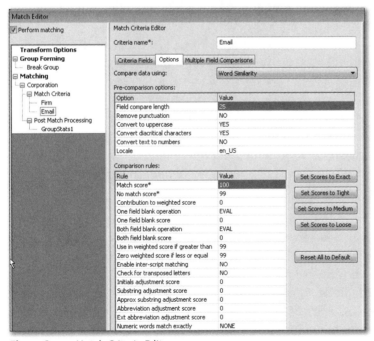

Figure 8.30 Match Criteria Editor

9. Double-click on the individual criteria and select the OPTIONS tab to see detailed match comparison options as a result of the Match Wizard (see Figure 8.30). For

more information on the match comparison options, see Appendix A (available for download from the book's page at *www.sap-press.com*). Having profiled their data during the data assessment phase of their data quality initiative, NeedsEIM, Inc. knows that their email contact data is less complete than they would like. So we want to make an adjustment to their match criteria to accommodate null or blank email fields.

> **Note**
>
> If you want help with the Match Wizard or Match Editor options, mouse over the right pane of the Wizard or Editor to access the embedded, online help.

10. In the MATCH CRITERIA EDITOR area, the ONE/BOTH FIELD BLANK OPERATION comparison rules should be set to IGNORE so the email match criteria is ignored in the comparison process if one or both record's email field is blank (see Figure 8.30). Because we are using a rule-based matching strategy, this means that in the case of blank email fields, it will fall completely to the firm match criteria to determine whether or not two records match.

11. Another adjustment that is needed is to lower the match score for the firm criteria. Currently, the Match Wizard has set the match score to 101, which means the criteria by itself is never enough to consider two records a match. Lower the match score to 90 (in the MATCH CRITERIA EDITOR area, shown in Figure 8.30) so that if data in two records is 90% similar or higher, the records will be considered a match. The email match criteria will then determine a match if the firm similarity score is somewhere in the gray area (in this case, between 77 and 90) or eliminate a match if two nonblank email fields are not an exact match.

Table 8.11 shows the results of the matching process. Match group numbers, match scores for each subordinate record, the match group count, and a match group rank (M = master record and S = subordinate record) are all available to post as output from the match transform as long as the *group statistics* post-matching operation is enabled. An example of group statistics is group_order. With group_order the master record receives a value of 1. Subordinate records receive a value of 2 through the number of records in the match group.

Group Number	Group Count	Match Score	Match Group Rank	Organization	Email Domain
10	2	<Null>	M	Grossman Forgals Inc.	Grossman
10	2	97	S	Grossman Forgal	Grossman
11	4	<Null>	M	Precision Woodwork	<Null>
11	4	100	S	Precision Woodwork	Precision
11	4	98	S	Precision Woodwork Co.	<Null>
11	4	93	S	Precision	<Null>
12	6	<Null>	M	M & I Bank	Mibank
12	6	92	S	M&I Bank	<Null>
12	6	92	S	M & I Bank	<Null>
12	6	100	S	M&I Bank of Beloit	Mibank
12	6	100	S	M&I Bank of Beloit	<Null>
12	6	92	S	MI	Mibank
13	2	<Null>	M	Smith & Harris Mach.	<Null>
13	2	92	S	S & H Mach.	<Null>
14	2	<Null>	M	Valk & Fragger	Vaulkfrager
14	2	99	S	Valk & Frager	<Null>

Table 8.11 Match Transform Example Output

Based on the initial results, NeedsEIM, Inc. can make adjustments to the match criteria, comparison options, and/or match and no-match thresholds to fine-tune the match result set. For information on additional options for supporting your matching business requirements and tweaking your match results, see Appendix A (available for download from the book's page at *www.sap-press.com*).

Once the matching has occurred, the data must be consolidated, which we discuss next.

8.3.4 Data Consolidation

Data consolidation either eliminates, filters, or combines duplicate records utilizing configurable rules. Once matches have been identified, data from the match groups can be salvaged and posted to form a single best record, or posted to update all matching records. Best record selection is based on your data priorities—in terms of source, frequency, completeness, timeliness (most current or up-to-date), and so on. Consolidation can also build reference keys to track individual records and their associations across multiple databases or sources. Figure 8.31 shows an example of data consolidation across three records in the same match group.

Figure 8.31 Data Consolidation Example

You can perform data consolidation by adding a best record post-match operation. The functions you perform with the best record operation involve manipulating or moving data contained in the master and subordinate records of match groups.

Table 8.12 shows a match group. As you can see, each record is slightly different. Some records have blank fields, some have a new date, and all have different phone numbers. An example of a best record strategy that could be applied would be to move the most current (based on date) phone data to all of the records in the match group (master and subordinate records).

Record	Name	Phone	Date	Group Rank
1	John Smith		11 Apr 2001	Master
2	John Smyth	608-788-8700	12 Oct 1999	Subordinate
3	John E. Smith	608-788-1234	22 Feb 1997	Subordinate
4	J. Smith	608-788-3271		Subordinate

Table 8.12 Best Record Creation Example

Another example might be to salvage useful data from matching records before discarding them. For example, when you run a drivers license file against your house file, you might pick up gender or date-of-birth data to add to your house record.

Using the best record operation, you can control when to populate a specific data element, whether data is populated in the master and/or the subordinate records in the match group, and how to populate a specific data element. Data Services provides strategies to help you set up the more common best record operations quickly and easily. If the prebuilt strategies do not meet your needs, you can always create a custom best record strategy. In our example of updating a phone field with the most recent data (Table 8.12), we can use the date strategy with the newest priority to update the master record with the latest phone number in the match group. This latter part (updating the master record with the latest phone number) is the action. You can also update all of the records in the match group (master and all subordinates) or only the subordinates. The best record strategies available out-of-the-box are:

▶ **Date**
With priority on the newest or oldest date in the strategy field.

▶ **Length**
With priority on the shortest or longest string in the strategy field.

▶ **Priority number**
With priority on the highest or lowest number in the strategy field.

▶ **Priority string**
Priority on the string with the most ascending or descending string order in the strategy field.

▶ **Non-blank**
Bases the strategy on the completeness of the data in the strategy field.

Once the best record strategy and strategy priority are selected, just choose a field that contains the data that you need to execute your strategy on and whether you want to post to the master only, subordinates only, or all records in a match group.

To work toward NeedsEIM, Inc.'s goal of consolidated supplier data, they will need to implement a best record strategy to work toward a single "golden" master record. You can take a step in that direction by adding a post-match operation to the match transform.

The following steps show a best record strategy using the post-match processing option:

1. Double-click on the MATCH transform. Click on the EDIT OPTIONS button on the OPTIONS tab.

2. Right-click POST MATCH PROCESSING in the left pane of the Match Editor and select ADD and then BEST RECORD.

3. Select a best record strategy based on NON_BLANK data in the EMAIL_DOMAIN_ HOST strategy field to be posted to the EMAIL_DOMAIN_HOST destination field in the master record of each group. Figure 8.32 shows the settings described.

Figure 8.32 Best Record Editor

After rerunning the data flow, you can see that the master records of each match group are now more complete with the addition of email data for each supplier (see Table 8.13). NeedsEIM, Inc. would go through a similar process for those data fields or attributes that they want to consolidate in their match groups to form a best record view of each of their suppliers, based on finance and procurements business needs.

Group Number	Group Count	Match Score	Match Group Rank	Organization	Email Domain
10	2	<Null>	M	Grossman Forgals Inc.	grossman
11	4	<Null>	M	Precision Woodwork	precision
12	6	<Null>	M	M & I Bank	mibank
13	2	<Null>	M	Smith & Harris Mach.	<Null>
14	2	<Null>	M	Valk & Fragger	vaulkfrager

Table 8.13 Best Record Example Output

8.4   Other Important Data Quality Capabilities

So far we have discussed how you can get started with data quality with the creation of a data quality job the performs data cleansing, data enrichment, and data matching. There are other important data quality capabilities that we must mention. The first is the embedding of data quality in SAP applications such as SAP ERP, SAP CRM, and SAP Master Data Governance. Additionally, there are blueprints you can download; these include example data and the data quality transforms, and provide a complete example for using data quality. Next discussed is the importance of data quality for other data domains such as product, service, and financial data.

8.4.1   SAP Data Quality Management, Version for SAP Solutions

This chapter would not be complete without discussing the integration provided for data quality management in SAP applications, specifically in SAP ERP, SAP CRM, and SAP Master Data Governance (hereafter SAP MDG). The embedded solution is called *SAP Data Quality Management, version for SAP solutions*, and it provides a transparent, out-of-the-box data quality solution within SAP applications. The key capabilities include address cleansing, address enhancements, and duplicate check-ing. As you enter a new business partner in the SAP application, an immediate check is done to cleanse the address and check for duplicates. Figure 8.33 shows how the solution works. The solution is embedded in the Business Address Services (BAS) layer provided in SAP NetWeaver Application Server ABAP.

First, the user enters the address data, and then a check is done with the data quality capabilities in Data Services. This provides an immediate response to the user. A validated address is provided, and the user can decide to use the validated address or the original address. After the address validation is completed, a duplicate check is performed to identify any potential duplicates. The user can then open an existing business partner or select to create a new one based on the duplicate list.

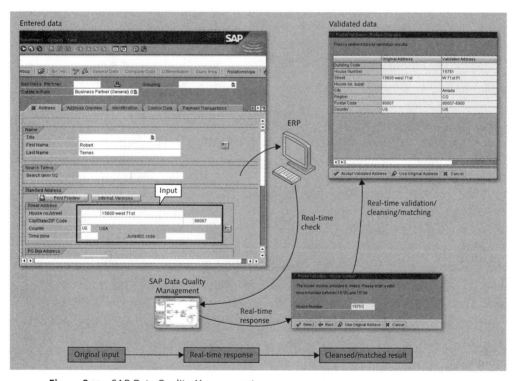

Figure 8.33 SAP Data Quality Management

In addition to the data quality capabilities provided as the user enters the informa-tion, you can also perform data quality cleansing and matching in batch mode.

This provides reports, such as matching reports that identify potential duplicates. Also, preexisting records can be detected during data loads. This can be especially helpful with SAP CRM if you are loading prospects from service bureaus or leads gathered during trade shows, webinars, or other marketing events. Additional support for marketing includes matching on marketing attributes such as age, hobbies, and salary.

SAP Data Quality Management also includes data quality in SAP MDG. You can customize which fields you want to match on, for example, plant data, material type, net weight for materials. This capability enables you to take advantage of robust data quality capabilities with the SAP CRM, SAP ERP, and SAP MDG native user interfaces.

8.4.2 Data Quality Blueprints

A blueprint is a sample Data Services job that is configured with best practices to solve a specific scenario. Each blueprint is an end-to-end job that includes sample data and can be run in the customer environment with only a few modifications. Some jobs include batch data flows, and some include real-time data flows; some jobs include party data, and some include product data. Data quality jobs include structured data, and text data processing jobs include unstructured data.

Data quality blueprints include sample jobs configured to illustrate best practice settings for common data quality use cases involving party (e.g., customer, supplier, business partner) data across the globe, including blueprints specifically tuned for Brazil, France, Germany, India, Japan, Mexico, and the United States and with international data sets. The blueprints also include miscellaneous jobs configured to illustrate best practice settings for specific matching use cases including integration with Dun and Bradstreet data as well as using Direct Marketing Association suppression lists.

There are also blueprints available to demonstrate the use of text data processing in conjunction with data quality, as well as custom functions that perform additional manipulation of data that are not part of the functionality of data quality transforms but are common functions that assist with the cleansing and matching of party data (*party data* is the name and address of a person or firm). Data Services blueprints are available from the SAP Community Network (SCN) at *http://www.sdn.sap.com/irj/boc/blueprints*.

8.4.3   Using Data Quality Beyond Customer Data

For the examples in this chapter, the focus was on cleansing party data (e.g., consumer, customer, supplier, business partner). Let's shift gears and take a look at data quality for data that is not names and addresses (commonly referred to as *nonparty data*). There is a unique challenge to cleansing nonparty data such as product or operational data. The problem is that SAP cannot necessarily ship you predefined cleansing packages that represent your products, services, or operations. These are unique to your business. Instead, there needs to be a way for your organization to describe and define custom cleansing rules that represent your business.

Imagine that you are a part of an office supply store chain. You offer a variety of paper products. In your systems, your paper product data is represented in an assortment of formats and descriptions. The box below shows a common example of how such data looks. However, the business is building a new website, and as a part of the requirements there needs to be the ability to browse products by manufacturer. How are you going to make the link between manufacturers and what is in your various point-of-sales systems that describes your company's products?

Product Data

Office Max multipurpose paper 96 bright 20 lb paper 2500 sheets 8 ½" x 11" OM44011

The answer is data quality—parsing and standardizing your business' product data stored in your point-of-sales systems to meet your new business requirements. And the critical piece of the solution is a tool in Information Steward called *cleansing package builder*. Cleansing package builder allows you to develop the necessary custom data parsing and standardization rules to cleanse your business' unique product and operational data. Cleansing package builder provides a user interface that allows a data steward to visualize how the data is parsed and standardized and evaluate the impact of their customized logic.

Cleansing package builder automatically creates the data dictionary, rules, and patterns that make up a cleansing package, which is then consumed by a Data Services data cleanse transform to parse, standardize, and cleanse business data such as account numbers, product codes and descriptions, part numbers, SKUs, and so on. Once the custom data parsing and standardization rules are in place to perform data cleansing on the product data, data cleanse can output discrete, standardized data attributes (such as manufacturer), which can be used in the matching process to support business goals around consistent, quality data to support that single view across the enterprise.

8.5   Summary

This chapter provided details on data quality and how to get started using data quality transforms. In this chapter you have learned how data cleansing, data enrichment, and data matching work in Data Services. You know how to get started using the address cleanse, data cleanse, and matching transforms. You've gained insight into options for parsing, standardizing, and creating match groups to improve the quality of your data. For more details, including a detailed list of all data quality transforms in Data Services, see Appendix A, available for download from the book's page at *www.sap-press.com*.

Data quality scorecards provide historic trends and the ability to prevent problems by quickly learning about new patterns or trends that can impact the business.

9 Monitoring Data Quality with Scorecards in SAP Information Steward

Chapter 6 introduced validation rules in SAP Information Steward (hereafter Information Steward) to measure the current status of data quality. The validation rules created in Information Steward can be executed either directly from Information Steward, or they can be exported to SAP Data Services (hereafter Data Services) to be used in data quality jobs. In Data Services, the validation transform uses the validation rules. (The validation transform is discussed in Chapter 8.)

So far, we have discussed the ad hoc and scheduled execution of validation rules to get the most current information about the level of quality. This allows users to review the data quality level from a technical perspective, answering questions such as:

▶ How good is the data content in the database system, application, or table that I am responsible for?

▶ What is the overall quality level for the file that we have processed during an ETL (extraction, transformation, and loading) batch job?

But beyond the data quality scores associated with individual technical objects such as database tables, applications, or batch jobs, the business users in a company need to visualize and drill down along other paths of information, answering questions such as:

▶ Can I immediately see the overall quality level of our product master data, independent of where it is stored?

▶ What are the different data quality levels of my customer records by regions?

▶ How did the data quality level change over time for my supplier data? Can I identify early drops of quality level before it is recognized by operational processes?

Information Steward answers these kinds of questions with *data quality scorecards.* A data quality scorecard allows a data steward—for example, the person responsible for the supplier data at NeedsEIM, Inc.—to get one central starting point to immediately see the consolidated data quality score of the supplier data *independent* of all applications that contain supplier data. This includes the most current data quality score as well as historical trends. From this high-level overall score, the data steward can drill down into further details such as the data quality dimensions, the individual rules, and the technical objects to which the rules have been bound for the supplier domain.

This chapter will go through the major steps in creating a data quality scorecard using NeedsEIM, Inc. as an example to monitor supplier and customer data. In addition to data quality monitoring discussed in this chapter, there are also some reports for data quality available in Data Services. These reports are discussed in Appendix A (available for download from the book's page at *www.sap-press.com*). This chapter will focus exclusively on Information Steward.

9.1 Components of a Data Quality Scorecard

Data quality scorecards are based on the consolidation of individual data quality scores calculated during the rule task execution. One data quality scorecard with multiple key data domains can be defined for each data insight project (data insight projects were introduced in Chapter 6). A data quality scorecard consists of at least of one tile that is linked to a specific key data domain. Additional key data domains can be included, each with their own tile. Figure 9.1 shows one tile linked to the customer data domain.

The number of tiles that are used on the data quality scorecard depends on the multiple key data domains or data entities that are used in the project. Customers also create different data quality score tiles for departmental or regional separation of the same data entities; for example, defining key data domains for customers in different regions such as North America, Europe, the Middle East and Africa (EMEA), and Asia Pacific Japan (APJ).

Figure 9.1 General Data Quality Scorecard Tile

Each data quality scorecard tile includes the name of the key data domain as a headline and the quality score that has been aggregated based on the calculation formula defined during the data quality scorecard setup. The data quality scorecard has three major areas, as shown in Figure 9.1 and described below:

❶ The overall data quality score, which is 7.88 in Figure 9.1. The scorecard includes traffic light color code information based on the thresholds defined for excellent, acceptable, and bad quality scores for the overall quality score. In this example the overall scorecard (the quality score) is yellow.

❷ The next level of detail information is based on the different quality dimensions that have been configured for the key data domain. They are color coded for quick information and support tooltip information on the individual score value when the user moves the mouse over the bars. In Figure 9.1, each data quality dimension has a different color based on the score. *Accuracy* is yellow, *completeness* is green, and *conformity* is red.

❸ In the bottom area, the quality trend diagram shows how the quality score changed over time and different measurements.

Color Figures

Although the print version of *Enterprise Information Management with SAP* is in black and white, the online version has full-color figures. Please visit *www.sap-press.com* for online book access.

From this high-level representation you can see the most important information about the current quality status. The user can drill down into a further detailed representation by clicking on the SHOW MORE... link in the upper-right corner of each data quality scorecard tile. Once you drill into further detail of the scorecard, you see a detailed view as shown in Figure 9.2.

Figure 9.2 Data Quality Scorecard Detail View

The detail screen has a drill-down hierarchy starting on the highest level with the key data domains of the data quality scorecard. By clicking on the individual levels on one of the entries, you can filter the next level of information to get from the key data domain to the linked data quality dimensions, to the linked validation rules, down to the individual rule bindings for the filtered validation rule. For all areas, the quality score itself as well as the color-coded category is printed and allows you to get a quick visual picture to easily identify the biggest data quality issues. The bottom-left area represents the quality trend over time for the highlighted hierarchy level.

On the most detailed level of the scorecard, you can either view the failed data itself or view the impact or the data lineage of the bound data fields based on the metadata management information collected for the data source.

9.2   Defining and Setting Up a Data Quality Scorecard

The starting point for the definition and setup of a data quality scorecard is determining what key data domains should be used for individual scorecard components. You must define which individual data quality scores related to the defined validation rules and data assets in the data insight project should be consolidated and aggregated to the key data domain.

In this section, we will start by explaining how to model the high-level data quality domains and map these domains to data quality dimensions. Then you will learn how to add validation rules, and finally, how to bind the data sources to the data quality scorecard.

9.2.1   Modeling the High-Level Key Data Domains

The key data domain is the highest level of the whole data scorecard perspective. For each key data domain, a separate data quality scorecard element will be added to the overview. There are several options to define these key data domains and create side-by-side tiles visualizing the data quality level of these business-related data domains. Example of domains used to create scorecards include:

▶ Classical data objects such as customer, supplier, employee, product, financial data

▶ Regional data domains such as North America, South America, EME, APJ

▶ Department, line of business or brand data domains such as finance, sales, marketing, human resources

This definition of the first level of separation of individual data quality scores depends on your business requirements and the data that will be assessed.

The steps below explain how to define the key data domains for a data quality scorecard:

1. On the DATA INSIGHT tab, choose the project for the new scorecard and click on the WORKSPACE hyperlink.

2. Click on the SCORECARD SETUP tab.

3. Click on the ADD button in the key data domain to open the KEY DATA DOMAIN DEFINITION window.

4. Enter the key data domain NAME and DESCRIPTION, and edit the lower and higher threshold for the traffic light color coding of the calculated score.

5. Click on the SAVE button to close the key data domain DEFINITION window.

Figure 9.3 shows an example of the customer key domain for a data quality scorecard.

Figure 9.3 Defining a Key Data Domain for a Data Quality Scorecard

Notice the name, description, and threshold settings in Figure 9.3. Although it is not pictured in the print version of this book, red is the color up to score 6.3, then yellow between 6.3 and 8.5. Any score above 8.5 is green. (Again, you can access a full-color online book at *www.sap-press.com*.)

9.2.2 Defining Data Quality Dimensions for the Key Data Domains

After setting up the key data domain for the scorecard, you defined the data quality dimensions to calculate the overall data quality score. Remember that the data quality dimensions have already been assigned to the individual validation rules (validation rules were introduced in Chapter 6). The data quality dimensions represent the next level grouping of calculated data quality scores. For a data steward responsible for a specific data domain, it is important to be able to drill down into multiple dimensions for further details to identify where the biggest problem areas for his overall data quality score are.

The data quality dimensions are described below:

▶ **Accuracy**
Determines the extent to which data objects correctly represent the real-world values for which they were designed. For example, the sales orders for the Northeast region must be assigned a Northeast sales representative.

▸ **Completeness**

Determines the extent to which data is not missing. For example, an order is not complete without a price and quantity.

▸ **Conformity**

Determines the extent to which data conforms to a specified format. For example, the order date must be in the format YYYY/MM/DD.

▸ **Consistency**

Determines the extent to which distinct data instances provide nonconflicting information about the same underlying data object. For example, the salary range for level 4 employees must be between $40,000 and $65,000.

▸ **Integrity**

Determines the extent to which data is not missing important relationship linkages. For example, the launch date for a new product must be valid and must be the first week of any quarter, since all new products are launched in the first week of each quarter.

▸ **Timeliness**

Determines the extent to which data is sufficiently up-to-date for the task at hand. For example, hats, mittens, and scarves are in stock by November.

▸ **Uniqueness**

Determines the extent to which the data for a set of columns is not repeated. For example, the new product name must be unique (the same name cannot be in the product master table).

In the future there could be an option for customers to define their own data quality dimensions.

The steps below teach you how to associate quality dimensions for a key data domain.

1. Highlight the key data domain in the SCORECARD SETUP tab where you want to add the quality dimensions.

2. Click on the ADD button in the QUALITY DIMENSIONS area to open the ASSOCIATE DIMENSIONS window.

3. Check the quality dimensions you want to add, as shown in Figure 9.4.

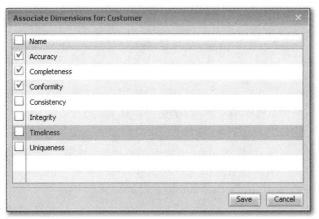

Figure 9.4 Associating Quality Dimensions to a Key Data Domain of a Data Quality Scorecard

4. Click on the SAVE button to close the ASSOCIATE DIMENSIONS window.

5. Review the weighting that you want to assign to the individual quality dimensions. By default it is an equal weighting, but you can also set up fixed weighting by changing from auto value to fixed and editing the fixed value. (Note: Weighting is also discussed in the next section.)

Returning to NeedsEIM, Inc., they have defined two key data domains for the data quality scorecard, one for the supplier data domain and one for the customer data domain. For each of the two key data domains, the data steward adds the following quality dimensions: accuracy, completeness, and conformity.

9.2.3 Adding the Validation Rules and Quality Dimensions for a Key Data Domain

The next step of the data quality scorecard setup is to add all the generic validation rules that you want to use for calculating the data quality scorecard. During the definition of the generic validation rules, the data quality dimensions were assigned to the rule. This means that within the data quality scorecard setup, the set of available validation rules to be added to a specific key data domain and possible data quality dimensions are limited based on the assignment done during the validation rule creation.

The steps below explain how to associate rules for a quality dimension:

1. Select the quality dimension in the Scorecard Setup tab where you want to add the validation rule.

2. Click on the Add button in the Rules area to open the Associate Rules window.

3. The Associate Rules window shows all the validation rules that have been defined for the quality dimensions you have selected. Check the rules you want to add from the list.

4. Click on the Save button to close the Associate Rules window.

5. Review the weighting that you want to assign to the individual rules. By default it is an equal weighting, but you can also set up fixed weighting by changing from auto value to fixed and editing the fixed value. Figure 9.5 shows an example.

Quality Dimensions				Rules		
Name	Weight		Score	Name	Weight	Score
Accuracy	Auto ▾	34	7.93	Customer telephone number must conform to std	Fixed ▾ 80	5.53
Completeness	Auto ▾	33	9.80	Customer_Postcode must be valid	Auto ▾ 20	7.67
Conformity	Auto ▾	33	5.95			
☑ Total Weight: 100%		Add	Remove	☑ Total Weight: 100%	Add	Remove

Figure 9.5 Review the Weighting of Validation Rules for a Quality Dimension on a Data Quality Scorecard

In Figure 9.5 notice that the quality dimension Conformity has two rules, one for the telephone number conformity and a second for the zip code. Also notice in Figure 9.5 that the weight for the postal code is automatically set to 20 and the telephone number rule has a fixed rating of 80. You can also see the existing score of the rule. This score is from the last execution of the validation rules.

NeedsEIM, Inc. can use this capability to define a generic validation rule called "An email address needs to have a specific pattern," which was linked to the conformity data quality dimension. The data steward creating the data quality scorecard adds this validation rule to the conformity data quality dimension for the key data domains for supplier and customer.

9.2.4 Binding the Data Sources to the Data Quality Scorecard

After the validation rules are added to the data quality dimensions for each key data domain, the last step is to bind the data sources to the individual validation rules. Remember from Chapter 6 that a core concept in Information Steward is to allow companies to define and approve the validation rules once and manage them centrally, abstracted from specific data sources. These validation rules are then bound to individual data sources that can be stored in multiple locations throughout the enterprise. For the data quality scorecard setup, the same validation rule might be used for multiple key data domains, but only bindings to individual data sources and the data quality scores from these data sources should be used to calculate the overall score of a key data domain.

The steps below explain how to associate a validation rule with a specific data source:

1. Select the rule in the SCORECARD SETUP tab where you want to add the rule binding. In Figure 9.6, the rule about the telephone number has been selected.

2. Click on the ADD button in the RULE BINDINGS area to open the ASSOCIATE RULE BINDINGS window.

3. The ASSOCIATE RULE BINDINGS window shows all the source connections that have been defined for the rule you have selected. Check the RULE BINDINGS you want to add from the list.

Figure 9.6 Data Quality Scorecard Setup

4. Click on the SAVE button to close the ASSOCIATE RULE BINDINGS window. Figure 9.6 shows the results where the telephone number rule has been associated with two views: the major U.S. customer view and the individual customer view.

5. Review the weighting that you want to assign to the individual rule bindings. By default, it is an equal weighting, but you can also set up fixed weighting by changing from auto value to fixed and editing the fixed value.

You have successfully completed the data quality scorecard setup if none of the elements on the scorecard setup panel has a warning symbol indicating that the next hierarchy level has not been set up.

In the case of NeedsEIM, Inc., they have bound the generic validation rule called "An email address needs to have a specific pattern" to the email columns of the customer, supplier, and employee database tables. For the data quality scorecard, they have chosen to represent only the supplier and the customer key data domain. The data steward at NeedsEIM, Inc. added the validation rule "An email address needs to have a specific pattern" to the conformity data quality dimension for each of the two key data domains, customer and supplier, and bound them to the respective tables. This automatically ensures that the data quality scores calculated for the generic validation rule on the different database tables will be correctly assigned to the right data quality scorecard tile.

9.3   Viewing the Data Quality Scorecard

The data quality scorecard is the central entry point to gain quick insight into the current and historical data quality level of specific data domains. From the data quality scorecard, you can drill down to detailed-level information, even down to the failed record sample data. The data quality scorecard includes an additional perspective on the data quality scores calculated during the rule task execution. Compared to the more technical perspectives already described in Chapter 6, this perspective is intended for the business user or data steward who wants to view data for a given data domain, independent of the technical objects and tables where the corresponding data is stored within the applications and databases.

Once the scorecard is set up, you just select the SCORECARD link in the data insight project. An example is shown in Figure 9.7 for the conformity data quality dimension for the postal code rule.

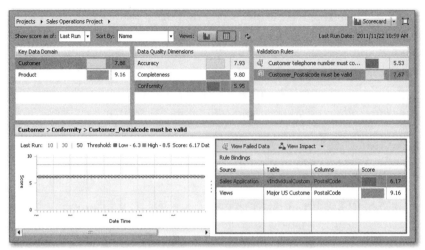

Figure 9.7 Drill Down to the Individual Rule Binding Level in the Data Quality Scorecard Detail View

For each of the key data domains, you can now review the overall quality score value between 0 and 10 with a quick indicator of traffic light colors (not shown in the print book, but viewable in the full-color online book) based on the defined thresholds. This gives you a very good first insight into the current level of data quality of the data related to the key data domain. As the quality score is calculated from the different quality dimensions, you can see the status of those quality dimensions in a bar chart as well. While the diagram shows only the color codes for quick insight, you can move the mouse over the individual bars to get detailed information from the tool tips. The quality trend for the quality score of the key data domain is also presented on this data quality scorecard tile, giving you information about how the quality score has changed over time and the last data quality assessments. This also gives you an early indicator if the quality score has increased (e.g., after a data cleansing activity) or decreased (e.g., after a new data load) over time.

This section explains how to drill into the scorecard details and analyze the failed record sample.

9.3.1 Drilling Down into Data Quality Scorecard Details

Follow the steps below to drill down into the data quality scorecard details:

1. Click on the SHOW MORE... hyperlink in the key data domain scorecard tile.

2. Review the quality score of each of the key data domains.

3. Select the key data domain into which you want to drill down further, and view how the rest of the information on the scorecard is filtered based on your selection. You will see only the data quality dimensions, validation rules, and rule bindings that are assigned to your selected key data domain. Also, the Score Trend chart now represents the trend over time for your selected key data domain.

4. Select the data quality dimension in which you want to drill down further, and view how the rest of the information on the scorecard is filtered based on your selection. You will see only the validation rules and rule bindings that are assigned to your selected data quality dimension. Also, the Score Trend chart now represents the trend over time for your selected data quality dimension.

5. Select the validation rule into which you want to drill down further, and view how the rest of the information on the scorecard is filtered based on your selection. You will see only the rule bindings that are assigned to your selected validation rule. Also, the Score Trend chart now represents the trend over time for your selected validation rule.

6. Select the rule binding into which you want to drill down further, and view how the trend chart changes. Hover the mouse over the score value for the rule binding and get further information on the number of failed and total records for score calculation.

In Figure 9.7, notice the scorecard for the sales operation project that has a conformity score of 5.95 with two rules: the telephone number rule and the postal code rule. By selecting the postal code rule, you can see that in the sales application individual custom table it has a score of 6.17; for the postal U.S. customer table it has a score of 9.16.

From the scorecard in Figure 9.7, you can see that the trend of the postal code rule has remained the same over the time measured and that the quality in the individual customer table is much lower than the major U.S. customer table.

9.3.2 Analyze Failed Record Sample Data

At this point you need to analyze the failed records. The steps for this process are as follows:

1. Click on the VIEW FAILED DATA button (shown in Figure 9.8) to view the failed record sample data in a separate window (shown in Figure 9.8).

2. Click on the column headlines to sort the records or click on the SHOW COLUMNS or FILTER CRITERIA button to change the layout of the table.

3. Click on the EXPORT TO EXCEL button to save the table to a spreadsheet for further review or processing.

Figure 9.8 shows an example of failed data.

Figure 9.8 View the Failed Record Sample Data from the Data Quality Scorecard Detail View

Once you have viewed the failed data, you can use this information to fix the data issues as well as identify the root cause and impact of the poor data quality in your enterprise.

9.4 Identifying Data Quality Issue Impact or Data Quality Root Causes in the System Landscape

As mentioned previously, you can drill down from the data quality scorecard to the individual validation rule scores and inspect the failed record sample data. This provides insight into the content of the data source that is assessed by the data quality project and allows you to identify how good or bad the data in the data sources really is.

But successfully managing data quality does not only mean identifying that the data in a specific data store is not meeting the given requirements. It is also important to identify what impact this bad data has on any other application or system in the enterprise. With the direct linkage of data quality monitoring and metadata management capabilities, it is possible to follow how data elements are moved between or within different applications.

This means, for example, you can drill down in a data quality scorecard to the current quality scores on the staging area of an SAP NetWeaver Business Warehouse (BW) system to analyze the impact of the bad data in the warehouse down to the report level. This section explains the process of reviewing the data quality issue impact on downstream processes or reports, as well as analyzing the data quality root causes.

9.4.1 Reviewing Data Quality Issue Impact on Downstream Processes or Reports

Follow the steps below to determine the data quality issue impact on downstream processes or reports:

1. In the data quality scorecard DETAIL VIEW select the RULE BINDING, including the data source and column to see the impact information.
2. Click on VIEW IMPACT. This opens a separate screen, including the impact analysis diagram representing the relationships among the technical objects such as the tables, mappings, queries, and reports of an SAP NetWeaver BW installation.

Figure 9.9 shows an example of an impact analysis for the telephone validation rule.

In Figure 9.9, the impact analysis shows what data fields have been selected based on the rule binding and the quality score that has been measured for the field. In the figure notice that the link is mapped to Data Services from the application for the ETL relationships, which is then mapped to a Rapid Mart. This was done based on the metadata information that has been integrated into Information Steward. This impact analysis can help answer the following questions:

► What ETL tool or process is moving data from this data field to other databases or applications?

► How is a data warehouse using this field? (For example, in SAP NetWeaver BW, what InfoCube or query in a data warehouse application is using this data field for calculating KPI information?)

▶ What report in my data warehouse application is showing information based on the source data field?

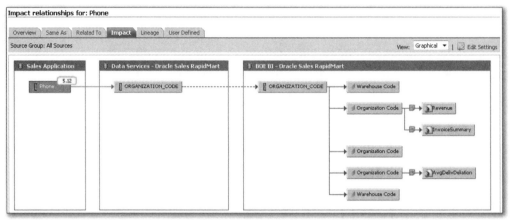

Figure 9.9 Data Quality Issue Impact Analysis

Based on this impact analysis diagram, you can precisely track down which other applications further downstream in the data flow or process chain are using the identified bad data. This allows you to identify the priority of necessary data cleansing or improvement activities on the bad data. For example, the data quality issue impact analysis shows that some of the most important business processes or reports are using data from data source fields that have a very low data quality score.

Another important use case for the direct linkage between the data quality scorecard and metadata management is the data quality root cause analysis. While a data steward is drilling down into the detail view of the data quality scorecard for a master data table, he can choose to view the lineage analysis functionality from metadata management directly from the data quality scorecard as well. In this case, the lineage analysis diagram shows the highlighted data field from the rule binding area on the right-hand side of the diagram, and also shows how this field was populated by an ETL solution from any data source system (including the mapping and data movement information). This allows you to track back and determine from what source field the bad data was populated. Based on this data quality root cause analysis, further data quality assessment activities or data cleansing activities at the entry point of the bad data can be set up to improve the overall data quality level.

9.4.2 Analyzing Data Quality Root Causes

The following steps describe how to analyze data quality root causes. (The result was shown in Figure 9.9.)

1. On the data quality scorecard detail view, select the rule binding, including the data source and column where you are interested in getting impact information.

2. Click on the VIEW IMPACT button dropdown and choose VIEW LINEAGE. This opens a separate screen, including the data lineage diagram shown in Figure 9.9. This represents the relationships of the technical objects, such as source tables, ETL processes that moved the data, and so on.

This analysis is important to NeedsEIM, Inc. They start by drilling down the data quality scorecard of the supplier data to the binding of the validation rule "An email address needs to have a specific pattern" to the supplier master table. As the quality score is quite low, the view lineage functionality is used to identify how the data field email_address has been populated by Data Services, and from what operational source systems the data has been extracted. This allows them to get insight into where the bad data can come from. The data lineage graph indicates that two Data Services jobs have moved email address information from the operational SAP ERP Central Component (ECC) system as well as from the additional Microsoft SQL Server database system. As a next step, they can initiate a data quality assessment on these source systems to verify if only one or both systems include bad email address information. They just need to add these systems to the data insight project and apply the already defined validation rules to the operational systems as well.

9.5 Summary

In this chapter we added the concept of data quality scorecards in Information Steward to the set of capabilities of SAP's EIM solutions. Data quality scorecards allow business users to get easy and direct access to the quality score of the key data domains for which they are responsible. In addition to the overview, data stewards can drill into various detail levels, down to individual data sources violating the defined validation rules. They can browse and review the failed record sample data. In addition, with the integrated linkage to the metadata management capabilities, they can also identify either from what source system failed data is populated into the systems, or where the bad data is being used. This provides an organization with not only information about the content quality level of their data assets, but also transparency and confidence in the data used by its operational applications. It allows an organization to know it can track where its data is coming from, and the quality of that data.

This chapter provides an example of using EIM capabilities for effective text analytics. In this chapter, you will learn about the text data processing capabilities delivered with SAP Data Services.

10   Processing Text Data with SAP Data Services

Text analytics, or text data processing, is the process of taking unstructured text data and turning it into something you can analyze and act on. It allows you to deal with information overload by mining very large bodies of text and making sense of all of the information without having to read every sentence. Simply put, text analytics automates research analysis from data sources that were previously unprocessable.

It is generally known that up to 80% or more of enterprise-relevant information originates in unstructured data, including email, customer response inquiries, blogs, forum postings, social media, surveys, and warranty claims. It may seem unfathomable, but the sheer amount of this unstructured data is doubling in increments of months, not years. Millions of Internet pages are being added by the day. How can businesses attempt to tame this textual tsunami? Building business intelligence requires more than simply searching for and finding vast amounts of information. The ability to perform accurate, large-scale, and rapid detection of key information trapped in enterprise, electronic, or social media is vital. Businesses need to automatically identify salient information in this tsunami—entities such as people, products, places, dates, and other information—by filtering out the noise in unstructured text sources and providing structure for use in routing, searching, and business intelligence applications.

Text analytics can assist the enterprise by pinpointing the who, what, where, when, and how much in unstructured text. The primary benefit of locating these atomic elements and transforming them into structured types is that businesses can spend more time analyzing and less time searching text. IT can unlock trends, issues, and opportunities concealed by unstructured text data. This information discovery facilitates enterprise decision-making processes by extending the value of your business intelligence investments that report from structured data.

Chapter 4 mentioned a few use cases for text data processing. Table 10.1 provides a more comprehensive list.

Use Case	Description
Electronic discovery	Discovery is a pretrial phase in a lawsuit, in which each party makes information available to the other. A lawyer's time is expensive. Accelerate the process of analyzing documents for evidence.
Brand monitoring	Someone wants to know what people are saying about their products and brands. Are they creating a "buzz," and is it positive or negative?
Employee morale	Use sentiment analysis of collaboration spaces to detect employee problems early.
Investigative case management	Analyze criminal records to discover connections among suspects, organizations, and events.
Innovation management	It's a labor-intensive process to evaluate ideas. Find related variances and group them together.
Patent research	Classify invention disclosure forms (IDF) according to topic maps.
Customer service	Optimize call center operations by routing topics in questions to the right person.
Information governance, risk, and compliance	Detect leaks of confidential data.
Recruiting	Help HR departments best match applicants to open positions.
Public sector	Analyze field reports for connections between people, organizations, bank accounts, and so on to discover terrorist networks and other threats.
Life sciences and pharmaceutical research	Aid scientists in finding related research documents.

Table 10.1 Use Cases for Text Data Processing

Use Case	Description
Health care informatics	Scrutinize patient records to assist hospitals with identifying drug dosages from freeform notes.
Personalized newsfeeds	Use reader interests to identify news articles they may want to read.
Customer satisfaction	Predict customer churn and detect product defects from customer complaints.
Contract management	Author, negotiate, audit, and continuously improve contracts to help organizations establish strategic long-term agreements.

Table 10.1 Use Cases for Text Data Processing (Cont.)

In this chapter, you will get an introduction to the text data processing capabilities provided by SAP. After that, we will dive into the details of the entity extraction transform, which is the transform for text data processing capabilities.

10.1 Introduction to Text Data Processing Capabilities in SAP Data Services

SAP Data Services (hereafter Data Services) is a unified, fully integrated platform for doing data integration and data quality on unstructured text data as well as structured data. This unique data foundation enables businesses to gain insights and make decisions on the basis of high-quality, reliable data that leverages both structured and unstructured sources.

In Data Services, text data processing (TDP) refers to transforms that extract information from unstructured data in multiple languages and create structured data that can be used by business intelligence tools. TDP analyzes text and automatically identifies and extracts entities, including people, dates, places, organizations, and so on. It also looks for patterns, activities, events, and relationships among entities and enables their extraction. Identifying such information tells you what the text is about.

> **Note**
>
> Data Services provides, by default, out-of-the-box core entities, relations, and events preconfigured to extract key information from text in numerous languages. You can get more details about these language modules in the text data processing Language Reference Guide at *http://help.sap.com/boeim*.

TDP goes beyond conventional string matching tools for information retrieval, which seek exact or fuzzy matches for specific sequences of characters. It applies full linguistic and statistical techniques to ensure that the entities and relationships that get returned are correct.

First, TDP performs grammatical parsing on the input text, for example:

▶ Can we *bill* you?

▶ *Bill* was the president.

As a result, it linguistically figures out if the word *bill* is a verb or a noun in the first bullet and not a person. In the second bullet, *Bill* is a proper noun.

Second, TDP performs semantic disambiguation, which is the process of resolving conflicts that arise when a term is ambiguous. For example:

▶ I talked to *Bill* yesterday.

▶ The duck has a *bill*.

▶ The *bill* was signed into law.

As a result, TDP figures out which noun is a person and core entity. In the first bullet, *Bill* is a proper noun, which is the name of a person. In the second bullet, *bill* is a common noun with one meaning. In the third bullet, *bill* is a common noun with a completely different meaning.

TDP automates the extraction of key information from text sources to reduce manual review and tagging. Access to relevant information in unstructured text can help streamline operations and reduce unnecessary costs by enabling you to understand important insights hidden in text.

In Chapters 7 and 8 you learned that there are several types of transforms in Data Services. There are transforms for cleansing, data validation, the query transform, and so on. Text data processing capabilities are also tied to a transform. Text data processing happens via the entity extraction transform. Next we will provide an overview of the entity extraction transform and discuss how it works.

10.1.1 Entity Extraction Transform Overview

Extracting entities and relationships among entities from unstructured text is accomplished in the Data Services designer using the entity extraction transform under the TEXT DATA PROCESSING folder. This is shown in Figure 10.1 and was accessed via the method shown in Section 7.5.3. The entity extraction transform is another transform found in the TRANSFORMS tab in the Local Object Library in Data Services.

Figure 10.1 Entity Extraction Transform under the "Text Data Processing" Folder in the Data Services Designer

Extraction involves grammatically parsing and semantically disambiguating the text, discovering entities of interest, classifying them to the appropriate type, and providing this metadata in a standard format. By using dictionaries and rules, you can customize your pattern extraction output.

Entities denote names of things that can be extracted and categorized by type. Entities may have subtypes that indicate further classification; this is a hierarchical specification of an entity type that enables the distinction between different semantic varieties of the same entity type. A subtype can be described as a subcategory of an entity.

Here are some examples of entities and subtypes:

▶ Boeing 747 is an entity of type VEHICLE with a subtype AIR.

▶ BMW X5 is an entity of type VEHICLE with a subtype LAND.

▶ SAP is an entity of type ORGANIZATION with a subtype COMMERCIAL.

Facts are umbrella terms covering extractions of more complex patterns, including one or more entities, a relationship between one or more entities, or some sort of state involving an entity. Entities by themselves only show that they are present in the text corpora, but facts provide information on how these entities are related. Facts are extracted using custom extraction rules. Fact types identify the category of a fact; for example, sentiments and requests.

Here are some examples of facts:

▶ *Business Objects acquired Inxight in a friendly takeover.* This is a relationship of type MERGER AND ACQUISITION.

▶ *Ms. Jane Smith is very upset with her reservation.* This is a relationship of type SENTIMENT.

10.1.2   How Extraction Works

The extraction process uses its inherent knowledge of the semantics of words and the linguistic context in which these words occur to find entities and facts. It creates specific patterns to extract entities and facts based on system rules. You can add entries in a dictionary as well as write custom rules to customize extraction output. The following sample text and sample output (Table 10.2) show how unstructured text data can be transformed into structured information for further processing and analysis.

> *Steven Paul Jobs (born February 24, 1955) is an American business magnate and inventor. He is well known for being the co-founder and chief executive*

officer of Apple. Jobs also previously served as chief executive of Pixar Animation Studios; he became a member of the board of The Walt Disney Company in 2006, following the acquisition of Pixar by Disney.

Entities	Type
Steven Paul Jobs; Jobs	PERSON
February 24, 1955; 2006	DATE
Co-founder; chief executive officer; chief executive; member of the board	TITLE
Apple; Pixar Animation Studios; Pixar; The Walt Disney Company; Disney	ORGANIZATION@COMMERCIAL
American business magnate; inventor; acquisition	NOUN_GROUP or Concept
Facts	Type
Jobs also previously served as chief executive of Pixar...	EXECUTIVE JOB CHANGE
Acquisition of Pixar by Disney	MERGER AND ACQUISITION

Table 10.2 Conversion of Unstructured Text To Structured Entity and Fact Types

The entity and fact extraction process is based on the use of dictionaries and rules:

▶ **Dictionary**
A dictionary for TDP is a user-defined list of entities. It allows for specifying entities that the entity extraction transform should always extract while processing text. The information is classified under the standard form and the variant of an entity. A standard form may have one or more variants. For example, *American Telephone and Telegraph* may be the standard form for a company, and *AT&T* is a variant of the same company. However, many would agree it is the other way around.

▶ **Rule**
A rule for TDP defines custom patterns to extract entities, sentiments, events, and other relationships between entities that are together referred to as facts. You write custom extraction rules to perform extraction that is customized to your specific domain; for example, to identify entities in unusual or

industry-specific language, such as the use of the word *crash* in computer software versus insurance statistics.

10.2   Text Data Processing and NeedsEIM, Inc.

Now that you have a general understanding of the technology, uses cases, and content, the following step-by-step example will get you started with TDP in Data Services.

The entity extraction transform can extract information from any text, HTML, or XML content and generate structured output. You can use the output in several ways: You can use it as an input to another transform or write to multiple output sources such as a database table or a flat file.

The following sections provide an overview of this functionality in light of some challenges facing NeedsEIM, Inc.

10.2.1   NeedsEIM, Inc. Pain Points

NeedsEIM, Inc. has seen an uptick in product quality issues as reported through the warranty channels in their complex supplier network. Fearing that this could lead to a widespread product recall, which would result in lost revenues and damage the brand, the risk management team must evaluate and mitigate the risks.

However, their data warehouse does not contain any information about the root cause of the quality issues, which is locked inside field technicians' free-form text notes. They also do not have the staff to read every repair log file and tag them for root causes.

After IT processes the text data fields using the TDP entity extraction transform to detect root causes, the dashboard shown in Figure 10.2 enables the risk management team to drill down into the results, explore the data, and discover correlations between products and models and the top 10 quality issues affecting them. Notice the most common concepts, by product line, which TDP has detected and extracted from the technicians' comment fields. TDP has pulled these concepts into a new field, making analysis of the root causes possible, where there was no visibility before.

Figure 10.2 shows an example of what a report might look like.

Figure 10.2 Top Defects Report Extracted from Technicians' Free-Form Notes

In Figure 10.2 notice the list of the top 10 defects and a summary of the types of defects. Data Services made this possible by:

▶ Integrating the warranty repair data into the warehouse.

▶ Processing the text data to discover the most mentioned concepts.

▶ Matching the discovered concepts to determine the most common root causes.

Figure 10.3 shows a job in Data Services that is used for text data processing to create the dashboard shown in Figure 10.2.

Figure 10.3 Data Flow in Data Services that Extracts Entities from the Technicians' Integrated Repair Log

Figure 10.3 is the entire job required to extract the data, cleanse, match, process the text data, and prepare the data for the dashboard. Next we describe how the text data processing transform highlighted in Figure 10.3 was built, including the key requirement for text data processing, the entity extraction transform.

10.2.2   Using the Entity Extraction Transform

From a very high level, NeedsEIM, Inc. requires processing of unstructured text data from a database that IT set up to integrate all the repair logs. To do this, they have to do the following:

1. Configure a connection to the database via a datastore.
2. Build a data flow with the database table as the source, an entity extraction transform, and a target.
3. Configure the transform to process the text.

Next we describe the step-by-step instructions for using the entity extraction transform. This includes adding it to a data flow, configuring the transform, and hints for working with the entity extraction transform.

> **Note**
>
> Before reading the next sections, you should first read Chapter 7 to understand the basics of Data Services.

How to Add an Entity Extraction Transform to a Data Flow

This section describes the steps necessary to add an entity extraction transform to a data flow.

> **Note**
>
> A transform configuration is preconfigured with best practices for input fields, output fields, and options. These are useful if you repeatedly use a transform with specific options and fields. You can also create your own transform configuration, either by replicating an existing configuration or creating a new one.

The steps below use a transform configuration provided out-of-the box for the entity extraction transform. This transform configuration is called BASE_ENTITYEXTRACTION.

1. Open a data flow object.

2. Open the Local Object Library if it is not already open.

3. Go to the TRANSFORMS tab.

4. Expand the TEXT DATA PROCESSING folder and select the transform or transform configuration that you want to add to the data flow.

   In Figure 10.4 ENTITY_EXTRACTION is the transform and BASE_ENTITYEXTRACTION is the transform configuration.

Figure 10.4   Entity Extraction Transform and Transform Configuration as Base_EntityExtraction

5. Drag the transform ENTITY_EXTRACTION or the transform configuration BASE_ ENTITYEXTRACTION onto the data flow workspace.

6. Draw the data flow connections.

7. Double-click on the name of the transform. This opens the Transform Editor, which lets you complete the definition of the transform.

8. In the SCHEMA IN field, select the input field that you want to map and drag it to the appropriate field in the INPUT tab. This is shown in Figure 10.5.

9. This maps the input field to a field name that the transform recognizes so that the transform knows how to process it correctly. For example, an input field that is named TEXT would be mapped to the TEXT input field. It is important to know that the TEXT input field for input mapping can have the data type *long*, *blob*, or *varchar*. The content to be processed must be in text, HTML, or XML format.

367

Figure 10.5 Mapping of the TEXT Input Field for the Entity Extraction Transform.

10. In the OPTIONS tab, select the appropriate option values to determine how the transform will process your data. This is shown in Figure 10.6.

11. Make sure that you map input fields before you set option values.

12. If you change an option value from its default value, a green triangle appears next to the option name to indicate that you made an override.

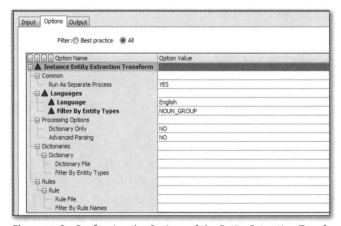

Figure 10.6 Configuring the Options of the Entity Extraction Transform

The settings are shown in Figure 10.6. Below we offer some hints for configuring the transform:

▶ Notice the field RUN AS SEPARATE PROCESS. You cannot change the value of this option. The entity extraction transform always spawns into a separate process.

▶ LANGUAGE specifies the language of your input data. You must select a language from the list of available languages in the dropdown menu.

▶ FILTER BY ENTITY TYPES is used to limit the extraction output to include only selected entities for this language.

▶ DICTIONARY ONLY limits the extraction process to use entities defined only in the specified dictionaries. You must specify a dictionary file to use this option. TDP includes the dictionary schema file *extraction-dictionary.xsd*. By default, this file is installed in the *LINK_DIR/bin* folder, where *LINK_DIR* is your Data Services installation directory. Refer to this schema to create your own dictionary files.

▶ ADVANCED PARSING is used to produce metadata for richer noun phrase structure, noun phrase coordination, and syntactic attributes that can be leveraged in custom rules. This is only available in English.

Configuring the Output Tab of the Entity Extraction Transform

1. In the OUTPUT tab, double-click on the fields that you want to output from the transform. The transform can generate fields in addition to the input fields that the transform processes, so you can output many fields. This is shown in Figure 10.7.

Figure 10.7 Output Fields that You Can Use in the Output Mapping for the Entity Extraction

2. Make sure that you set options before you map output fields.

3. The selected fields appear in the output schema. The output schema of this transform becomes the input schema of the next transform in the data flow.

The following are hints for working with output fields:

▶ STANDARD_FORM is the official or normalized name associated with the value of the corresponding TYPE.

▶ TYPE is the type of entity or fact. It may also represent subtypes.

▶ LENGTH is the character length of an entity or a fact.

At this point you have:

▶ Configured a connection to the database via a datastore.

▶ Built a data flow with the database table as the source, an entity extraction transform, and a target.

▶ Configured the transform to process the text.

Now you can run the job so that TDP parses the unstructured text input in the field technicians' notes, identifies the concepts mentioned, and pulls these concepts into a new field, making analysis of root causes possible. We can now access a qualitatively different type of information, where there was no visibility before. First look at the example input data shown in Figure 10.8.

DATE	CASE	MODEL	SERIAL	PRODUCT	TEXT
2006.11.27	3103441	ZIC360NMBLH	ZDO30595	11	"leaking from fill tube at ba...
2006.11.29	3103473	JT952BFBB	ML608657Q	21	lot of grease on the oven fl...
2006.11.28	3103472	GSS22QGMWW	FD224746	11	tech reports new doors wer...
2006.11.29	3103475	ZISB360DRB	LG033436	11	"Warm ff. Check all the ba...
2006.11.29	3103479	SCA1001KSS02	TL900491K	27	"The cavity is dented on th...
2006.11.30	3103480	PDW9800J10BB	RH717747	41	"Leaking from the top tub s...
2006.11.28	3103482	JVM2070SK02	EL903119B	27	tech reports control freezes...
2006.11.29	3103485	SCA2000BAA	AZ900092	27	"new smart board not oper...
2006.11.29	3103484	FUF20DPJRWH	SLT71980	13	consumer complains of moi...
2006.11.25	3103489	GSD4330Z00WW	HT752896B	41	"tech reports harness caug...
2006.11.25	3103488	GSD5500G02CC	LG800836B	41	"tech reports that call was ...
2006.11.28	3103490	FCM20DPFWH	LL171525	13	"tech 582 reports he replac...
2006.11.29	3103496	PDW8280J10SS	RL825724B	41	"left side hinge failed on fra...
2006.11.24	3103500	PFS22SISBSS	VH047253	11	"REPAIRABLE Tech state...
2006.11.29	3103503	GTS18FBSWW	RH778315	11	"There was a leak in the e...
2007.01.02	3193507	JVM1851BD002	GD994218S	27	"Bob. Burnt wave guide. u...
2007.01.02	3193508	JVM1441WD	TA919262S	27	"glass broke, repairable ...
2006.12.01	3103442	SCA1000HWW04	GL901955K	27	"tech states the unit was dr...
2006.11.28	3103502	JVM1790WK01	RL901683	27	tech 332 reports that tone ...

Figure 10.8 Input Data from the Technicians' Notes in the Text Column

In Figure 10.8, notice the unstructured input data from the field technicians' notes in the TEXT column; for example, the NEW SMART BOARD NOT OPER... record. This record has a serial number, product number, and text. In Figure 10.9, notice how this changes after the execution of text data processing in Data Services.

DATE	CASE	MODEL	SERIAL	PRODUCT	STANDARD_FORM	TYPE	LENGTH
2006.11.29 00:00:00.0000...	3103485	SCA2000BAA	AZ900092	27	new smart board	NOUN_GROUP	15
2006.11.29 00:00:00.0000...	3103485	SCA2000BAA	AZ900092	27	NON REPAIRABLE o/w	NOUN_GROUP	18
2006.11.29 00:00:00.0000...	3103485	SCA2000BAA	AZ900092	27	return unit	NOUN_GROUP	11
2006.11.29 00:00:00.0000...	3103484	FUF20DPJRWH	SL171980	13	environmental issues	NOUN_GROUP	20
2006.11.25 00:00:00.0000...	3103489	GSD4330Z00WW	HT752896B	41	caught fire	NOUN_GROUP	11
2006.11.25 00:00:00.0000...	3103488	GSD5500G02CC	LG800836B	41	top rack binding	NOUN_GROUP	16
2006.11.28 00:00:00.0000...	3103482	JVM2070SK02	FL903119B	27	known suggestions	NOUN_GROUP	17
2006.11.28 00:00:00.0000...	3103482	JVM2070SK02	FL903119B	27	smart board	NOUN_GROUP	11
2006.11.28 00:00:00.0000...	3103482	JVM2070SK02	FL903119B	27	vent louver motor runs	NOUN_GROUP	22
2006.11.28 00:00:00.0000...	3103472	GSS22QGMWW	FD224746	11	consumer uses alot	NOUN_GROUP	18
2006.11.28 00:00:00.0000...	3103472	GSS22QGMWW	FD224746	11	crushed ice	NOUN_GROUP	11
2006.11.28 00:00:00.0000...	3103472	GSS22QGMWW	FD224746	11	air leaks	NOUN_GROUP	9
2006.11.29 00:00:00.0000...	3103475	ZISB360DRB	LG033436	11	cold air return	NOUN_GROUP	15
2006.11.29 00:00:00.0000...	3103479	SCA1001KSS02	TL900491K	27	left side wall	NOUN_GROUP	14
2006.11.30 00:00:00.0000...	3103480	PDW9800J10BB	RH717747	41	top tub seams	NOUN_GROUP	13
2006.11.28 00:00:00.0000...	3103472	GSS22QGMWW	FD224746	11	new doors	NOUN_GROUP	9
2006.11.28 00:00:00.0000...	3103490	FCM20DPFWH	LL171525	13	returned appl	NOUN_GROUP	13
2006.11.28 00:00:00.0000...	3103502	JVM1790WK01	RL901683	27	possible volume levels	NOUN_GROUP	22
2006.11.28 00:00:00.0000...	3103502	JVM1790WK01	RL901683	27	middle volume level	NOUN_GROUP	19
2006.11.28 00:00:00.0000...	3103502	JVM1790WK01	RL901683	27	OVEN LIGHT	NOUN_GROUP	10

Figure 10.9 Extracted Entities from the Technicians' Notes in the STANDARD_FORM Column Limited to NOUN_GROUP as Indicated in the TYPE Column

In Figure 10.9, notice that after processing the technicians' free-form notes, the entity extraction transform has pulled out the concepts or NOUN_GROUP entities into a new field. For example, on the top row in the STANDARD_FORM column, the NEW SMART BOARD concept is highlighted. We now have the information that the smart board is a return unit and is nonrepairable.

Without processing the text fields, our reporting could only work with the structured fields in the data: DATE, MODEL NUMBER, PRODUCT LINE, and REGION. There was nothing explaining root cause, severity, or what was done to address the issue. This has changed since performing text data processing. Figure 10.10 shows a dashboard aggregating the entities including their various variations.

The use of text data processing enables companies like NeedsEIM, Inc. to turn service technicians' logs into proof-points of product quality issues they are facing. Trends and issues can now be addressed without requiring the staff to read every repair log file and tag them for root cause.

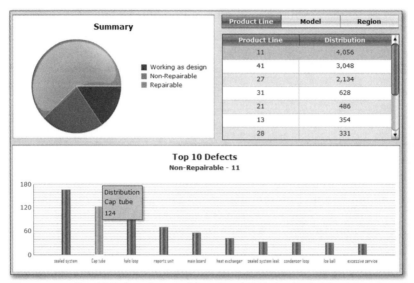

Figure 10.10 Top 10 Defects Extracted from NeedsEIM, Inc. Technicians' Free-Form Text

10.3 Summary

In this chapter you have successfully used TDP to sort through the noise of manually entered text and automatically distill the meaningful bits from it. Because the transformation of unstructured text is automated, it provides a means to handle a high volume of data.

In the next chapter you will learn about the use of Data Services for migrating data to new applications.

This chapter explains how to use Data Services for effective data migration. In this chapter you will learn details about what SAP delivers for data migration and how you can get going quickly on your data migration projects.

11 Migrating Data with SAP Data Services

Data migration has been mentioned several times thus far in the book, and was discussed in some detail in Chapter 4. Chapter 7 also discussed data migration as a typical use case for using data integration capabilities delivered with SAP Data Services (hereafter Data Services). This chapter will expand upon previous discussions by walking you through both the SAP products and migration content SAP provides for data migration projects. Specifically, Section 11.1 will discuss use cases for data migration, then describe solutions available for data migration; Section 11.2 will teach you about migration content delivered by SAP to accelerate migration projects; Section 11.3 will walk through a specific example of migrating customer data to SAP ERP; and finally, Section 11.4 will describe systems migration.

11.1 Introduction to Data Migration

Chapter 4 discussed business reasons why you need to migrate data, but we also should examine technical reasons for data migration projects. Some common reasons include:

▶ **Implementing a new SAP application system**
This includes any new SAP ERP or SAP Customer Relationship Management (CRM) implementation, adding a line of business to an existing SAP application, or an industry implementation such as SAP for utilities or SAP for banking. This could also include a new data warehouse application from SAP.

▶ **Database vendor consolidation**
Database vendor consolidation requires a data migration if companies want to

reduce the number of databases they need to support; for example, migrating your existing SAP ERP systems to SAP Sybase ASE.

▶ **System consolidation**
System consolidation projects can be driven from a green-IT or sustainability project, by the business to simplify the business processes, or by IT to reduce the total cost of ownership through the reduction of systems that require maintenance and ongoing production support.

In all of these scenarios, you need to migrate data from one system to another. Data migration is often a first entry point to enterprise information management. Normally you need to do more than just relocate the data. You also need to cleanse, validate, de-duplicate, and possibly enrich the data. Additionally, data migration projects include a definition of rules for the quality of the data, and these rules can be reused for ongoing data integration as well as ongoing data assessment. The governance that is required in migration projects will hopefully evolve to ongoing information governance. (Information governance projects are discussed in Chapter 2; data quality rules and assessments are discussed in Chapters 6 and 9.)

SAP has several solutions for data migration; each one is listed below:

▶ **SAP Data Migration**
SAP Data Migration uses Data Services and SAP Information Steward (hereafter Information Steward) for assessing and migrating your data. This solution is the focus of this chapter and SAP's recommendation when migrating from non-SAP applications to SAP.

▶ **Legacy System Migration Workbench**
Legacy System Migration Workbench (LSMW) is a data loader tool available in SAP NetWeaver Application Server ABAP. It is a tool for loading the data and does not extract, cleanse, govern, or provide data quality capabilities.

▶ **SAP NetWeaver Information Lifecycle Management (ILM)**
For a system consolidation scenario, once you move to a central and harmonized system, you need to decommission your source data. From a data migration perspective, this includes a data migration of your source systems to SAP NetWeaver ILM. System decommissioning is discussed in more detail in Chapter 13.

▶ **SAP Landscape Transformation**
SAP Landscape Transformation is used to migrate specific data from one SAP system to another SAP system. A common example is an older 4.6c system where

you want to migrate one company code or one profit center to another SAP system. SAP Landscape Transformation performs these types of migrations for companies with multiple SAP systems.

> **Note**
>
> For those experienced with LSMW who want to also extract, cleanse, and get the full benefit from using Data Services, you can use Data Services for extraction, transformation, and then you can call LSMW to load the data.

SAP Data Migration software is the focus of this chapter because it includes migration of non-SAP data and migration from any target to any source. It offers (via Data Services) rich capabilities for extraction, cleansing, transformation, validation, and de-duplication of data prior to loading. The work done for data migration can be leveraged for ongoing integration as well as ongoing data cleansing.

Using SAP's solutions for EIM in your data migration projects enables you to:

1. Profile and extract from diverse source systems.
2. Map the source data to the target data structures, including simple and complex transformations of the data.
3. Standardize, parse, cleanse, and validate data. This includes data validation against the target business context (i.e., the business rules of the target system, such as if plants are required or if the country codes are correct).
4. Load data into the target system.
5. Reconcile loaded data to know what was loaded versus what was expected to be loaded.

When referring to SAP Data Migration software, we are specifically referring to Data Services and Information Steward used for data migration projects.

11.2   Data Migration Content Delivered by SAP Best Practices and Rapid Deployment Solutions

If all you needed for successful data migration projects was software tooling, we would not provide a separate chapter for data migration. The primary software products you need for data migration are Data Services and Information Steward.

Data migration projects require deep knowledge of and expertise in the target data structures: understanding what system you are migrating to, the requirements for the data in the new system, and the expectations for the data to be successful in the new system. When migrating to SAP applications, the source system is completely unknown to SAP. You could be migrating from a home-grown application, another vendor's software solution, a mainframe application, or any other datastores that were used prior to your SAP application. While SAP cannot provide accelerators or deep knowledge of your legacy source systems, SAP can and certainly does provide details on your target system for data migration. This knowledge, provided for you as out-of-the-box migration content, accelerates your SAP implementation.

Migration content that accelerates data migration projects is provided as Rapid Deployment Solutions, referred to as Rapid Data Migration Solutions, and SAP Best Practices. Many Rapid Deployment Solutions (hereafter RDS) are available today. A full list is available at *http://service.sap.com/solutionpackages*. These rapid data migration solutions provide migration content that is used with Data Services. This chapter provides a specific example of using the migration content that will enable you to understand what the migration content is and what is delivered with the migration content.

Next we discuss further details on the migration content and how data migration works with Data Services.

11.2.1 Data Migration Content

When we refer to data migration content, we are referring to several things you can download from the service marketplace and use with SAP software to accelerate your data migration projects. This migration content includes:

▶ Specific jobs, workflows, and cleansing packages provided in Data Services. For example, over 100 jobs are provided in Data Services for different data domains in SAP, such as material, sales order, employee, and so on. Each job extracts, maps, and validates the data against the SAP business context. This will be explained in more detail in the next section.

▶ A migration services tool that reads the SAP IMG configuration for mapping source to target values in a translation table (e.g., map U.S.A. in legacy system to US in target).

▶ SAP BusinessObjects Web intelligence reports for reporting on the progress of the migration.

▶ SAP BusinessObjects Dashboards reports for matching and merging duplicate records.

▶ Information governance project tracking for data migration projects.

As mentioned, the content is delivered for specific SAP data domains such as material, sales order, employee, and so on. While Appendix B (available for download from the book's page at *www.sap-press.com*) provides a complete list of migration content, the following provides a few more details on migration content delivered by application area:

▶ **Migration content in Data Services for SAP ERP**

    ▶ Business partner content such as customer and vendor masters

    ▶ Logistics content such as material master, bills of material (BOMs), purchasing documents, sales documents, employee information, cost centers

    ▶ Financial content such as receivables, payables, and cost elements

▶ **Migration content in Data Services for SAP CRM**

    ▶ Business partner content such as customer and vendor masters

    ▶ Sales content such as activities, leads, opportunities, and contracts

▶ **Migration content in Data Services for utilities**

    ▶ Content such as meter readings, move-in dates, equipment, devices

▶ **Migration content in Data Services for banking**

    ▶ Content such as business partner, loan information

Since new migration content is added a few times each year, you should check *http://service.sap.com/bp-datamigration* and *http://service.sap.com/solutionpackages* for additional data migration content. In addition to the migration content by object that includes integration and data quality transforms for some objects, there is also content for data remediation and for information governance for data migration projects.

11.2.2 Architecture of SAP Best Practices and Data Services for Data Migration to SAP Applications

Figure 11.1 shows how data migration works using the content provided with SAP Best Practices and RDS.

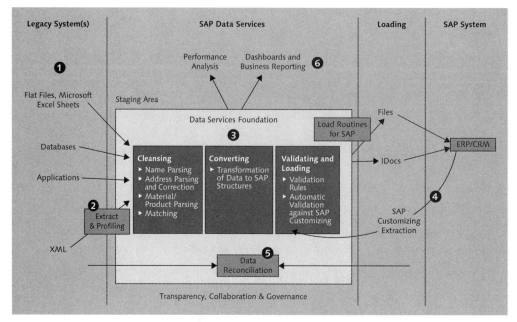

Figure 11.1 Architecture for SAP Best Practices for Data Migration

Each area in Figure 11.1 is explained below.

❶ Legacy data environment

The legacy data environment refers to the source systems for the migration. The legacy environment can be any source system that is supported by Data Services connectivity (connectivity options for Data Services were discussed in Chapter 7).

❷ Extract and profile

Data is extracted from the source and placed in a staging area in Data Services. At this point you can conduct technical profiling with Data Services. Additionally, you can start profiling very early on the source systems using Information Steward. Data profiling in Information Steward was discussed in Chapter 6.

❸ Cleanse, transform, and validate

This includes updating the data so that it meets specific patterns, mapping and transforming the data according to rules, and validating data against the SAP business context. This can involve combining two fields into one, splitting fields, updating the data in a field to match certain rules (for example, telephone number formats), and validating data against required fields and lookup values from the SAP business context and configuration. Cleanse, transform, and validate were discussed in Chapter 7 and Chapter 8.

❹ **SAP configuration extraction**

As part of an SAP implementation, the SAP system is configured with many values such as plants, material types and groups, and sales territories. Mapping of the source data normally requires mapping fields that comply with the SAP configuration. The extraction of SAP configuration data takes the settings in the SAP system so that the source data can conform to the required format in the target system.

❺ **Reconciliation**

Reconciliation looks at what was actually loaded versus what was expected to be loaded.

❻ **Dashboards and business reporting**

Throughout the process, dashboards are available for people involved with the project to stay informed about the status of the migration. Additionally, the migration project often sets data quality expectations and governance around data management.

11.3   Migrating Customer Data to SAP ERP

Now that you have an understanding of the solution, including the migration content, you are ready for an example of how to get started with data migration using Data Services and the migration content. Use the steps discussed next to get started with the software and the content.

11.3.1   Step 1: Download the Migration Content

To download the migration content to be used in Data Services, your first step is to go to *http://service.sap.com/bp-datamigration* (requires login credentials). This is where you can get most of the data migration content. However, in the future, RDS solutions will provide more migration content than the existing content at *http://service.sap.com/bp-datamigration*. This example will download all migration content from the service marketplace, but in the future you can also use *http://service.sap.com/solutionpackages* to get the most recent migration content.

At *http://service.sap.com/bp-datamigration* you can see the migration content for data migration. In addition to the core migration content, there is also migration content for data quality and information governance. This section will focus on the core migration content. You can review the overview presentation and watch the demo. Then select DATA MIGRATION DVD. This takes you to the location to download the content. You can download the DVD even if you do not own the software. If you do have a key for the software, the installer will install both Data Services and the SAP Best Practices migration content.

Once you complete the download and unzip the file, select INDEX.HTM. This brings up a page with access to the getting-starting guides and the documentation. Alternatively, you can get the same information in online help. To use the guides from online help, go to *http://help.sap.com* and follow the menu path SAP BEST PRACTICES • CROSS-INDUSTRY PACKAGES • ENTERPRISE INFORMATION MANAGEMENT. Online help provides quick guides for SAP ERP and SAP Customer Relationship Management (CRM) and walks you through manually loading the migration content into Data Services.

At this point, even without the software installed, there are still key guides and places to start planning for the migration. The migration content has Word documents and Excel templates for each of the objects in the SAP system (e.g., a document on materials, and another on customers). You can read the document to understand the object and use the Excel spreadsheet to start the research on how the source data maps to the target.

11.3.2 Step 2: Install the Software

When it's time to install the software, get a temporary key from *http://service.sap.com/licensekey*. As mentioned above, the download includes an installer that installs both the software and the migration content. (However, if you already have Data Services installed, you can use the documentation guides provided at *http://service.sap.com/bp-datamigration* to install the content manually into your existing Data Services installation.)

If you are new to Data Services, you might want to start by going through the Data Services tutorial that is included in the documentation when you install the product. You will also want to go through the examples provided in Chapter 7 on data integration and Chapter 8 on data quality.

11.3.3 Step 3: Review the Jobs in Data Services

Once everything is installed, you can see a project called AIO_BPFDM_IDOC in Data Services. This project has jobs for each of the objects, including Job_AIO_CustomerMaster_IDOC for the customer master and Job_AIO_MaterialMaster_IDOC (Figure 11.2).

Figure 11.2 Migration Content in Data Services

Drill into the customer job and you can see the mapping and validation that takes place (Figure 11.3). The validation is against required lookup fields in the SAP system, validating mandatory fields as well as the format (e.g., all phone numbers should have a country code; all U.S. ZIP codes should be in 5+4 format).

Figure 11.3 Mapping and Validation in the Customer Basic Data Job

The mapping within the job, as shown in Figure 11.4, has the source fields on the left and the target fields on the right. The pop-up screen in Figure 11.4 is produced by double-clicking on MapLegacy. This example shows the mapping of the country from the source to the target.

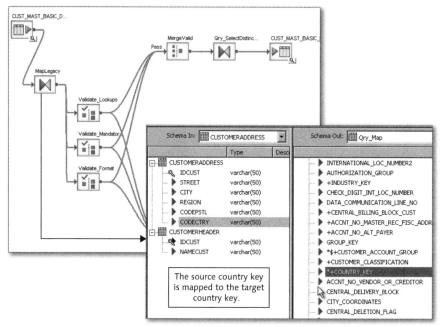

Figure 11.4 Mapping the Source Data to Target SAP Structures

The migration content includes Word documents explaining each IDoc, as well as spreadsheets for mapping the legacy customer data to the SAP IDoc structure. You can use the Excel template to start the mapping research of the source to the target (i.e., the source system table customer and FirstName field will be mapped to SAP table KNA1 Name1) prior to the mapping in Data Services.

The other component that is important during the migration is the migration services tool. This tool reads the SAP system and extracts values that are then used to map source values to values required in the SAP system. In this example, U.S.A., US, and Vereinigte Staaten von Amerika in the source system should map to US in the target system (Figure 11.5).

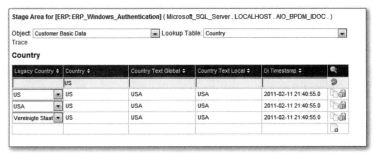

Figure 11.5 Migration Services Tool Provided by SAP Best Practices

Following the steps above, you can get started using the migration content and Data Services for your data migration project. For a complete demo of data migration, go to *http://service.sap.com/bp-datamigration* and select DEMO.

11.4 Systems Migration

In Chapter 4, *systems migration* was defined as the migration of data and associated document content from one or more existing stores of information to a new application deployment, including the retirement and decommissioning of legacy data stores. *Information* is both data and rich content (text and binary documents, pdf, email, pictures). It includes data, metadata, unstructured content, and information required to support application migration projects. It also includes the decommissioning of source systems no longer required.

So far we have focused on the migration of structured data to a new application, specifically to a new SAP Business Suite application. However, when implementing a new SAP ERP system, you might want to also consider the concept of systems migration, which includes migrating unstructured data such as contracts, emails, and other documents to SAP ERP, especially if you are implementing SAP Extended Enterprise Content Management by OpenText (discussed in Chapter 14). Additionally, once the migration project is done, what will happen with the source system? Does it remain for ongoing integration? What will you do with all the data and information not migrated? As you migrate data to SAP ERP, what are the legal requirements for how long you need to keep the data? Do you need to set up retention policies? Systems migration extends data migration to answer these questions and to look further than the initial data migration.

Systems migration naturally complements every SAP Business Suite implementation. It combines data migration with SAP NetWeaver ILM and SAP Document Access by OpenText to ensure that data and information are migrated, retained as long as needed, and decommissioned when they become a liability to the company. An example is shown in Figure 11.6.

Figure 11.6 Systems Migration

The preceding figure shows systems migration, including the migration to SAP ERP and the migration to SAP NetWeaver ILM for system decommissioning of source systems. Notice that SAP NetWeaver ILM stores the data in ILM-aware storage and can be used for reporting; for example, for a tax audit. You will learn more about system decommissioning in Chapter 13.

11.5   Summary

This chapter has introduced you to data migration, including the use of Data Services for data migration, the migration content delivered by the RDS and SAP Best Practices group, an example of the migration content provided for migrating customer data to SAP ERP, and information on systems migration.

In the next chapter, we will discuss SAP Master Data Governance.

This chapter introduces out-of-the-box, domain-specific master data governance to centrally create, maintain, and distribute master data with a focus on SAP Business Suite.

12 Introducing SAP Master Data Governance

Most organizations face complex master data governance challenges. Without an integrated and centralized approach to master data governance, companies have ad hoc and unplanned data processes that are not sufficiently controlled or guided. Management of corporate master data in such cases can become quite time-consuming, slow, and error-prone.

Companies need correct and complete master data to maximize the efficiencies of their business processes. Availability of such data across the business network needs to be accelerated. Fortunately, *SAP Master Data Governance* (hereafter SAP MDG) can help by providing prebuilt scenarios for centralized governance of master data domains. The prebuilt scenarios can be customized and extended, and new scenarios can be developed. Because SAP MDG also allows for customized processes, it ensures a consistent definition and governance of master data in the organization. This, together with the distribution of the master data to the relevant business systems in the landscape, can replace the often error-prone process of manually maintaining master data in multiple systems.

> **Note**
>
> Although the focus of this chapter is SAP MDG, SAP's master data management offering covers broad customer needs with a comprehensive portfolio of master data infrastructures and applications. This includes *SAP NetWeaver Master Data Management (MDM)* with a proven multidomain infrastructure for analytical master data scenarios, and *SAP Data Services* (hereafter Data Services) to support integration and data quality improvements such as address cleansing and duplicate detection.

SAP MDG runs on the SAP Business Suite and uses existing business logic and customer-specific configuration to ensure the quality of master data at the point of creation. It supports centralized maintenance processes that ensure that the master data is always fit for use in the SAP Business Suite's business processes and beyond. The native integration means that SAP MDG is capable of reusing the existing data models, validations, business logic, and configurations for managing master data from the underlying SAP applications. There is no need to rewrite all of these from scratch.

Note

All master data managed through SAP MDG is ready for use in the SAP Business Suite's business processes. However, it is important to note that this data can be distributed and used in non-SAP systems as well.

SAP MDG works very well with other SAP solutions for EIM. SAP MDG complements the capabilities of SAP NetWeaver MDM, for example, when customers want to consolidate master data from disparate sources, and use SAP NetWeaver MDM as the hub for integration and consolidation of globally relevant master data. Later in this chapter you will also learn how SAP MDG uses Data Services natively and also supports SAP Information Steward (hereafter Information Steward).

This chapter starts by introducing SAP MDG, including the key concepts and a typical process flow. You will learn how to get started with key configuration required in SAP MDG. After learning about the default governance processes provided, we will discuss governance for custom objects and walk through an example of master data governance for a custom object. We will introduce the concept of a rule-based workflow and then provide an example of the integration of SAP MDG and Information Steward.

12.1 SAP Master Data Governance Overview

SAP MDG enables collaborative governance of master data through integrated workflows using a *change request process*. The workflows orchestrate the governance process across multiple users who each contribute their knowledge to the creation or change of master data. It starts with a request to maintain master data, continues with validation and processing by various stakeholders, and ends with approval or rejection by authorized experts. This entire process is supported by *SAP Business Workflow,* together with the *Business Rules Framework* (hereafter BRFplus), which is an ABAP-based rule engine.

The change request process ensures that the data needs to be maintained only once centrally. Thereafter, it is replicated to all connected systems in the landscape. SAP MDG comes with a *data replication framework* (DRF) that supports the organization and execution of this data replication and eliminates the need for manual maintenance multiple times in different systems. It is important to note that by providing DRF, SAP MDG has not invented another way of doing data replication. Rather, the intention is to better support customers in managing the replication they already do today. DRF sits on top of the established replication mechanisms, such as application link enabling (ALE), intermediate documents (IDocs), and enterprise services. The purpose of SAP MDG's DRF is to keep track of what data needs to be distributed where and what has been distributed successfully or not, regardless of the replication mechanism. In the DRF, systems can also subscribe to distribution of master data based on certain filter criteria; for example, only materials for plant 1000 with material type finished goods should be distributed to a system TRN.

The scenarios provided out-of-the-box have been built using the *master data governance application framework*. This framework is also available for customers to build their own custom-defined SAP MDG scenarios based on their own master data models. These custom models can be completely self-defined by the customer, can be extensions of the standard models in SAP MDG, or can be based on standard SAP data domains where there is not yet standard SAP MDG content for the data domain.

Customers can use the framework to define the appropriate data models and then generate the persistence and user interfaces based on these models. They can define appropriate workflows and the roles that will provide access to the user interfaces. They can use the DRF to distribute the data that has been maintained. Also, they can build their own validations or extend existing ones based on BRFplus. Finally, Business Add-Ins (BAdIs) are also provided to include custom ABAP code in SAP MDG's processes. Later in this chapter you will see a simple example of configuring a custom-defined object from scratch in SAP MDG.

SAP MDG supports flexible deployment options. It can be deployed either as a stand-alone system or on top of an SAP ERP system. An end user can access SAP MDG using either the SAP NetWeaver Portal or the SAP NetWeaver Business Client.

In this section, we will introduce some of the most important elements of SAP MDG, including deployment options, change request and staging, and an example process flow.

12.1.1 Deployment Options

SAP MDG was delivered starting with enhancement package 5 for SAP ERP 6.0. As shown in Figure 12.1, there are two typical ways for customers to deploy SAP MDG in relation to their existing system landscape.

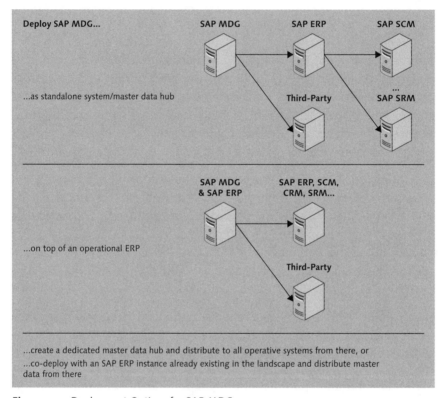

Figure 12.1 Deployment Options for SAP MDG

The first way is to introduce a completely new system as a dedicated master data hub, using only the master data governance functionality in this system and distributing the master data from it to other SAP or third-party systems that run the various business processes. This approach has the advantage that SAP MDG can be deployed without disturbing the existing system landscape and can service multiple domains with a single hub. Existing SAP ERP systems do not require an upgrade to a release supporting SAP MDG, as the hub itself handles distribution of governed master data to older SAP or third-party systems in the landscape.

The second approach is to run SAP MDG on an existing SAP ERP system where you have the domain you want to govern. This system then governs data for that particular domain; for example, material data. The governed data from such an SAP MDG system is then directly available to the business processes running on that system, and is also distributed to all other systems that need it.

A special flavor of the second case could be customers who only run one SAP ERP system. In such cases, SAP MDG can be deployed with that single SAP ERP system by upgrading it to at least enhancement package 5 and turning on SAP MDG's business functions. Even if you do not want to distribute the master data to any receiving system (which would rarely be the case), SAP MDG will still allow you to:

▶ Separate incomplete or not-approved data from the production data through staging.

▶ Use workflows to distribute maintenance of data to multiple people.

▶ Enhance validations beyond the existing business process rules.

▶ Benefit from the improved prevention of duplicates and data quality enrichment.

▶ More easily track key performance indicators (KPIs) for master data creation and maintain an audit trail of completed change requests.

Both the deployment options detailed allow customers to efficiently govern their corporate master data. The approach that a customer chooses should depend upon his specific business needs and cost considerations.

12.1.2 Change Request and Staging

Now that you understand the deployment options in SAP MDG, let's talk a little more about some of the most important concepts involved in SAP MDG. The data governed in SAP MDG goes through a change request process involving an approval workflow. Until the changes are approved, they must be kept separate from data used in the business process execution on the system. Such changes must become visible to the business processes only after they are approved. In other words, you need to separate data entry from data approval.

This is where the concepts of *change request* and *staging* come into the picture. Change request and staging are core concepts for SAP MDG and are used to drive collaboration between the various users; for example, the requester of changes and the approver.

A change request is a container for new and changed master data of one change process. It determines the approval process flow and the processors. Changes are carried by the change request until they are approved, for example, by a data steward. It is possible to configure change requests to add or remove steps or processors, include objects to be changed at request creation, or handle multiple or single master data object instances.

Figure 12.2 shows the steps involved in a typical change request process. An example is the maintenance of master data, its validation and approval, and finally its replication to the various target systems in the landscape.

Figure 12.2 Change Request and Staging

Data that is still in process is stored in a separate temporary repository known as the staging area. The staging area does not impact any business processes running on the system. A complete audit trail of changes is maintained by the system. Once the changes are finally approved, this data is transferred to the operational database, which is known as the *active area*. All business processes and applications refer only to the master data that is held in the active area. From SAP MDG's active area, the data can be distributed to other systems to be used by business processes running on them.

SAP MDG provides two modes for active area persistence:

▶ **Reuse active area (reuse mode)**
In this mode, existing database tables of the related applications are used for storing the active master data. For example, SAP MDG for materials uses the MARA table in SAP ERP Central Component (ECC). Reuse mode is best suited for customers who want to use the existing data dictionary structures provided by SAP, including extended or previously created custom structures.

▶ **Generated active area (flex mode)**
In this mode, the database tables generated by SAP MDG are used for storing the active data. This mode provides additional flexibility, as it does not need any additional data dictionary structures to be created. Customers can simply model (in SAP MDG) the attributes they do not need in the SAP ERP system but only want to maintain and store centrally for distribution to other SAP or non-SAP systems. The benefit is that the additional attributes need to be modeled in SAP MDG only once, and then SAP MDG itself takes care of generating the active area.

12.1.3 Process Flow in SAP Master Data Governance

Figure 12.3 shows a typical process flow in SAP MDG using the *create or change material* scenario. This is one example of the standard content SAP ships with SAP MDG.

Figure 12.3 Material Governance Process

In master data governance for material, the default approval process follows the two-man rule:

- ▶ The process begins with a *business user* requesting creation of a material or change of material data. After completing his input, the business user *submits* the request.

- ▶ The *master data expert* is notified of this new request through his work list. He reviews the changes, after which he may add further changes or enhancements and send the review back to the business user for *revision* or clarification.

- ▶ The *business user* can decide to cancel the request (for example, in cases where a suitable material already exists) or adjust the data and *resubmit* his request.

- ▶ The *master data expert* can again review and revise the request. If the data is complete and correct, he approves the request.

All changes are carried by a change request as discussed in the previous section. These are validated for correctness against the existing business logic, using the validations defined in the underlying SAP Business Suite. In addition to these, external validations may be used as well. Custom validations may be modeled using BRFplus or programmed using code lists or simple coding checks. Once the data has been validated and found to be error free, it is approved by a master data expert.

The approved data can then be replicated to all connected systems in the landscape. The replication can be automatic as part of the last step in the workflow, or it can be triggered manually by the user.

The entire governance process is controlled by adaptable workflows that can be configured based on business requirements. In the workflow section of this chapter, you will learn how the workflow can be configured.

After the data has been replicated to other systems, it can be adapted or enriched in the local client systems.

12.2 Getting Started with SAP Master Data Governance

You can get SAP MDG up and running in a short span of time and with only some minimal configuration. The required settings can be found in the implementation guide (Transaction SPRO) by following the path CROSS-APPLICATION COMPONENTS • PROCESSES AND TOOLS FOR ENTERPRISE APPLICATIONS • MASTER DATA GOVERNANCE.

This section provides an overview of the most important configuration steps.

12.2.1 Data Modeling

Establishing the data model is the first step in getting started with SAP MDG. A data model represents the master data in the system. It consists of entity types and relationships to enable modeling master data structures of any complexity in the system. You have the option to use the data models provided, to enhance existing data models, or to create your own data models.

There are a few key terms you need to know when working with data models. The first is *entity types*. Entity types are master data objects that have a collection of fields. For example, the MM data model has multiple entity types that relate to a material. The material entity type relates to the material basic data and contains fields such as weight, material group, and base unit of measure. EAN, which is the international article number, is an entity type that is not changeable. Entity types are defined for each type of master data that will be used and potentially changed in the data model. The system generates database tables for each entity type required for processing the master data in SAP MDG. There are also fields that are part of a data model but should never be changed in SAP MDG (for example, local details such as plant data). The definition of an entity type includes a storage/use type "do not change in MDG." This property determines whether and how master data can be changed in SAP MDG and the type of tables that are generated by the system for storing the master data.

Recommendations for SAP Master Data Governance Data Models
▶ Use the SAP-delivered data models when possible; this will save implementation time.
▶ Extend the SAP data model when needed.
▶ Before creating your own data model, check the SAP roadmap of data models in the SAP MDG area of the SAP Community Network (SCN).

The validity of entity types can be restricted using *editions*. An edition is important if the master data object has a time-dependency element. Editions are delivered by default in the financial domain; for example, centers, profit centers, and cost elements. You may want to add a time dependency to general ledger (GL) accounts, company, and/or consolidation structures. Using an edition requires some additional configuration in the model so that the time dependency is included in the persistence layer. (You can find more details on editions by performing a search for "MDG editions" at *http://help.sap.com*.)

Entity types can be linked using relationships. Relationships can be of types *leading,* *qualifying,* or *referencing*. A leading or qualifying relationship specifies the *from-entity* *type* on a higher level than the *to-entity type*. The from-entity type is automatically taken as the key in the generated tables. A referencing relationship specifies the from-entity type as an attribute of the to-entity type. An example is material leading to a GTIN (global trade number) where the material becomes part of the key field for the GTIN entity. An example of a referencing relationship is a country code that is checked for a supplier address but is not part of the key field. For more information see the SAP MDG documentation at *http://help.sap.com.*

12.2.2   User Interface (UI) Modeling

UI modeling is done when defining the UI configuration of the web user interface for creating and processing a change request. If you want to use the existing user interface models, no further configuration is required for the user interface. You only need to do the UI modeling if you choose to customize existing models or create your own.

For example, it is possible to specify whether the system hides certain entity types and fields on the selection screens, in the results of a search, or in data cleansing. The settings for UI modeling can be found under GENERAL SETTINGS • UI MODELING.

In addition to using the delivered user interface logic, you can use Business Add-Ins (BAdIs) to change the user interface for individual processing of an entity type. Changes can be made in the following areas:

▶ Adjust the definition of attributes or add new attributes.

▶ Initialize the displayed data (when creating a new entity, for example).

▶ Restrict the values displayed in a dropdown box or selection field group.

▶ Restrict the values displayed in the input help.

▶ Dynamically control the visibility of fields on the user interface and of the property that determines if fields are required or display-only.

▶ Define navigation destinations of UI elements of the type hyperlink or pushbutton.

▶ Check if the lead selection of a table may be changed.

12.2.3 Data Quality and Search

Several important configurations for data quality and search are done in this step. First, *validations* and *derivations* are defined for the data models. Just as with the other areas, no configuration is required if you want to use the validations and derivations provided out-of-the-box. Validations ensure that the master data is consistent. Derivations are used to calculate values for resolved attributes from other resolved attributes, thereby simplifying data entry. A resolved attribute enables you to derive one value from the other. For example, the tax jurisdiction code for a business partner is derived from the address.

The GENERAL SETTINGS • DATA QUALITY AND SEARCH • DEFINE VALIDATION AND DERIVATION RULES customizing activity is used to configure validation and derivation rules. In addition to this, a BAdI is provided to create customer-specific checks on entities and change requests. This BAdI can also be used to define that certain field values are to be derived from the values of other fields in the master data.

Second, the search providers available for the different types of search used in SAP MDG are defined in this step. The available search applications are Business Address Search (BAS), Database Search, Enterprise Search, and Remote Key Search.

Types of Searches available in SAP MDG

- Business Address Search (BAS) enables you to search by an address, including fuzzy search and similar values.
- Database Search is an exact search method based on values or ranges stored in a database.
- Enterprise Search is for free text and fuzzy search.
- Remote Key Search searches from a client system to the SAP MDG central system.

The other important feature in this customizing activity is the configuration for a duplicate check. On the basis of the data model (for example, business partner or material), you can define which search mode the system must use and which thresholds (percentages) are to apply to determine duplicates.

Records that have a matching score lower than the low threshold are not considered duplicates. Records that have a matching score that lies between the defined low and high thresholds are considered potential duplicates. Records that have a matching score higher than the high threshold are not allowed by the system, as they are considered to be identical.

> **Note**
>
> Data quality duplicate checks and thresholds are discussed in more detail in Chapter 8.

Finally, the enrichment capabilities are defined in this customization activity. An example is an external address directory for address cleansing. Both internal and external service calls are supported. For example, with enrichment of the address data, Data Services can be called as an external service.

12.2.4 Process Modeling

Process modeling defines the relationship between the business activity change request types, the workflows, and the entities. The customizing activities for process modeling create edition types and configure business activities, change requests, and workflows. Process modeling configurations can be found under GENERAL SETTINGS • PROCESS MODELING.

A *business activity* is a business operation you can perform in SAP MDG. (Examples of delivered business activities are CREATE MATERIAL, DISPLAY MATERIAL, CREATE SUPPLIER, BLOCK/UNBLOCK SUPPLIER, etc. Additional business activities can be created using the configuration under GENERAL SETTINGS • PROCESS MODELING • BUSINESS ACTIVITIES • CREATE BUSINESS ACTIVITY.) Change request types are assigned to specific data models, and a business activity can be associated with one or more change request types. Each change request type can have a different workflow template and different service-level agreement and is capable of processing single or multiple objects. For example, the create supplier business activity can be associated with a change request type "create supplier" and change request type "create supplier, simplified workflow."

If you use the data model for business partner or material, the business activities (such as create, change, approve) are already defined and assigned to the data models; you only need to assign the right people to the workflow in the process modeling configuration steps. The customizing activity for creating business activities allows you to create your own business activity and assign it to a data model for cases in which you want to process your own entity types for which SAP delivers no business activity.

Customizing activities are available in the process modeling node for configuring a rule-based workflow and defining steps in it. When you configure a rule-based workflow, separate settings are provided for each change request type. SAP delivers BRFplus decision tables as example content for each change request type. This SAP-proposed content is imported into client 000. To use this content, you need to export the decision tables from client 000 to an Excel file and then import them into your client. The decision tables in the customer system are then filled with the example content. It is also possible to define the decision tables manually. If the Excel import is recorded in a customizing request, it can also be used to import these decision tables to other systems. SAP also delivers predefined change request steps for rule-based workflows with corresponding application scenarios.

12.2.5 Data Replication

The customizing activities for data replication are used to specify how data is replicated to one or more target systems. For example, the filters for selecting data to be transferred (only materials for plant 1000) can be specified here. Using the customizing activities for data replication, the business object settings and the communication-relevant settings (for example, services, ALE, IDocs) for business systems involved in data replication are defined, and replication models are created. Each replication model can consist of one or more outbound implementations. For the configuration of data replication, existing outbound implementations are referenced or user-specific ones are defined.

To add custom implementations, BAdIs are available for changing the default system behavior for transferring language-dependent texts, formatting the file for downloading data from SAP MDG, uploading master data to SAP MDG, and creating SAP MDG change pointers from ALE change pointers for selected message types.

12.2.6 Key and Value Mapping

Mapping is needed in various scenarios where the same business object is created in different systems with different identifiers. *Key mapping* is when the primary key for an object (such as business partner or material) is different in various systems; the key mapping ensures that we know which object IDs represent the same thing in different systems. *Value mapping* is used when codes between systems are different, and they should be translated when distributing data between systems.

Two typical scenarios for key mapping are described below:

▶ **Scenario 1**

A business partner is created in one system (system A) with business partner ID 4711. Afterward it is replicated to a second system (system B) with internal number creation for business partner. In this system the business partner is created with number 0815. Using key mapping, it is possible to store the information and know that partner 4711 in system A is the same as business partner 0815 in system B.

▶ **Scenario 2**

One material was created in several systems, independently from each other. For analytic reasons it is necessary to accumulate the information from all systems about this material. Therefore, the analytic report needs to know all the different identifiers of the various systems. This information can be retrieved out of the key mapping data.

The configuration settings for key mapping can be used to:

▶ Change the default key mapping settings.

▶ Extend key mapping settings for existing business objects, typically by adding new object IDs.

▶ Extend key mapping settings for new business objects.

Common examples of value mapping include payment terms and country codes (USA versus US versus United States in different systems). Value mapping is an alternative to synchronizing the customizing entries and their corresponding master data across all systems. Table 12.1 shows a use case in which the Form of Address customizing element uses one set of codes in SAP MDG and a different set of values in an external system.

Form of Address	Code Value in SAP MDG	Code Value in External Code List
Mr.	0001	0004
Ms.	0002	0003
Company	0003	0002
Mr. and Ms.	0004	0001

Table 12.1 Example of Different Values Between Systems

12.2.7 Data Transfer

SAP MDG supports import of data from the master data client systems. These inbound channels are a part of the data transfer functionality. The following three capabilities are provided for data transfer:

▶ **Export master data**
To export various types of master data from client systems in enterprise service XML format.

▶ **Import master data**
To import various types of master data (available in enterprise service XML or IDoc formats) into SAP MDG.

▶ **Convert master data**
To convert various types of master data (available in non-XML or third-party formats) into enterprise service XML format for subsequent import into SAP MDG.

The customizing activities in the data transfer area set up the ABAP class that should be called to convert to the proper XML format, configuration for the service call such as the message type, and the import sequence for objects with dependencies.

From among the logical directories defined in the system (Transaction FILE), a subset needs to be defined in the customizing for data transfer. Only these logical directories can then be used by the data transfer applications as the destination for exported XML files and the source for files to be imported or converted. Once the system has imported or converted files for a selected object type, they are moved to an archive directory that must also be defined in the customizing for each object type used in data transfer.

12.2.8 Activities Beyond Customizing

A few other activities are required beyond customizing to get started with SAP MDG. These are primarily related to the creation and maintenance of user roles and configuration of SAP NetWeaver Portal or SAP NetWeaver Business Client. The roles need to be assigned to users. Data model user interface configurations are assigned to the roles. For SAP NetWeaver Portal, the following business packages are available as templates:

- Business package for financial master data
- Business package for material governance
- Business package for master data governance for supplier

Once these settings have been made, you can start using SAP MDG.

12.3 Governance for Custom-Defined Objects: Example

As mentioned earlier, it is possible for customers to extend SAP MDG by adding their own business logic, or even to use SAP MDG for governance of their own objects. For example, in the context of standard SAP MDG domains (financials, supplier, material, etc.), subordinate entity types that are not yet delivered with the data model may be added. You can include Z-tables, extended fields, and other customer enhancements to the SAP MDG data model. You can also extend an existing model with additional reference data, such as bank codes, additional material information sales, or plant data.

To extend SAP MDG, you can create a data model completely from scratch or extend the data models delivered by SAP, along with the corresponding configuration. In the former case, you have to create all the configurations for the new object type. Configurations such as data modeling, UI modeling, process modeling, data replication, and so on need to be performed. However, when you extend the provided SAP MDG model, you just need to extend the existing configuration.

In the previous section, we discussed at length the various configuration options available. Now you will learn how to use these options for configuring a custom-defined object in SAP MDG. The example will implement a simple model of an airline carrier that should be governed using SAP MDG and includes the following fields and attributes:

- Airline ID
- Text description of the airline
- Airline's URL
- Existing lookup table for currency

Planning the data model is the first step toward implementing this custom-defined object in SAP MDG. This involves asking questions such as: How many and what entity types are needed? What is their relationship? Which of the fields are automatically available via an entity type, and which additional fields need to be modeled? Once these questions are answered, data modeling can be performed. As discussed in the previous section, the customizing activity for data modeling in SAP MDG is available under GENERAL SETTINGS • DATA MODELING • EDIT DATA MODEL.

In this section, we discuss the various steps involved in creating a new custom object.

12.3.1 Define New Models for Airline Entity and Currency Entity

First, you need to create a new data model. Figure 12.4 shows how the new entity is defined. This example defines a new entity called CARR for the airline carrier.

1. Navigate in the IMG (Transaction SPRO) settings for SAP MDG to GENERAL SETTINGS • DATA MODELING • EDIT DATA MODEL.

2. Create a new entity type called CARR for the airline object, and a database table will be generated for it.

3. The identification is defined with the data element S_CARR_ID.

4. The text is 20 characters in length, is associated with the carrier, and is not language-dependent.

5. For other properties, leave the default values.

6. Add an attribute URL with data element S_CARRURL.

Figure 12.4 Define Entity Type CARR for the Data Model

After creating the entity type CARR, follow similar steps to create the entity type CURRENCY for the possible currency codes that can be assigned to an airline.

> **Note**
>
> One important difference is that the table of currency codes should not be changeable via SAP MDG. This needs to be indicated during creation of the entity type by setting the STORAGE / USE TYPE to NOT CHANGEABLE VIA MDG; NO GENERATED TABLES.

The table of currency codes to be used already exists. It is defined with the data element S_CURRCODE. Figure 12.5 shows how the entity type CURRENCY is defined.

Figure 12.5 Define Entity Type CURRENCY for Data Model

12.3.2 Define Relationship Between the Airline and Currency Entity Types

The next step is to define a relationship between the entity types:

1. Still in the EDIT DATA MODEL window, select the data model and entity type. Then select RELATIONSHIPS and NEW ENTRIES.

2. Define a relationship from the entity type CURRENCY to the entity type CARR, so that exactly one currency must be assigned to every airline. This is shown in Figure 12.6.

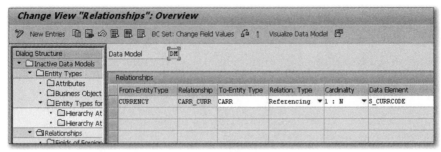

Figure 12.6 Define Relationship from CURRENCY to CARR

3. Save and activate the data model.

4. You can visualize the created data model by selecting the data model name and clicking on the VISUALIZE DATA MODEL button shown in Figure 12.6. The results are shown in Figure 12.7.

Figure 12.7 Data Model Visualization

Notice in Figure 12.7 that the data model is visualized with the airline carrier and the fields in the airline carrier.

12.3.3 Define User Interface

Once the data model has been created in SAP MDG, the next step is to define a user interface configuration for the single-object maintenance of an airline with a change request:

1. Access the customizing activity for data modeling in SAP MDG, which is available under GENERAL SETTINGS • UI MODELING • EDIT UI CONFIGURATION.

2. A UI configuration can be created either from scratch, or by using an existing template. In Figure 12.8, an existing configuration, ZDEMO_AK_FLIGHT, is used.

> **Note**
>
> If there is not an existing user interface template, then this needs to be developed using ABAP Web Dynpro Floorplan Manager. For more details on creating custom UI templates, search for "Floorplan Manager for WD ABAP Developer's Guide (SAP NW 7.03)" on the SAP Community Network (SCN).

Figure 12.8 Create UI Configuration with Template

3. In the window shown in Figure 12.8 select the row with the XY model and select CREATE WITH TEMPLATE.

4. Overwrite the proposed names for the target configuration and select START DEEP-COPY, as shown in Figure 12.9.

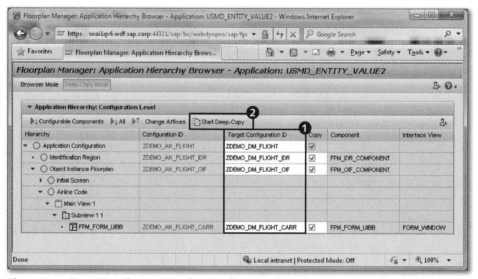

Figure 12.9 Deep-Copy the User Interface Configuration from the Template

The data model is assigned to the new configuration ZDEMO_DM_FLIGHT.

12.3.4 Link the User Interface Configuration to the Data Model

The next step is to link the user interface configuration to the data model. We started by copying an existing user configuration; now we must link the UI to the data model. This creates the persistence layer required for the airline entity. Follow the steps below:

1. To edit the configuration, select the UI configuration ZDEMO_DM_FLIGHT and choose EDIT from the screen shown in Figure 12.8.

2. Edit the configuration and change the value of the field USMD_MODEL to DM. This is shown in Figure 12.10.

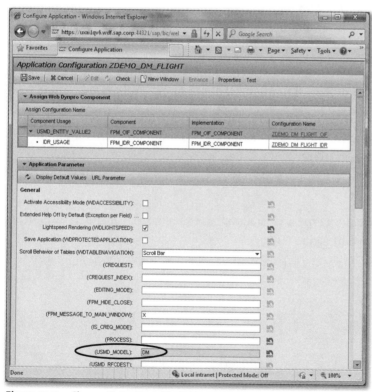

Figure 12.10   Change Data Model to DM

Figure 12.10 assigns the Web Dynpro components and creates the required database persistence layer. It also associates the copied UI template with the new data model. Based on the data model, the system generates the DB tables and creates a persistence level through the data model definition.

12.3.5 Create a Change Request Process

Now that the data model and UI configuration have been created, we need to define a change process for the maintenance of the airline with an SAP MDG change request. The definition of the change process consists of the following:

▶ Submission of request for changes to the airline data.

▶ Processing by a data expert to enhance the airline data.

▶ Final check by an approver.

▶ Revision potential if the approver rejects and sends the request back to the initiator.

We begin by creating a change request type that will be linked to an SAP Business Workflow template (described in more detail in Section 12.4):

1. Access the customizing activity for creating a change request type, which can be found under GENERAL SETTINGS • PROCESS MODELING • CHANGE REQUESTS • CREATE CHANGE REQUEST TYPE.

2. Create a change request type ZDMCRTYP. Name the new change request "DM Airline Single".

3. A new change request type is created for data model DM using this customizing activity, as shown in Figure 12.11.

4. Enter "CARR" in the MAIN ENTITY TYPE column and "WS7570004" under WORKFLOW.

New Entries: Overview of Added Entries

Type of Chg. Request	Edition Type	Data Model	Description (medium text)	Objects Required	Single Object	Main Entity T...	Workflow
ZDMCRTYP		DM	DM Airline single	☐	☑	CARR	WS75700040
				☐	☐		
				☐	☐		

Dialog Structure
▾ ☐ Type of Change Reque
  • ☐ Entity Types
  • ☐ Business Activities
  • ☐ Service Level Agree

Figure 12.11 Create Change Request Type

12.3.6 Assign Processors to Workflow

The next step for configuring the airline object in SAP MDG is to assign processors to workflow steps:

1. Navigate to the customizing activity GENERAL SETTINGS • PROCESS MODELING • WORKFLOW • OTHER MDG WORKFLOWS • ASSIGN PROCESSOR TO WORKFLOW STEP NUMBER (SIMPLE WORKFLOW), as shown in Figure 12.12.

Type of Chg. Request	Step	Description (medium)	Ob	Agent ID	Complete name	
ZDMCRTYP	1	Processing	US	SINHAAK	Akshay Sinha	
ZDMCRTYP	2	Final Check	US	SINHAAK	Akshay Sinha	
ZDMCRTYP	3	Revision	US	SINHAAK	Akshay Sinha	

Figure 12.12 Assign Processor to Workflow Steps

In Figure 12.12 notice that there are four steps and that for this example we assigned the same user ID to all steps. In reality you would not assign this to a user, but use a variable such as a position, job, or organizational unit.

> **Standard Workflow versus Rule-Based Workflow**
>
> This example uses a standard workflow, which always includes steps for reviewing, approving, and revising the change request. In this example, a person, job, or organizational unit is assigned as a processor. Later you will learn about using a rule-based workflow, which extends the standard delivered workflow.

This completes the configuration for the airline object. You can now test the creation of the airline in SAP MDG using the change request type defined above, which is what we discuss next.

12.3.7 Test the New Airline Change Request

For testing, you can use the Web Dynpro application USMD_CREQUEST_CREATE provided by SAP:

1. Launch the Web Dynpro application USMD_CREQUEST_CREATE. This is a generic Web Dynpro application used to test any change request. The request is displayed as shown in Figure 12.13.

Figure 12.13 Test Using USMD_CREQUEST_CREATE

2. Click on the CHANGE MODEL button on the USMD_CREQUEST_CREATE screen to change the personalization; that is, the UI configuration and change request type associated with the airline data model.

3. Enter a description, the change request type, and the new airline code to create. Perform the steps as shown by the workflow.

4. Add the currency, description, and URL as shown in Figure 12.14, and submit the change request.

Figure 12.14 Add Airline Currency, Description, and URL Before Submission

As shown in Figure 12.12, users have also been assigned for the revision and approval steps (in our example we only assigned one user, but normally you would assign different users or roles). These activities can now be performed, thereby completing the process of governance for the airline master data change request in SAP MDG.

Each request is routed to the inbox. We recommend that you use the SAP NetWeaver Business Client for processing SAP MDG change requests. It includes out-of-the-box configuration for the SAP MDG-provided domains. Custom objects, such as the airline we created, are approved via the Universal Worklist or a Web Dynpro application, as shown in Figure 12.15.

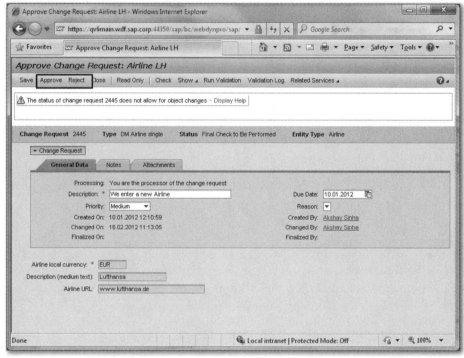

Figure 12.15 Approval of Custom Change Request

Once the approval is done, it is stored in the active area and is ready for use by business processes.

12.4 Rule-Based Workflows in SAP Master Data Governance

This section provides an overview of how SAP MDG uses SAP Business Workflow together with BRFplus for workflows that are dynamically controlled at runtime by decisions based on rules.

> **Details of SAP Business Workflow and BRFplus**
>
> This section will only provide a general overview of SAP Business Workflow and BRFplus. If you would like to know more about these solutions, please reference the following SAP books: *Practical Workflow for SAP, Second Edition* (Ginger Gatling et al., SAP PRESS, 2009) and *BRFplus—Business Rule Management for ABAP Applications* (Thomas Albrecht, Carsten Ziegler, SAP PRESS, 2011).

Workflows are critical to managing master data because without some type of process control, the management of master data is often completely unstructured: neither guided nor controlled. Workflows guide users through the master data process, as well as monitoring the progress and providing governance. Change processing and issue resolution, integrated with workflow, keeps data, process, and issue resolution in one place. Expensive, hard-coded, inflexible, semi-automated processes can be replaced by a flexible process, especially if the workflow is based on an integrated rules management.

SAP MDG provides a predefined set of default workflows for master data governance processes. These processes and roles can be adapted and tailored based on customer needs and can span the enterprise to accommodate your master data governance requirements.

This section uses a concrete example based on the default workflow process provided by SAP for material governance. This section also includes information about how to get started with the required SAP MDG-specific configuration.

12.4.1 Classic SAP Business Workflow and Rule-Based Workflow using SAP Business Workflow and BRFplus

SAP MDG allows companies to use workflow in two flavors. One option is to use traditional SAP Business Workflow and to model all workflow branches for one governance process in the workflow modeling environment. The other option is to combine SAP Business Workflow with the capabilities of BRFplus. Using BRFplus enables one fixed workflow template with parallel branches. At runtime, BRFplus defines which of the parallel branches to execute. The runtime decisions happen iteratively based on the current state of the workflow, the status of the change request, and user interactions. The flow is determined by decision tables. This combination of SAP Business Workflow and BRFplus is often referred to as *rule-based workflow*.

Rule-based workflow is a good match for master data governance processes. Rule-based workflow provides flexible processing and easy configuration. The following are typical requirements for master data governance processes that require flexibility and easy configuration:

▶ Adding or removing a workflow step (e.g., adding an additional approval or notification step).

▶ Changing the order of workflow steps (e.g., moving a first level of approval before a special data enhancement step).

▶ Skipping workflow steps based on certain rules (e.g., a MATERIAL CREATE request coming from a product lifecycle management system can skip an approval step).

▶ Routing rules based on change request type (e.g., regional data enhancement/ approvals).

▶ Routing rules based on the content of the master data (e.g., secondary approval for special customer payment terms).

These configurations are usually driven by business users who want to make changes to the master data governance processes over time. The combination of SAP Business Workflow and BRFplus fulfills the requirement for a powerful yet easily configurable governance process.

SAP Business Workflow is the core technical engine used to run the process. It is used to trigger the execution and distribution of the steps of the workflow. BRFplus is the coordinator and decision maker for every step of the workflow. Before executing the next step, the rules engine determines the next step and the next processor (who should do the step, whether human or system).

To allow for this flexibility, the base workflow for SAP MDG has been designed as shown in Figure 12.16. In Figure 12.16, the process starts when a change request is created. Once the process starts, some preparation is done based on the change request type and other variables. Then the decision tables are read. Based on the decision tables, a workflow task is created using the parallel processing branch, and it is either executed as a backend process activity (executed automatically) or executed by a user. Once one step is completed, the rules engine is used to determine the next step. This happens iteratively until the process is completed, cancelled, or requires error handling.

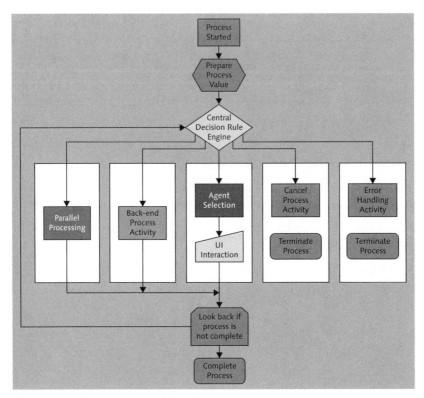

Figure 12.16 Flow of Rule-Based Workflow

The rules engine requires several inputs for the decisions. These decision inputs include:

▶ **Object type and request type**
For example: object type material, request type create or change.

▶ **Request status**
For example: to be considered and approved, changes to be executed, to be revised.

▶ **Previous step and rule/role**
For example: the previous step was requested by the data steward, or previous step was rejected by the plant manager.

▶ **Data entered in the request**
The data includes attributes that can be used for routing tasks to users; for example, material type, MRP controller.

▶ **Initiator**
This is the user who initiated the request.

▶ **User action**
For example: approve, reject, finalize processing.

All design-time configuration of the process is reflected in BRFplus decision tables, which can be maintained by nontechnical users. At runtime, each process loops back to the rules engine to decide on the next step. The content maintained in the decision tables reflects your governance process.

Three decision tables are available:

▶ Single-value decision table (DT_SINGLE_VAL_<CR_type>)

▶ User agent decision table (DT_USER_AGT_GRP_<CR_type>)

▶ Non–user agent decision table (DT_USER_AGT_GRP_<CR_type>)

It is critical to understand these three tables and how they work together because all three are required for decision processing in BRFplus. The text in parentheses in the list of tables above is the technical name of the table. The appendage of <CR_type> to the end of each table indicates the change request type appended to the table. The change request type is important because the workflow template is common across all change requests. The same workflow leverages the rules for all change request types. It is the content of the decision tables for each change request type (CR_type) that differentiates one governance scenario from another. For example, change request type MAT01 is a change request type to create a material. Change request type MAT06 is a change request type to mark a material for deletion. The decision table is related to the change request type; for example, DT_SINGLE_VAL_MAT01 has the single-value decisions for the material creation process. Decision table DT_SINGLE_VAL_MAT06 has the single decision values for the mark material for deletion change request.

Each of the three decision tables is discussed in more detail next.

Single-Value Decision Table or DT_SINGLE_VAL_<CR Type>

The single-value decision table reflects the governance process flow. The combination of previous step and previous action determine the new step and the new change request status. Examples of the change request include changes to be executed, final check approved, and to be revised.

The single-value decision table also holds the link between the three tables. This is referred to as a *condition alias*. Each condition alias needs at least one processor. The processor can be a person, or it can be the system (meaning it is processed automatically with no human interaction required). This means that for each condition alias, there is a related entry in one of the other tables. For condition aliases requiring a person, the link is in the user agent decision table. For automatic condition aliases, the link is in the non-user agent decision table.

User Agent Decision Table or DT_USER_AGT_GRP_<CR_Type>

The user agent decision table holds the users and the type of steps they execute. The user can be defined as an actual user ID, a role, or an organization unit. Examples include "data stewards approve," "plant managers revise," "Bob checks the data." In this case, "data steward" and "plant manager" could be positions in the organizational structure or a role such as a security role. And Bob, of course, is an actual person.

The agents are assigned to the following step types: check, approve, process, revise, and activate. In the example where data stewards approve, the step type APPROVE is assigned to the data steward role.

This means a condition alias in the single value decision table could point to a processor as a data steward. The user agent decision table indicates that the data steward is a specific security role and that data stewards approve. The result is that users with the role data steward receive an approval task. Likewise, if the condition alias has Bob as a processor, then the user agent decision table knows that Bob is a specific user ID and needs a check data task.

Non–User Agent Decision Table or DT_NON_USER_AGT_GRP_<CR_Type>

Just as the user agent decision table links the user to the step type, the non-user agent decision table links the automatic steps (not requiring user action) to the type of action it needs to perform. In this case, the action is referred to as a process pattern. Process patterns are abstractions of business activities. Some examples of process patterns include:

▶ Background processing pattern (call of a service, function, etc.)

▶ Error-handling pattern

▶ Notification pattern (sending a notification to a user or system)

Additional process patterns can be added if necessary, either to achieve parallel processing or to combine multiple workflow steps to one process pattern.

The configuration of the rules content via the three tables can be done by uploading a Microsoft Excel file. This allows a business user to work in a known environment rather than learning a new user interface to configure a master data governance process. A summary of how the decision tables build the process workflow is shown in Figure 12.17.

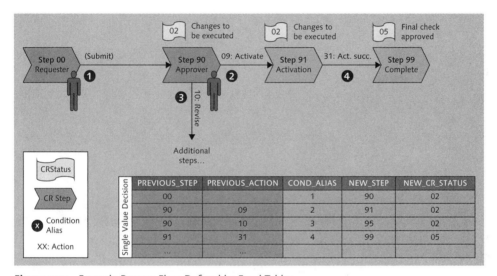

Figure 12.17 Example Process Flow Defined by Excel Tables

Figure 12.17 shows an example of the Microsoft Excel process that is used to define a workflow and update the single-value decision table. In the table shown in Figure 12.17, the previous step is 00, there is no previous action, the condition alias is 1, the new step is 90 (which is "final check," explained in the next section), and the new change request status is 02. What does this mean? It means that in the single-value decision table, after step 00, the next step should be step 90, and the new change request status should be 02. Notice in the workflow that step 90 is APPROVE and change request status 02 is CHANGES TO BE EXECUTED. In the second row, if the previous step is 90, which is the APPROVE step, and the previous action is 09, which is ACTIVATE, then the next step should be 91, which is the activation of the change request. In the third row, if the previous action is 10 (action 10 is SEND FOR REVISION), then the next step is 95 (not shown in the figure, but it would be a step to REVISE). By configuring the previous step and next step in the Excel spreadsheet, the user can configure the workflow. This means the users can change the flow of the workflow with less IT involvement.

As an example of changing the flow without IT involvement, let's say that in Figure 12.17 you want to add an additional expert to review the material. Assuming that there is a step type and user assigned for this additional review step in the user agent decision table (for example, check by MRP controller), you just need to update the Excel spreadsheet or update the single-value decision table. This is shown in Figure 12.18.

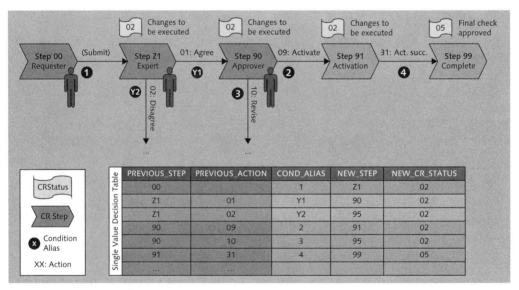

Figure 12.18 Enhance Process Flow

Figure 12.18 shows new step Z1, previous action 01, and condition alias Y1. Assuming Y1 is in the user agent table to check by the MRP controller, just by adding Z1 to the single-value decision table or the Excel spreadsheet, the workflow is enhanced with a new step for review. Remember that the condition alias will link Z1 and 01 to the user agent table for check by the MRP controller. If the Z1 step has an action of 02 (which is DISAGREE; the actions are described in the next section), then the next step is now different, and the user involved is different as well.

12.4.2 Designing Your First Rule-Based Workflow in SAP Master Data Governance

This section explains the most important steps involved in getting started with the configuration of your own rule-based workflow. A more detailed step-by-step process is included in the online help and guides available (search for "Extensibility Options for SAP Master Data Governance" on the SCN). This section provides an overview of the key areas involved in the creation of your own rule-based workflow in SAP MDG.

Before You Start, Configure Basic Workflow Settings

Before using SAP Business Workflow or a rule-based workflow, some configuration is required in the IMG. This includes basic configuration of SAP Business Workflow and extended configuration of SAP MDG. These settings can be found under SAP NETWEAVER • APPLICATION SERVER • BUSINESS MANAGEMENT • SAP BUSINESS WORKFLOW and in the SAP MDG customizing section, GENERAL SETTINGS • PROCESS MODELING • WORKFLOW.

Before designing your own rule-based workflow, there are a couple of basics you need to understand. From the section above, you know that the design of a rule-based workflow requires building the three tables: single value, user agent and non-user agent. The update to these tables determines the process, actions allowed, step types, and agents. You also must understand:

▶ There are specific step types and actions that you will use to design your rule-based process. The allowed step types and actions are listed in the following tables.

▶ Each change request type has a defined set of change request steps and numbers associated with each step.

Next we discuss step types/actions and change request types in more detail.

Step Types and Actions

The user agent decision table contains the users and the step types they can execute. In the earlier example, the data stewards could approve, where APPROVE was the step type defined for the data steward in the user agent decision table. Examples of step types and actions are provided in Figure 12.19.

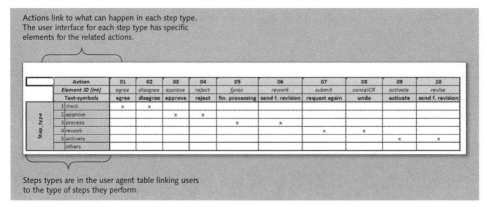

Actions link to what can happen in each step type.
The user interface for each step type has specific
elements for the related actions.

		Action	01	02	03	04	05	06	07	08	09	10
		Element ID (int)	agree	disagree	approve	reject	fproc	rework	submit	cancelCR	activate	revise
		Text-symbols	agree	disagree	approve	reject	fin. processing	send f. revision	request again	undo	activate	send f. revision
	1	check	x	x								
Step type	2	approve			x	x						
	3	process					x	x				
	4	rework							x	x		
	5	activate									x	x
		others										

Steps types are in the user agent table linking users
to the type of steps they perform.

Figure 12.19   Step Types, Actions, and User Interface

The step types are used in the user agent decision table. The actions are used in the PREVIOUS ACTION column of the single-value decision table. Back in Figure 12.17 and Figure 12.18, the actions shown are 09, 10, and 31. In Figure 12.19, you can see that 09 is ACTIVATE, and 10 is SEND FOR REVISION. Action 31 (not shown in the table) is ACTIVATION SUCCESSFUL.

Each of the step types determines the user interface and the related action options the users will have. For example, for step type 1, which is CHECK, the user interface gives the user two options: AGREE and DISAGREE. For step type 2, which is APPROVE, the user can approve or reject. For step type 5, which is ACTIVATE, the user can activate or send for revision. When you configure the step types, you are actually configuring the user interface options for the user.

Change Request Type and Change Request Numbers

It is also important that you know the change request steps allowed for each change request. Table 12.2 shows an example of the CREATE MATERIAL CHANGE request.

Type of Change Request	Change Request Step	Description
MAT01 (create material)	00	Processing
MAT01	90	Final check
MAT01	91	Activation
MAT01	92	Revision

Table 12.2   Material Change Request Step Types

Type of Change Request	Change Request Step	Description
MAT01	93	Validation
MAT01	95	Revision processing

Table 12.2 Material Change Request Step Types (Cont.)

Table 12.2 states that for change request type MAT01, which is the create material change request type, the allowed steps are 00, 90, 91, and so on. The table indicates that 90 is FINAL CHECK, 91 is for ACTIVATION. These numbers are SAP-delivered steps, used for configuring the single-value decision table, are what is configured in BRFplus to configure the workflow (shown in Figure 12.17 and Figure 12.18).

If you have a custom change request (such as the airline request described in Section 12.3) you will configure which change request steps you want for your change request. In the configuration for SAP MDG, you will add entries similar to those shown in Table 12.2 for your change request type.

Now that you understand the major configuration steps involved, you can begin to design your own rule-based workflow. The following lists the steps that need to be performed:

1. Design the flow and decide which steps and loops are needed. This should be done with the data stewards and business experts who know what is needed for a particular change request type.

2. Decide which step types are needed, understanding that each step type relates to the options the users will have (approve, reject, activate, etc.).

3. Enhance the flow diagram with resulting actions of each step. This is where you start to tie in the numbers. So if a resulting action is "send back for revision," this is mapped to action 10.

4. Enhance the flow diagram with the condition alias. Remember that the condition alias links the action to who will perform the action.

5. Enhance the flow diagram with statuses; for example: TO BE CONSIDERED AND APPROVED, CHANGES TO BE EXECUTED, TO BE REVISED.

6. Build the decision tables in SAP MDG configuration (single-value decision table, user agent table, and non-user agent table). The single-value decision table can be built with the *Microsoft Excel* upload. The user table and non-user tables need to be updated directly in SAP MDG.

For more details on workflow configuration, refer to the online help and guides available in the SAP MDG extensibility center on the SAP Community Network (SCN).

12.5   NeedsEIM, Inc.: Master Data Remediation

Now that you have a better understanding of SAP MDG and have seen how it works, we will apply the capabilities of SAP MDG to NeedsEIM, Inc. (introduced in Chapter 1).

Cleansing supplier master data is one of the requirements outlined by the procurement business function at NeedsEIM, Inc. The problem is that until now, supplier naming in this organization has been all over the board, with no rules in place. This has led to dissatisfaction on the part of the suppliers, as their names and general information are incorrectly printed in correspondence. Moreover, payments to suppliers have failed in the past because the supplier name was not legally correct. NeedsEIM, Inc. wants to correct the supplier data as part of an overall effort to reduce the number of total suppliers and increase the percentage of discounts they received from their top-tier suppliers. To overcome these issues, a new process has been introduced at NeedsEIM, Inc. for standardizing the names of all new and existing suppliers.

One of the rules that are part of this new process is that supplier names may not contain special characters. Therefore, the supplier master data needs to be cleaned up by removing any special characters used in the name fields. The changed names will have to be approved before they can be used in any business transaction. Therefore, this activity not only needs a large number of master data changes, but also collaboration between the data specialist, who is responsible for making the name changes, and the approver. A combination of Information Steward and SAP MDG provides a perfect solution for this problem.

Figure 12.20 shows how Information Steward can be integrated with SAP MDG. Information Steward sits on top of Data Services and provides an end-user environment for visualizing data quality analysis results. The core of Information Steward is a set of rules defined by the user. Information can be exported from a master data source and be imported into Information Steward. After this import, the information can be checked for compliance against the set of rules defined by the user. The integration of SAP MDG and Information Steward will be available as a Rapid Deployment Solution (Rapid Deployment Solutions were introduced in Chapter 4).

At NeedsEIM, Inc., the source of this master data is the vendor master table. Data is exported from this table, imported into Information Steward, and matched against a set of user-defined rules.

Figure 12.20 Integration of Information Steward with SAP MDG

The result of the data quality evaluation is available as a scorecard in Information Steward. A *scorecard* is an aggregation over several quality dimensions. One quality dimension consists of one or more validation rules. A failed record database table holds information about which records failed which rules. This is basically a list of vendor numbers.

For the records that do not comply with a validation rule, a change request can be created directly in SAP MDG. The change request is processed in SAP MDG, and during this period the changes are stored in the staging area, as explained above. After approval, the changes are made active and are reflected back into the vendor master table. Upon looking at the updated data in Information Steward, it is possible to see the data quality improvements in the dashboard.

Figure 12.21 shows a data quality work center in SAP MDG. At the top of Figure 12.21 are the validation rules. (Validation rules are discussed in Chapters 6 and 9.) For each validation rule, the failed records can be viewed in the table at the bottom. The validation rule and failed record information is read from Information Steward using a web service call. The CREATE CHANGE REQUEST button above the failed records enables the creation of a change request in SAP MDG for one or more selected records.

Figure 12.21 Data Quality Work Center in SAP MDG

At this point, the failed records are stored in SAP MDG, which provides many options for interacting directly with the SAP MDG APIs. For each failed record, it is possible to see if it is a part of another change request, and if so, then what the status of that change request is. What follows is a normal change request approval workflow process, at the end of which corrected data becomes available in the active area. Thus, using this technique, remediation of the supplier master data at NeedsEIM, Inc. can be performed very efficiently.

12.6 Summary

This chapter covered SAP MDG and how it provides centralized governance for selected master data domains; for example, supplier, material, customer, and financials. In addition to the provided master data domains, this chapter also discussed how you can extend SAP MDG for custom-defined objects. You also learned how the combination of Information Steward and SAP MDG supports the clean-up of existing supplier master data. For all new suppliers not yet in the system, SAP MDG ensures that the data is entered correctly during the creation process. To learn more about SAP MDG, see the Master Data Governance wiki on the SCN.

The next chapter discusses data archiving, retention management, and system decommissioning available with SAP NetWeaver Information Lifecycle Management.

In this chapter you will learn how to leverage SAP solutions for information lifecycle management (ILM) to establish a holistic ILM strategy for your organization that covers the entire information universe: structured and unstructured content, SAP and non-SAP systems, live and legacy systems.

13 Introducing SAP NetWeaver Information Lifecycle Management

Mentioning the fact that we are living in an information age or information society may sound like a cliché, but it's absolutely true. And it becomes more obvious every day as the influx of information, particularly that companies have to deal with, increases at an amazing speed. Therefore, every organization needs a strategy to cope with the challenges of managing the lifecycle of its business information.

Such an information lifecycle management (ILM) strategy must be holistic in a way that takes into account several factors, such as managing information from both live and legacy systems, and covering both structured and unstructured information. And, of course, it must be compliant with legal retention requirements.

SAP solutions for information lifecycle management support you in building a holistic ILM strategy that covers the entire spectrum of information management: information of structured and unstructured types, from live and legacy systems, as well as from SAP and non-SAP systems. SAP therefore truly considers itself a "one-stop shop" for companies seeking to establish a holistic ILM solution for their business.

SAP NetWeaver Information Lifecycle Management contains the following capabilities:

▸ **Retention management**
Enables you to set retention rules and retain business records for different periods of time according to policy or legal requirements. This holds true for all previously mentioned information types and systems. You also can collect and preserve records related to ongoing legal cases.

- **System decommissioning**
  Supports the decommissioning of legacy systems. This includes the transfer of data from the legacy system to the retention warehouse and reporting on this data using SAP NetWeaver Business Warehouse (BW) or local reporting. Retention management actions can also be applied to legacy data residing in the retention warehouse.

In addition to the core capabilities of retention management and system decommissioning included in SAP NetWeaver ILM, it also uses the following products within the retention management and system decomissioning capabilities:

- **SAP Data Services (hereafter Data Services)**
  Data Services enables the integration, transformation, improvement, and delivery of trusted data to support critical business processes and decisions. In a system decommissioning scenario, this product also provides the required extraction, transformation, and loading (ETL) capabilities for decommissioning non-SAP systems.

- **SAP Archiving by OpenText**
  SAP Archiving by OpenText provides archiving functionality for the storage of data and documents via SAP ArchiveLink. The product contains the OpenText Enterprise Library, which implements the WebDAV (Web-based Distributed Authoring and Versioning) interface of SAP NetWeaver ILM and secures the retention of data files stored with SAP NetWeaver ILM.

- **SAP Document Access by OpenText (hereafter SAP Document Access)**
  SAP Document Access is an enterprise content management (ECM) solution that provides easy access to SAP data, such as archive files and SAP ArchiveLink documents for both live and legacy content. It also includes basic extended content management (ECM) functions, such as scanning, optical character recognition (OCR), and bar-coding.

> **Note on Terminology**
>
> SAP NetWeaver ILM is the core component in the suite of SAP solutions for information lifecycle management. Therefore, in this chapter most processes and examples refer to this solution.

In this chapter we will provide more insight into how to use the SAP solutions for information lifecycle management to implement a solid ILM strategy and meet your ILM goals. Specifically, we discuss the history of SAP NetWeaver ILM, offer a brief general introduction to the tool, and then take a closer look at managing the information lifecycle in your SAP systems, both for legacy systems and during a system decommissioning.

Given the limited space available in this book, this chapter can only provide you with a brief overview of the SAP solutions for information lifecycle management. For more in-depth information, you can refer to the official SAP NetWeaver ILM documentation on the SAP Help Portal, attend the training course BIT665, or read the book *Archiving Your SAP Data* (Helmut Stefani, SAP PRESS, 2007).

Note on Versions

The information, screenshots, and examples provided in this chapter are based on SAP NetWeaver ILM 7.03, delivered with SAP NetWeaver 7.0 EHP3 and SAP ERP 6.0 EHP6. You can also use previous versions of SAP NetWeaver ILM if you are on the following releases: SAP NetWeaver 7.0 EHP2/SAP ERP 6.0 EHP5 and SAP NetWeaver 7.0 EHP1/ SAP ERP 6.0 EHP4.

13.1 The Basics of Information Lifecycle Management

In this section, we discuss what ILM means and why it's needed.

13.1.1 What Does ILM Mean?

Over the last few years, ILM has transformed from being a mere buzzword to representing a solid strategy and concept with a clear definition that most agree upon. According to the definition at SAP today, *information lifecycle management* is comprised of the policies, processes, practices, and tools used to align the business value of information with the most appropriate and cost-effective IT infrastructure from the time information is created through its final destruction. This definition reflects an application-centric, rather than technology-centric, approach.

13.1.2 Why Is ILM Needed?

Let's take a look at the drivers or pain points that have led to the existence of ILM. ILM was not invented without reason; rather, it is a result of various developments and global trends over the last decade (for example, the high cost of data management, increased legal risks associated with information management, and poor system usage and performance).

The drivers that make ILM necessary can be grouped into two categories: external drivers and internal drivers. We discuss both of these next.

External Drivers

Due to disasters such as 9/11 and economic scandals such as Enron and World-Com, the number of laws and regulations governing the retention of information has increased dramatically on a worldwide scale—and so have related lawsuits. This clearly shows that there is a huge demand for this kind of data handling; for example, e-discovery and legal hold management (both features that are included in SAP NetWeaver ILM).

Internal Drivers

One of the major internal drivers can be labeled *system landscape harmonization*. In today's highly globalized economy, the number of mergers and acquisitions (M&A) increases on a worldwide scale, making it necessary for the parties involved to consolidate their IT landscape accordingly. The selling party, for example, needs to hand data pertaining to the sold business over to the buyer, and—provided that all legal retention obligations are met—can then shut down the system. But system landscape harmonization is not only about M&A, it has also to do with companies' need to reduce the complexity of their system landscape in order to keep it manageable.

The bottom line for all internal drivers is cost. It is a waste of money and resources to maintain systems that are not needed for operational use and that are only accessed sporadically. Relocating retention-relevant data from old systems to a safe place and shutting down these systems for good can save companies large amounts of money in terms of hardware, energy, and personnel costs.

13.2 Overview of SAP NetWeaver Information Lifecycle Management

SAP NetWeaver ILM has not emerged out of the blue. Its foundation was laid in close cooperation with the Americas' SAP Users' Group (ASUG) years ago. Several of the basic functions were partly designed in conjunction with the ASUG ILM Influence Council. Through this close cooperation with its customers, SAP was able to obtain specific feedback on the pain points companies face in their ILM and legal compliance strategies. As a result, development of the new retention management and system decommissioning functions has been directly aimed at solving these pain points, and has been developed with a special focus on enhancing or building on existing capabilities.

SAP NetWeaver ILM addresses many of the pain points associated with information lifecycle management (discussed in Section 13.1 and shown in Figure 13.1). It does this by providing adequate tools and processes that enable you to control the lifecycle of your data from the time it is created until its final destruction at the end of its life. When this data is no longer needed for daily operations, it is moved from the database to the archive to keep the database volume at a reasonable level. While the data resides in the archive, retention policies ensure that it is retained and deleted in a legally compliant way. SAP NetWeaver ILM also enables you to decommission obsolete systems and move retention-relevant data to the ILM retention warehouse for long-term storage.

Figure 13.1 Customer Pain Points and How SAP NetWeaver ILM Helps

Next we will introduce the major capabilities included with SAP NetWeaver ILM.

13.2.1   Cornerstones of SAP NetWeaver ILM

SAP NetWeaver ILM includes the following cornerstones:

▸ SAP Data Archiving

▸ Retention management

▸ System decommissioning

We discuss each of these in more detail next.

SAP Data Archiving

This cornerstone is at the heart of SAP NetWeaver ILM and focuses mainly on managing database volumes. SAP Data Archiving is a tried and tested standard method for relocating business-complete data from the database to the archive. With several hundred archiving objects across the SAP Business Suite having been developed in the last 15 years, it is an indispensable means for fighting data growth, reducing storage costs, and ensuring the performance of applications. With SAP NetWeaver ILM the classical data archiving functions have been enhanced to support new ILM requirements; for example, data destruction or the archiving of data from open business processes (snapshots, which are copies of data from the database). The archive files created as a result of an SAP NetWeaver ILM process have the same format as files created in classical data archiving.

Retention Management

This cornerstone supports the business scenario for *end-of-life data*. It is aligned with the typical lifecycle of data in an SAP application and involves functions to control the retention of data from creation to destruction, based on policies and rules defined in SAP NetWeaver ILM. It also allows you to perform e-discovery actions and place legal holds on data that needs to be protected from destruction for litigation reasons.

System Decommissioning

This cornerstone focuses on the business scenario for an *end-of-life system*. Using a standardized methodology for system decommissioning, it enables you to shut down obsolete systems for good. This includes extracting retention-relevant data from the legacy system, transferring it to the ILM retention warehouse, and applying the ILM retention rules to it. And finally, it enables you to report on the retained data, for instance, during a tax audit.

13.2.2 Data Archiving Basics

As mentioned above, SAP NetWeaver ILM is deeply rooted in SAP Data Archiving, the de facto standard for data archiving in an SAP environment. To avoid the negative effects of large data volumes on costs, performance, and system availability, *business complete data* — which is nonchangeable data no longer needed in everyday business processes — needs to be removed from the database and stored in such a way that it can be accessed in read-only mode at a later time. SAP Data Archiving is the only method supported by SAP for this process, and is particularly suited for processing mass data. Before we look at the data archiving process in more detail, let's briefly define some technical terms.

▶ **Archiving object**
The archiving object is a logical grouping of related business data. In other words, it contains the definition of the logical units in business processes. It also contains the programs necessary for processing the data (primarily write and delete programs), as well as the definition of the required customizing settings. In the context of SAP NetWeaver ILM, the concept of archiving objects has transformed into the notion of *ILM object*, which in most cases corresponds 100% to the underlying classical archiving object; for example, FI_DOCUMNT.

▶ **Archive Development Kit (ADK)**
The vast majority of archiving objects are based on the Archive Development Kit (ADK) technology. ADK is the fundamental technology on which SAP Data Archiving is built (for the ABAP environment). It provides the necessary runtime environment for all archiving processes and programs and is used by both SAP development and customers to develop new archiving objects. In addition, it is responsible for ensuring, for example, that data is retrieved correctly when accessed in the archive, irrespective of the application release at the time of archiving. It can handle data archived before and after a Unicode conversion. Other technical issues, such as the compression of the data that is archived and file handling, also fall under the responsibility of ADK.

As of SAP Web AS 6.40, SAP offers an additional technology especially designed for XML-based archiving. Both ADK-based and XML-based archiving is performed using Archive Administration, Transaction SARA. Archive Administration is the main tool used for most user activities in data archiving, such as scheduling write and delete jobs, building and deleting the archive index, and storing or retrieving archive files.

The Data Lifecycle

It is important to visualize the lifecycle that data records created in an SAP application typically follow. Figure 13.2 shows the lifecycle and the frequency with which SAP data is usually accessed over its lifetime.

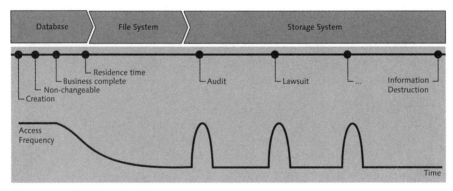

Figure 13.2 The Lifecycle of Data

When a business document, such as an accounting document or a sales order, is created in an SAP application, it is stored in the database, from where it can be accessed any time. After its creation, the document is usually accessed quite frequently; however, as the business process to which the document belongs is completed, it will be less frequently accessed, then may only require read-only access, and perhaps should eventually be destroyed. There are some important terms related to these time periods that you should understand:

- ▸ **Residence time**
  In SAP Data Archiving, this is the length of time that must be exceeded before application data can be archived.

- ▸ **Retention period**
  This is the length of time up to the point at which the data or documents can be destroyed. In SAP NetWeaver ILM, we also speak of minimum and maximum retention periods. The minimum retention period is the least amount of time that data has to be kept due to legal requirements before it can be destroyed.

The maximum retention period is the amount of time data has to be kept before it must be destroyed due to legal or other requirements.

> **Residence Time versus Retention Period**
>
> For the retention time it does not matter where the data resides, that is, in the database or a storage system. Therefore, the residence time always falls within the retention period.

In the context of the entire lifecycle, data is only modifiable and relevant for operational use for a short period of time. The largest portion of the lifecycle is the retention period, during which the data cannot be deleted due to legal requirements. In this period the data is only accessed infrequently; for example, in case of a tax audit or if a product liability issue arises.

From an EIM perspective, data also has its own lifecycle with regard to the investment required for managing the data during its life. In the on-boarding phase, right after the data is created or when it arrives in the system—for instance, due to a migration or consolidation project—the investment effort is low. Most activities are performed during the active use of the data. For example, the data is subject to data quality or data governance activities, or it is loaded into the data warehouse for reporting. After its active use, the data is only processed infrequently, mainly during archiving or retention management activities or when the system is decommissioned. (Refer back to Figure 1.2 in Chapter 1 for a visual image of this process.)

Data Archiving Process

Figure 13.3 depicts the basic process of data archiving in an SAP system.

The process can be divided into the following steps:

1. **Write data to archive files**
   The data to be archived is read from the database and written sequentially to newly created archive files. This step is performed by the write program of the archiving object.

2. **Delete data from the database**
   The delete program deletes the data from the database after it has been completely written to the archive files. To ensure the integrity of the archived data, the delete run is not started until the created archive files have been read and confirmed.

Figure 13.3 Data Archiving Process

3. **Store archive files**

   The archive files that were created during the write phase can be moved to storage systems or to tertiary storage media. The storage phase is not part of the actual archiving process. As an option, the user can start the storage phase before the deletion phase.

13.2.3 ILM-Aware Storage

An ILM strategy would be incomplete without taking into account the storage of the data in a secure environment that prevents the data from being deleted or manipulated in any way. To comply with legal rules and regulations, SAP NetWeaver ILM uses a concept called *ILM-aware storage*.

ILM-aware storage is based on the new WebDAV interface, which, in contrast to SAP ArchiveLink, has the ability to create complex storage hierarchies and to attach properties to each node in the hierarchy and the content (archive file) itself. SAP NetWeaver ILM uses an ILM-enhanced WebDAV interface for information transfer between the application system and the storage system. This ensures that not only the actual content is passed to the storage, but also metadata in the form of WebDAV properties, such as expiration dates or legal holds.

For the storage system to understand and allow actions on the stored data based on the retention rules, it must be able to receive this metadata and act accordingly. If it does, it is considered ILM-aware. Storage vendors can obtain an ILM certification from SAP to show their customers that their system is ILM-aware. New certifications are currently based on version ILM-BC 3.0.

To fulfill the requirements of ILM, the storage system must meet certain criteria. On the one hand, it must ensure that the data it harbors is protected against deletion, as long as its retention time has not expired. On the other hand, it must support the destruction of data on request. WORM-like magnetic storage technology is particularly suited for this purpose.

From an ILM perspective, unstructured documents, such as scanned invoices, incoming or outgoing documents, or print lists, are as important as structured data. The reason is that the information they contain also needs to be retained, as it complements the information included in structured data. SAP NetWeaver ILM supports the handling of SAP ArchiveLink documents and print lists that are stored on a storage system using the SAP ArchiveLink interface. SAP ArchiveLink documents are linked to their corresponding structured documents (the link information is stored in the TOAx tables); hence they are often referred to as attachments. SAP ArchiveLink documents are handled in both the retention management and the system decommissioning scenarios.

While structured data (archived data) managed by ILM is stored on an ILM-aware storage system, unstructured documents (such as *.pdf, .tif, .jpg,* etc.) are stored as before via SAP ArchiveLink. In ILM only the references to the SAP ArchiveLink documents are stored in the archive hierarchy (see Figure 13.4).

Print lists may be difficult to locate and retrieve because of the restricted set of available selection criteria. SAP Document Access by OpenText provides for easier print list retrieval through its virtual folder technology, generated indices, and the ability to add search fields and grouping definitions.

Figure 13.4 shows how structured and unstructured data is stored in separate hierarchies based on retention rules.

With the ILM-enhanced WebDAV interface, the archive files and snapshots (copies of data from the database) are stored in a hierarchy that reflects the parameters determined by the ILM retention rules and that is built at the time of storage. The system distinguishes between archived data and snapshots. As you can see in Figure 13.4, archived data is stored under the node AD, whereas snapshots are stored under the node SN.

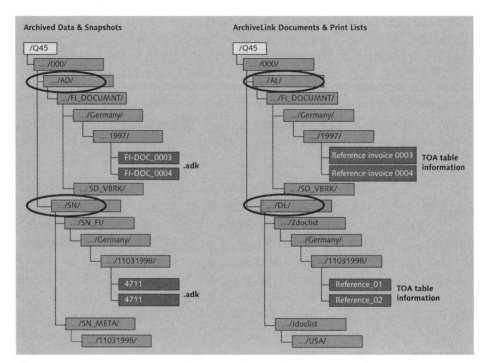

Figure 13.4 ILM-Aware Storage: Archive Hierarchy Based on Retention Rules

References to SAP ArchiveLink documents and print lists are stored in a "shadow" hierarchy that corresponds to that of the structured data. This way, the unstructured data is placed opposite of its corresponding structured data and inherits the same lifecycle metadata. In Figure 13.4, you can see that SAP ArchiveLink documents are stored under the node AL, and print lists are stored under the node DL (DL stands for the German word *Drucklisten*).

The archive hierarchy is built according to the rules specified in SAP NetWeaver ILM and the type of data archived.

13.2.4 Architecture—What You Need to Run SAP NetWeaver ILM

The core functions of SAP NetWeaver ILM are provided with SAP NetWeaver enhancement packages, whereas the application-specific content, such as the ILM-enabled archiving objects, is contained in SAP ERP enhancement packages (see SAP Notes 1168187 and 1494347). Figure 13.5 and Figure 13.6 provide an architectural overview of the ILM scenarios, including the system components and landscape layers involved.

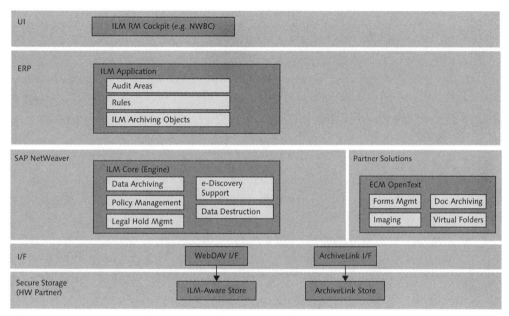

Figure 13.5 Architecture of the Retention Management Scenario

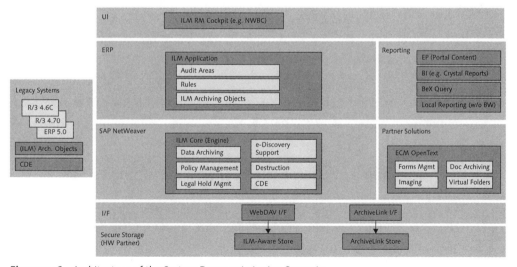

Figure 13.6 Architecture of the System Decommissioning Scenario

To use SAP NetWeaver ILM, you need to activate the relevant ILM business functions in the switch framework (Transaction SFW5), depending on the ILM scenario. The activation of SAP NetWeaver ILM cannot be revoked.

Retention Management

You use the ILM retention management functions in a live ERP application system (AS ABAP) that uses SAP NetWeaver 7.0 enhancement package 3 as its technology platform. To be able to control the communication of the ABAP application instance with the external ILM store, you require a storage service. You have the following options:

► You can use the storage and retention service (SRS) that runs on the application system (AS ABAP). The SRS can run either locally on the application system or centrally on a different AS ABAP instance. In the latter case, several application systems can share it.

► You use the XML data archiving service (XML DAS) that runs on an application server Java (AS Java). Select an appropriate system with the usage type AS Java from your system landscape. Several AS ABAP instances can share the XML DAS running on this system.

System Decommissioning

To manage the lifecycle of legacy data in the ILM retention warehouse, you need to set up a dedicated system (AS ABAP) with SAP ERP 6.0 enhancement package 6 based on SAP NetWeaver 7.0 enhancement package 3. You also need SAP NetWeaver BW for reporting and an ILM-aware storage system. For the administration of the ILM store, the same options apply as described for retention management.

For more information on how to use SAP NetWeaver ILM on SAP ERP 6.0 enhancement package 6, see SAP Note 1648883.

13.3   Managing the Lifecycle of Information in Live Systems

SAP NetWeaver ILM enables you to control the lifecycle of information in a live SAP environment. This includes online data that is still available in the database, but also nonoperational data that has been moved to the archive. SAP NetWeaver ILM includes the following retention management capabilities:

▶ **Manage audit areas**

    ▶ Create audit areas at the beginning of the process

▶ **Manage and enforce retention policies**

    ▶ Set policies for automatic data retention and subsequent destruction

    ▶ Retain data according to set policies

    ▶ Responsibly destroy data when the expiration date has been reached

▶ **Maintain separate archives per retention period**

    ▶ Create multiple archive files for each calculated expiration date

▶ **Perform e-discovery**

    ▶ Search for information in response to legal requests

▶ **Apply legal holds on data**

    ▶ Automatically prevent data destruction

    ▶ Apply hold to online and archived data

In this section, we explain some basic concepts, such as audit areas, data destruction, and legal hold management.

13.3.1 Audit Area

The audit area is another central concept in SAP NetWeaver ILM. It bundles data according to the reason for keeping the data. For example, financial data needs to be kept for tax reasons and would therefore belong to the audit area TAX. SAP delivers the following audit areas with SAP ERP 6.0 enhancement package 6:

▶ **TAX**
Covers the minimum scope for tax auditing in the United States or Germany. This scope was defined with the help of SAP user groups. The German *Braunschweig* model can be used from a reporting perspective as a guideline for the scope of the TAX audit area.

▶ **PRODLIABIL**
Contains the data required for processing product liability claims. The scope of this audit area includes pick lists and batch where-used lists reports. The audit areas for tax and product liability also include objects for SAP for Utilities and SAP for Oil & Gas.

► **DEMO**

This is a sample audit area to which the ILM object FLIGHT_BOOKINGS is assigned. It also contains a DEMO policy. This audit area can be used for test purposes because it does not deal with business-relevant data. Therefore, it is not assigned to a switch, and no SAP NetWeaver BW queries are delivered for it.

► **GENERAL**

This audit area is delivered empty, which means no ILM objects are assigned to it. The aim is to assign objects to this audit area that are not assigned to a different audit area. This approach is ideal if you want to have the retention rules from different application areas in a consolidated form. Any objects assigned to the audit area GENERAL cannot be assigned to another audit area.

Standard audit areas delivered by SAP cannot be modified. To use these audit areas you can copy them into the customer namespace and edit them as required.

Using the policy management or "policy engine" component, you can specify policies and rules according to which data will be segregated into different files during archiving, shown in Figure 13.7. This holds true for structured data as well as for unstructured documents. Archive files created before the implementation of SAP NetWeaver ILM can also be integrated. A conversion tool helps you "re-archive" such files, thereby applying the retention rules on them.

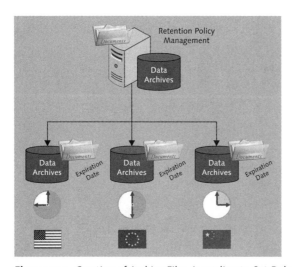

Figure 13.7 Creation of Archive Files According to Set Rules

Simply put, *policy management* (in previous releases of SAP NetWeaver ILM, this was also referred to as the *information retention manager*, or IRM) lets you define the amount of time data will be kept and the location where it will be stored. Apart from retention rules, you can also define residence rules to specify how long data resides in the database before it can be archived.

Section 13.5 will show how to set up a policy and define rules. In the example, this is shown from the perspective of system decommissioning, but the same procedure would also apply for live systems.

Retention Management of Unstructured Data

In SAP NetWeaver ILM, retention rules can also be applied to unstructured documents linked via SAP ArchiveLink. However, they are not applied to the documents themselves, but rather to their references as stored in the archive hierarchy of the ILM-aware storage (see Section 13.2.3). That way, unstructured documents can inherit the retention times of their parent object. If, for example, an accounting document receives a retention time of seven years, the corresponding scanned invoice would also receive a retention time of seven years.

You can propagate retention times for SAP ArchiveLink documents and print lists in the store by running the following reports:

▶ ARLNK_SET_PROXYS_ALDOCUMENTS

▶ ARLNK_SET_PROXYS_PRINTLISTS

As a prerequisite for the enforcement of retention times, the storage system must have the correct compliance class. This means, for example, that a document will be destroyed when it has reached its expiration date *only* if the SAP ArchiveLink storage system supports the destruction of documents and understands the SAP destroy command.

13.3.2 Data Destruction

Retention management would be incomplete without being able to destroy data whose minimum retention period has passed or whose maximum retention period has been reached. With SAP NetWeaver ILM, you can destroy data in the database, but also archived data and SAP ArchiveLink documents kept in the store. In either case, data cannot be destroyed if it has a legal hold placed on it. In the destruction function, you can select online data, archive files, attachments, and print lists whose retention period has expired, transfer them into a destruction work list, and execute the destruction run.

To destroy data in the database of a live system, you simply choose the DATA DESTRUCTION option offered in the write program variant of ILM-enabled archiving objects (shown in Figure 13.8).

Figure 13.8 Data Destruction in the Live Database (Transaction SARA)

Destruction of data in the database is carried out with an archiving write run and a subsequent delete run. In this process, temporary archive files are created and then deleted at the end of the delete phase. These files, together with the administration data that relates to them, are automatically deleted by the system.

With SAP NetWeaver ILM you can also destroy data in the archive, including attachments and print lists. For more information, please refer to Section 13.5.

13.3.3 Legal Hold Management

Legal hold management is a tool specially developed for use in SAP NetWeaver ILM scenarios. Although it provides functions similar to SAP Case Management, it can be used independently from the latter. With legal hold management, you can create legal cases, place legal holds on archived data business object repository (BOR) objects and SAP ArchiveLink documents, and run e-discovery reports. Together with the BOR objects to be locked, you can also display the related attachments and include them in the hold.

Let's assume that your company is currently going through a lawsuit and that the related data, including a specific accounting document, has been secured by placing a legal hold on it. In this case, the system would not allow you to destroy the document, even if it has reached its expiration date and is ready for destruction.

Legal hold management comes with a history function that allows you to find out, for example, which reports have been executed or which objects have been deleted. By using a personalization function, you can specify which object types will be used in the e-discovery search.

> **Note**
>
> The SAP NetWeaver ILM-specific function for setting legal holds (as an alternative to SAP Case Management) is currently available only for use in live application systems. The complete availability of this function in the retention warehouse system (system decommissioning scenario) is planned for future deliveries.

The following is a summary of the retention management functions provided by SAP NetWeaver ILM:

▶ Audit area management

▶ Policy and rule management

▶ Archiving programs that integrate with the policy and rule management functions

▶ Destroy function (for databases, archiving, and attachments)

▶ Legal hold management

▶ ILM-aware storage for secure and legally compliant retention of data

▶ An ILM-certified storage system

Retention management always occurs in a live system environment. To be able to use the latest version of the retention management functions, you must be on SAP ERP 6.0 enhancement package 6. See also Section 13.2.4.

13.4 Managing the Lifecycle of Information from Legacy Systems

SAP NetWeaver ILM provides a standardized method for decommissioning legacy systems, including SAP and non-SAP systems. As a basic principle, you first need to analyze the data in the legacy system you want to decommission (part of the preliminary project steps). Then you transfer the selected data from the legacy system to the SAP NetWeaver ILM retention warehouse system, where you apply retention rules on it to ensure legally compliant storage. From the store, the data can be accessed at any time; for example, to respond to tax audits or create financial reports. Figure 13.9 shows the basic process, including the system prerequisites.

Figure 13.9 Process Overview and System Prerequisites

In the following sections we go through the main steps required for decommissioning legacy systems.

13.4.1 Preliminary Steps

Before you start to decommission a legacy system, there are a number of preliminary steps that need to be completed. We discuss these next.

Analyze the Data in the Legacy System

Typically, you only want to extract data from the legacy system that needs to be retained; for example, for legal reasons. In this step you analyze the data volume in your legacy system to identify exactly which data is eligible for extraction.

Questions to be answered include:

▶ What data does the legacy system contain?

▶ What data is relevant for reporting (for example, for tax audits or product liability claims)?

▶ Are the relevant archiving objects available in the system?

In the SAP system you can find a variety of tools that help you analyze the content of your system, such as:

▶ Database analysis (Transaction DB02)

▶ Database tools such as SAPDBA and BR for Oracle and Informix

▶ Tables and archiving objects (Transaction DB15)

▶ Table analysis (Transaction TAANA)

SAP also offers services to support you in your system analysis. As a result of your analysis, you should have a clear picture of what data must be transferred to the retention warehouse and what data can be left behind.

Enable Your Legacy System for SAP NetWeaver ILM

Since your legacy system does not have any ILM functions, you must enable it for use with SAP NetWeaver ILM. This includes importing ILM-enabled archiving write programs and the context data extractor (CDE) extraction services.

You need to implement SAP Notes to install the CDE (see Note 1089434) and ILM-enable any archiving objects (see Note 1180653) to cover all the data you need to transfer to the retention warehouse.

If your legacy system is on SAP R/3 4.6C or SAP R/3 Enterprise 4.70, you can use the related ILM add-on to import this content:

▶ BC-ILM-ADO-46C: see SAP Note 1402693

▶ BC-ILM-ADO-47: see SAP Note 1614029

For other releases or non-SAP systems, contact the SAP System Landscape Optimization (SLO) group at *http://service.sap.com/slo*.

Configure the Retention Warehouse System

Before you can start reporting on the data transferred from the legacy system, you need to configure the retention warehouse system. To do so, you need to install and set up an SAP ERP 6.0 enhancement package 6 system and connect it to an ILM-aware storage system. The main step here is setting up and configuring the archive store, as described in the SAP NetWeaver ILM documentation. You also need an SAP NetWeaver BW system for reporting. See also Section 13.2.4.

The process of managing the lifecycle of information from legacy systems requires different steps in each phase and for each system involved. Figure 13.10 provides an overview of the process steps involved in system decommissioning.

Figure 13.10 System Decommissioning Process Steps

13.4.2 Steps Performed in the Legacy System

Once the preliminary steps of analyzing the data and preparing the legacy system for SAP NetWeaver ILM are completed, the next step is to archive the data.

Before shutting down the legacy system for good, you have to ensure that you have archived all the data you need to retain. This entails archiving business-complete data (that is, data from closed business processes), but also data from still open processes that might be worth keeping for retention reasons. Apart from this transactional data, you also need to archive context data, such as master data and metadata like ABAP Dictionary records, customizing settings, and so on. You use different functions for each of these types:

▶ Business complete data: standard archiving objects

▶ Business incomplete data: snapshot option provided by SAP NetWeaver ILM-enabled archiving objects

▶ Master data for which an archiving object exists: snapshot option provided by SAP NetWeaver ILM-enabled archiving objects

▶ Master data for which no archiving object exists: CDE extraction services

▶ Metadata: CDE extraction services

13.4.3 Steps Performed in the Retention Warehouse System

In addition to the steps in the legacy system, there are several steps that must be done in the retention warehouse in SAP NetWeaver ILM:

▶ **Define audit areas and retention policies**
To ensure that the data coming from the legacy system will be stored safely according to its retention time, you must define adequate audit areas and retention policies. You can then transfer the data from the legacy system and apply the retention rules to it.

▶ **Transfer the data from the legacy system to the retention warehouse system and convert the data**
You can now transfer the archived (structured) data and the SAP ArchiveLink information (for the unstructured data) to the retention warehouse system and convert it for use in SAP NetWeaver ILM (ILM conversion). You must also transfer the related archive administration data so that archiving sessions are made available to the retention warehouse system. After the data has been transferred, you can start the ILM conversion, during which the retention rules are applied to the data. As an optional step, you can create checksums to compare the data before and after conversion.

▶ **Use reporting in SAP NetWeaver BW or use local reporting**
After you have decommissioned the legacy system, you can use the data stored in the retention warehouse to report on it. This can be done using either SAP NetWeaver BW or local reporting, a function that does not require SAP NetWeaver BW.

SAP NetWeaver ILM Cockpit Roles for the SAP NetWeaver Business Client

To help you perform the process steps of the ILM scenarios (retention management and system decommissioning) faster and in the recommended order, SAP delivers the following SAP NetWeaver ILM cockpit roles for the SAP NetWeaver Business Client (NWBC):

▶ **Retention Management Cockpit—Administrator**
Contains all steps an administrator needs for all retention management functions.

▶ **Retention Management Cockpit—Line of Business**
Contains only those functions that are relevant for line of business (LoB) staff; for example, accountants.

▶ **System Decommissioning Cockpit—Administrator**
Contains all steps an administrator needs for all system decommissioning functions performed in the retention warehouse.

▶ **System Decommissioning Cockpit—Line of Business**
Contains only those functions that are relevant for LoB staff; for example, accountants, with a main focus on reporting.

Using the SAP NetWeaver ILM cockpits, you do not have to remember all the transactions that are required in an SAP NetWeaver ILM scenario; the cockpits will guide you through the process in the right sequence. The cockpit roles are delivered as templates and can be adjusted as needed. It is still possible to use the transactions in the system; for example, Transaction SARA.

Figure 13.11 shows the SAP NetWeaver ILM cockpits in SAP NetWeaver Business Client (NWBC). The SAP NetWeaver ILM retention warehouse cockpit for administrators has been opened.

Figure 13.11 ILM Cockpits in SAP NetWeaver Business Client

13.4.4 Handling Data from Non-SAP Systems During Decommissioning

The SAP solutions for information lifecycle management also support the decommissioning of non-SAP systems. The main difference to SAP system decommissioning is the handling of the original data to be extracted from the legacy system. Since the definition of this data may follow a data model that is totally different from that of SAP data, the legacy data needs some special treatment before it can be transferred to the retention warehouse for further use.

By leveraging the extract, transform, and load (ETL) capabilities of Data Services, it is possible to extract the data from a non-SAP system, map it onto SAP structures, and convert it into Archive Development Kit (ADK) archive files with an identical format, like archive files created from native SAP data. The ADK mapping is performed using adapted ADK write programs (non-SAP write programs), in which, for instance, the archiving checks are disabled. Data Services does the technical profiling and data auditing to help assess the state of the data from the data conversion and archiving readiness. Additionally, Information Steward can be used for business data assessment on the legacy system as well as a single view of data lineage and impact analysis.

Once the data from the non-SAP system has been processed this way, you can use it in the retention warehouse in a similar way as you would do with native SAP data. For example, you would apply retention rules to the freshly created ADK files and move them to the store for long-term preservation. For reporting, you would simply load the data into SAP NetWeaver BW and use predefined queries for tax audits or product liability. Of course, you can also use local reporting tools.

13.5   System Decommissioning—Detailed Example

Now that you are familiar with the SAP NetWeaver ILM retention warehouse and know the basic concept of system decommissioning, we will present a detailed example of how the process works in the system. Given the large number of steps that a system decommissioning project may involve, we will only focus on the most important steps.

For this scenario we assume that you have analyzed the data in your legacy system and that you have enabled the system for use with SAP NetWeaver ILM. You have also configured the retention warehouse system as needed. For more information, see Section 13.4.1.

In this section, we explain the steps required to extract data from the legacy system, transfer it to the retention warehouse, and report on this data.

13.5.1 Data Extraction

To be compliant with legal or business requirements, it is necessary to extract the transactional data, master data, and context data from the legacy system before it is shut down.

We recommend that you perform the necessary archiving steps in the following order:

1. Archive business-complete data (transactional data).

2. Archive business-incomplete data (transactional data).

3. Archive master data for which archiving objects exist.

4. Archive master data for which no archiving objects exist and other context information.

5. Archive all other data not covered above.

Let's start with archiving the transactional data. This includes both the settings to archive transactional data and to archive the related context using the context data extractor.

Archive Transactional Data

In this step we first archive business-complete data using the standard write program, and then we archive business-incomplete data via the snapshot function. In this example, we archive financial accounting documents using the archiving object FI_DOCUMNT.

1. In Transaction SARA, create a variant for the write program and specify the archiving range:

```
Company code: 1000
Fiscal year: 2000
Document number range: 100001350 - 100001399
```

This is shown in Figure 13.12.

Note the ILM ACTIONS section. It only appears for SAP NetWeaver ILM–enabled archiving objects. To archive data from closed processes, select ARCHIVING. Enter a comment on the archiving session for later easier spotting in archive management.

Maintain Variant: Report ILMFI_DOCUMNT_WRI, Variant EIMBOOK

Variant attributes

Financial records

Company Codes	1000	to	
Document Numbers	100001350	to	100001399
From Fiscal Year	2000		
From Fiscal Period	1		
To Fiscal Year	2000		
To Fiscal Period	99		
Document Type		to	

Restrictions

Min.No.of Days in the System	
Key date	17.11.2011

ILM actions
- ⦿ Archiving
- ○ Snapshot

Processing Options
- ○ Test Mode
- ⦿ Productive Mode   ☐ Delete with Test Variant

☑ Detail log
Comment on archiving run   EIM book

Figure 13.12 Maintain the Write Program Variant

2. Specify that the archiving session should run in productive mode and request a detailed log. Then schedule the session as usual.

   After the write job is finished, check in the log to see whether the documents are archived (Figure 13.13).

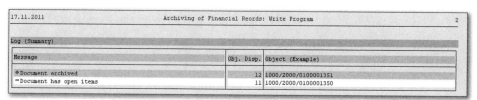

17.11.2011	Archiving of Financial Reords: Write Program		2

Log (Summary)

Message	Obj. Disp.	Object (Example)
⊛ Document archived	12	1000/2000/0100001351
▬ Document has open items	11	1000/2000/0100001350

Figure 13.13 Log of Write Program

As you can see, 12 documents were archived, and 11 documents could not be archived because they have open items. We now need to archive these 11 documents using the snapshot function:

1. In Transaction SARA, use the same variant for the write program as above.

2. Choose SNAPSHOT in the ILM ACTION section and execute the run as you would normally do.

3. After the write job is finished, check in the log to see whether the documents are archived (Figure 13.14).

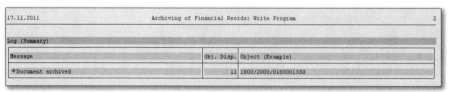

17.11.2011	Archiving of Financial Reords: Write Program		2
Log (Summary)			
Message	Obj. Disp.	Object (Example)	
◆Document archived	11	1000/2000/0100001350	

Figure 13.14 Log of Write Program—Snapshots

The log states that the remaining 11 documents with open items were also archived. Remember that snapshots are taken with no archivability checks on. This enables the archiving of data that, in classical archiving, would not be eligible for archiving.

In this example, we chose to have the delete program start automatically when the write job is finished (START AUTOMATICALLY checkbox in ARCHIVING-OBJECT SPECIFIC CUSTOMIZING). Therefore, we do not need to schedule a delete run right now.

Next, we need to archive the context information.

Archive Data Using the Context Data Extractor

Once you have archived the transactional data, you must ensure that the associated context information that is required for the later interpretation of the transactional data is also transferred to the retention warehouse. This is done by using the context data extractor (CDE). In this example, we archive context data from Financial Accounting in SAP ERP and the fiscal year 2004.

1. Call Transaction ILM. Select ARCHIVE DATA FOR ILM from the EXTRACTION folder.

2. Enter the required parameters; for example, the application FI. Figure 13.15 shows an example.

Selection screen program for ILM

Selection Criteria

General

Extract Name	EIM BOOK			
Company code	1000	to		⇨
Fiscal year	2004			
Language	DE	to	EN	⇨

Application Areas

Applications	FI	⇨

Replace existing Archive

☐ Replace existing Extraction

Figure 13.15 CDE Selection Screen

3. Execute your run. The archiving object that is used in the background is SN_FI (snapshot of financial accounting data).

4. In archive management (access via Transaction SARA) the CDE run is listed as a complete archiving session (Figure 13.16).

Archive Administation: Archiving Session Overview

Archiving object	SN_FI	FI segments for Information Lifecycle Management

Sessions and files for archiving object	Note
▾ ◯◯◼ Complete archiving sessions	
▾ 734 - 797 (11.08.2011 - 17.11.2011)	
▾ 797 - 17.11.2011	EIM book 1000 2004 DE EN
• 🔒 000797-001SN_FI	
▸ 782 - 18.10.2011	1000 2002 DE EN
▸ 781 - 18.10.2011	1000 2001 DE EN
▸ 755 - 25.08.2011	1000 1998 DE
▸ 749 - 24.08.2011	1000 1997 DE
▸ 739 - 16.08.2011	1000 2000
▸ 734 - 11.08.2011	1000 2000

Figure 13.16   CDE Session in Archive Management

By taking a look at the statistics you will see that you have archived 135 data objects (Figure 13.17).

```
Selection screen program for ILM

Statistics of archived objects

Archive file:      000797-001SN_FI     Number of objects:  [    135 ]
Size in MB:                    0,566
```

Table	Number	Description
TXI_CONTROL	135	Control Record for ILM archives
TXI_FM01	5	Financial Management Areas
TXI_FMFPO	1.130	FIFM: Commitment Item
TXI_INDEXD	3	Index definition (security index)
TXI_LFBK	267	Vendor Master (Bank Details)
TXI_PTRV_DOC_HD	69	Transfer Travel -> FI/CO: Header o
TXI_PTRV_DOC_IT	280	Transfer Travel -> FI/CO: Lines of
TXI_PTRV_DOC_TAX	90	Transfer Travel -> FI/CO: Tax line

Figure 13.17   Statistics of Archived Objects

5. To view the result of the CDE run, call Transaction ILM and select DATA EXTRACT BROWSER from the EXTRACTION folder.

The content of your CDE extract is displayed in the DART Browser (Figure 13.18). You can see that in your session you have extracted context data related to transactional data and master data, both from financial accounting.

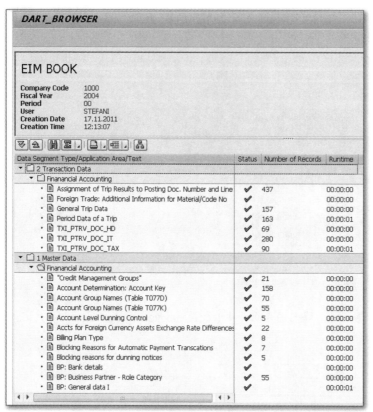

Figure 13.18 Content of CDE Archive File

Now that you have archived all the data (business-complete data, business-incomplete data, and context data) from the legacy system that you need to retain for later access, you are ready to transfer the resulting archive files to the retention warehouse and, once they have arrived there, apply retention rules on them in the ILM conversion step.

13.5.2 Data Transfer and Conversion

Before you start transfer and conversion, you need to set up audit areas and retention rules. During conversion, the rules will be applied to the transferred data to make sure it is stored with its appropriate expiration date in the ILM-aware storage. Remember that only the retention warehouse has the SAP NetWeaver ILM functionality required to perform these steps; the legacy system is totally unaware of SAP NetWeaver ILM (with the exception of the ILM-enabled archiving objects and the CDE extraction services being available in the legacy system).

Let's take a look at the steps involved in setting up audit areas and rules. First will be the actual setup of the audit areas and rules, then the transfer of data using the audit areas and rules, and, finally, the transfer and conversion of the data to archive files.

Set Up Audit Areas and Rules

You can access the required functions using the SAP NetWeaver Business Client (NWBC) ILM Retention Warehouse cockpit for administrators, under AUDIT AREAS and ILM RULES. You can also use the corresponding transactions.

Before you can create policies, you must have at least one audit area set up. For this example, we have copied the standard audit area TAX and created the new audit area ZILMTAX in the customer namespace. We have assigned the following ILM objects to the new audit area:

FI_DOCUMNT, AL_DOCUMENTS, SN_META, SN_GEN, SN_GENC, SN_FI, SN_FIC

These ILM objects belong to our example. We need them to view a complete SAP NetWeaver BW query at the end of the process, including the original documents:

1. To create a policy, go to AUDIT AREAS • PROCESS AUDIT AREAS, or use Transaction IRMPOL.

2. Make the necessary entries as shown in Figure 13.19, and then choose NEW.

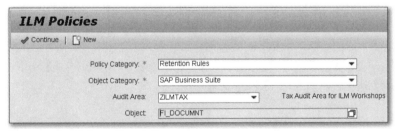

Figure 13.19 Define a New Policy

Since this example is about managing the retention of data, we choose the policy category RETENTION RULES. ILM policy management also supports the policy category RESIDENCE RULES, which lets you define residence periods for your archiving objects.

3. Enter a policy name. In this example, we choose EIMBOOK.

4. Select the field BUKRS (company code), and then use the ADD ITEM arrow to move it into the selected condition fields table (see Figure 13.20). We will need this field later in the reporting phase.

Figure 13.20 Define a New Policy (Cont.)

5. Save your new retention policy. You need to have a customizing transport request ready.

6. For your new policy, enter a retention rule like the one we created for this example (see Figure 13.21).

Figure 13.21 Define a Rule

7. Once you have saved your retention rule, select CHANGE STATUS to set the policy status to live (shown in Figure 13.22).

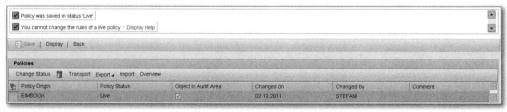

Figure 13.22 Set the Policy Status to Live

What You Should Know about Retention Rules

When you create a new retention policy, you can choose the fields that are to appear during rule maintenance. There are mandatory fields (e.g., system, client) that are always part of the rule, and other fields that can be selected from a list of available fields, such as the company code. The available fields are set up in Customizing by SAP development and vary per ILM object. If you create your own ILM objects, you must also set up available fields in Customizing (Transaction IRM_CUST).

For the system to determine the expiration date during archiving, you must specify certain criteria when setting up a new rule. It is possible to enter a minimum and a maximum retention period, as well as a retention time unit (e.g., year, day, and month) and a time reference. The minimum retention period indicates how long the data must at least be kept. The maximum retention period indicates after what date the data must be destroyed. The time reference criterion tells the system from what point in time the retention times are to start counting (e.g., end of year, end of fiscal year).

By entering a storage system, you specify the location at which the data will be stored in the ILM-aware storage.

Your retention policy and rule have now been activated, which means that, during archiving, the system will route the data to the correct storage location and will store the calculated expiration date.

Transfer and Convert the Archive Files

In the next phase, you transfer the actual data and the archive administration data (information about the archiving sessions, such as session number, etc.) from the legacy system to the retention warehouse. If the legacy system and the retention warehouse system are connected to the same file system, it is only necessary to transfer the administration data. You also transfer the link information of SAP ArchiveLink attachments and propagate the retentions onto the references. This will enable you to include your attachments in your ILM strategy.

After you have transferred all the data, you apply the retention rules you set up earlier to the data using the ILM conversion function. An important part of this process is filling the repository from the SN_META file. This file contains the necessary metadata that allows for the interpretation of the data once the original system has been shut down.

Note

As an optional step, you can use the checksum function to compare the data before and after the rules have been applied. In this example we will not cover this step.

Figure 13.23 shows the steps of the data transfer process.

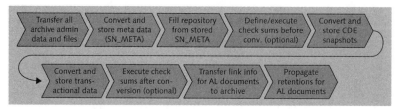

Figure 13.23 Transferring Data Step-by-Step

The transfer is triggered from within the retention warehouse system and requires an RFC connection between the legacy system and the retention warehouse system. In this example we perform the transfer from the SAP NetWeaver Business Client (NWBC) ILM Retention Warehouse cockpit for administrators. Our retention warehouse system and the legacy system share the same file system, so we only need to transfer the archive administration data.

To transfer the archive administration data for the archiving sessions performed in the legacy system, proceed as follows:

1. Go to ARCHIVE FILES TRANSFERS • TRANSFER ARCHIVE ADMINISTRATION DATA (Transaction ILM_TRANS_ADMIN_ONLY).

2. Double-click on the legacy system (in our example, "ILM" is the name of the legacy system we want to decommission) to call up the work list of available archiving objects and sessions (see Figure 13.24).

Figure 13.24 Transfer Archive Administration Data

In Figure 13.24, we have highlighted the two archiving sessions that we created in the legacy system. The first one contains the business-complete data, and the second one the snapshot data (shown in the bottom portion of Figure 13.24). You can see that the transfer of these sessions has not started.

3. To start the transfer, select the required sessions (multiple selection is possible by holding down the ⎡Shift⎤ or ⎡Ctrl⎤ key on your keyboard) and choose DATA TRANSFER.

4. Fill up the pop-up screen providing the required information and schedule the run in live mode. When the job is finished (see Figure 13.25), you can see in the overview screen that two new sessions have been created during the transfer: 1453 and 1454.

Sessions and Files	Status	Process Status	New...	New...	No. of Obje...	Transferred...	Session Note
▼ FI_DOCUMNT	△	Data transfer partially finished			714	38	
▼ 000 Complete Archiving Sessions	△	Data transfer partially finished			602	26	
▼ 528 - 795 (20.05.1999 - 17.11.2011)	△	Data transfer partially finished			602	26	
▶ 795 - 17.11.2011	■	Data transfer finished	1453		12	12	EIM book buiness-complete
▶ 794 - 17.11.2011	◇	Data transfer has not started			58	0	EIM book (Test)
▶ 776 - 12.10.2011	■	Data transfer finished	1416		9	9	BIT665 Demo 1000 100005
▶ 774 - 26.09.2011	■	Data transfer finished	1365		1	1	1000, 100005997 1997
▶ 773 - 26.09.2011	■	Data transfer finished	1373		1	1	1000, 100005998 1997
▶ 767 - 08.09.2011	■	Data transfer finished	1337		1	1	1000, 100005999 1997
▶ 745 - 24.08.2011	■	Data transfer finished	1311		1	1	1000, 100000011 2001
▶ 733 - 09.08.2011	■	Data transfer finished	1296		1	1	1000, 100000010 2001
▶ 655 - 24.03.2000	◇	Data transfer has not started			493	0	Archivierung 1995
▶ 530 - 20.05.1999	◇	Data transfer has not started			2	0	
▶ 529 - 20.05.1999	◇	Data transfer has not started			11	0	
▶ 528 - 20.05.1999	◇	Data transfer has not started			12	0	
▼ 🗋 Snapshots	△	Data transfer partially finished			112	12	
▼ 731 - 796 (09.08.2011 - 17.11.2011)	△	Data transfer partially finished			112	12	
▶ 796 - 17.11.2011	■	Data transfer finished	1454		11	11	EIM book snapshot
▶ 793 - 17.11.2011	◇	Data transfer has not started			100	0	EIM book (Test)
▶ 731 - 09.08.2011	■	Data transfer finished	1295	1291	1	1	1000, 100000000 2001

Figure 13.25   Data Transfer Finished

5. By taking a look at the job log, you can see the two new session numbers, 1453 and 1454, that were created for the transferred sessions 795 and 796, respectively (see Figure 13.26).

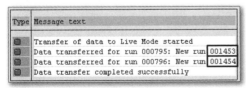

Type	Message text
▣	Transfer of data to Live Mode started
▣	Data transferred for run 000795: New run 001453
▣	Data transferred for run 000796: New run 001454
▣	Data transfer completed successfully

Figure 13.26   New Sessions Created During the Transfer

Now you need to convert and store your newly created archiving sessions:

1. Proceed as described above for the transfer, but choose CONVERT & STORE TRANS-ACTIONAL DATA.

2. In the CONVERT FILES tab strip, select your sessions, fill in the required information (select the WITH CONVERSION checkbox), and schedule the job in live mode.

3. In ARCHIVE MANAGEMENT, in the section with complete archiving sessions, you can see the names of the new sessions after conversion.

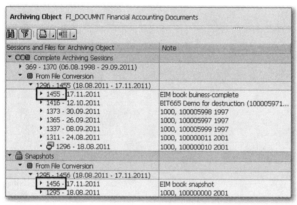

Figure 13.27 New Sessions Created During Conversion

The old sessions that were replaced, 1453 and 1454, appear in the section with replaced archiving sessions (Figure 13.28).

▾ ☐ Replaced Archiving Sessions	
▾ 365 - 1454 (06.08.1998 - 17.11.2011)	
▸ 1454 - 17.11.2011	EIM book snapshot
▸ 1453 - 17.11.2011	EIM book buiness-complete

Figure 13.28 Replaced Archiving Sessions

Each of these steps created new archiving sessions. This is the standard procedure in data archiving to ensure full tracking of the entire process and to guarantee that the original sessions and files are not modified.

In this example, we chose to have the storage start automatically when the conversion is finished (START AUTOMATICALLY checkbox in ARCHIVING-OBJECT SPECIFIC CUSTOMIZING). Therefore, we do not need to store the data at this stage. You can also store your archiving sessions manually, by clicking on the FILE STORAGE button in the STORE FILES tab of the transfer tool, see Figure 13.29.

When the storage job has finished, you can see that sessions 1455 and 1456, which we created during conversion, have now been stored.

Sessions and Files	Status	Process Status	Run ...	No. of Obje...	Stored Obj...	Session Note
▼ FI_DOCUMNT	◼	File storage finished		37	37	
▼ COB Complete Archiving Sessions	◼	File storage finished		25	25	
▼ ▣ From File Conversion	◼	File storage finished		25	25	
▼ 1311 - 1455 (24.08.2011 - 17.11.2011)	◼	File storage finished		25	25	
▶ 1455 - 17.11.2011	◼	File storage finished	795	12	12	EIM book buiness-complete
▶ 1416 - 12.10.2011	◼	File storage finished	776	9	9	BIT665 Demo for destruction
▶ 1373 - 30.09.2011	◼	File storage finished	773	1	1	1000, 100005998 1997
▶ 1365 - 26.09.2011	◼	File storage finished	774	1	1	1000, 100005997 1997
▶ 1337 - 08.09.2011	◼	File storage finished	767	1	1	1000, 100005999 1997
▶ 1311 - 24.08.2011	◼	File storage finished	745	1	1	1000, 100000011 2001
▼ 🔒 Snapshots	◼	File storage finished		12	12	
▼ ▣ From File Conversion	◼	File storage finished		12	12	
▼ 1295 - 1456 (18.08.2011 - 17.11.2011)	◼	File storage finished		12	12	
▼ 1456 - 17.11.2011	◼	File storage finished	796	11	11	EIM book snapshot
• 🔒 001456-001FI_DOCUMNT	◼	File storage finished		11	11	

System ID of Legacy Syst: ILM
Legacy System Client: 800
Convert Files / Store Files

Figure 13.29 File Storage Finished

This is also indicated accordingly in ARCHIVE MANAGEMENT under COMPLETE ARCHIVING SESSIONS • FROM FILE CONVERSION.

The transfer of data from the legacy system to the retention warehouse storage system is now complete. There, the data is stored safely and can be accessed any time should the need arise.

13.5.3 Reporting

If you need to access archived data—for example, due to an upcoming audit or if end users need to view historic data—you can run reporting operations on the data in the archive using different reporting options:

▶ SAP NetWeaver BW using any BW frontend, including SAP Crystal Reports

▶ Local reporting (without SAP NetWeaver BW)

In the reporting phase, you select the data from the archive and extract it into SAP NetWeaver BW structures or the table browser for the local reporting functions. The data selection is based on the previously defined audit area through the audit package template. The data is extracted through the audit packages and transferred from the archive files into the BW structures. Based on the audit package, you can view the data either in SAP NetWeaver BW or in local reporting. In SAP NetWeaver BW, you can use the queries that SAP predelivers to support tax audits.

Figure 13.30 provides an overview of the steps required for both reporting options.

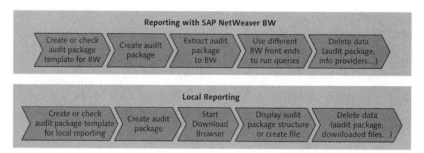

Figure 13.30 Process Steps for Reporting

Reporting with SAP NetWeaver BW

For this example, we assume that an audit package template has already been created for the upcoming audit. An audit package template contains a subset of the objects, tables, and fields of the corresponding audit area, with relevance for the audit.

Next, we go through the main steps required for reporting.

Create Audit Package

Create an audit package using the audit package template previously set up.

1. From the NWBC ILM Retention Warehouse cockpit for administrators choose AUDIT PACKAGES • PROCESS AUDIT PACKAGES.

2. Choose NEW and enter the required information, such as the audit package template and the source system details.

3. In the second step of this guided procedure, select the archived data to be processed. In this example, we want to report on financial accounting data (FI_DOCUMNT), so we need to specify the document type, the company code, and the fiscal year.

4. In the next screen, you enter additional parameters, such as the name of the audit package, whether it will be used for SAP NetWeaver BW reporting or local reporting, and the execution type.

5. Now you have the opportunity to review your entries and finally create the audit package.

6. The newly created audit package (EIMBOOK in our example; see Figure 13.31) should now appear with the status NEW in the overview screen of Audit Package Handling.

Audit Package Handling

Audit Packages

AudPkg	Audit Package	Description	Created By	Created On	AuthGrp	Status	Usage type	Template
6	BIT665_TEMPLATE	BIT665 Template for InfoObject Reuse I	WOJCICKA	27.09.2011		Generated	BI Reporting	ZILMTAX_BIT665
9	ZILMTAX_BIT665T	BIT665 Template for InfoObject Reuse II	WOJCICKA	20.10.2011		Generated	BI Reporting	ZILMTAX_BIT665T
10	BIT665_GR_0	BIT665 Demo	WOJCICKA	20.10.2011		Successfully Loaded	BI Reporting	ZILMTAX_BIT665T
11	EIMBOOK	EIM book	STEFANI	18.11.2011		New	BI Reporting	ZEIMBOOK

Figure 13.31 New Audit Package Created

Extract Audit Package to BI

To extract an audit package to BI, proceed as follows:

1. From the overview screen of AUDIT PACKAGE HANDLING, select your audit package. Choose BI REPORTING • EXTRACT AUDIT PACKAGE TO BI.

2. In the next steps of the guided procedure, you define technical parameters, such as the target SAP NetWeaver BW structure (datastore object or InfoCube), and you analyze the results of your selection and define the job parameters, such as server group and start time. Schedule the job as required.

When the extraction job has successfully finished, your audit package appears with the status SUCCESSFULLY LOADED in the overview screen of AUDIT PACKAGE HANDLING (see Figure 13.32).

Audit Package Handling

Audit Packages

AudPkg	Audit Package	Description	Created By	Created On	AuthGrp	Status	Usage type	Template
6	BIT665_TEMPLATE	BIT665 Template for InfoObject Reuse I	WOJCICKA	27.09.2011		Generated	BI Reporting	ZILMTAX_BIT665
9	ZILMTAX_BIT665T	BIT665 Template for InfoObject Reuse II	WOJCICKA	20.10.2011		Generated	BI Reporting	ZILMTAX_BIT665T
10	BIT665_GR_0	BIT665 Demo	WOJCICKA	20.10.2011		Successfully Loaded	BI Reporting	ZILMTAX_BIT665T
11	EIMBOOK	EIM book	STEFANI	18.11.2011		Successfully Loaded	BI Reporting	ZEIMBOOK

Figure 13.32 Audit Package Loaded to SAP NetWeaver BW

Run Reporting in SAP NetWeaver BW

Now that the archived data is available in SAP NetWeaver BW, you can use the predelivered queries to view the data:

1. Use the query ACCOUNTING DOCUMENT HEADERS to display the accounting documents from the decommissioned system. You will find it from within the NWBC ILM Retention Warehouse cockpit for line of business under BI REPORTING • TAX REPORTS • ACCOUNTING DOCUMENT.

2. After you have called up the query, the ACCOUNTING DOCUMENT HEADERS window with the subtitle VARIABLE ENTRY appears. Select your audit package and execute.

   Now you see, in Figure 13.33, the accounting document headers from the legacy system according to your previous selections.

Figure 13.33 Display Accounting Document Headers from SAP NetWeaver BW

From this screen, you also have direct access to any original documents attached to the accounting documents. These attachments must also have been made available to the retention warehouse storage system. Simply select the line with the document header in question and choose DOCUMENTS • DISPLAY DOCUMENTS from the context menu (right-click).

Once you are done with reporting, you can delete the audit package in the SAP NetWeaver BW system to release the occupied storage space.

Local Reporting

With local reporting, you can view the data from the archive in a table browser format. You do not need SAP NetWeaver BW for this option. Here also, the retrieval starts with the creation of an audit package template and then an audit package. You can view the contents of the audit package in the download browser and then decide which tables you want to view. Data can only be viewed per table.

An important aspect of local reporting is that you can export data in the SAP Audit Format (AIS). This is important for tax audits, as many financial authorities require companies to hand over tax-relevant data for evaluation in their own tools (such as IDEA in Germany).

Due to the limited space in this chapter, we do not cover local reporting in this example.

13.5.4 Data Destruction

Data destruction is not one of the core activities performed during a system decommissioning project. However, since legacy data that resides in the retention warehouse is subject to the same aging process as data in a live system, it is just as important to control the lifecycle of legacy data as it is for live data. And this includes the destruction of archived data that has reached its expiration date.

You can reach the data destruction function for archived data through the link in the NWBC ILM cockpit role for the scenario you are using. You can also call up the function directly by using Transaction ILM_DESTRUCTION. This is regardless of whether data is to be destroyed in a live system environment or in the retention warehouse.

In this example we want to destroy accounting documents from legacy system ILM, client 800, that we archived and moved to the retention warehouse as part of the system decommissioning process (see Figure 13.24, earlier in the chapter).

1. From the NWBC ILM Retention Warehouse cockpit for administrators choose DATA DESTRUCTION • DESTROY DATA IN ILM STORE.

2. Choose ARCHIVE FILES (ADK) and specify the ILM object, the SAP system, and the client (see Figure 13.34).

Figure 13.34 Data Destruction Selection Criteria

3. Choose Execute.

4. In the screen with expired resources, drill down to find the archive files you want to destroy (see Figure 13.35). You will not see snapshots, as they have an unknown expiration date and are therefore not shown here. (A special function allows you to set the expiration date of snapshots to Today. As a result, these snapshots can be destroyed through the standard destruction transaction on the next day.)

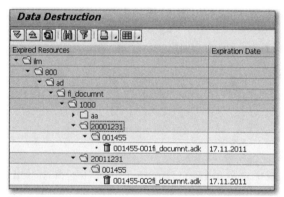

Figure 13.35 Archive Files Eligible for Destruction

Remember that the archive files of session 1455 were created as a result of the file conversion (refer back to Figure 13.27). The trash can symbol indicates that the archive file has reached its expiration data and is ready for destruction.

5. In the DATA DESTRUCTION main screen (see Figure 13.36) select the archive file to be destroyed and drag it to the CREATION OF DESTRUCTION WORKLIST container (see Figure 13.37). Save your destruction work list.

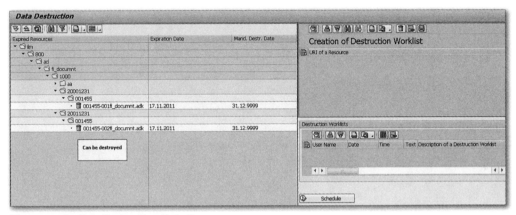

Figure 13.36 Data Destruction Main Screen

Figure 13.37 Destruction Work List

6. In the lower DESTRUCTION WORKLIST container, select your destruction work list and schedule the destruction job in live mode.

Security Considerations

To comply with security standards, two individuals can perform the compilation of the work list and the execution of the destruction run steps ("four-eye principle"). This concept is supported by suitable user roles provided with the SAP NetWeaver ILM software.

7. When the job is finished, you can verify the destruction result in the ILM STORE BROWSER or in ARCHIVE MANAGEMENT. This is shown in Figure 13.38.

The destroyed archiving session is listed as complete, but it is marked with a special icon to signal that its archive files have been destroyed.

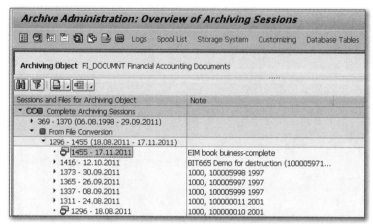

Figure 13.38 Destruction Result in Archive Management

13.6 Summary

In this chapter, we provided you with an overview of the SAP solutions for information lifecycle management, and showed you how you can best leverage them to build a holistic ILM strategy. With SAP NetWeaver ILM being the pivotal component of this solution suite, we took a more thorough look at the features and inner workings of this product. By following our practical examples, complemented by screenshots from a real system environment, you saw see how SAP NetWeaver ILM works in real life. No matter whether you want to manage the lifecycle of your data in a live system environment or whether you need to retire an SAP or non-SAP system in a standardized and legally compliant way, SAP's ILM solutions will help you to succeed.

Any company that wants to be successful in today's globalized world needs to ensure that its IT-related costs don't go over the top. It must also ensure adherence to an ever increasing number of laws and regulations. Therefore, to stay on the safe side, having a holistic ILM strategy in place is not an option but a must.

> **Note**
>
> For more information on getting started with data archiving projects, see Appendix C (available for download from the book's website at *www.sap-press.com*).

This chapter provides an overview of the business process for managing unstructured content such as pictures, word documents, mails, spreadsheets, and so on.

14 Introducing SAP Extended Enterprise Content Management by OpenText

Enterprise content management (hereafter ECM) is a broad area that includes the capturing, managing, preservation, and delivery of content and documents to organizations and business processes. Chapter 4 provided a high-level description of SAP's offering for ECM. This chapter will focus on ECM as it relates to the business process, which we will call *integrated* ECM. Integrated ECM allows you to associate and manage unstructured information (such as documents or emails) with structured information (such as application data) in the context of business processes.

Integrated ECM has a twofold meaning. The obvious one is that ECM supports seamless integration of unstructured content with application data. The second meaning is that ECM offers content management capabilities within an application system.

> **Twofold Meaning of Integrated ECM**
>
> ▸ *Integration* as support of unstructured content with application data or application systems
> ▸ ECM capabilities as *integrated within* an application system

Along with data integration (Chapter 7), data quality (Chapter 8), and master data governance (Chapter 12), integrated ECM plays an important role in improving business processes and, in the end, is the underlying strategic key performance indicator (KPI) by which the efficiency and efficacy of those processes are measured.

An example from the German telecom industry can help to illustrate how poor content management can hurt a business process. Suppose Franz wants to remodel his house but would like to disconnect his home phone during construction. He writes a letter to the phone company (a letter is required in Germany when changing telephone service) explaining that he will need to disconnect his phone during construction.

A week later, Franz gets a message for the phone company—on the answering machine for to the line he wants disconnected. He calls the phone company call center, and the agent asks why he is disconnecting his phone service, worried that he has a complaint about their service.

Franz tells the agent that he wrote a letter explaining his need to have the phone disconnected due to demolition and construction, but the call center agent cannot see the letter because the telephone company does not have integrated ECM. Franz must again explain why he must discontinue phone service and supply his temporary address, and the time of both Franz and the call center agent is wasted. Furthermore, the call center agent changes his home address to the temporary address he has given but unfortunately neglects to update his billing address, resulting in his invoices being sent to the wrong address.

Because the call center agent was not able to see all of the documents associated with Franz' account, the net result was poor customer service and damage to the customer relationship. Documents and unstructured content play an important role not only in call center scenarios, but in all customer-centric business processes.

And that's true not only for business processes that rely on customer data, but any business process where unstructured content is relevant. Think back to NeedsEIM, Inc. (introduced in Chapter 1): it outsources manufacturing and has a diverse supplier network. ECM tools are needed in various business areas to cover important business challenges, especially in those where unstructured content plays an important role, such as contracts, engineering drawings, specification designs, invoicing, and so on.

In addition to better-run business processes with unstructured content, managing the unstructured content is also important for meeting internal and external compliance and reporting demands.

A single, reliable version of the truth for both structured and unstructured content, with careful version and access control, should be available for any part of a business process or end-user decision point. Both types of information should also be part of a thoughtful strategy for retention management. These principles, which assure compliance and minimize legal fines, are the foundation of effective, process-centric information management.

SAP Extended ECM by OpenText delivers the basis for the seamless and frictionless integration of unstructured content into the business processes supported by the SAP Business Suite and should be an integral part of any information management initiative.

This chapter describes integrated ECM based on SAP Extended Enterprise Content Management by OpenText (hereafter SAP Extended ECM). The discussion includes details of what is offered, core components, and technical integration options supported, and explains how to get started using a workspace, which is a key concept for SAP Extended ECM. (Chapter 5 includes examples of real-world use of SAP Extended ECM.)

14.1 Capabilities of SAP Extended ECM

SAP Extended ECM is a complete enterprise content management solution. Even though it is offered by OpenText, it is a complete solution extension provided by SAP. SAP Extended ECM, as well as the other solutions offered by OpenText, has dedicated product teams on both sides, adheres to SAP requirements for support and upgrades, has deep technology integration with SAP, and includes committed codevelopment efforts.

Figure 14.1 shows an overview of the core capabilities required to deliver an integrated ECM project. These capabilities are delivered with SAP Extended ECM.

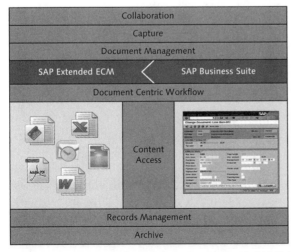

Figure 14.1 Overview of Capabilities Provided with SAP Extended ECM

Each of the capabilities shown in Figure 14.1 are described below, starting with the bottom and moving toward the top.

▶ **Archive**
Refers to data and document archiving. In this context, an archive is the secure storage for all unstructured content.

▶ **Records management**
Controls the complete lifecycle of unstructured content with functionality certified by the U.S. Department of Defense 5015.2 certification.

▶ **Content access**
Enables users to have a personalized view of unstructured content. This includes retrieval of content from authorized sources and viewing of content through a choice of user interfaces.

▶ **Document-centric workflow**
Enables electronic document approval and signing processes.

▶ **Document management**
Enables basic content handling capabilities such as retrieval, storage, versioning, check-in/check-out, metadata handling, and security handling.

▶ **Capture**
Enables scanning of paper documents.

▶ **Collaboration**
Enables users to brainstorm, develop, share, and comment about document and file collaboration in the SAP business process context.

Each of these is so important that it warrants further discussion of how the capability works and the business problem it addresses.

14.1.1   Data and Document Archiving

All unstructured content must have a repository for storage. OpenText provides this storage. The storage is used to store content such as images, scanned documents, manuals, and all content that is associated with an SAP business process.

As mentioned in Chapter 4 and again in Chapter 13, archiving also refers to the removal of information that is no longer required. SAP Extended ECM also supports retention policies and the archiving of information that is no longer required for productive use. It works with SAP NetWeaver Information Lifecycle Management

(ILM) (discussed in Chapter 13), for archiving data that is no longer needed. SAP NetWeaver ILM handles the archiving of all structured documents as well as SAP ArchiveLink documents associated with the SAP business context. This means that if you scan invoices for FI documents, associate documents and manuals with equipment, or associate résumés and pictures with employees using SAP Extended ECM, then when it is time to retire that data, SAP NetWeaver ILM will retire both the SAP structured content and associated SAP ArchiveLink documents. If you are already using SAP Extended ECM, then you can use the OpenText repository as the ILM-aware storage discusses in Chapter 13. Section 14.3.1 discussed SAP Archive-Link as the service inside the SAP NetWeaver Application Server ABAP for linking archived documents and the application documents entered in the SAP system. SAP ArchiveLink is fully supported by OpenText as well as by SAP NetWeaver ILM.

14.1.2 Records Management

Records management is the discipline of managing the lifecycle of documents in physical and electronic format, from creation to deletion. Records management is relevant for all industries to support compliance with financial reporting, auditing standards, and Sarbanes-Oxley requirements.

Records management also plays an important role in many business processes and industries: developing new product, managing public health and public organization records, and managing all records required for government compliance.

The U.S. Department of Defense (DoD) 5015.2 certification is the gold standard for software solutions supporting records management. Even though this certification is only compulsory for organizations associated with the Department of Defense in the United States, it is also used as the records management benchmark in other public sector and non-public sector organizations globally.

SAP Extended ECM is certified to the DoD 5015.2 standard and also complies with the international ISO 15489 standard for records management systems. Records management is applied to any document created by any process in SAP Extended ECM. This includes the support of all documents in a classification scheme that defines document types, document lifecycle, and security information for all related documents.

14.1.3 Content Access

Content needs to be made available to the end user, in the user's preferred interface, and independent of the application that initially generated the content. For example, as mentioned previously, a call center agent needs access to all content related to a customer, including content that originated from paper, emails, calls, or other sources.

14.1.4 Document-Centric Workflow

Document-centric workflow is an important capability of SAP Extended ECM to support document-driven processes. For NeedsEIM, Inc., contracts for each outsourced manufacturer and each supplier must be created in a collaborative fashion and go through a series of approvals before being sent to the supplier or manufacturer for their signature.

Document-centric workflow templates can easily be created in a graphical interface and conveniently used by the end user. All workflow steps and decisions are logged in a complete audit trail, so before a contract is sent out, all changes to the contract and the approval process can be tracked in SAP Extended ECM.

14.1.5 Document Management

Document management is the core element of SAP Extended ECM. Document management delivers basic content-handling capabilities such as retrieval, storage, versioning, check-in and check-out, metadata handling, and security handling.

Document management is where you start when moving away from storing your files in various file shares or on laptops, which often makes it impossible to find the latest version of a file. Versioning in file shares is often managed by file name, so names like *contract_final.doc, contract_final_final.doc,* and *contract_final_final_last.doc* are often found in a file share location, and often hierarchies are very complicated. With SAP Extended ECM, versions of files/documents can be easily managed and the change history easily understood. Major and minor versioning is supported, and access rights can be easily managed.

It is well known that employees spend a significant amount of time searching for documents. Support for users to search for documents is a key functionality of SAP Extended ECM. When searching for a document, you often may only know the author or a keyword from the content. Searching by both document metadata and by full text is fully supported in SAP Extended ECM.

Document management is extended by records management, which extends document management to all the compliance regulations supported by records management.

14.1.6 Capture

Capture is a key element of SAP Extended ECM. Capture refers to the scanning of documents in formats such as TIF, PDF, and JPG; indexing the document; providing metadata for search and discovery; attaching the document to the right transaction or business process; and generating searchable PDF documents using OCR (optical character recognition).

SAP Extended ECM supports barcode scenarios out-of-the-box, and all SAP Archive-Link capture scenarios are supported as well. This will be discussed in more detail in the next section.

The following explains one specific bar-coding example for outgoing documents that is supported by default: Many scenarios, such as contract signing and closing documents, require paper copies to be sent by mail and may require a handwritten signature. Computer-generated signatures are not allowed in some scenarios; for example, in correspondence with public sector organizations. The approval workflow in SAP Extended ECM supports hand signatures. The user prints the document with an automatic generated barcode and signs it. Before being mailed, the signed document is scanned and automatically added as signed version.

14.1.7 Collaboration and Social Media

Collaboration is very important for knowledge workers. It happens with or without a system in place to support it. SAP Extended ECM enables the capture of the collaboration to be associated with a business process. This includes social media behavior such as commenting, activity feeds, user notification, users following other users, and so on.

SAP Extended ECM moves collaboration out of email tools and into a true collaborative environment for tasks such as creating a contract for a new supplier or manufacturer.

14.2 How SAP Extended ECM Works with the SAP Business Suite

As explained in the introduction, integrated ECM has a twofold meaning: supporting seamless integration of unstructured content with application data, and offering ECM capabilities as an integrated part of an application system.

Figure 14.2 shows the integration of SAP Extended ECM with the SAP Business Suite.

Figure 14.2 Integrated Unstructured Content

Figure 14.2 can be divided into three sections: user interface, application integration, and detailed application synchronization. The user interfaces at the top of the figure reference the types of user experiences available to interact with the content associated with the SAP Business Suite. SAP Extended ECM unstructured content can be associated with application data—for example, a hierarchy of customer documents—and displayed together with the application data in user interfaces used by the SAP Business Suite (SAP GUI, SAP CRM WebClient, SAP NetWeaver Portal, SAP Supplier Relationship Management [SRM]) as well as with non-SAP user interfaces such as Microsoft Outlook, Lotus Notes, Microsoft Windows Explorer, and SAP Extended ECM's native web interface. Integration of unstructured content with application data is brought to any user via the interface best fitted to the role and task.

The middle portion of Figure 14.2 depicts SAP Extended ECM and SAP Business Suite in the same box because they are so seamlessly integrated as to appear as the same application.

The lower part of Figure 14.2 shows synchronization details of the integrated platform approach of SAP Extended ECM together with the SAP Business Suite. This includes tight integration and synchronization of data references, metadata, users, and their security access and controls. Each of these is explained below in more detail:

▶ **User synchronization and single sign-on support**
Ensures a consistent and seamless user experience for end users. It also lowers the cost of maintaining various user identities in different systems.

▶ **Access control synchronization**
Ensures that access control rights maintained in the SAP Business Suite are also applied on SAP Extended ECM. For example, when a user is not allowed to see certain customer data in an SAP CRM system, the user also cannot access the same details in SAP Extended ECM. SAP authorization objects are synchronized with the access policies in SAP Extended ECM.

▶ **Metadata synchronization**
Pushes SAP application data to SAP Extended ECM. This means SAP Extended ECM is always up-to-date and in sync with the SAP application data. This tight synchronization ensures high-quality document and folder attribute data and enables searching in offline scenarios, such as providing customer data offline for a sales visit.

▶ **Data references**
Ensure referential integrity of the data in SAP Extended ECM and the SAP Business Suite. For example, the unstructured content for a specific supplier is associated with the correct supplier in SAP ERP. It also provides the representation of SAP object relationships, such as the equipment hierarchy or project hierarchy in the SAP Extended ECM user interface. The result is that ECM users can leverage the "business model" of SAP applications for browsing, searching, and content classification, providing them the business context for content.

14.3 Integration Content for SAP Business Suite and SAP Extended ECM

SAP Extended ECM supports various options to integrate content in the SAP Business Suite: SAP ArchiveLink, the SAP ECM integration layer, and workspaces within SAP Extended ECM. (SAP ArchiveLink and the SAP ECM integration layer are part of the SAP core offering, and workspaces are part of SAP Extended ECM.) We discuss these three options in this section.

14.3.1 SAP ArchiveLink

SAP ArchiveLink is a building block of SAP Extended ECM. The SAP ArchiveLink interface was the first integration approach developed by SAP to attach documents and scanned images to transactions in SAP; for example, attaching scanned invoices to financial transactions in SAP ERP. It creates a link in SAP to associate content stored in a document archive repository. This is shown in Figure 14.3.

Figure 14.3 SAP ArchiveLink Integration

Figure 14.3 demonstrates the link between the SAP database and the content store. In this example, a document is stored in the application table BSEG. SAP Archive-Link creates a reference to this in table TOA00. This table stores the link between the object in SAP and the document in the content store. With SAP ArchiveLink, a user must be logged into the SAP system to access the content. The SAP system and the external content store communicate via a standardized *http* interface.

Hint

SAP ArchiveLink is used for associating content with business objects. SAP ArchiveLink also supports SAP Data Archiving, which relocates information from production systems (discussed in Chapter 13).

The basic architectural guidance for SAP ArchiveLink is to enable attaching one or more documents (such as scanned images) to an SAP transaction. The content is stored not in the SAP database, but in an external content store designed to hold unstructured content.

There are several advantages of using external storage for storing content:

▶ External content stores reduce the size of the SAP database.

▶ External content stores are designed to manage unstructured content.

▶ External content stores support any sort of physical storage media.

▶ External content stores often come with their own viewer technology.

SAP ArchiveLink supports many scenarios. The most common ones include:

▶ Automated storage and management of incoming documents based on SAP Business Workflow.

▶ Automated linkage and storage of incoming documents using bar codes.

▶ Ad hoc processing of incoming documents.

▶ Storage of outgoing documents such as SAP SmartForms or Adobe print forms. SAP ArchiveLink can attach the outgoing document to the SAP business object, whether it is printed, faxed, or emailed.

▶ Print lists (reports); for example, an annual report. Examples of print lists are account update logs in finance, warehouse stock, and logs.

SAP Extended ECM enhances the base SAP ArchiveLink capabilities with the use of metadata management, version support, audit trail, searching, and other capabilities, to provide full management of all content associated with SAP.

14.3.2 Content Management Interoperability Standard (CMIS) and SAP ECM Integration Layer

Content Management Interoperability Services (CMIS) is an OASIS open standard that works to standardize "a Web services interface specification that will enable greater interoperability of Enterprise Content Management (ECM) systems. CMIS uses Web services and Web 2.0 interfaces to enable rich information to be shared across Internet protocols in vendor-neutral formats, among document systems, publishers and repositories, within one enterprise and between companies."[1]

To understand how this is supported with Extended ECM by OpenText, refer to Figure 14.4. Notice that the user interface on the top represents the user interfaces supported by SAP. The user interface on the bottom represents the user interfaces supported by the document management system. Next, notice the SAP ECM integration layer; the ECM integration layer is provided by SAP for support for ECM for all ECM vendors. Also notice the ECM store within the SAP Business Suite; this store would be required if you wanted to leverage the ECM integration layer without an external content store. Finally, notice the CMIS protocol is used to integrate with the document management system.

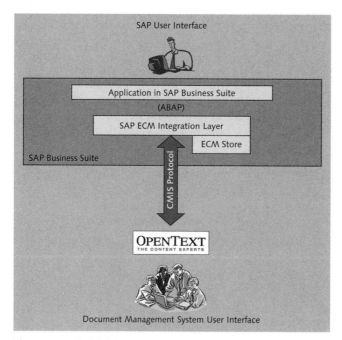

Figure 14.4 SAP ECM Integration Layer and CMIS Standard

In Figure 14.4, the ECM integration layer also enables customers to leverage the features of document management systems for documents created in their SAP applications. Documents created by an SAP business application should be accessible

---

1   Source: *http://www.oasis-open.org/committees/tc_home.php?wg_abbrev=cmis*

not only via the business application, but also via the user interfaces and services provided by the third-party document management system.

To be able to use the powerful features of a document management system such as searching, document-centric processes, or classification mechanisms, you have to enrich the documents stored in the third-party systems with additional metadata from the business application. This metadata enables a user, working directly in the document management system, to understand the business object or business process to which a document belongs without launching the business application. In addition, the application assigns properties to documents or folders that can be used for searching or classification of documents. An application can even add access rights to the documents created in the external system to ensure that only authorized actors are able to access the documents in the third-party system.

The SAP ECM integration layer is supported from SAP NetWeaver 7.03 on. SAP also provides a JAVA version for the integration layer, which will be used by SAP NetWeaver Process Orchestration (including SAP NetWeaver Business Process Management) and is supported with SAP NetWeaver 7.2 Java Application Server 7.2 and higher.

14.3.3 SAP Extended ECM Workspaces

Extended ECM's most advanced and innovative integration option with SAP is based on the *ECM workspace*. While the term *ECM workspace* is well known in the enterprise content management market, our reference to ECM workspaces will be specific to the workspaces provided by the *ECMLink* technology from OpenText.

Figure 14.5 shows an example of a workspace. Each workspace is attached to an SAP object and links all relevant content. Figure 14.5 is a workspace for a piece of equipment. This includes SAP ArchiveLink documents, non-SAP documents, images, or emails. All content is provided in a single view. The power of workspaces lies in the ubiquitous access from all relevant SAP user interfaces, including the SAP GUI, SAP NetWeaver Portal, SAP GUI for HTML, and specific web user interfaces provided by SAP CRM, SAP SRM, and the SAP NetWeaver Business Client. In addition to SAP user interfaces, non-SAP user interfaces include the SAP Extended ECM web interface, Microsoft Windows Explorer, Microsoft Office, and email clients such as Microsoft Outlook and Lotus Notes.

Figure 14.5 SAP Extended ECM Workspace

In Figure 14.5 the workspace includes metadata, folder structures, and documents and forms. Each of these is explained below.

❶ **Metadata**

Metadata provides information about the object that can be displayed in SAP and non-SAP user interfaces. The metadata is used to identify the workspace in non-SAP user interfaces as well. Metadata defined for a workspace is available in the web UI of SAP Extended ECM. Metadata is data duplicated from SAP to the SAP Extended ECM user interfaces. Examples of metadata in Figure 14.5 include the attributes on the pump such as the pump number, description, plant, and so on.

❷ **Folder structures**

Folder structures reflect how the content is organized. Default folder structures are provided out-of-the-box, and you can create your own as well.

❸ **Documents and forms**

These include all related documents for the workspace. This can include pictures, scanned images, videos, contracts, and so on. Additionally, the forms in the workspace can be used as templates to create other documents; for example, an email draft to send to a customer.

❹ Business relationships

Business relationships allow you to link the business workspace to predefined business object structures in the SAP system. An example is the relationship of a customer to sales orders. In Figure 14.5, the business relationships shown are the relation of the pump to locations and equipment. Document activity feeds display activities such as NEW DOCUMENT CREATED and NEW VERSION CREATED by certain users.

The full content of a workspace (metadata, folder structure, business relationships) is dependent on the user's business role. The business role in SAP Extended ECM depends on the user's authorizations in the SAP system. For example, for NeedsEIM, Inc., there is a workspace for each manufacture, including detailed specifications, drawings, and so on. Internally, the design engineers can only access workspaces for the projects they are assigned to with external manufactures. An employee working in the contract department would only see the contract-relevant document/folder in the workspace.

Each workspace provides core ECM capabilities, such as collaboration, document-centric workflow, document management, records management, and capture capabilities, each discussed in the previous section. The layout of the ECM workspace for a certain SAP business object is based on fully configurable business workspace templates that define the folder structure, metadata structures, roles, permissions, and user interface elements.

SAP Extended ECM supports three workspace types: *business workspaces, case workspaces,* and *binder workspaces*. Case workspaces have additional characteristics, such as a status field used to define a beginning and end of the workspace. Case workspaces support defined phases and typically have a list of processors. They are used to support collaboration, including follow-up actions such as setting a reminder to review a document in two weeks. Binder workspaces only allow attaching a folder structure to SAP objects.

To give you a better understanding of an ECM workspace, Figure 14.6 shows an equipment business workspace in the WebGUI for SAP Extended ECM. We have chosen to show a business workspace, as this the most commonly used ECM workspace type.

The user can see the folder structure and the attached documents in the middle and all relevant SAP data and the related SAP objects on the right-hand side. On the left, all changes to documents in the business workspace are shown as document and folder activities and feeds. In addition, a powerful faceted full text search within the documents in a business workspace is available.

Figure 14.6 Business Workspace for Equipment in SAP Extended ECM WebGUI

As shown in Figure 14.7, the same information can be accessed via the Windows Explorer frontend. Documents can be added easily in the Windows Explorer by drag and drop. All functions available in the WebGUI can be performed in this frontend via context menus. For example, the user can display and maintain document attributes in the Windows Explorer frontend.

The same information is available for a user accessing the information via a transaction in the SAP system, as displayed in Figure 14.8. The pump information is now displayed in the SAP GUI, including all content, such as the manufacturing plant inspection report shown in Figure 14.8.

Figure 14.7 Business Workspace for Equipment Displayed in Microsoft Windows Explorer

Figure 14.8 Business Workspace for Material via SAP GUI

As you get started with SAP Extended ECM, customizing the workspace is a very common activity. Therefore, next we will discuss the basics of how to create your own workspace and where you can get a step-by-step example of workspace creation.

Configuring Your Own Workspace in SAP Extended ECM

When designing a workspace, you need to know the objects (for example. material, equipment, vendor) that require workspaces. You need to define the data that should be metadata for the workspace. Remember that the metadata will be displayed in all user interfaces. Folder structures are provided for you, but you can also customize your own. You also need to consider security aspects, document types, and relationships between workspaces.

Step-by-step instructions for configuring a workspace can be found in the Open-Text Knowledge Center. The guide for creation of workspaces can be found here: *https://knowledge.opentext.com/knowledge/piroot/erx/v100000/erx-acs/en/erx-acs-en.pdf.*

Once the base configuration is done, business users can create workspaces. This can happen from the SAP GUI, the SAP Extended ECM user interface, the SAP CRM Web Client, or the SAP CRM Interaction Center Web Client. Figure 14.9 shows an example of how a user can create a workspace from the SAP GUI.

Figure 14.9 Creating a Workspace from the SAP GUI

If you are already familiar with the generic object services available in the SAP NetWeaver Application Server ABAP, you will notice how workspaces are associated with the generic object services.

Workspaces can be generated manually (as shown in Figure 14.9) or automatically. Automatic creation is common if you want to create a workspace for each business object of a certain type; for example, objects used in a plant maintenance application in an SAP system. The configuration for workspaces does require some setup in the SAP IMG (Transaction SPRO) as well as in SAP Extended ECM. Once a workspace is created, it can easily be viewed in the SAP GUI, as shown in Figure 14.10.

Figure 14.10 Easy Navigation to Workspace in SAP GUI

In Figure 14.10, notice that the user can use the generic object services and select DISPLAY WORKSPACE while viewing ny transaction in the SAP system that has a workspace. In Figure 14.10, the example shows a workspace from a material. The user is in the material for the pump, and selects to view the workspace. He can immediately see documents stored in SAP Extended ECM related to the material.

14.4   Summary

In this chapter, you learned that SAP delivers integrated enterprise content management. You now understand that SAP ArchiveLink is an important foundation for SAP Extended ECM. You learned about the role of the ECM integration layer, and the CMIS OASIS standard for content. You learned about the major features of SAP Extended ECM and how to get started using and configuring workspaces to relate content to the SAP business processes.

This chapter combined with the ECM discussion in Chapter 5, by Belgian Railways, gives you a good starting point for understanding ECM.

The Authors

Corrie Brague is the director of Information Quality and Insight (IQI) Product Management for SAP, where she leads a product management team to define software solutions that help businesses improve their data quality. She participates in ASUG and works with a broad range of customers and partners to support market-driven product direction, as well as enhance the insight of the customer and market space within the IQI development organization. She has over 12 years of experience in data quality and mail automation software solutions gained through positions in software engineering, project management, development management, and product management.

George Bryce is an enterprise data architect at Procter & Gamble, which has more than 300 consumer brands marketed in 160 countries with global sales exceeding $85 billion annually. He has been a leader in P&G's master data capabilities, with over 20 years of experience architecting, designing, and supporting the management of data as an asset through the creation of a single global master data client. His current focus is the creation of an enterprise architecture that enables business-led data governance with clear accountability for data ownership.

Ryan Champlin has over 12 years of experience in the field of information management, having worked within both engineering and product management organizations. At Business Objects and SAP, he played an instrumental role as a product manager on the industry's first single platform for data quality and data integration: SAP Data Services. He currently works as a director of engineering within the EIM team at SAP, where he is responsible for the data quality management solutions for various SAP applications (for example, SAP ECC, SAP CRM, and SAP MDG).

Dr. Andreas Engel is an expert in enterprise information management focusing on integrated enterprise content management. He has more than 15 years of experience in the software industry. Currently working as a solution expert in the SAP global go-to-market organization, he drives innovation from market requirements to market adoption.

Srikant Dharwad is an enterprise data architect for Lexmark International, Inc., responsible for developing solutions for customer/vendor master data management and the enterprise data warehouse. He has more than 15 years of experience in solution development/architecture, technology consulting, product development, and EIM solution development for industry verticals. Prior to joining Lexmark, he worked at Teradata Corporation in various roles, including product development and solutions consulting.

Ina L. Felsheim is a director of solution management for SAP's EIM products. She has been with SAP since 1997, and currently works on information governance and end-to-end use scenarios. She has managed a diverse set of EIM products, and is the SAP point person for both the Data Governance and Data Management SIGs, as well as the EIM Influence Council.

Will Gardella leads the Cloud and Big Data technology innovation team at SAP Labs in Palo Alto, California. He is the technical advisor for SAP's global big data strategy, and has focused on applying Hadoop technology in the enterprise context since 2010.

Ginger Gatling currently works in the solution management group for EIM at SAP. She has been with SAP since 1997, and has experience that ranges from teaching Basis and technical courses to working in solution management, covering topics from SAP Business Workflow to data migration. She co-authored the book *Practical Workflow for SAP* (SAP PRESS, 2009), which has donated over $20,000 to Doctors Without Borders—and she looks forward to doing the same with this book! She is an active member of her local North Texas ASUG chapter.

Simer Grewal joined SAP in 2004 as an application developer in the ERP master data area, and has since worked as an architect, project manager, and product owner. As a member of the North America EIM Center of Excellence, he has product knowledge spanning the EIM portfolio, with specialization in the MDM/MDG area. His current focus is to help customers understand their business processes and build an enterprise-wide information governance strategy.

Stéphane Haelterman has been working with SAP since 1997, leading process improvements, process automation, and invoice management projects in Europe. After successfully implementing SAP Invoice Management by OpenText to optimize the purchase-to-pay platform at Belgian Railways, he was asked to build a vision and strategy to bridge the gap between business processes and the most tangible asset left behind: the business documents. He now leads the four-year implementation program for SAP Extended Enterprise Content Management by OpenText.

Eric Hamer has worked at Intel Corporation for 28 years, and has experience in wafer fab lithography engineering and factory automation software development and architecture. Currently, he is an enterprise architect for IT solutions. His contribution to Chapter 5, Practical Examples of EIM, reflects his own opinions and experiences, and does not necessarily represent Intel's positions, strategies, or opinions.

Rob Jackson has over 14 years' experience archiving SAP documents and data, and was the founder and chairman of the ASUG Data Archiving and ILM Special Interest Group from 1998 to 2012. As part of the ASUG influence council, he was very involved in the joint initiative with SAP for the creation of SAP NetWeaver ILM. He has worked as an imaging systems engineer at Eastman Kodak Company and as a solutions architect at Owens Corning, and is currently a solutions architect at a consulting company that specializes in imaging and data archiving projects.

Mike Keilen is a senior director of solution management in the EIM group at SAP, and has been with SAP since 1991. Over this time, Mike has provided leadership across both the EIM and enterprise content management topics in various engineering, product, solution, and partner management roles. Mike is currently responsible for SAP's EIM rapid deployment solutions, EIM within the Business Suite, data migration, and enterprise content management solutions.

Markus Kuppe is vice president and chief solution architect for master data management solutions in the SAP Business Suite. Since joining SAP development in 1997, he has led various programs across the SAP Business Suite in topics like reporting, user experience, and architecture, always in close collaboration with customers. He is a frequent author and speaker at business events.

Terry McFadden is the principle enterprise architect responsible for enterprise information architecture at Procter & Gamble, which has more than 300 consumer brands marketed in 160 countries with global sales exceeding $85 billion annually. Having moved from corporate data architect to enterprise architect, his focus is now on enterprise information management. He also leads P&G's Global Business Services benchmarking practice.

Louann Seguin has worked for National Vision, an Atlanta-based optical retailer with over 700 locations and e-commerce, since 2003. She is currently the vice president of Information Technology and Strategy, and is responsible for overseeing all corporate applications and development, enterprise data/information architecture and management, business intelligence, and web development.

Akshay Sinha holds a Master's degree in Computer Science from Birla Institute of Technology & Science in India, and has been working at SAP for over six years. He has extensive software development experience on ABAP and Java/J2EE technologies, and currently works with the SAP MDG development team at SAP Labs.

Helmut Stefani joined SAP in 1997, working on the documentation, product management, solution management, and roll-out of data archiving and information lifecycle management topics. He has authored several publications, including a book on data management, data archiving, and ILM. He can be reached at *helmut.stefani@sap.com*.

Eric Stridinger has been a leader in IT, supply chain, business intelligence, and data management for 22 years. In addition to holding several technical and functional positions and leading many high-profile global SAP projects, he has been involved with ASUG and worked as the chairman of the Data Governance Committee for a global tooling manufacturer. He is currently the director of the SAP supply chain for a global pharmaceutical company.

Anthony Waite is the product manager for text analytics products, and works out of the SAP Labs office in Cambridge, MA. He has been involved in SAP's EIM solutions for over four years, evangelizing data integration and data quality on structured and unstructured data at SAP. Before joining SAP, he worked for seven years as an OLAP product manager at Oracle.

Niels Weigel is a member of the GTM Solutions team for EIM, and is responsible for the roll-out- and roll-in-related activities of SAP Information Steward. Prior to this appointment, Niels was the product manager for the global-address cleanse solution within SAP Data Quality Management.

All authors have chosen to donate their royalties from this book to Doctors Without Borders/Médecins Sans Frontières.

Doctors Without Borders / Médecins Sans Frontières (MSF) is an international independent medical humanitarian organization that delivers emergency aid to people affected by armed conflict, epidemics, natural and man-made disasters, and exclusion from health care in more than 60 countries. A private, non-profit organization, Doctors Without Borders was founded in 1971 as the first non-governmental organization to both provide emergency medical assistance and bear witness publicly to the plight of people it assists. The work of Doctors Without Borders is based on the humanitarian principles of medical ethics and impartiality. The organization is committed to bringing quality medical care to people caught in crisis regardless of race, religion, or political affiliation, and operates independently of any political, military, or religious agendas. The organization received the Nobel Peace Prize in 1999.

Index